...From Time Immemorial

...From Time
]IMMEMORIAL

Indigenous

Peoples

and

State

Systems

Richard J. Perry

University of Texas Press / Austin

Copyright © 1996 by the University of Texas Press
All rights reserved
Printed in the United States of America
First edition, 1996

Requests for permission to reproduce material from this work
should be sent to Permissions, University of Texas Press, Box 7819,
Austin, TX 78713-7819.

⊛ The paper used in this publication meets the minimum requirements
of American National Standard for Information Sciences—Permanence of
Paper for Printed Library Materials, ANSI Z39.48-1984.

Perry, Richard John, 1942–
—from time immemorial : indigenous peoples and state
systems / Richard J. Perry. —1st ed.
    p.   cm.
  Includes bibliographical references and index.
   ISBN 0-292-76598-3 (cloth : alk. paper). —ISBN 0-292-76599-1
(pbk. : alk. paper)
   1. Indigenous peoples.   2. State, The.   3. Indians of North
America—Government relations.   I. Title.
GN380.P48   1996
306' .08—dc20   96-903

...For Rick, Jaya, Travis, and Gregory May you grow old and content in a world in which the troubles in this book are nothing more than history.

Contents

. . . .

List of Maps   ix

Preface   xi

Part One: Starting Premises 1. A Long View   3

                                 2. Ideas and Ideology 25

Part Two: The States   3. Mexico   45

                                 4. United States   85

                                 5. Canada   124

                                 6. Australia   161

Part Three: Comparisons   7. Other States and Indigenous
                                    Peoples   201

                                 8. Conclusions from Cases Compared 223

                                 References Cited   253

                                 Recommended Sources on
                                    Indigenous Groups 279

                                 Index   283

Maps

. . . .

European Intrusions in North America   **41**

Indigenous Mexico   **46**

Mexican States Mentioned in Chapter 3   **72**

Some Indigenous Groups in the
      United States   **89**

Indian Territory as Defined by the
      Royal Proclamation of 1763   **130**

Canada   **147**

Australia with Aboriginal Reserves   **175**

Indonesia   **204**

Namibia, Botswana, South Africa,
      Tanzania, and Kenya   **214**

Preface

. . . .

This is about what happens when people whose ancestors have lived for centuries in small, autonomous societies find themselves encompassed within state systems. Whether we refer to them as "previous inhabitants," "native peoples," "First Nations," "Aboriginals," or "indigenous peoples," many of their experiences have been comparable. State conquest and incorporation have happened in diverse places to millions of indigenous people over the past few centuries. The process has many histories. But as different as these histories are, they seem to share certain features.

These similarities raise a rather obvious question. Are the various episodes of state incorporation nothing more than a multitude of discrete events with little in common, or are there underlying patterns that human actions have followed over and over again, regardless of who the actors were or where and when they acted? Basically, this is one version of a broader anthropological question: Why do people do what they do? Why do they do what they do to each other? Do individuals make any difference in the flow of events, or do impersonal forces sweep them along? How free are the choices people make? And to what extent do they act within the constraints of conditions that they have not created and of which they may not be fully aware? These are some of the hoariest, most vexing, and most fundamental questions in the social sciences.

To approach some of these issues, we shall compare the ways in which radically different societies—expanding states and small populations organized on the basis of kinship—have interacted within a global context in a variety of instances.

Through a couple of decades of anthropology courses, my students and I have used scores of ethnographic works. Most of them describe the internal workings of small communities. They dissect the dynamics of interpersonal relationships, the intricacies of belief systems, the ways in which people produce and distribute their food and how they raise their children. In many cases, the authors of such works devote a short chapter or so to "outside influences"—an almost reluctant acknowledgment that these communities are immersed in a wider sea of human interaction. Often this comes across as an extraneous addendum—a dissonant interference with our absorption in the intimate lives of the people.

It hardly needs pointing out, though, that relationships beyond the local community are usually important enough to warrant a mood-breaking interruption in our focus on local cultural systems. As many writers have argued—some of them quite forcefully—the cultures we try to understand through these ethnographies are products, in many ways, of these wider influences and outside dynamics. To a great extent, anthropology has focused especially on small populations that have been captured by state systems through economic involvement, displacement, or most commonly, through force.

This book looks beyond the study of particular local populations, an approach that has characterized anthropology throughout most of its history and has produced some of its greatest contributions. The intention here is to build on those contributions. Following the advice of Eric Wolf and others, we shall step back and use the perspectives of history and the other social sciences in the hope of making some sense of the small by looking at the large. It is an attempt to see how things fit together, or whether, in fact, they do.

The trail that led to this book wanders through a number of stops. A lifetime of studying the human experience through anthropology, an interest in Native American cultures, and an attempt to analyze the nature of the reservation system in the United States all led to the project. Trying to understand what the reservation system is all about meant needing to see Native American cultures not only for what they are in themselves, but in terms of the circumstances in which their communities exist.

They have survived in a global arena of ponderous political, economic, and social dynamics. To understand their situations requires attention to power relationships and the ways in which these impinge on people's lives. In my work in the San Carlos Apache community, it was clear that many aspects of people's lives there would have been almost inexplicable without some consideration of the American state and the reservation system (Perry 1993).

It also was evident in looking beyond the reservation system in the United States that such power relationships are not unique to Native American communities. Similar patterns shape the experience of other indigenous peoples in different state systems. Some of the international parallels, in fact, seem so striking that they call for more detailed comparison.

A number of studies already have drawn some limited comparisons, especially between Canada or the United States and Australia (see, e.g., Libby 1989, Wilmsen 1989, Morse 1984, Armitage 1995). At this juncture, though, it seems useful to broaden the scope of these inquiries and consider why the course of state-indigenous relationships has come to look so much alike in so many different places.

The context is a large part of the picture, even though we tend to see it as background rather than as the main subject. Close studies of communities remain the essential bedrock of anthropology, but the purpose here is to offer a bit more of the context.

The basic questions we face in this book are deceptively simple. Why do states deal with indigenous populations the way they do? Why do indigenous peoples within states behave the way they do? But these broad questions lead us into a range of further inquiries that turn out to be more complicated. How can we account for similar patterns of interaction that seem to have developed in states with different histories, geographic areas, and indigenous populations? Similar patterns that result from identical causes may not be all that puzzling. But similarities that arise from different beginnings raise more questions. Can different causes produce parallel effects?

Or is it possible that the differences we perceive among these states are superficial? Do they hide more profound underlying similarities? Conversely, are patterns of interaction that look similar in the various cases misleading? If similar patterns do occur over and over, what about the cultural differences that we anthropologists consider so important? Do they matter much in the long run?

To deal with these issues and to sort out some of the more useful questions, we shall compare the histories of four different states in North America and Australia and consider a range of other global cases more briefly.

A preface is the place where the author not only explains the purpose of the book but defines its limitations. I hasten to do so. Specialists in any of the four regions with which we deal in a single chapter will find that some of the sources and issues that they would have included are missing. This is inevitable. It does seem, however, that the available information tends to substantiate the general patterns. Should anyone offer sources that would drastically revise these rather pessimistic conclusions, I, for one, would be most grateful and relieved.

It would be impossible here to offer extensive or detailed histories of these states. These are readily accessible in many fine historical works, and any attempt to replicate them would be unrealistic in a book of this length. The complexities of these states and the indigenous peoples they encompass have already generated many volumes. Even if I or any author were capable of offering complete coverage of each case, the result would be a massive tome through which few readers would persevere. The rare achievements of that sort all too often result in books that "everyone should read" but few actually do.

The purpose here is somewhat different. The point is to consider these cases in order to perceive patterns and relationships. Closer analyses of each case in its own right would be desirable, but the approach here is to juxtapose examples for comparison and to look for larger patterns, rather than to explore the minute details of such matters as court cases and legislation. I have tried to include such events when they represent major shifts in policy or epitomize ongoing tendencies, but the reader must look elsewhere for fine-focused analysis.

Nor can we explore detailed ethnographic studies of any of the hundreds of diverse indigenous cultures involved in this process. These, too, are available and would be useful parallel reading. Here we can glance only cursorily at the universe of peoples whose fortunes are, after all, the ultimate concern. Once again, though, the interplay between these populations and other interests within their states is the primary subject. To help compensate for this, I have included a selection of recommended ethnographies for indigenous peoples in each state.

In any case, there is much more to say on all of the issues this book touches upon, and I look forward to benefiting from others' continued discussion of them. I also hope that even specialists in these regions will find it useful to compare the circumstances of indigenous peoples in their own areas of study with those in others.

We know that finding the right questions can be as difficult as getting to the answers. We can begin with some of the more apparent similarities in state behavior. Why do states invade indigenous territories? Many populations have lived adjacent to one another for millennia without doing that. Probably many have not even felt the motivation to do so. What accounts for the general sequence of policies from genocide, to assimilation, to recognition of special status that most states have followed from first contact to the present? How much difference does the ability of indigenous peoples to defend themselves make? Does it matter how they choose to respond to invasion?

At the time of European contact, for example, Mexico had a population of millions and considerable military power but fell quickly to the Spanish. Australia, with a small scattered population but few resources that interested early invaders, remained mostly in the possession of its indigenous people for a much longer period. Does it matter whether the resources that indigenous peoples possess happen to be valuable? One would think so, although ultimately, it seems only to be a matter of time before outside interests find that even the sparsest areas have some value, whether it be for subsurface minerals, for bombing practice, or for hazardous waste dumps. The most important question, perhaps, is how most indigenous populations have managed to survive the numerous and concerted attempts to make them disappear. Generally, the range of tactics from genocide to assimilation have failed to get rid of them.

In many ways, this has been a discouraging project. It has involved immersion in case after case of injustice, cruelty, and exploitation. I have not been able to include all of the ghastly examples on record, even in this limited number of cases. There are far too many. But we shall encounter enough to make the situation amply clear.

It seems important to remember, though, that throughout this bloody history, many heroic and humane individuals have made efforts to redress wrongs and make things better—often at great personal cost. In most cases, however, their success has depended on the extent to which their views coincided or conflicted with those of powerful constituencies. Usually this has led to their failure. But the frequent appearance of these divergent views offers some hope, if we care to seize it. These occurrences imply a human potential for positive change. They also underscore the fact that it will not be enough to view the history of state-indigenous interaction in terms of good people and bad people, regardless of how we might define those qualities. In most times and places, there seem to have been plenty of both. The task facing us is to explore the conditions in which this assortment of characters have acted and to fathom why some have been more successful than others in various instances.

The book consists of three sections. In the first section, Chapter 1 offers a broad, historic view of the development of states in general and their behavior toward indigenous peoples. Chapter 2 is a discussion of possible approaches to the questions that the first chapter introduces. In the second section, chapters 3 through 6 examine the cases of Mexico, the United States, Canada, and Australia. In the third part, Chapter 7 discusses examples of other state systems ranging from Namibia to Siberia. Chapter 8 compares the various cases and discusses what we might conclude from them.

This project rests on the shoulders of many and has tried the patience of a few—particularly those closest to the author. Some have listened to ideas during the early stages and made useful suggestions. Professor Robert Tonkinson of the University of Western Australia, Professor Emerita Jane Goodale of Bryn Mawr College, and many others lent their support. I express my gratitude without holding them responsible for any erroneous conclusions I may have reached. I must thank Professor Charles Bishop of the State University of New York at Oswego for an initial reading and excellent critical advice. I also thank St. Lawrence University for a series of Faculty Research Grants that allowed me to pursue these issues over the past several years and which made it possible for me to spend some time in northern Kenya examining development schemes in the Samburu, Turkana, West Pokot, and Baringo Districts. Most of all, I am grateful to Alice Pomponio, Professor of Anthropology at St. Lawrence University, my wife and colleague. If this work has merit, it owes a great deal to her tireless capacity to let me try out ideas and to point out some of the bad ones—and occasionally send me to great heights by writing "good!" in the margins.

Starting Premises

. . . .

I

A Long View

. . . .

1

I n A.D. 1500, an Aranda elder in a desert of the Southern Hemisphere was about as different from a Zapotec villager growing corn on the other side of the world as two human beings could be. A few centuries later, their descendants had much more in common. By the twentieth century, they were living within state systems. They were Australians and Mexicans.

Their languages, beliefs, and ways of life remained distinct, but the imposition of states had placed them in situations with profound, and in some ways very similar, implications. Their states were different, but for the indigenous peoples within them, autonomy, with its choices and access to resources, had foundered within a wider arena.

For much of human history, local populations have been autonomous in important respects. This does not mean that they were isolated. It has always been part of the human experience to interact—to communicate, trade, intermarry, and sometimes fight. These populations were autonomous in the sense that they were free from the imposition of power arising from the framework of a wider political structure. Virtually all human beings today, whether they descend from invading populations

3

or from the aboriginal inhabitants of the land, live within the constraints of one or another state system.

This book is about what it means for formerly autonomous peoples to become encompassed within states while managing to retain their distinct identities. It is an enormous issue. Such populations, although they make up only a tiny portion of the world's peoples, exist within states in every region of the globe.

To deal with them comprehensively would require an encyclopedic approach far beyond the capacities of a single book or an individual author. But the fact that we can even discuss the issue of "indigenous peoples and the state" implies that despite the diversity of these thousands of cases, certain patterns and processes give them something in common. Before going on, though, we should establish some conceptual basis for the ensuing discussion. What is a "state"? It will be useful to consider some of the characteristics of states in a general sense before we proceed to comparison of particular cases.

States

If we take a long view of human history, states are fairly new. The first state probably arose about five thousand years ago between the rivers draining into the Persian Gulf. Since that time, states have developed in many places from the Andean Highlands to the low river courses of Southeast Asia. They have grown and collapsed, expanded, contracted, and disappeared, and other states have grown on their ruins.

States represent a mode of existence radically different in many ways from the experience of most human societies in the past. If persistence indicates success, though, the state has been one of the most successful human developments to date. Although particular states have come and gone, the state as a mode of existence has proliferated inexorably since its first appearance.

We need not bog ourselves down here in the long-standing question of why states arose in the first place. That issue has occupied generations of scholars (see , e.g., Steward 1955, Service 1975, Fried 1967, 1968a, 1968b, Cohen and Service 1978, Claessen and Skalnik 1979, Claessen and van de Velde 1991). As far as we know, states have arisen only among agricultural populations, although food production in itself is not sufficient to produce a state. People have grown crops and raised animals for thousands of years without developing anything resembling a state. Many of them, even now, could exist quite easily without being involved with a state—except that they may need one of their own to protect them from the attentions of other states.

A good deal of discussion has addressed the ways in which states differ from other sorts of human social organization. Half a century ago, V. Gordon Childe (1942) enumerated their characteristics, listing monumental public works, the development of science, long-distance trade, social classes, craft specialization, large, dense populations, and other features.

States require large numbers of people—or is it, perhaps, more accurate to say that large populations require states? Some writers have argued in various ways that large, dense populations require a state as a means of organizing complex activities on a large scale (see, e.g., Wittfogel 1957, Boserup 1965). The populations of states, in any case, usually are far greater than those of societies that organize themselves on the basis of kinship and whose members know each other's names and faces. We should be cautious about this correlation, however, since some large populations, such as the Dani of Irian Jaya, may include tens of thousands of people who share a language and cultural system without developing a state (see Heider 1991).

One characteristic of state systems is that they coordinate and regulate important economic activities and access to resources—farmland, irrigation water, mineral deposits, or whatever. Whether the need for such coordination brought states into existence is a matter of conjecture. Once states did come to exist, though, they produced a different set of circumstances for populations within and outside their boundaries.

States and Interest Groups

The most salient aspect of states is not merely that they encompass large numbers of people, but that they include multiple *categories* of people. Whether these categories amount to social classes, ethnic groups, or other constituencies, states involve internal differentiation. Therein, perhaps, lies their essence. States not only incorporate populations that are different from one another to begin with, but often, despite a tendency to eradicate cultural differences within the populace, they foster internal differentiation in power and wealth.

This implies multiple activities and roles in production, as well as an unequal distribution of wealth and access to resources. Inevitably, it means conflicts of interest. States coordinate these interests and the groups that embrace them in an arena that tends to be as competitive as it is cooperative.

Interest groups, as we use the term here, are categories of individuals who perceive that they have some wishes or needs in common and who are likely to try to influence events in a manner they consider favorable to themselves. The life process of the state lies in the dynamics of its various constituencies. Nikos Poulantzas (1980) and others have pointed out that the state is more than the apparatus of government; it exists at the nexus of these competing interests.

But the situation is more complicated than that. Some interest groups are powerful; some are weak. Some may broaden their bases of influence or power by allying themselves with other constituencies. Some, on the other hand, may misperceive their own best interests. Large numbers of individuals with similar concerns may not even perceive that they have interests in common and fail, therefore, to act as an interest group. This can also happen when animosities prevent their acting in concert—a situation that ruling interest groups often promote. "Divide and rule" is a strategy at least as old as the state itself.

Interest groups that acquire predominant access to resources or influence over state policies—both of which tend to converge—are sometimes referred to as elites. Gaetano Mosca (1939) refers to what he calls a "political class," by which he apparently means the intellectual component of the ruling elite, whose attempts to manipulate state policy on their own behalf nonetheless encounters constraints by "social forces," including the demands of other interests. C. Wright Mills (1956) uses the term "power elite" as an alternative to "ruling class," partly because power can manifest itself in many ways outside the formal mechanisms of government.

It is clear that competing interest groups may supplant one another from time to time in elite positions and that the boundaries of elites are sometimes permeable. R. Michels (1948) notes that the leadership of radical parties, representing nonelite interest groups, tend eventually to moderate their goals and become more distanced from their constituencies. To some extent, he suggests, this is the effect of their acquiring greater experience and sophistication, which distances them from the "incompetence" of the masses. As Nikolai Bukharin ([1925] 1961) argues in response, though, this "incompetence" is often a consequence of social and economic conditions. The separation of leadership from its constituents may also involve co-optation, in which elites cultivate the leaders of disadvantaged groups. This pattern is not infrequent among indigenous populations.

Ernesto Laclau (1979) and others have criticized Poulantzas's position on the grounds that it seems to deny the state any autonomy in its own right and depicts it as merely suspended among the tensions of competing interests. Instances in which states manifest autonomy vis-à-vis other interests, though, often seem to involve situations in which one interest group or elite has managed to acquire control of the state's governing apparatus and, consequently, is able to guide policy on its own behalf. In such cases, the state is far from being a driverless vehicle.

Ideology is an important aspect of state stability. Louis Althusser argues that *"no class can hold State power over a long period without at the same time exercising its hegemony over the State Ideological Apparatuses"* (1971:139). States often reinforce their legitimacy through ideology that claims the universal inclusion of all or most citizens. They may adopt a posture of impartial attention to the broad range of interests that the population represents. State ideology may also rationalize the advantages of powerful interests by appeals to the common good, offering internal order or military protection. Prevailing ideology often disguises the ways in which powerful interest groups influence the state's policies and actions. In general, the state's pose as an entity that exists over and above special interests is an essential aspect of its capacity to mediate and balance these interests or to broker the interests of some over others.

When we refer to the state as an entity of some sort, we must avoid the pitfall of reification, the "fallacy of misplaced concreteness," even though we might teeter perilously close to the brink. There is, in some respects, a tendency for the state to reify itself. This occurs through the manipulation of symbols ranging from flags to monumental structures to divine leadership.

The state actually represents a pattern of relationships. In that sense, a state is less concrete than the population it subsumes or the perceptible infrastructure associated with it. But although this constellation of relationships may be abstract, it is not imaginary. It is real enough to make some things happen and to inhibit other things from happening.

The pattern of relationships within a state can change while the population and perhaps even the infrastructure remains, as has sometimes occurred as a result of military coups or revolutions. More than a thousand years after the fall of the Classic Maya city-states, the Maya people continue to go about their business in Guatemala, El Salvador, Honduras, Belize, and Mexico. But as long as the pattern of relationships composing the state exists, it produces a compelling situation. The state not only monopolizes the legitimate use of power, as Max Weber (1949) points out. It amounts to a set of social, political, and economic circumstances that motivate and constrain the actions of people collectively and individually. It constitutes a field of conditions within which human behavior occurs.

Interest groups within the state involve their own sets of internal relationships, though usually on a more restricted scale. Interest groups may be highly structured, as the Church was in Spain at the time of the

Mexican invasion. They can be loose categories such as rural peasants or *campesinos* who may share certain concerns without forming organizations. They can be ephemeral, like the temperance movement in the United States, or relatively stable, like the farm lobby. Ultimately interest groups consist of individuals who collectively seek to influence events in a manner they prefer. But their actions occur within a social, political, and ideological context.

The state comprises the major arena for these actions and defines the parameters of feasibility through incentives and constraints, allocating power and advantage and imposing restrictions, allowing and repressing options.

The state systems that have arisen, developed, and declined throughout recent human history have shown similarities in these respects and others. The Inca Empire, Sumer, Great Britain, and most other states have had to deal with the demands of merchants, the priesthood, the underclass, and other constituencies while the ruling interests attempted to retain enough order to perpetuate their own positions.

In later chapters, we shall examine the processes through which four state systems—Mexico, the United States, Canada, and Australia—have incorporated local indigenous populations. The ways in which the formal structures of the state and the interest groups within it have affected the lives and circumstances of indigenous populations is one important part of this discussion. Another is the responses of the indigenous peoples themselves as they have attempted to act in their own interests within this arena.

States and Indigenous Peoples

While the term "indigenous peoples" refers here to local populations that existed in place before a state system incorporated them, the phrase "in place" requires some qualification. Small autonomous populations in some areas have inhabited vast tracts of land, utilizing widely scattered resources in a systematic manner from season to season. In this sense, the "place" that they were "in" implies far more than the locality where they happened to be smoking meat over a fire at the time outsiders first encountered them.

The connections of indigenous peoples to land has often been intricate, subtle, and tremendously complex in ways that make the European criteria of ownership seem simplistic. In any case, they were the prior occupants of the region that subsequently fell within the bounds of a state. They have been there, as many state documents acknowledge, "from time immemorial."

Many writers refer to state power as "hegemony." This has at least two meanings. The most straightforward, perhaps—and the meaning of the term in this discussion—is simply the extension and range of state power. Other writers, following the work of Antonio Gramsci (1971), take hegemony to imply the acceptance of state power by the populace. Since we are discussing cases here in which the extension and maintenance of power has involved violence and repression, the issue of acceptance—especially if it implies a willing choice on the part of the people—is highly problematic. For that reason, hegemony here means only that the state has encompassed an indigenous population. This meaning of the term leaves open the complex issues of acceptance, acquiescence, and resistance for further discussion.

Because states exist in a matrix of intersecting interests, an indigenous population that a state incorporates enters this milieu and becomes still another group facing the need to compete on its own behalf. Other interest groups often pursue a variety of ways to weaken indigenous populations' capacity to compete. Powerful interests sometimes achieve this by influencing state policies, which government agencies implement in the state's name.

Ways to weaken local indigenous peoples might involve dispersing them or relocating them collectively, which frees their land or other resources for exploitation by others. In some cases, interest groups have subjected indigenous populations to attempts at genocide as happened in the United States and Australia during the nineteenth century and in Brazil, Irian Jaya, East Timor, and other places in the twentieth.

Short of annihilation, the surviving individuals may simply become citizens of the state without special status. This occurred in Mexico, as many indigenous peoples merged through intermarriage and altered identity into the general population through the process of *mestizaje*. Such a process can result in the de facto disappearance of the population altogether, since their scattered members no longer constitute a collectivity with enough cohesion to act effectively on their own behalf. As indigenous collectivities lose their identities, the process may involve the loss of language and the eradication of cultural phenomena such as kinship systems, ceremonials, and so forth, that had lent coherence to the population. The dissolution of indigenous communities through absorbing their members into the general populace has been the political aim in many states.

Often, though, this process has not gone to completion. For many reasons that we shall explore below, indigenous peoples often persist as discernible and self-conscious groups within state systems. Their ways of life may change; their boundaries may blur; and their status may be subject to challenge. But in many cases—sometimes after centuries of beleaguered existence—they have remained.

Cases for Comparison

In the past few thousand years, the encompassment of indigenous peoples by states has occurred too many times to permit any comprehensive discussion here. Yet beyond the details of historic circumstances, certain dynamics recur. The United States, Australia, Canada, and Mexico offer prominent examples of these processes.

This set of cases has important limitations. The four states not only have much in common, but they also differ in many ways from other possible examples of state systems. All four began as colonies of invading European states and subsequently became independent states in their own right. All have been associated with the extension of global capitalism and have participated in its growth.

During the course of their histories, moreover, they influenced one another considerably. All were part of a shared global system of ideas, commerce, and political forces. In that sense, we might perceive them as four local manifestations of the same global process (see, e.g., Frank 1975, Wallerstein 1974, 1984).

On the other hand, while the United States, Canada, and Australia developed on the British model, Mexico arose from the Spanish state. All of them have distinct aspects and histories. In the final chapter, we shall also briefly discuss a range of other examples. At this point, however, the four cases will serve to identify certain patterns.

The indigenous peoples in these states differed widely from one another, even within the bounds of individual states. Spanish invaders in Mexico found dense populations with their own indigenous states that were founded on a heritage of over two thousand years of political processes. Beyond the margins of these Mexican states, many small agrarian communities and nomadic bands had retained their autonomy.

In Australia the British encountered a vast continent with a sparse, generally mobile population that relied entirely on wild foods. In the northern region of North America that later became Canada, there were a few agricultural villages in the Great Lakes and St. Lawrence Valley area in the sixteenth century, but most of the indigenous peoples throughout the great expanse of boreal forest, prairies, and tundra relied on wild foods.

The area that eventually came to be the United States shared many indigenous peoples with Canada and Mexico, both because of changing state boundaries and because of indigenous territories that overlapped them. Encompassing a range of ecological zones, including many well suited for agriculture, the region included mobile hunters and gatherers, sedentary villages, political confederations, and some densely populated societies with many of the characteristics of states (see, e.g., Smith 1990, Fowler 1975).

States, Nations, Tribes, and Bands

Although we have noted that a state consists of more than the structure of government, states inevitably *have* governmental structures. Some sort of political mechanism mediates and exercises power, regulates access to resources, imposes a degree of order, and so on. This is one way in which the concept of the state differs from the concept of "nation."

The terms "nation" and "state" are often interchangeable in contemporary usage, but they are not the same. "Nation," in the archaic sense, has the same roots as "natal" or "native." In Europe through the seventeenth century, the term often simply meant "the people of" some particular place or region—the people born there, the inhabitants (Rustow 1968:8).

This did not necessarily imply that they had a state with a formal apparatus of governance or even that they shared any overall coordination of activity. Thus, we have biblical references to the "nations" of various regions and colonial allusions to "Indian nations" by the same Europeans who often denied that these people had any true societies, let alone state systems. Fray Alonso Benavides, writing in New Spain in the early 1600s, refers to the "huge Apache nation," even as he makes it clear that they are scattered, mobile, and diverse with no overall political structure (quoted in Bolton 1916).

This dichotomy between nation and state was pivotal in the refusal of many colonial authorities, such as the British in Canada, the United States, and Australia, to acknowledge that indigenous inhabitants possessed organized societies. The principle was a central basis upon which the Crown denied indigenous rights to land based on prior ownership (Asch 1984:43, Williams 1986:110).

Blending the ideas of state and nation became more frequent in eighteenth-century Europe as thinkers of the Enlightenment pondered the issues of social contract and rational governance. Yet even now, the difference remains. We have many examples of "nationalist movements" involving populations who seek independence from the states that incorporate them. In such cases, groups that consider themselves nations often hope to establish states of their own that do not yet exist, and perhaps never did (see Hobsbawm 1989:12).

Benedict Anderson (1983) has referred to nations as "imagined communities"—that is, collectivities that come to feel that they share some common essence that distinguishes them from all others. He notes that in some cases the growth of literacy and the mass publication of popular fiction in the vernacular has played an important role in generating this collective sense of identity.

In the interest of state cohesion, it is desirable for concepts of nationhood to coincide with the extent of state boundaries. The term "nation-state" suggests such a correspondence. As the events of the world in the late twentieth century make amply clear, though, this does not always reflect reality. We need only review the roster of separatist movements in Europe alone to underscore the frequency of this disjuncture.

In the United States after independence from Britain, the new American state became more self-conscious regarding the issue of nationhood as it tried to deal with the obstreperous regional interests of the former colonies. In references to indigenous peoples, the term "nation" fell to disuse, and "tribe" came to be more common. "Tribe" tended to demote indigenous peoples to a more primitive social order than the term "nation" implied (see Lewis 1968:146).

In Canada the term "band" became the equivalent of "tribe" and, if anything, further diminished the sense of indigenous social complexity. This shift in terminology coincided with the notion of universal, but differentiated, progress in human affairs that had come into vogue among Euro-American intellectuals by the beginning of the nineteenth century.

In Mexico after independence from Spain, there was more inclination to stress the fiction of universal incorporation into the new state. The United States and Canada continued to hold indigenous societies at an ambivalent arm's length. Chief Justice John Marshall's "Cherokee Nation" decisions referred to them as "domestic dependent nations." The Mexican government, however, tried to incorporate *indios* as full citizens, which, no doubt, had something to do with the fact that indigenous peoples in Mexico at the time constituted the majority of the population. The term *indios* applied in a comprehensive sense to the diverse range of indigenous peoples, while names of specific aggregations—Yaqui or Tepehuane—referred to particular groups. Only in the relatively uncontrolled regions to the north, where the Apache, Yaqui, and a few others were more successful in resisting incorporation by the Mexican state, do we find frequent generic reference to *los tribus barbaros* ("barbarous tribes") who were less likely candidates for full citizenship.

By the mid-nineteenth century, though, the intellectual *científicos*, positivists who favored a scientific approach to government, subscribed to the widely shared Euro-American view that *indios* represented a more primitive stage of human development. The *científicos* were openly pessimistic about the capacity of these people for civilization.

In Australia the term "nation" never did apply to indigenous peoples, who for the first century or so were considered all but irrelevant to the affairs of the state. In keeping with the nineteenth-century evolutionary thinking of intellectuals in Europe, Canada, the United States, and Mexico, prevailing Australian opinion agreed that Aboriginal peoples represented a lower stage of existence. Many assumed that they were doomed to disappear before long and therefore did not warrant much attention. At most, the more tender-hearted expressed some sympathy for them and urged that humane policies help to "smooth the dying pillow." Others, often of a less intellectual bent, tried their best to hasten Aboriginal disappearance.

The term "Aboriginal," with its neutral tone, merely acknowledged that they had existed prior to the European arrival. Classification of their social or political organization was not a matter of much concern until the twentieth century. The term "horde," with its implication of a minimally organized collection of individuals, appeared in some writings by the turn of the century. "Tribe" gained currency in the early twentieth century, although not without some discussion among scholars (Williams 1986:232n, Berndt and Berndt 1992:25).

The Expansion of States

States have tended to expand, although this process has often been episodic, interspersed with periods of consolidation and even retreat. One aspect of this tendency to expand has been the need to establish order at the margins of state territory, incorporating troublesome populations that clash or compete with peoples within the state's boundaries. This, however, does not account for the expansion of England, Spain, and other European states that claimed regions far beyond their boundaries. What did the movers of state expansion in these cases hope to acquire for their efforts?

In general, their motives involved material considerations. In Mexico the Spanish were after precious metals, particularly gold and silver. Individual Spaniards sought personal fortunes, generally in the form of land and the indigenous labor to work it. The Crown and the Church endeavored to extend Christendom among nonbelievers.

In Canada and along the Atlantic Coast, the British wanted fish, furs, timber, and land for settlement. In Australia the British sought an out-of-the-way repository for convicts after the American colonies were no longer available for that purpose. Other resources, such as gold and grazing land for livestock, became more important later.

In each case, expansion benefited some, but by no means all, of the state's home population. The invasion of Mexico served the immediate interests of the Church, the Crown, and an elite handful of adventurers in its service. Most of the forces behind colonization were powerful constituencies within the Spanish state. But the invasion did little to serve the vast numbers of rural Spanish peasants and the urban underclass that constituted the majority of Spain's population.

In England the quest for furs and timber, the later appropriation of land in North America, and the establishment of a penal colony in Australia also favored relatively special interests. In every case, particular constituencies were powerful enough, or astute enough, to promote policies of state expansion for their own benefit, but these policies often ignored or conflicted with the interests of others within the same state. Fernand Braudel remarks that

> the first territorial state to complete its transformation into a national economy or national market, England, fell under the domination of its merchants fairly soon after the 1288 revolution. It is hardly surprising that in preindustrial Europe a certain determinance seems to have brought about the coincidence of political power and economic power. (1979:51)

By the sixteenth century, the ability of European commercial interests to influence states on their behalf had led to violent interstate conflicts. The French, English, Spanish, Dutch, and even the Danish states vied with each other in the Caribbean and the coastal areas of North and South America on behalf of their trading interests. But in many respects, the majority of the populations within these states, who benefited little from these maneuverings, had more in common with the indigenous peoples in conquered areas than with their own elite who exploited both.

Within these conquered regions, the interests of various state constituencies also found themselves at odds with one another. The Jesuits in New Spain opposed *encomenderos* and mine owners regarding the use of indigenous labor. Planters in the Caribbean vehemently opposed the restrictive trade policies the English Parliament imposed to protect domestic industries. Conflicts arose in Australia between British immigrants who were established in towns and freed convicts who raised sheep in the Outback. Generally, the incentives and positions of various constituencies regarding indigenous peoples and each other reflected their perceptions of their own advantage and the aims they wished to fulfill, whether these were the acquisition of raw materials, labor, souls, or land.

The Appropriation of Land

State colonial expansion generated kaleidoscopic processes and myriad motivations, but most often land was a central concern. Appropriation of land took various forms, ranging from the violent eradication of the inhabitants to a bland disregard of their presence. As we have noted, European colonial states often claimed vast tracts of territory as uninhabited, particularly when they were the domain of hunting and foraging peoples who did not settle in permanent locations.

At times this may have been based on genuine misunderstanding. European invaders came from densely populated agrarian societies whose lands already were short of timber and other resources. No doubt they were unfamiliar with land-use patterns of people who exploited widely scattered wild foods on a methodical and sustainable basis, although there is little evidence that most of them would have cared in any case. The British applied the principle, expressed in the arguments of John Locke, that true ownership of land required the transformation of nature through the investment of human labor. In this view, one had to farm land in order to claim it (Williams 1986:112).

But more often than not, this posture amounted to a rationale for appropriation rather than a misunderstanding in good faith. In North America, the British claimed sovereignty over lands in which indigenous peoples had grown crops for many centuries. During the early years of colonial expansion, in the "Age of Discovery," European heads of state developed a "Law of Nations," but this dealt mainly with the principles by which states would recognize each other's claims of the territories they invaded. There was little suggestion that indigenous populations might have prior and more legitimate claims to the lands they inhabited (Green and Dickason 1989).

Although the British Crown denied rights of land ownership even to highly visible, stable indigenous populations, it usually acknowledged, nonetheless, that these people had been present from time immemorial. The British state admitted that they had been *using* the land and therefore might warrant consideration based on that occupancy. But the Crown offered this more as a gesture of benevolence than as a recognition of inalienable rights. In the United States, it was conventional to describe indigenous peoples as having "roamed" the land, suggesting something more comparable to wildlife than to established societies.

In Mexico, although the Spanish took over sedentary, hierarchical indigenous societies practicing intensive agriculture, local populations also lost control over their use of land. In this case, however, with the establishment of plantation-like *encomiendas* and the policies of *reducción*, which gathered local populations into centralized communities, the Spanish appropriated not only the land but the labor of the inhabitants to farm it (see Spicer 1967:13).

To many indigenous populations, individual exclusive ownership of land in the European sense was an alien concept. Many had developed intricate means of assuring collective access to vital and scattered resources. Often—particularly among those who placed substantial reliance on wild foods—these patterns acted to prevent individual monopolization of particular localities. Even in the few cases when agents of the state were aware of this, however, these patterns received little recognition. In the face of pressures by interests that applied the rationales of state acquisition by conquest or that defined the lands as "unoccupied" or "undeveloped," the intricacies of indigenous land tenure were of little concern.

The governing interests of expanding states usually took the claims of indigenous peoples seriously only when the latter were able to mount practical resistance, or when there was some other perceived advantage to the state in respecting their sovereignty. In the early phases of encroachment, negotiated settlements often involved agreements for peaceful coexistence or compensation for land. As long as the British in Canada were engaged in struggles with other European powers, they sought the assistance, or at least the neutrality, of indigenous peoples. In Australia the early colonial government of New South Wales saw the possibility of trouble with the Aboriginals as an irritant that could only complicate the problems of dealing with convict labor (Hughes 1986:94, 273).

Agreements with indigenous peoples often arose from widely differing assumptions about human relationships to land, about the relationship of the contractual parties to one another, and in general, about what the exchanges entailed. While in many cases inadequate communication introduced inadvertent confusion to these agreements, sometimes they involved outright deceit. As the invading populations became more numerous and indigenous populations declined—often ravaged by diseases that arrived with Europeans—shifts in the balance of power led states to abrogate or disregard many such agreements.

In Australia most indigenous populations were not numerous enough to defend the territories they held. Their density in some regions amounted to one person per tens or even hundreds of square miles, although recent estimates suggest a greater population along the east coast. Notwithstanding their complex systems of rules specifying the rights of local groups to land and their responsibilities for its resources, and despite their sporadic attempts at resistance, in the long run they simply were pushed aside with little pretense of legitimate transfer.

Where larger and more concentrated indigenous populations were capable of retaining possession of their territories in the face of pressure, as they were in the United States and a few parts of Australia, they often became targets of overt policies of genocide. Failing that outcome, interest groups influenced the government to displace them through force and relocate them to less desirable areas.

The outcome in all four states has been the massive loss of indigenous peoples' land base, particularly when there was no immediate use for their labor. In some instances, however, it served the purposes of other interests to leave indigenous populations on their land, though not necessarily in control of it. This was the case in parts of Mexico, in North American plantations, and in the Canadian fur trade areas, where the products of indigenous labor were of economic value.

Processes of Incorporation

With invaders having appropriated most of their land, surviving indigenous peoples have often been relegated to enclaves with little access to most of their resources. Once it was no longer possible for other constituencies to portray these remnant populations as a serious threat, calls for annihilation usually lost favor. Instead, powerful interests within each state promoted policies inhibiting the ability of indigenous peoples to compete within the wider arena of state hegemony. The most obvious of these measures has usually been outright exclusion from access to wealth and power within the state system. Racism and ethnic discrimination in their various forms have often constituted ideological devices in implementing this strategy.

On the other hand, such exclusion presented a paradox. It generally stopped short of total rejection from the state, which would have amounted to independence. Indigenous peoples have not been allowed to escape the bounds of state hegemony. To this end, various assimilation policies have developed to promote the incorporation of indigenous populations into the state on terms acceptable to more powerful interests within the state system. Generally this has involved marginalization and relegation to the role of surplus cheap, self-reproducing labor.

This process has meant induction into the labor force at the lowest levels, often on an occasional basis. Having lost their resource bases, indigenous peoples have found themselves relegated to a situation in which they could not survive without money, but had nothing to sell but their labor. They have often remained in situations of chronic underemployment, with little choice but to accept menial or dangerous jobs that more well-situated constituencies find undesirable.

Indigenous enclaves, whether state-administered reserves or simply de facto indigenous communities, are self-reproducing with little cost to potential employers and provide a reserve pool of labor for use whenever needed (see Burawoy 1976). Whether for harvesting crops, working in mines, or herding livestock, the labor pool is available or dispensable at the convenience of the employer, depending upon the season or the vagaries of world commodity prices. In colonial Chiapas, by 1790 "the central altiplano was transformed into a reservoir of unused Indian labor, a reservoir that might be tapped during moments of expansion and dammed up at moments of contraction" (Wasserstrom 1983:105).

Other measures tended to perpetuate this situation and inhibit the capacity of indigenous peoples to pursue their collective interests effectively. Many states have intervened in the political structure of indigenous populations, appointing leaders who are willing to act as liaisons with the government and with more powerful interest groups. This lends a semblance of legitimacy to agreements that may not resonate well with the interests of the indigenous population.

The Spanish appointed indigenous *caciques* to represent state authority in local communities. The United States and Canada imposed local governing structures, "tribal" or "band" governments that were articulated to the state's government. In some cases, this arrangement can facilitate the expression of indigenous concerns to the state. It may also, however, tend to blunt the possibility of effective resistance and render indigenous communities more vulnerable to the initiatives of other interests.

Formal education has also played an important role in this process. Presented as a benefit to help indigenous peoples overcome their problems of poverty, the ideology behind these initiatives often involves an implicit assumption that the dire situation of indigenous populations stems from their own ignorance. This has resulted in aggressive measures to alienate children from their indigenous heritage and social milieu and to undermine their sense of collective identity.

In the United States, Canada, and Australia at various periods, indigenous education has entailed sending children to boarding schools far from their communities. In these schools, the emphasis usually has been on such things as discipline, speaking English (or French), and the value of hard work. Generally this has meant menial labor that the instructors would not choose to do themselves (see Littlefield 1989, 1993a). It has also involved rigorous segregation by sex, which some writers have suggested was intended to depress indigenous birth rates (Morris 1989:110).

For the most part, these institutions have been designed to prepare students to enter the labor force at the "appropriate" (lowest) levels, rather than offering the type of education accessible to the elite, which offers avenues to positions of power and economic advantage.

Indigenous populations have managed to persist, despite these assaults, and states have developed counterstrategies in response to their persistence. Once indigenous populations have found themselves in relatively powerless positions, other interest groups within the state have often begun to appropriate cultural symbols of their identity rather than suppress them. Music, graphic designs, elements of costume, and religious effigies have become objects of "appreciation" by the elite. They may even become celebrated emblems of the collective "national heritage."

Thus, replications of Aboriginal designs decorate the walls of Australian corporate executives. Aztec motifs grace a facade on the campus of the National University of Mexico. Carved poles from the Pacific Coast tower over Canadian municipal parks. And on United States television, a braided Native American man dressed in beaded, fringed buckskin wipes away a tear as a passing motorist flings trash onto the roadside.

Indigenous Strategies of Resistance and Survival

Indigenous peoples have not been passive victims. Overpowered through violence in all four states and vastly outnumbered except in Mexico, where they are nonetheless fragmented and often dispersed, they have altered their strategies to pursue their own interests as best they can. Their initial responses to the appearance of invading populations varied according to their circumstances. In Mexico, Cortés encountered armed resistance among smaller states at the margins of the Aztec Empire and, eventually, by the Aztecs themselves. In most cases, though, violent reaction came later. In Australia indigenous peoples met the first Europeans with mild curiosity but, for the most part, went about their business until they faced unacceptable encroachment and attacks.

Australian indigenous cultures had established intricate relationships among humans, the land, and its resources. These systems had developed in a manner that prevented the likelihood of one group's unwelcome incursion into another's territory. Much of this involved concepts of spiritual association with sacred sites within the domain of various local groups. Although the extent and limits of group territories were precise and well defined, mutually understood protocol nonetheless kept these territories accessible to others.

The people were fully capable of violent measures in response to hostility or to breaches of acceptable behavior, but their populations were small. Their subsistence required frequent movement within their ranges, and they were widely scattered across vast regions. Many fought in skirmishes and held out through guerrilla tactics, but in the long run, concerted action to defend the boundaries of their territories from armed, encroaching Europeans was not a feasible solution for them (see Reynolds 1982, Rowley 1970).

In Canada and the United States, indigenous reactions also varied. Many groups on the Atlantic Coast countenanced Europeans without initial resistance or overt hostility. Their reactions seem to have ranged from friendly curiosity to aloof disdain for the short, hairy, and rather foul-smelling strangers who had arrived after months at sea. Some were willing to enter into trade relationships or even to accept Europeans as allies in opposition to other indigenous groups.

North of the St. Lawrence River, the hunters that Europeans later called Naskapi, Montagnais, and Cree utilized vast territories in small, mobile groups. In the Great Lakes and Atlantic Coast regions, agricultural peoples had more densely populated stable towns and cultivated fields. For the most part, their customary territories were well established, although they often exploited overlapping hunting territories. They had been accustomed to carrying on extensive trade among themselves for many centuries, some of it over great distances.

In the Southeast, much the same situation prevailed with regard to European contacts from the Atlantic Coast. Hernando de Soto's expedition in the 1500s ravaged and destroyed many populations to such an extent, however, that there is little record of indigenous response. These episodes of contact had their own trajectories, which we shall consider in more detail in later chapters. But once the invading populations had secured control or possession of most of the land and indigenous peoples were relegated to reduced enclaves, their strategies took other forms.

Indigenous peoples who were unable either to resist encroachment or to retreat faced the need to adapt to the new context. Where they had lost their resource bases and suffered attrition through disease or warfare, their most compelling need was for physical survival, which meant acquiring adequate nutrition.

Most attempted to participate in the cash economy that engulfed them. In the United States, the Apache, in the aftermath of fierce resistance, became the major source of unskilled labor in the Southwest by the end of the nineteenth century. In the Great Basin and Intermontane Plateau, the Washo, Paiute, Shuswap, and others took jobs as laborers on ranches and farms. In Australia some Aboriginal groups took on short-term seasonal work on sheep and cattle stations and ranches, although well into the twentieth century this was often for food rather than for wages. Most, if they were able, retained considerable reliance on "bush tucker" during much of the year.

The forms of indigenous labor in various instances ranged from outright chattel slavery to wage work. Mexican *encomiendas* and later, *haciendas*, often involved feudal types of arrangements. Missions and *haciendas* also used the *repartimiento* system of sporadically drafting labor from the countryside. Debt peonage, which demanded labor to pay off the costs of food or other supplies, took various forms in regions ranging from southern Mexico to the Subarctic fur trade. Bonded servants worked as domestics and farm labor in many areas. Where wage work was technically voluntary, as in the United States, it often amounted to coercion through impoverishment.

Indigenous peoples in Canada supplemented their bush foods and the rations promised in treaties by acting as hunting and fishing guides and as laborers in the timber, construction, and coastal fishing industries. Indigenous communities in Mexico raised crops for sale. Many worked on European establishments such as *haciendas* in the north or henequen plantations in Yucatán. As early as the sixteenth century, *tamemes* ("load carriers") were a major source of transport (Chance 1989:22). Tlaxcalans established a role as carriers and messengers throughout New Spain (Chance 1989:33). During the eighteenth and nineteenth centuries, many indigenous peoples in Mexico continued to work as *cargadores*, providing human labor for the transport of goods.

Much of this labor was compulsory—either through force or in the sense that few alternatives remained for subsistence. In many cases, though, indigenous peoples actively sought employment. Some also pursued the formal education that might allow them to operate more effectively within the context in which they found themselves.

In all cases, however, competition with other groups tended to exclude indigenous peoples from the most lucrative employment and often prevented them from pursuing their educational goals beyond rudimentary levels. Chronic underemployment tended to become an established fact of life for most indigenous people in all four states.

At the same time, many indigenous populations sought to reaffirm and strengthen their collective identities. Generally, they attempted to retain group cohesion as a source of mutual support among themselves. Such cohesion often meant attempts to maintain their systems of kin ties, albeit with adjustments in many cases, their ceremonial life, ideology, and language. This process often gained impetus as a result of the frustration arising from inadequate opportunities within the wider arena, although a commitment to indigenous cultural systems in their own right was a significant factor.

These cultural systems not only provided networks of support but also defined personal identity and offered coherent ideology that in times of stress became all the more important. It also became apparent to many of them that the dispersal of their populations would bring about severe vulnerability to the machinations of outside interests. To many, the greatest hope for an acceptable mode of survival lay in maintaining their identity as a basis for collective action. Throughout this process, their collective identity remained under persistent assault by missionaries, government agents, and other functionaries of the state.

Some indigenous strategies for survival posed threats to their cohesion. Acceptance of wage labor, for example, often meant dispersal and the adoption of different modes of behavior and personal interaction. It sometimes meant a downplaying of cultural identity. Many, nonetheless, attempted to balance and accommodate these essentially contradictory demands.

Indigenous peoples also attempted to deal with the state through its own structures. In the 1730s, for example, a delegation of Yaqui leaders traveled to the capital of Sonora to express their concerns to Spanish officials (Spicer 1980). In the United States, Native Americans sent numerous delegations to Washington, often addressing Congress about grievances. Similar delegations of native peoples in Canada visited Ottawa and the provincial capitals. In Australia, Aboriginal organizations on numerous occasions chided the government for failing to live up to its stated ideals of equality and justice.

If such appeals seldom achieved their intended results, access to the legal system of the state sometimes proved to be more successful. Although legal systems of states have tended to reflect the interests and concerns of the most powerful constituencies, their legitimacy usually rests on the supposition that laws are universally applicable (Unger 1986, Kairys 1982). Once in place, they are accessible, at least theoretically, to all constituencies. Some indigenous peoples have utilized this opportunity to gain rulings that have worked in their favor, although their overall success has been mixed. Even in South Africa during the grimmest days of apartheid, however, the courts offered more hope of redress than other bodies of government.

Indigenous peoples also have attempted to broaden the bases of their interest groups. In most cases, to the extent that they have maintained some cohesion, indigenous communities have constituted clusters of tiny minorities within the state's population. In the aggregate, however, these scattered populations constitute larger potential constituencies.

Indigenous coalitions for resistance developed as early as the seventeenth century in New England, when Metacom of the Wampanoags headed an alliance that the English eventually destroyed in King Philip's War. The Creeks joined the Yamasee in the Southeast against the British but failed partly because they were unable to secure the alliance of the Cherokee towns. In the Midwest, Black Hawk's and Pontiac's coalitions had dramatic but brief successes.

In Mexico the Mixtón Wars beginning in the first few years after Conquest involved loosely concerted action against the Spanish by indigenous peoples in the regions north of Mexico City. Local populations carried out sporadic raids for years against the mining operations at Zacatecas. The "Caste Wars" of the late nineteenth century in the Maya region involved a new religious order containing Christian elements and continued sporadically for decades. In 1994 the Zapatista Army of National Liberation in Chiapas threatened to spread rebellion to other states and caused the ruling party much concern.

Militant coalitions did not play a major role in Australia. Most resistance was on a small local scale, often in response to atrocities committed by local settlers (see, e.g., Rowley 1970, Reece 1974, Reynolds 1982). By the early twentieth century, however, a number of organizations had formed to represent Aboriginal interests. By that time, many local populations in Australia had lost possession of their territories and gathered around sheep or cattle stations, mining operations, or mission stations. Many of these groups consisted of remnants of different local populations. Their aggregation may have helped to foster some sense of common purpose with regard to the state.

Most indigenous coalitions in Canada before the twentieth century formed within populations with similar cultural and linguistic identity, although even in the 1860s and 1870s, Cree, Assiniboin, Métis, and others in southern Saskatchewan pressed their grievances in concert to the Canadian government (Miller 1991:173). In the early twentieth century, a number of indigenous organizations in Canada formed to represent their concerns collectively across ethnic lines, both on a regional basis and in some cases on a national scale. Similar developments occurred in the United States during that period. The National Congress of American Indians began in the 1940s. And more recently, Native Hawaiians have explored common issues with other indigenous peoples in the United States.

In the latter half of this century, indigenous peoples have attempted to expand their base of support beyond the bounds of their own state systems. Canadian and United States indigenous groups have sent delegations to the United Nations to appeal for international support. Representatives of Australian Aboriginal peoples have conferred regularly with Native groups in Canada. Native American groups in the United States and Canada have also taken a strong interest in the cause of indigenous peoples in Latin America, Australia, and New Zealand. In 1994 the United Nations passed a resolution endorsing the recognition of indigenous rights on a global scale.

These developments characterize the continuing flow of interaction among indigenous peoples and state systems. In some instances, these events have led to forceful assertions of group identity and to some redefinition of that identity. Among other things, they suggest that indigenous peoples will continue to assert their interests, explore strategies, and perhaps recast their concerns with increasing consideration of other peoples with whom they share common issues.

The chapters in Part 2 will examine in more detail the historical development of the four state systems, the indigenous peoples of each state, the processes of incorporation, and the actions of indigenous peoples in response. Finally, we shall compare these cases with other examples. Before doing so, however, we must consider some of the ways in which we might approach this inquiry. What sorts of questions should we ask?

Ideas and
Ideology

. . . .

2

Episodes of states incorporating indigenous populations constitute historic tales acted out in numerous locales, and the dynamic principles involved in these processes are not entirely self-evident. To understand what happened and why it happened requires interpretation. Interpretation, in turn, demands a framework of assumptions that unavoidably reflects a point of view.

In dealing with ideological issues that involve state relationships with indigenous peoples, we confront a problem with two faces. On the one hand, we must attend to the ideology that states have generated with regard to their own actions in the colonial enterprise. This has often amounted to self-justifying rationalization. On the other hand, we need to try to take a position beyond this and to adopt a more detached perspective. Our job is to understand in reasonably disinterested fashion the reasons for these events, the processes involved, and their consequences.

We face this task, however, imbued with ideology that arises from and is immersed inextricably in one of the colonial states under discussion.

We derive our epistemology from the very intellectual milieu that gave rise to colonialism in the first place.

Having taken note of this problem, however, we have little choice but to push on—ever on the alert for distorting bias. Perhaps one ray of hope within the depths of this dilemma lies in the internal contradictions that plagued European thought throughout the historic era we are considering. While some aspects of colonialist ideology countenanced the policies of the period and served to justify them, very few apologists constructed arguments that expressly favored cruelty, exploitation, and genocide for their own sake. Most European thinkers of the time would have agreed that these aspects of colonialism were unfortunate, at best. The task of rationalizers, then, was to justify the inevitable occurrences of these evils in the quest for a greater good.

This exercise always entailed a rather shaky juxtaposition of means and ends. We have the advantage now, though, of letting some of these contradictory premises fall asunder as they have always tended to do. We can deplore the horrors of colonialism, indulging our own ideological preference, without having to justify them as others did in the past. It may not be fair, but it does free our hands a bit from some dead issues.

At the outset, we face a series of "why" questions. Why did European states begin the process of colonization in the first place? Why did they interact with indigenous peoples the way they did? Why did indigenous peoples respond in the ways they did? How have so many indigenous populations managed to remain distinct within existing states? Why, having survived, are they so consistently beset by poverty and relative powerlessness?

These questions have many different specific answers arising from a range of historic cases. We can address those only through fuller discussion of the four cases in later chapters. But the questions also evoke different responses according to the framework of suppositions from which we approach them.

Ideological Opposition: Christian versus Pagan

For many Europeans of past centuries, the "why" of colonial expansion would not have amounted to a simple drive to rob and exploit populations in other parts of the world without reference to some further underlying motivation. Most such motivations would have rested on what seemed to be the more positive aspects of colonialism. Colonialism not only enriched the state but brought Christianity, or civilization, or some other supposed benefit to the unenlightened inhabitants of those far-off lands. At times isolated voices such as that of Bartolomeo de Las Casas decried the injustices that occurred. But even Las Casas's objections were not to colonialism in itself but to unnecessarily harsh treatment of the colonized. Most people who gave it much thought at the time would have rationalized colonialism as a beneficent enterprise.

This tendency to take a positive view of colonialism has appeared in many versions. There are a few writers even in the mid-1990s who would argue that colonialism brought many benefits to what is now called the Third World (see Said's 1993 discussion).

The Spanish who invaded Mexico in the early sixteenth century had just driven the Moorish occupiers from the Iberian Peninsula. The ideology associated with that struggle emphasized religious conflict expressed through the violent use of arms. In the succeeding decades, the concept of a militant Christianity overcoming infidels through force—whether they be Muslims, Jews, or indigenous peoples who had never heard of Jesus—became a well-established precedent that required no additional justification.

The spread of Christianity often took a back seat to the appropriation of precious metals, but it was a significant factor throughout the Spanish colonial period. In many respects, the two motivations were hardly separable. Despite conflicts between the clergy and other Spanish interests, Christianity in many ways served to rationalize and facilitate the pursuit of wealth.

The ideology and practice of Spanish conquest involved internal contradictions, though, and the actors in the colonial arena were not monolithic in their views. Columbus is one of our best examples of one who apparently could not have cared less about the well-being of the inhabitants of the Indies and wreaked countless horrors on them (see Todorov 1984). The Church and the Crown soon came to the conclusion, though, that the indigenous peoples of Mexico were human beings with souls capable of salvation and therefore had some right to protection by the state.

There was some disparity between Royal decrees of the Spanish Court and the behavior of colonials across the Atlantic. The phrase *obezco pero no cumplo* ("I obey but I do not comply") has a long history in Mexico. At least some of them, nonetheless, objected to widespread forced labor and oppression, ineffective as these protests may have been.

The Spanish also encouraged intermarriage with high-ranking Aztec women as a means of consolidating the Spaniards' position within the existing political structure. This would seem to be a clear recognition of the humanity of indigenous Mexicans, however pragmatic the motivation. There were some parallels between the strongly hierarchical structures of Spanish and Aztec societies, and perhaps even some sense of affinity between the elites of both. This was rather different from the simplistic racism that later became so prominent throughout North America.

The Spanish case is also an interesting contrast, incidentally, to the sexual interaction between British and indigenous peoples in the rest of North America and Australia, which generally was far more exploitative, depersonalized, and frowned upon when it was impossible for state officialdom to ignore it.

The Ideology of Resource Appropriation

Religion played a lesser role in the British policies in North America, possibly because of the greater religious diversity in England and because the Protestant churches could not exert the same degree of political power there as the Roman Catholic Church did in Spain. It would be difficult to argue that the Spanish and British differed much in the degree of their acquisitiveness, but the resources the British sought were different and perhaps less glamorous, in a sense, than the gold and silver that found its way to the Spanish Court. For the British, codfish, timber, beaver furs, and agricultural land drove them in search of adventure and the magisterial favor of the Crown.

The British desire for land took two major forms. Many individuals, fleeing a crowded agrarian society, hoped to establish the farms they could never have had in England. But entrepreneurs also established commercial tobacco and sugar plantations along the South Atlantic Coast. In addition to the simple farms that many English colonials coveted to produce a comfortable life for themselves, the production of commodities—cod, furs, tobacco, and sugar—also impelled British enterprises. Both the individual farms and the plantations, in any case, involved the appropriation of lands that indigenous peoples occupied.

Plantation owners tried for a time to use indigenous slave labor, but that was never very successful. Individual small farmers, on the other hand, merely wanted to be rid of the inhabitants of the land. The British denigrated indigenous peoples to some extent for being non-Christian, but their relegation to undesirable status had more to do with direct competition for their resources than with their beliefs.

The number of indigenous peoples compared to the English immigrant population, and the complexity of the competitive arena among Europeans and their indigenous allies, tempered relationships in some regions—especially in the early years. The English could ill afford to provoke needless antagonisms where other Europeans constituted a significant presence, or where indigenous peoples outnumbered them.

This situation changed when the French and Spanish lost most of their territorial bases in eastern North America and waves of European-introduced diseases had devastated indigenous populations (see, e.g., Dobyns 1966, 1988).

The Birth of the Primitive

The ideological basis for relegating indigenous peoples to "primitive" status underwent some refinement with the European Enlightenment in the eighteenth century, although there was considerable curiosity about "savages" in earlier times. Various explorers and entrepreneurs, beginning with Columbus, had brought indigenous people from far-off lands to display in Europe. Jacques Cartier kidnapped some Laurentian Iroquois in the early sixteenth century to show to the king of France. The practice of importing indigenous people for display continued through the late nineteenth century when Buffalo Bill Cody's Wild West Show, boasting genuine Plains Indian warriors, performed before the queen of England (see Kehoe 1989:57).

Some Enlightenment figures such as Jean-Jacques Rousseau took a somewhat positive, if whimsical, view of the "savages" and "barbarous races" that were becoming more and more familiar to Europeans. Even in the late sixteenth century, Michel de Montaigne had the opportunity to chat with some Tupinambá from Brazil. Apparently this inspired him to comment that "I do not believe, from what I have been told about this people, that there is anything barbarous or savage about them, except that we all call barbarous anything that is contrary to our own habits" (Darnell 1974:130).

The Enlightenment involved a secularization of thinking, a turning away from theological explanation that coincided with a weakening of the Church as a political power. It embraced the idea of intellectual progress. Humanity, in this view, had advanced and would continue to do so through rational thought and scientific discovery.

The notion of progress through rational thought did not, however, do much to improve European attitudes toward indigenous peoples. Even fantasies of the "noble savage" employed negative categories as positive features, focusing on what they did *not* have. Savages supposedly had no prisons, no taxes, no laws, no financial worries, no clothing, or whatever else the writer considered particularly irksome about his own society. But these positive-negatives also implied that the "savage" fell short as well in the rational thought department. The image of childlike, fancy-free qualities conveyed an appealing innocence, but not necessarily great intellect.

Eventually this early version of the primitive would develop harsher aspects. In the eighteenth century, the "savage" was not as advanced as the European in rational terms, but was somewhat attractive on that account. And there was a sense that these "children of nature" could, and probably would, some day advance in rationality, even if that might mean a loss of innocence. The sense of linear progression, of becoming more like Europeans, was implicit.

This view took a different turn in the nineteenth century when the idea of progress through rationality lost ground to the idea of progress through competition. The Enlightenment with its lively optimism had tended to include all humankind in the hope for increased rationality. The nineteenth century gave birth to the dour and oppressive Social Darwinism that saw progress in terms of winners and losers.

Nineteenth-century ideas of progress lost much of the wry social critique of Voltaire and his contemporaries and instead, took on the burden (some would say the white man's) of justifying the contemporary structure of power. These ideas in their many versions held that competition is an inexorable law of nature and that human populations are no different in this regard from the rest of Creation. Some are more "fit" than others, and in a competitive arena it is not only inevitable, but ultimately just, that the fittest survive.

These ideas had important implications that may help to explain their appeal. They tended to deaden whatever qualms of conscience or misgivings one might have about social inequality or the exploitation of one group by another. One could argue that such inequalities, by their very existence, justified themselves. Domination was prima facie evidence of superior fitness.

The arch Social Darwinist Herbert Spencer decried the unnecessary slaughter when the Royal Navy bombarded an African village of thatch huts with salvos of heavy artillery (quoted in Harris 1968:136). But in the long run, Spencer argued, humanity would be better off when the strong prevailed and the weak were eliminated (see, e.g., Spencer 1896: 233). Apparently he just felt that there was no need for such wretched excess.

Much of the academic discussion regarding relative progress rested on the idea of the "psychic unity" of humankind. That term may have a pleasing egalitarian ring to modern readers, but in the era of "scientific racism" it was the basis for rampant ethnocentrism. Psychic unity expressed the assumption that the human mind everywhere works in the same fashion—that is, that logic and rational thought, as Europeans understand them, are universals. Why, then, were the lives of people in far-off lands so different from those of Europeans? Not because they were operating in some sort of different intellectual fashion of equal validity or value. It was because they had not yet arrived at the same solutions to problems that "civilized" Europeans had solved long ago.

Eventually, many assumed, indigenous peoples would get to it, but in the meantime they lagged far behind. The other side of the coin was that "savage races" represented what Europeans had been like in the distant past. But in the present, and for the foreseeable future, these populations were different from Europeans mainly because they had not yet advanced far enough.

These ideas found raw expression in the work of such writers as Daniel Brinton (1896), who was more explicit than many about the absolute superiority or inferiority of various peoples on the globe. Other scholars of the day measured skull shapes and the sizes of brain cavities from various populations in order to document the inferiority of various "races" (Gould 1981, Stanton 1960). By the mid-nineteenth century, the process of linking cultural differences with inherent biological traits was well under way.

Out in the "field," as it were, Europeans collected specimens for further study. Hundreds of Tasmanian skulls lined the shelves of laboratories, becoming irreplaceable after the last Tasmanian died near the turn of the century. In the southwestern United States, army troops murdered the Apache leader Mangas Coloradas while he was in custody and decapitated the body. They boiled his head to send the skull East for scientific analysis. In the Pacific, dried Maori heads with their elaborate facial tattoos became valued collectors' items. Australian Aboriginal skulls also found their way into laboratory collections, sometimes after the massacre of their former owners. This era seems to have involved the highest frequency of head-hunting among English speakers since expansion of the Roman state had subjugated their ancestral Celtic tribes.

Social Darwinism came about in an era when the Industrial Revolution in England was imposing greater demands on labor at home and generating tremendous profits for the few. While Karl Marx could peer through his grimy window and see rampant exploitation, Herbert Spencer in his comfortable study contemplated a vigorous and productive division of labor. While Spencer held forth in the drawing rooms of English society, Marx, as we know, received fewer social invitations from the elite.

It was an age when colonial empires had all but divided the world among themselves. In England the economic system rested on the cheap labor of the domestic populace and the "triangular trade" of manufactured goods shipped from Liverpool to the coast of Africa for slaves. Entrepreneurs shipped the slaves from Africa to Charleston and the West

Indies, trading them for sugar, cotton, tobacco, and other New World produce. The customhouse in Liverpool celebrated this prosperity with carved heads of Africans decorating the facade (Williams 1984:150). England abolished the slave trade in the early nineteenth century, but its weaving industry continued to depend on the slave labor of U.S. cotton plantations until the Civil War interrupted the supply (Wolf 1983).

It seems ironic that the Enlightenment corresponded with the burgeoning of the slave trade, while Social Darwinism arose in its aftermath in England. Enlightenment thinkers, though, had tended to use notions of "savages" as abstract heuristic devices, often as a means to illustrate points about their own societies or about humankind in general. If they were inclined at all toward activism, their attentions tended to focus more on internal politics than on offshore enterprises.

With the Industrial Revolution well under way by the early nineteenth century, though, the Social Darwinists lived in societies whose economic underpinnings depended on resource extraction and commodity production in many far-off regions of the world. Colonialism had, in effect, become a domestic issue (see Said 1993). The end of the slave trade by no means meant the end of foreign or domestic labor exploitation. In many respects, the use of cheap, self-reproducing local workforces had become more profitable. The "scientific racism" of the time offered justification for what passed as the development of resources in regions where the "primitive" inhabitants were incapable of making full use of them on their own.

Beyond Social Darwinism?

Neither the relatively benevolent perspective of the Enlightenment nor the nineteenth-century framework of Social Darwinism granted indigenous peoples status or worth that was equivalent to that of Europeans. Since then, academic views have advanced a great deal and have relegated most of these concepts to the dustheap. Unfortunately, though, some of these older assumptions continue to influence popular thought and some intellectual perspectives. Some of the ideas we might have expected to be discarded have merely been recycled. In 1994, for example, a book arguing that populations in the United States differ genetically in their intellectual capacities received favorable reviews and much public attention (Murray and Herrnstein 1994).

It is not surprising, perhaps, to see some of these ideas appear from time to time in the mass media—although it might have disappointed some to have seen the staid *New York Times* in the 1970s refer to the Tasaday of the Philippines as a "Stone Age Tribe," or to see that "Gray

Lady" of the media refer to the people of Papua New Guinea in the same way in the mid-1990s (Shenon 1994, Howe 1995).

Some of the old notions of unilinear progress are implicit in conventional economic models that portray indigenous peoples as "underdeveloped." We all know, of course, that the term "underdeveloped" essentially means that people are poor. Or does it?

Development implies change on a linear scale. Underdeveloped means less developed than some entity that is more developed. More important, the terms "developed" or "underdeveloped" focus solely on the population in question rather than on the conditions that engulf them. They suggest some inherent quality, or lack of it, that is internal to the entity or the society itself.

Underdevelopment indicates inadequacy and does not take account of external causes. In some ways, it is comparable to describing a robbery victim as being underfinanced. This may be accurate, but it leaves out a great deal.

The concept of underdevelopment is closely linked with the idea of modernization. In many respects, they amount to complementary aspects of the same perspective. One distinction between them, however, is that while the concept of underdevelopment rests most firmly on straightforward material issues such as per capita income, mortality rates, and so on, modernization implies a more encompassing range of social and cultural issues.

Modernity, according to David Lerner, is "primarily a *state of mind*—expectation of progress, propensity to growth, readiness to adapt oneself to change" (1964:iix). In the 1960s, David C. McClelland (1961) developed the idea of "achievement motivation" (nAch) that differentiated Third World societies poised for advancement from those bogged down with unproductive attitudes.

Implicitly, at least, the state of modernity assumes the presence of "modern" (which generally is a euphemism for "Western") social institutions ranging from the nuclear family to elected leadership to appropriate values. From this perspective, aspects of indigenous social organization such as clans, extended family households, or the egalitarian distribution of resources are not merely different from predominant European modes of living. There is also a sense that such patterns are anathema to modernism and that they retard healthy growth, advancement, and progress. They are "inefficient" and "archaic." In a word, they are "traditional."

"Traditional" in the parlance of modernization models implies a mindless replication of cultural patterns generation after generation simply because "this is the way we've always done it" or because "the ancestors taught us to do it this way." Those who embrace modernization models tend to consider "Western thinking" to be founded on rational thought, careful assessment, and openness to innovation. We have already noted the deep roots of these assumptions in the eighteenth century. The disquieting awareness that "Western thinking" has created devastating ecological and social problems for which it has yet to find rational solutions seems to have little impact on such models. As is often the case with magical premises in many societies, the reaction to apparent failure is not to question the underlying assumptions but to apply them all the more intensely.

Nor is there much acknowledgment that the so-called traditional ways of life of indigenous peoples have developed over centuries because they work fairly well in their local situations. This does not necessarily mean that these populations had achieved idyllic lives (cf. Edgerton 1992). All people have problems. Few, if any, have managed to solve all of them. But most, given the opportunity to make their own choices, have developed strategies that work better for them than do programs promoted by outsiders who are pursuing interests of their own. The disastrous effects of eradicating "traditional" practices in many parts of the world are well documented (see, e.g., Erasmus 1961, Bodley 1982).

Notwithstanding such evidence, though, many theorists—including those with great influence in powerful international development agencies—continue to view modernization as the high end on a linear scale of development. With minor changes in detail, the basic conceptual model has much in common with nineteenth-century views of cultural evolution.

True, most of the overt racism has been exorcised, and the harsh role of competition is a bit softer. The nineteenth-century view of competition to eliminate the weak has undergone an interesting transformation. Competition now has transformed into cooperative ventures involving the allocation of functions within a global economy that supposedly will help the weak develop new vigor. No longer is it "nature, red in tooth and claw" but an arena in which competition is a healthy stimulus for all, in which "a rising tide raises all boats." On the other hand, this framework still assumes that underdevelopment is the fault of the underdeveloped.

While these approaches do recognize the existence of relative deprivation among many of the world's peoples, including indigenous populations, they still tend to blame the victims. They downplay the effects of resource appropriation by powerful interests on creating impoverishment since the heyday of colonialism.

They also tend to ignore the disparities of power inherent in these situations. One could argue that if we wish to understand the causes of poverty among indigenous peoples, the appropriation of land, minerals, water, and timber and the forced relocation of communities might be at least as significant as backward attitudes on the part of the people.

Dependency Theories

Since the 1950s, a different perspective, much of it inspired by the insights of Karl Marx, offers a somewhat different view of global disparities in wealth and power. The most influential of these approaches are dependency theory and world systems theory.

Although there have been many versions and refinements in these models in the past few decades, the gist of the approach is that if we hope to understand the conditions that theorists refer to as underdevelopment, we must pay attention to the extraction of wealth from the poor by the wealthy. Rosa Luxemburg, writing in 1913 long before the formulation of dependency theory, expressed the issue succinctly:

> In its urge to appropriate productive forces for the purpose of exploitation, capital ransacks the entire world, provides itself with the means of production from all corners of the earth, obtaining these from all levels of civilization and from all forms of society. (quoted in Hout 1993:21)

Although dependency theorists have given most attention to relationships among states, the dynamics apply equally well to relationships among indigenous populations and interest groups within states (see, e.g., Lamphere 1976, White 1983).

Andre Gunder Frank (1972), discussing underdevelopment in Latin America, distinguishes metropolitan or First World countries from "satellite" Third World nations. Put simply, the dynamics involve the extraction of raw materials from the satellites—often through poorly paid and/or coerced labor—which interests in the metropolis acquire at low cost, convert into consumer goods, and sell at great profit. The local satellite population, divested of control over its own resources, has little choice but to enter the market as consumers and buy back manufactured commodities that the metropolis has produced from the satellites' own raw materials.

This relationship is inherently exploitative, since the satellite producers of raw materials derive little benefit from their labor or their raw materials. The powerful beneficiaries of this arrangement, moreover, often establish and maintain the system through the use of force.

Interests in the metropolis control the means of production—mining machinery, smelters, timber-harvesting equipment, shipping stock, or whatever. This model seems applicable to a range of cases, particularly with the burgeoning of transnational corporations that are based in the metropolis but own and control mines, plantations, and so on throughout the world.

Immanuel Wallerstein carried these ideas farther in constructing a model he calls "world system theory." According to Wallerstein, the spread of capitalism beginning in the fifteenth century has created a global division of labor that divides most of the world into "core," "periphery," and "semiperiphery." As Wil Hout observes, the core/periphery relationship involves unequal exchange and power disparities maintained by coercion. While sophisticated production methods and free wage labor characterize the core, labor in the periphery may involve outright slavery or "feudal" relationships (Hout 1993:118–120).

The concept of the semiperiphery is an essential component of this model. The semiperiphery is intermediate between the core and periphery with regard to the sophistication of production and the strength of the state structure. It acts as a "buffer between two opposing forces" (Hout 1993:119).

As Wallerstein notes, the semiperiphery can "deflect the political pressures which groups primarily located in the peripheral areas might otherwise direct against core states and the groups which operate within and through their state machineries" (1974:350). Peasant unrest might disrupt a coffee plantation in Latin America, but there is little chance that the problem will do serious harm to a New York–based conglomerate that not only owns that operation but many others like it.

In that vein, as societies become peripheral they are more likely to become hierarchical, with a small elite linking the larger population to the exploitative network. During the West African slave trade, for example, Fula and Mande societies became highly stratified. They were among the most deeply involved in the trade, yet they drew the majority of slaves from their own populace (Wallerstein 1986:332–334).

Recognizing the disparity of power that permits some interest groups to extract the wealth and command the labor of others is an essential aspect of these and similar models. Once this relationship is in place, it may become more elaborate, but as Frank (1972) points out, it is unlikely to end without massive uprisings that break the structure altogether.

The Human Component

Ultimately these structural relationships are the product of human action—the behavior of individuals. When we view the history of injustice that has occurred in association with them, we might be tempted to conclude that some evil conspiracy has been at work. This view, though, does little to help explain the situation. It certainly is true that scoundrels have appeared here and there, although probably with motives more often selfish than purely malevolent. But that takes us nowhere in understanding the differences among particular cases. It does not help us to fathom why certain courses of action have prevailed at one time but not at others. Nor does it help us understand how myriad individual choices, malevolent or benevolent, have produced the massive structures of relationships to which Frank, Wallerstein, and others refer.

As Walter Rodney and others have pointed out, humans are caught in "a web not of their own making" (Wallerstein 1986:332). But who, if not humans, made it? The relationship between human action and sociopolitical structure is one of the most fundamental and nagging issues in the social sciences. We can find some resolution, as Rodney notes, by incorporating a historic perspective.

As we all know, one thing leads to another. Human choices are not random. They arise from circumstance, existing knowledge, a sense of appropriateness, perceptions of what one can get away with, guesses at what might work best, and numerous other factors.

Most, if not all, of these considerations derive from experience. They are the consequences of history—long term and short term, collective and personal. We can rarely know for certain precisely what has motivated the actions of an individual. But we can understand to some extent why certain choices on the part of numerous individuals are more likely than others, considering the circumstances.

Choices build upon one another. The countless actions of individuals affect the context of further choices and, in that sense, affect these choices and the actions individuals are likely to take in the future. Humans do not create social structure on the spot. They act in the midst of it and affect it as they go along.

Perhaps, then, we can set the issue of motivation and human agency on the back burner and consider instead the fact that humans act within situations that already exist. People do not necessarily act in order to construct a sociopolitical system but to do the best they can in the one that engulfs them. As Johan Galtung observes:

> . . . for the concrete actors that happen to be performing roles in the structure in question *no specific motivation* is necessary. The basic assumption is that the *structure* (of imperialism) is extremely strong and has its own internal logic so that once it has started operating it is not necessary for those who are acting

within it to desire all the consequences. (Galtung 1983:183; quoted in Hout 1993:95–96)

We can apply many of the ideas associated with dependency models to the situation of indigenous peoples in state systems. For our purposes, however, the dependency and world systems models are not adequate. For one thing, they pay little attention to the populations at the "satellite" or "peripheral" end of the relationship. These tend to appear as faceless victims. From that perspective, it does not seem to make any difference what their cultures are like, what sorts of social organization they have, or for that matter, how they feel about their situations. As Peter Worsley has put it, culture becomes a residual category (1984: 41–44).

There is also a tendency, as Hout observes, for these approaches to embrace the same concept of economic development or progress inherent in underdevelopment and nineteenth-century evolutionary models (1993:48; see also Higgott 1983:74–75). While they point to exploitative relationships, the thrust of these models is that power disparities inhibit the exploited from developing along the lines of First World interests, with the implication that they would if they could. The assumption of developmental trajectory is subtle, but implicit nonetheless. This may or may not be valid, but in any case it remains to be demonstrated.

For the moment we can set that assumption aside. Given the diverse modes of existence that autonomous peoples have developed in the past, there seems little reason to assume at the outset that if left alone, they would follow some particular path. In that vein, understanding the situation of indigenous peoples in state systems requires that we take note of the people themselves—the ways in which they have used and related to the land, the ways in which they have organized themselves, and the ideas that have motivated their behavior.

Indigenous Peoples as Interest Groups

To approach this issue we can return to a view of the state as an arena of competing interest groups. We need not imagine any guiding principle or unseen hand steering the course of the state. It is enough for the moment merely to assume the underlying dynamics that arise from individuals and interest groups pressing their own advantage as they perceive it.

This is not to say that human beings are basically selfish and mean-spirited. They certainly can be, but they can be heroic and self-sacrificing as well. The main point is that collectively, through time, people tend to make choices that they feel will accrue to their benefit rather than to their detriment. Over the course of history, this simple factor has had ponderous consequences. At times we may encounter instances of "enlightened self-interest" that shed favor on others, although this is less common than we might hope.

Once immersed in a state, indigenous peoples have encountered the need to deal with other interests in order to protect their resources and, in some cases, their lives. Usually, powerful interests have been able to influence the mechanisms of the state to appropriate these resources or to secure indigenous labor.

At the same time, however, indigenous populations have developed strategies of their own—resisting dispersal, forming coalitions, utilizing the legal structures of the state, and seeking in other ways to secure power within the system. These strategies have had varying degrees of success. They continue to develop, even as other interest groups develop strategies of their own. Ultimately this complex game of strategies amounts to competition for resources. While many of us might prefer to believe that the power of ideas and values guides human affairs, these have tended to dance around the edges of material imperatives. Ideology has more often been a reflector than a cause of material concerns.

The Transcendence of Interest Groups

In viewing the state as an arena of interest groups, we must also keep in mind that it is not a closed field. Interest groups operate within state systems, but they are not necessarily captured within them. Even in the eighteenth and nineteenth centuries, the Hudson's Bay Company operated as a semi-independent entity outside the Canadian state, claiming ownership of a vast region of North America. British and Dutch trading companies in the seventeenth and eighteenth centuries not only wielded great influence over the governmental policies of their respective states but established quasi-autonomous political footholds in distant parts of the globe.

Major corporations have long since gone beyond state boundaries to the extent that they often use particular states primarily as convenient bases of operation (see Barrett and Cavanaugh 1994). This is consistent with the "interest group arena" model; it is essentially a case of interest groups having grown powerful enough to transcend states rather than merely competing within them and, in some cases, to play one state off against another.

Transnational economic activities involve competition and bargaining between international firms and states entailing a "triangular nexus comprising firm-firm, state-state, and firm-state relationships" (Dicken 1994:102). K. Cowling and R. Sygden define the transnational corporation as "the means of coordinating production from one centre of strategic decision making when this coordination takes a firm across national boundaries" (1987; quoted in Dicken 1994:105).

From the perspective of indigenous peoples, this is significant. These transnationals continue to be interested in their remaining resources. The power of these giant interests to compete for them—and to influence state policies on their own behalf—appears to be greater than ever.

Interests, Ideology, and Shifting Parameters

Perhaps another consideration requires comment. If we can argue that ideas tend to reflect material concerns and perceived interests, should we assume that the ideas we offer here are any different? Perhaps they are not. They may reflect a sense that our pertinent spheres of interest now have changed. Can it be that, for most of us, our interests coincide more closely with those of indigenous peoples we have never seen than with the powerful constituencies that would divest us and them alike of our vital resources?

Perhaps the parameters of interest groups have shifted, as they so often have in the past. Transnational corporations enrich the few by devastating rain forests, fouling water sources, spewing acid into the atmosphere, impoverishing labor in wealthy countries, and exploiting labor in poor ones. Do our interests ally us with them, or with the peoples of the earth whose resources they appropriate? What, in fact, are the operative interest groups for the present?

The Four Cases

Armed with these questions and perspectives, we can examine briefly the historic trajectories of the four state systems of Mexico, the United States, Australia, and Canada. Before doing so, however, we might summarize some comparative aspects of the four states. Of the two parent states that gave rise to them, Spain had a more centralized power vested in the Crown, while England's governance involved a tension between the Crown and Parliament. In the long run, it seems that this made little difference in the colonial process.

France and the Netherlands also were major players in the early arena of colonialism in the New World, but by the early nineteenth century both had relinquished most of their territorial holdings in North and South America. The same was true of Spain, although the uninterrupted

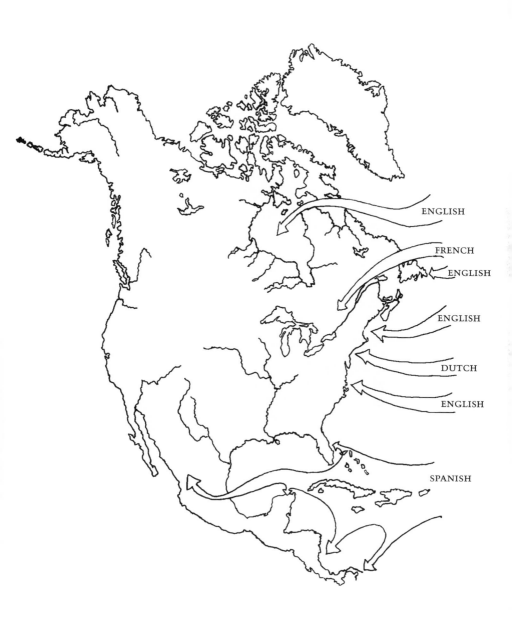

ENGLISH

FRENCH

ENGLISH

ENGLISH

DUTCH

ENGLISH

SPANISH

European Intrusions in North America

sovereignty of Spain in Mexico for three centuries induced a far deeper Spanish influence than did those resulting from the relatively briefer reigns of the French and Dutch in North America.

Residual French and Dutch cultural influences remain in regions of the United States. Quebec in Canada remains distinctly French, but British influence throughout most of Canada came to predominate in later centuries. Even the French legal system of Louisiana, which incorporated elements of the Napoleonic Code, has altered significantly toward an Anglo-American model (Friedman 1985).

All four states arose from invasions of occupied territories. We could class the United States, Canada, and Australia as "settler societies," "where the colonists revolted against the homeland yet maintained colonial patterns and relationships with indigenous populations" (Libby 1989:xii; see also Denoon 1983, Alexander 1989). Such situations seem most likely when the indigenous populations constitute a small minority within the state. Mexico, while sharing some of the characteristics of settler societies, has been far more influenced by a large indigenous presence.

Although indigenous states in Mexico contested the incursion, the Spanish encountered no significant resistance by other European powers there until much later. In the rest of North America, as we have noted, numerous European states and indigenous populations maneuvered for position in a complex choreography of wars and diplomacy. The English invasion of Australia, which occurred some two and a half centuries after Cortés entered Mexico, met little resistance.

All four states eventually became independent of their original states. In Mexico and the United States, independence occurred through violent revolution, while it occurred later, more peacefully, and in some ways more ambiguously in Canada and Australia. Since that time, indigenous peoples in all four states have continued to make their presence felt. This, however, is a matter for the next several chapters.

The States

. . . .

II

Mexico

. . . .

3

We cannot be tranquil,
and yet we certainly do not believe;
we do not accept your teachings as truth,
even though this may offend you.

(Aztec *tlamatinime* ["knowledgeable men"] to Spanish missionaries in 1524. León-Portilla 1963:66)

At the time of the Conquest of Mexico, the unity of the Spanish state was recent and rather tenuous. Spain was a collection of principalities and distinct regions that had recently freed themselves from Moorish invaders. The Crown, uniting the royal houses of Castile and Aragon under the dual monarchy of Ferdinand and Isabella, needed wealth to consolidate and maintain its position.

Numerous constituencies vied to influence state policies, and the government, though powerful, often had problems enforcing Crown policy in the colonial regions. When Hernán Cortés invaded the mainland of Mexico, he did it in defiance of his superior, the Spanish governor of Cuba. The governor had originally appointed Cortés for the job, but when Cortés's arrogance gave him second thoughts he sent a rescinding order—which Cortés avoided by a hasty departure from port.

The explorers and *conquistadores* who carried out the Spanish explorations had varied origins. Columbus, as every schoolchild should know, was not Spanish at all but Genoan. Like many *conquistadores*, Cortés was from Estremadura, a region whose affiliation with Castile was somewhat

APACHE
O'ODHAM
ÓPATA
YAQUI
TARAHUMARA
TEPEHUANE
MAYO

(Chichimec)

HUICHOL HUASTEC

Gulf of Mexico

Pacific Ocean

OTOMÍ
TOTONOC
TARASCAN AZTEC

Valley of Mexico

Yucatán

MIXTEC ZAPOTEC

MAYA

Indigenous Mexico

tenuous. The majority of later Spanish migrants to Mexico, however, came from Andalucia, a part of Castile (Ruiz 1992:28).

The Church, one of the more powerful constituencies in Spain, had a relationship with the Crown that was congenial but rather independent. At the beginning of the fifth century, the pope had given the Crown responsibility for the Spanish Church, which effectively placed the Church at the service of royal policies. This was a relationship that neither side cared to test too severely, however. The Church hierarchy was not averse to pressuring the sovereigns on various issues. The Church had, however, imposed a unifying element over the regional and economic diversity of the peninsula, particularly in the face of the Moorish enemy.

The Church itself was far from unified in many respects. Rivalries among the Jesuit, Augustinian, Franciscan, and Dominican orders were to play themselves out on the far side of the Atlantic as well as in Europe. The Crown also had to contend with noble families who had their own agendas and with merchants who applied pressure to institute policies favorable to their interests. Merchants, in fact, persuaded the royal house to fund Columbus's first expedition.

The Spanish Conquest of Mexico began on a small scale. The early sorties and probes often were fragmentary and the policies of occupation contradictory, representing the various interests involved. This divisive tendency grew over the years when an increasing number of Mexican-born Spaniards (*criollos*) found their interests at variance with those of native-born Spaniards (*peninsulares*) who in New Spain often wielded the authority of the Spanish Crown.

Indigenous Mexico

Mexico on the eve of the Conquest had a population of several million people, many of them living in and around major cities. Tenochtitlán, capital of the México (or Aztec) state, was five times the size of London when Cortés set foot on the coast. The city loomed in the center of a shallow lake, with causeways leading to it from the shore. Its market displayed commodities from hundreds of miles around. Caged jaguars, spectacular blue-green feathers of *quetzál* birds, cacao beans, foodstuffs, and woven cloth dazzled the Spanish troops. Aztec merchants (*pochtecas* or *oztomecas*) traveled throughout the México sphere of influence, negotiating trade and often acting as spies for the expansionist México state (Berdan 1982:31).

Tenochtitlán was only one of several major Aztec cities around Lake Texcoco and one of many urban centers scattered around the Valley of Mexico. Most of the surrounding peoples paid tribute to the México, although some, including the Totonoc state that Cortés first encountered on the coast, had managed to resist. Aztec chronicles recount that the people of Zózola in the Mixtec region to the south burned their city and fled into the mountains rather than submit to Aztec authority. Another Aztec account notes that still other subject states rebelled against pressure to trade their gold, jewels, and precious feathers for items they deemed to be worthless junk (Katz 1988:71). In the southern regions of Oaxaca, the Zapotec had also remained independent of Aztec hegemony. Many of them would later offer stubborn resistance to Spanish authorities as well.

Although the Aztec state was relatively new when Cortés arrived, urban living was already an ancient way of life in Mexico. The city of Teotihuacán, some fifty miles or so to the north, had been comparable in size and power to Imperial Rome before it fell seven centuries earlier (Millon 1967). To the southeast, most of the Maya cities lay neglected after their decline centuries before, some of them all but covered by rain forest vegetation. Sizable Maya communities continued to exist throughout the region, however, and hundreds of thousands of Maya people continued to tend their farm plots around small villages. Almost five hundred years later, descendants of these Maya farmers would still be resisting usurpation of their lands.

The small farming villages beyond the margins of city-states followed a way of life that had begun thousands of years earlier and would persist long after Cortés. North of the agricultural zone, in the deserts and in the mountains the Spanish would name the Sierra Madres, scattered peoples hunted, foraged, and grew a few crops. These people the Aztec referred to as Chichimec, "Children of Dogs." They had offered fierce resistance to the states of the south and would do the same with the Spanish and Mexican states that came after them. Their descendants are among the Yaqui, Tepehuane, Ópata, Tarahumara, and O'Odham.

Mexico's populations spoke hundreds of languages representing several major language families. The distribution of Uto-Aztecan languages, to which the Aztec language Nahuatl belongs, extends north up the Sierra Madres far into what later became the United States. Uto-Aztecan was probably the predominant language family among the Chichimec, from whom the Aztec claimed descent. The various Maya languages constitute another family. Hundreds of thousands of people in Mexico and Central America still speak Maya and Nahuatl. Other languages, including Otomian, Mixtecan, and Mazatecan make up the Otomanguean family.

The Conquest and Its Aftermath

Historians have debated the reasons for the Aztec state's rapid demise in the face of the Spanish invasion and have offered a range of explanations. The indigenous populations did, after all, vastly outnumber the European invaders. And in the sixteenth century, Spanish technology was not all that superior to that of the Aztec.

But technology was not the only factor. Smallpox and other diseases, new to the Mexican population, rapidly killed millions of indigenous people and did much to weaken the possibility of concerted, armed resistance (see Dobyns 1966). Opposition to the Aztec on the part of their threatened neighbors also, no doubt, inhibited their ability to fend off the Spanish. México foreign policy, it seems, had left them with few loyal allies. Soon after the Spanish appeared, the Aztec sent a delegation to their old Tarascan enemies in Michoacán to seek an alliance against the Spanish, but their reception was ambivalent, at best (Warren 1985:24).

Although horses terrorized Mexicans at first contact, it did not take the Aztec long to discover that indigenous weapons could disable and kill the animals. Certainly firearms gave the Spanish some advantage, but the guns of the time were far from reliable, slow to reload, and awkward to use in a close fight. It seems most likely that disease, local political divisions, and Spanish success in nullifying the Aztec leadership were most decisive.

Some assessments of the ease with which Cortés toppled the Aztec state are also misleading. After the death of the head of state, Moctezuma, in Spanish custody, the furious Aztec drove the Spanish from Tenochtitlán, killing many of them as they fled across the lake laden with booty. The Spanish later referred to the episode as *la noche triste* ("the sorrowful night"). Cortés fled to the coast and regrouped, assembling a force of eighty thousand, but only six hundred of these were Spanish. With this army of disaffected Aztec neighbors, Cortés finally succeeded in taking the cities of Texcoco, Ixtapalapa, Chalco, and Tacuba in 1521. Tenochtitlán fell after a three-month siege during which Spanish possession of the causeways cut off the Aztec food supply. Most of the defenders held out until they starved to death.

The Aztec and Spanish states each had significant religious underpinnings. Although the Aztec had not shown much interest in proselytizing during their conquests, Spanish history had produced a deep intolerance for other belief systems. The Church in Castile not only had promoted a holy war against the Moors but, as early as the thirteenth century, had challenged the legitimacy of Christianized Jews and Moors (*moriscos*). By the 1500s, in the overheated days of the Counter-Reformation, the principle of *limpieza de sangre* ("purity of blood") became an issue regarding the capacity of non-Europeans to become true Christians. This not only offered an ideological rationale for driving *moriscos* and Jews from Spain (and from much of their property) but also had ominous implications for indigenous peoples of the Americas.

Spanish condemnation of Aztec practices led to violent suppression. The Aztec propensity for human sacrifice lent considerable impetus to the Spanish measures, notwithstanding the European penchant for rather severe physical punishments. The Inquisition, after all, was gaining momentum in Europe at the time. The Spanish defaced temples, toppled stone carvings of deities, destroyed written texts, and, in general, desecrated the symbols of Aztec theology.

Aztec cosmology would have led many believers to expect that universal catastrophe would result from these desecrations. When this did not ensue, it is possible that many of the populace developed misgivings about their beliefs. It is also possible that this led to some receptivity to

Christianity. On the other hand, from the perspective of the Aztec and other peoples in Mexico, their world had indeed come to a catastrophic end along with the lives of millions of inhabitants. The raw use of force probably had as much as religious premises to do with the peoples' submission to Spanish authority, whether secular or clerical.

It is probably significant, too, that the Aztec state was probably as hierarchical as the Spanish. Most of the population had been subject to authority of one sort or another for generations. The imposition of Spanish power may have been repugnant to them, but it was not without precedent.

Interest groups in New Spain quickly began dividing the spoils. Cortés and his followers acquired *encomiendas,* plantation-like establishments that commandeered indigenous labor. Centuries earlier, the Crown had granted *encomiendas* in Spain as rewards for service against the Moors, and the practice continued briefly in New Spain. *Encomiendas* were not inheritable, supposedly, but reverted to the Crown at the death of the *encomendero.*

Predictably, this nontransferable aspect of *encomiendas* became an issue of some contention. Within a few years, the Crown abolished the granting of *encomiendas,* although Philip II acquiesced under pressure to allow their inheritance over three generations. *Encomiendas* thus became one of the earliest examples of conscripted labor in Mexico. Cortés also acquired the list of towns that had paid tribute to the Aztec and distributed them to his soldiers, providing them with another source of income from indigenous labor (Ruiz 1992:38).

The Spanish, for the most part, had a low opinion of manual work. In sixteenth-century Spanish values, physical labor was associated with the lower classes. *Conquistadores* with noble origins or aspirations were loath to till the soil themselves. As one writer of the time observed sardonically, "No one comes to the Indies to plow and sow, but only to eat and loaf" (Forbes 1960:112). Cortés himself supposedly quipped, "I did not come to till the land like a peasant" (Ruiz 1992:80).

We can only estimate the human costs of this process. By 1570 the Spanish population of New Spain was about seven thousand, but about three and a half million indigenous people had died (Ruiz 1992:85).

The Church

The Church, for its part, also mobilized the labor of the indigenous people. Missionaries pursued a policy of *reducción,* concentrating people from the countryside in mission villages. Local people supplied the labor for constructing the missions as well as for producing the crops to support them. In many cases, this also freed their abandoned lands for Spanish appropriation. Concentration of people in mission communities produced breeding grounds for the rapid spread of disease, further depleting the population. The missionaries, in return, offered Christian teaching—particularly the values of humility and obedience.

These policies met with varying degrees of success. The practices differed among missionaries and varied over the centuries of Spanish power. Father Eusebio Kino made strong inroads among the O'Odham, or Pima. By the late 1700s, the Spanish had established missions at Túbac, Tumacácori, and San Xavier del Bac in what is now southern Arizona. These settlements led a tenuous existence, however, in the face of Apache raids. In Oaxaca, on the other hand, the Dominicans took a more repressive stance toward the Zapotec and Mixtec and eventually stood accused of draining local resources for their own profit (Chance 1989:88, 157).

The Jesuits among the Yaqui approached their task by learning the language and generally refraining from gross interference in local practices, insofar as they considered these customs compatible with Christianity. Although the Yaqui at first drove off Spanish officials, in the eighteenth century a Yaqui delegation invited a priest to come live with them. Jesuits also obstructed the efforts of mine owners to levy workers from Yaqui villages (Spicer 1980:37–39).

By the end of the eighteenth century, the Crown felt it prudent to weaken the power of the Church in New Spain. It began by expelling the Jesuits, who were the most fiercely loyal to the pope. Reaction among the Church hierarchy and its supporters—involving alarm over the possible loss of Church property—inhibited further expulsions. Eventually the Franciscans replaced the Jesuits in the north.

Mines, *Haciendas,* and Indigenous Labor

Although the Church used indigenous labor, Church officials objected to some of the most egregious abuses by other interests. The early protests of the priest Bartolomeo de Las Casas were instrumental in persuading the Council of the Indies under Charles V to outlaw forced labor. As we have noted, however, landowners and other users of indigenous labor did not necessarily honor this decree.

After Cortés had claimed Mexico for the Crown and named it New Spain, the Spanish spent much energy searching for gold comparable to the riches of Peru. The quest for precious metals was an early and persistent theme throughout the Spanish domain in the Americas. As early as 1540, Francisco Vásquez de Coronado took an expedition to search for gold and traveled as far north as what is now Nebraska. He found little, but in the regions north of the Valley of Mexico silver turned out to be far more plentiful. By the mid-sixteenth century, mines were extracting the silver deposits at Zacatecas.

Mining was an especially destructive devourer of labor and lives, although pay in the mines generally was higher than in the agricultural sector or in other industries. Much of the most oppressive agricultural labor took place under the demands of local officials. In many cases, this involved coercion of the local population to produce cash crops. "Unlike religious corporations, provincial governors set out to organize a set of commercial enterprises based not on direct ownership of land but on the intensive exploitation of Indian labor" (Wasserstrom 1983:96).

Mines and *haciendas* never developed in the Sierra Zapoteca. The main indigenous resource was labor to produce cotton, textiles, and cochineal, a red dye made from insects that live on the maguey plant, for urban markets (Chance 1989:xiv). This was no less harsh or destructive of the population than other measures of exploitation, however. From the combined results of disease, food shortage, and the flight of displaced indigenous peoples, the remaining population in Chiapas by 1790 was about a third of what it had been before contact.

Silver enriched the Spanish state for a time, but its main use was to purchase goods from other European powers. Spain relied heavily on the mineral wealth of the New World in lieu of developing its home industries. As a consequence, silver extracted in Mexico passed through Spain and continued to flow eastward, ultimately leaving Spain impoverished (Wallerstein 1974). The cohesion of the Spanish state weakened in the aftermath, and Spain became incapable of retaining its far-flung holdings under continued harassment by other European powers. In the early nineteenth century, Mexico would break free.

Social Divisions in New Spain

While the Spanish exploited the indigenous population of Mexico through forced labor of various forms, Spanish landholders also formed liaisons with indigenous women, especially those of high rank. Cortés set an early example, fathering numerous children by indigenous women. He had two sons named Martín—one by the indigenous woman Malinche, who guided him to Tenochtitlán, and the other, whom he recognized as his heir, by his Spanish wife. The two Martíns offer an interesting metaphor for the social division between *mestizo* and *criollo* that was to become so central an aspect of Mexican life in the following centuries.

Many of the sexual relationships between Spaniards and indigenous women amounted to abduction and rape, but some unions were more stable. The state encouraged intermarriage, partly as a means of stabilizing the society. Such relationships were inevitable in any case, since few Spanish women came to Mexico during the first few years of the colony. By 1540, some twenty years after the Conquest, only 6 percent of the Spanish population were female (Ruiz 1992:87). As a result, the Mexican population soon included many people of mixed parentage.

For centuries, though, these remained a minority. Indigenous people still constituted 70 percent of the population of Mexico at the end of the eighteenth century. *Peninsulares* born in Spain amounted to a tiny segment of the population, despite their disproportionate access to power. By the nineteenth century, *criollos*, Spanish born in Mexico, referred to them derogatorily as *gachupines*. The term is a reference to spurs, perhaps evoking a sense of arrogance. *Criollos* formed a significant and growing category whose interests were increasingly at odds with those of the *peninsulares*, whose affectations of social superiority exacerbated the tensions.

As time passed and more Spanish women arrived in Mexico, a greater social stigma began to develop for those with indigenous backgrounds. *Peninsulares* and *criollos* alike increasingly looked down upon *mestizos* and *indios*. The racism familiar to other parts of Europe and North America, which had arisen in Spain with regard to Moors, Jews, and African slaves, took root in Mexico as well.

Indigenous Resistance

The extension of centralized power over an area as large and diverse as New Spain was to be a chronic problem that persisted long after independence. Spanish authorities in some areas, particularly the south, exerted power by co-opting local leadership. They recognized or instituted *caciques*, bestowing them with material advantages and, when necessary, reinforcing their power. Some of these leaders did their best to aid and protect their people in the face of Spanish rule. But as generations passed, state and local interests favored those who cooperated rather than those who resisted. In many regions, the structures of indigenous leadership were gone by 1560 (Chance 1989:30).

Indigenous peoples continued to be a troublesome factor to the ruling interests, though, especially at the margins of state hegemony. Yucatán, with its large and scattered Maya population, was difficult to bring under control. The apparent lack of minerals served to discourage large-scale colonization, and the population remained predominantly Maya. Attempts to commandeer labor for commercial agriculture met sporadic resistance, including a major uprising in 1761.

In Chiapas rebellion flared in the early eighteenth century among the Tzotzil and Tzeltal populations in reaction to the *repartimiento*, a system of coerced labor. Pressure on the local people to produce cotton and cacao for Spanish officials at the expense of their own food crops had led to widespread hunger and culminated in a regional uprising in 1712. This was only one episode among many in the region.

> In 1660, native people in Tehuantepec revolted against the provincial authorities of Oaxaca; within a few weeks, Indians throughout that jurisdiction had risen in arms. Thirty-three years later, in Tuxtla, Zoque people, disgusted by the onerous repartimientos to which they had been subjected, killed Chiapas's alcalde mayor, Manuel de Maisterra, in the public plaza. Similarly, in 1722, ten years after the Cancuc uprising, still other Zoques (in Ocozocuautla) forced their overzealous priest to flee for his life. And finally, in 1761, Yucatecan Indians attempted once again to end Spanish rule in southern Mexico. (Wasserstrom 1983:109–110)

In the north, where Spanish state hegemony was even more tenuous, Yaqui resistance outlasted the Spanish colonial regime. Between forty and fifty rebellions flared in that region between 1600 and 1750 (Spicer 1980:35). The Apache in the northern margins of New Spain harassed villages from the seventeenth century onward, preventing the establishment of more than a few Spanish settlements beyond northern Sonora and Chihuahua except for military outposts (*presidios*). Far from the seat of government in Mexico City, enclaves of struggling farmers in the north received little support from the state. Impoverished villagers often were left to defend themselves from Apache raids with bows and arrows and spears (see, e.g., Cortés 1989, Griffen 1988:167). Eusebio Kino and other Franciscans managed to establish missions in the area among the more congenial O'Odham people, whose receptivity to the Spanish may have arisen partly from their fears of the Apache.

East of Apache territory along the Rio Grande, the Spanish established a more secure presence through harsh measures among the sedentary agricultural Pueblo communities. The Pueblo villages, structured on the basis of priestly societies, suffered greatly under the tutelage of militant Christian priests whose approach to proselytization owed much to the Inquisition. The military commander Antonio de Zaldívar went beyond burning the occasional heretic and slaughtered all of the inhabitants of Acoma Pueblo—a process that took three days (Forbes 1960:92).

The Pueblo communities revolted in 1680 under a man named Popé, forcing the Spanish to withdraw temporarily from the region. The priest

Andres Pérez de Ribas discerned supernatural rather than political forces at work, referring to leaders of the revolt as "diabolical shamans who had intimate dealings with the Devil and were the instigators of the uprising" (Reff 1995:67). The Spanish subsequently reestablished control of the Pueblo, however.

In New Spain, the pattern of indigenous resistance, despite the variety of circumstances and localities, usually involved reaction to the imposition of intolerable oppression.

> As practiced by the provincial governors and their agents, these transactions were so unfavorable to the Indians—the recompense for their labor so far below current market prices and the size of the repartimiento often so excessive as to interfere with food production—that only the severest forms of physical coercion could induce the Indians to accept them. (Farriss 1983:8)

Many of the leaders of indigenous resistance utilized Christian symbols to help unite their followers, albeit in local versions. Earlier writers have referred to this as syncretism, a covert maintenance of old ways under a Christian veneer. There is some reason to believe, however, that many conversions to Christianity were genuine and that their local flavor was just that—the result of a foreign religion taking root in an existing cultural milieu.

Resistance, when it did occur, often amounted to people's attempts to change their material conditions for the better. In many ways, it was more an effort to solve problems than simply to assert cultural identity for its own sake. Short of violent resistance, though, most indigenous communities attempted to survive as best they could in their situations, often accepting aspects of Spanish custom and ideology while trying to maintain an acceptable mode of living.

Independence

By the nineteenth century, the complexities of New Spain and the increasing conflicts of interest between *criollos* and the Crown led to independence. To some extent, the eruption of revolution was a response to fortuitous events. Napoleon III of France had deposed King Ferdinand VII of Spain in 1808, giving the throne to his own brother Joseph. Some *criollos* applauded this action, believing that it would serve their vested interests. To many in Mexico, however, this was both an outrage and an opportunity.

Many were not prepared to disavow their ties to the weakened Spanish state, but the situation offered a rationale for them to assert their own interests by refusing to recognize Spanish authority until Ferdinand regained his crown. It also galvanized thousands of *indios, mestizos,* and *criollos* to act on their grievances against the *peninsulares*.

The symbolic beginning of the war of independence occurred in 1810 with the famous *grito* ("shout") of Dolores. Father Miguel Hidalgo y Costilla, priest in the small town of Dolores far to the north of Mexico City, had been involved in a small circle of political plotters who chafed under some of the grosser inequities of the colonial regime. When Hidalgo learned that the authorities had discovered the conspiracy, he mobilized his followers and released prisoners from the jail, locking up some local *peninsulares* in their place.

Addressing his forces from the pulpit, he exhorted them to recover the lands that the Spaniards had stolen from them. According to some versions, he cried "Mexicans! Long live Mexico! Death to the *gachupines!*" Whatever his actual words, the *grito* set off a response that eventually would cost 600,000 lives.

Hidalgo never lived to see the outcome of the rebellion. Spanish forces captured and executed him in 1811. Two years later, another priest in the south named José María Morelos led a rebellion against the Spanish and drafted a constitution that called for racial equality and land reform. The Spanish executed Morelos in 1815, but the southern region of Mexico, with its large indigenous population, continued to be explosive well over a century later.

Ensuing events highlighted many conflicting interests among the populace of New Spain. Hidalgo had established good relationships with the local indigenous population. For them, the vital concern was to regain lost lands and to protect those they retained. The many *criollos* who held these lands did not share this goal. For some *criollos*, the demands for indigenous recompense constituted a threat. Most *criollos* and *indios* alike, however, were more interested in redressing a variety of immediate grievances than with absolute independence from Spain.

When Ferdinand reascended the Spanish throne, he showed little gratitude to the rebels who had risen in his name and sent reinforcements to quell the revolution. The irony deepened, however, when liberals in Spain forced Ferdinand to accept the Constitution of Cádiz in 1820. *Criollos* and *peninsulares* in Mexico, finding the document far too liberal for their tastes, mounted a conservative resistance to forestall the reforms (Riding 1985:47). The war of independence in effect became an attempt to preserve the old order of power relationships within New Spain.

Mexico did achieve independence shortly thereafter. Agustín de Iturbide became the standard-bearer of conservative interests and negotiated a pact with one of the few rebel generals who had survived the conflict, Vicente Guerrero. Together they drew up the Plan of Iguala, a programmatic statement that included three "guarantees." These stated that Roman Catholicism was to be Mexico's only religion; that all Mexicans were equal; and that a constitutional monarch from Europe would rule Mexico.

The first of these guarantees was a clear bow to conservative interests that had long supported the Church, as well as to the Church itself as a wealthy and powerful interest. While the aim of this guarantee focused mainly on inhibiting the spread of Protestantism, it also had implications for indigenous beliefs.

The second guarantee—that all Mexicans were equal—was fanciful idealism at best. Few of those in power had any serious intention of relinquishing power or redistributing wealth. It did, however, preclude any special status or sovereignty for indigenous peoples. Equality under the Constitution could forestall any special attempts to compensate groups who had suffered past injustices or to give special protection to those who faced such threats in the future.

The third guarantee seems a rather plaintive acquiescence for a revolutionary manifesto. It amounted to a bow to the centuries-old authority of the Old World. Iturbide, as a *peninsular,* identified strongly with that heritage.

Spain, beleaguered on numerous fronts, agreed to Mexican independence in 1821 and acknowledged the three principles in the Treaty of Córdoba. Iturbide, now Generalísimo de Tierra y Mar, enjoyed the title emperor of Mexico for a brief time until political opposition forced him to flee to Europe in 1823. He returned to Mexico in 1824, apparently expecting his followers to rally around him. To his disappointment, he faced a firing squad on the same day (Green 1987).

The Effects of Independence on Indigenous Populations

The departure of Spanish authority did not bode well for indigenous peoples. Spanish protections may not have been particularly effective, but their loss left indigenous communities utterly at the mercy of local interests. During the colonial era, especially before the 1760s, even though the central state was weak the "Spanish judiciary . . . maintained in most areas sufficient independence from local elites to encourage Indian communities to pursue their disputes over land with private or competing interests through the courts" (Coatsworth 1988:59). The second guarantee of the Plan of Iguala, which laid out the philosophical position of the new government that all Mexicans were equal, had the effect of removing barriers to exploiting indigenous peoples and seizing their lands.

The interests of the Spanish Crown had always taken precedence over those of various constituencies in Mexico, and these various interests had been arrayed over a wide arena. But Spain had in theory, at least, recognized the corporate status of many indigenous *ejidos* (communal landholdings) (Wolf 1969:4). With the departure of this overall hegemony and the relative weakness of the Mexican central government, local indigenous communities had little protection from nearby landowners.

There were many regions where the authority of the Spanish Crown had been a faint echo to begin with, and where independence made little difference in the lives of indigenous peoples. In general, though, indigenous populations after independence probably were marginalized to a greater extent than they had been under the Spanish state. To the extent that the government gave them much concern at all, it often amounted to recognition that their cultural differences and extreme poverty presented a problem to Mexican unification and prosperity.

On the other hand, the indigenous heritage as an abstract concept became an important theme in emphasizing Mexico's distinctness from Spain. By the late nineteenth century, the grandeur of the Aztec (or Méxica) state had become a symbol of national identity. From the earliest years of independence, the glorification of *indigenismo* in the abstract, coupled with the marginalization of *indios* as living people, was a fundamental and troublesome contradiction.

Most of the political struggles and strategizing that affected the Mexican state took place within the circles of intellectual and economic elites. Among those occupying center stage in power debates during the early years of the republic, the conservative Lucas Alamán and the liberal Lorenzo Zavala were leading ideological adversaries. But their disagreement rested essentially on which faction of the elite should rule. "Of those in power, few wanted government, in accordance with current ideological dogmas, to interfere in economic matters. The criollo elite, as well as the tiny band of mestizos ready to join it, believed politics should be in their hands, both fearing the participation of Indians and country folk" (Ruiz 1993:87).

Sporadic eruptions continued among indigenous peoples who found conditions intolerable. In some cases, other interests provoked these reactions for their own ends. The Caste War of Yucatán, for example, was largely a creation of competing *ladino* or *mestizo* factions, one of which tried to incite the local Maya to attack the other (Rus 1983). The major consequence was that both *ladino* groups slaughtered thousands of Maya and promoted the myth of a widespread and brutal Indian uprising. During the period of 1846–1848, an estimated half of the Maya in the region were killed.

The Increasing Complexity of the Mexican Population

The cultural diversity of the Mexican population before the Conquest came to involve still more social divisions in the ensuing centuries as the Spanish state incorporated more territory within its effective hegemony. Significant conflicts of interest grew between the *peninsulares*, who held power and influence disproportionate to their numbers, and the increasing population of *criollos*. By the end of the eighteenth century, *criollos* tended to disclaim any indigenous background and defined themselves emphatically as Mexican-born of pure Spanish descent. They had became an interest group whose boundaries became more distinct but who also developed diverse and sometimes conflicting concerns among themselves.

The formation of a significant *criollo* class further marginalized *indios*, who had minimal power despite the fact that they still constituted a large majority. They were scattered in thousands of communities from Texas to Yucatán and spoke hundreds of different languages. The generic category *indio* had far more reality in the minds of *mestizos, criollos*, and *peninsulares* than it did for indigenous peoples themselves, whose affiliations centered more on locality, common language, kinship ties, and access to communal *ejido* lands.

Indigenous assertions of identity arose more often in response to threats to their lands than in defense of their culture. Cultural features served as unifying symbols, but these tended to support the more fundamental concerns of land and survival. Conflict among neighboring indigenous communities that spoke the same language was not uncommon (see, e.g., Chance 1989:28). Because the sense of affiliation and common identity did not extend far beyond the range of kinship and community, resistance remained local or, at most, regional, with a few important exceptions. Some of these exceptions occurred in the aftermath of massive dislocations, when indigenous peoples who were driven from their lands throughout wide regions found themselves thrown together and developed a sense of common cause.

Mestizaje

From the earliest years of New Spain, the most rapidly growing section of the population were *mestizos*, people of mixed Spanish and indigenous parentage. This was not a simple matter of genealogy. As generations passed, it became more a matter of cultural and social identification. People of mixed parentage who spoke indigenous languages rather than Spanish, who wore local rather than European styles of clothing, and who were part of indigenous communities generally were *indios*. But an individual who left an indigenous community, spoke Spanish, and adopted the clothing style of the larger society became *mestizo*.

In many locales, animosities grew between *mestizos* and *indios*. Although both were relatively disadvantaged compared to *criollos*, they came to constitute different interest groups and often found themselves in competition for land or other resources. As Eric Wolf notes, "The boundary between 'Indians' and non-Indians has never been static, but rather an arena contested by people on both sides of the labor reserve colony" (1986:327).

A consequence of this process of shifting identity was that while those identified as *indios* still constituted about 45 percent of the population early in the twentieth century, seventy years later they amounted to about 10 percent (Riding 1985:292). Among other things, this trend suggests the relative disadvantages of an *indio* identity. According to the 1940 census, about 6 percent of the Mexican population spoke only an indigenous language. By 1970 this had dropped to 2.1 percent (Kehoe 1992:94).

The Proliferation of Interest Groups

As the total population of Mexico increased and economic activities diversified during the centuries after Conquest, the numbers of interest groups burgeoned. Mines, manufacturing enterprises of various sorts, and *haciendas* and plantations proliferated. These developments not only pushed more indigenous peoples off their lands but left them with no choice but to provide cheap labor in order to survive. Complicating matters still further, foreign interests—particularly United States and British—invested in Mexican ventures and frequently interfered in the internal affairs of the state. Old interests such as the Church and wealthy landowning families continued to be major players in the arena.

Within this array of competing interests, we can see a range of oppositions. The interests of the wealthy opposed those of the poor. Liberals opposed the entrenched power of the Church with its large landholdings and numerous charges for religious services that sometimes amounted to extortion. Rural interests competed with urban. Regional interests persisted, perhaps most acutely between Mexico City and outlying regions and other growing cities. After independence, sharp fault lines developed between liberals and conservatives.

These issues overlapped various categories of the population. Indigenous peoples were more likely to be poor than wealthy and to be rural rather than urban, although in the twentieth century thousands of displaced *indios* migrated to Mexico City and other urban areas. Nineteenth-century conservatives were more supportive of the Church than were liberals, who opposed what they saw as the Church's anachronistic and oppressive power and who even sought to outlaw clerics.

Liberals also opposed special status for *los llamados indios* ("those called Indians"). They opposed the perpetuation of special status and communal indigenous landholdings. Liberals in general tended to endorse "fusion" rather than the recognition of a distinct indigenous identity (Hale 1989:220). Conservatives, on the other hand, were more prone to favor separatism for indigenous populations.

Some of these issues became sharper after independence, but they arose sporadically during the last years of Spanish hegemony. Ultimately, they contributed to its demise.

Trials of the New Mexican State

The early decades of the Mexican state saw governments change at the average rate of more than one per year, as presidents rose and fell. The vagaries of Mexican politics during the nineteenth and early twentieth centuries amount to a complex, fascinating tale, which many historians have recounted in detail.

We can view the era in terms of a swirl of interests vying for advantage, but a few individuals warrant special attention because of their personal impact on events. One of these is Antonio López de Santa Anna. Santa Anna was extraordinary if only because of the impact of his career on the course of Mexican history during this period—much of it to the detriment of the state. Santa Anna was instrumental in leading the opposition to Iturbide and became president himself—several times—in the turbulent aftermath of independence. He also played a key role in the loss of about half of Mexico's territory.

Mexico had encouraged settlers to develop the sparsely populated northern expanse of Texas in an effort to consolidate its claims along the border, although more settlers came from the United States than from Mexico (Miller 1989:210). Many of these continued to identify themselves with their place of origin. As their numbers grew, they chafed under the attempts of the remote government in Mexico City to become involved in their affairs—particularly to discourage slavery and to collect taxes. In 1829 Mexico abolished slavery altogether in an attempt to slow immigration into Texas from the United States. In 1830 the government prohibited immigration from the United States entirely.

Some Mexicans who had moved to Texas from other parts of the country shared resentment toward the government in Mexico City. Lorenzo

Zavala, for example, the prominent liberal politico, despised Santa Anna and left for Texas during one of Santa Anna's many short terms as president. Zavala supported some degree of Texas resistance, though probably not to the extent of the U.S. activists who declared secession from Mexico in 1834.

Texas rebels attacked a garrison in 1835, and Santa Anna led a force of federal troops to restore order. The campaign included the battle at El Álamo that became an incendiary part of United States folklore. More significantly for Mexico, though, Santa Anna found himself in a situation at San Jacinto that led to his capture by rebellious Texans under a man whose Cherokee acquaintances had named "Big Drunk," but whose real name was Sam Houston.

Negotiating to obtain his release from the Texan rebels, Santa Anna acquiesced to what became known as the Velasco Agreement in which he promised to support the independence of Texas from Mexico. When word of this accord reached Mexico City, the outraged Congress refused to recognize the agreement, and Santa Anna withdrew in temporary disgrace. Texas, on the other hand, considered itself independent. The United States annexed Texas in 1845, adding another slave state to the Union and beginning a war that resulted in Mexico's loss of the northern half of its territory.

France, observing Mexico's troubles, saw an opportunity to take advantage. The French demanded compensation from Mexico for damages that had occurred to the property of French citizens during an outbreak of civil disorder in Mexico City. In an attempt to intimidate the government, French ships blockaded the port of Veracruz in 1838.

The situation gave Santa Anna the chance to redeem himself, and he led troops to defend Veracruz. The French blockade turned out to be a fiasco, although their naval bombardment devastated the city, which they occupied until the Mexican troops under Santa Anna drove them back to their ships. Santa Anna lost a leg in the battle, which he later, as president, exhumed and buried with full military honors in Mexico City. Mexicans wryly dubbed the episode "la guerra de los pasteles" (the Pastry War) because the French demands had involved payments for damage to a French pastry shop.

Although Santa Anna lost his limb, he regained the public acclaim he cherished. Assuming the presidency one last time, he took the title "Most Serene Highness." His political career ended when he raised funds to quash a rebellion in Ayutla by selling half of the state of Sonora to the United States—a move that resulted in his banishment from Mexico for the remainder of his life.

Many of the newly independent state's vulnerabilities became starkly apparent during this era. Economic problems resulting from the eleven-year war of independence from Spain had exacerbated competition for sparse resources among various constituencies. The government was impoverished, but to raise taxes among the diverse populace would have risked further rebellion. Taxing the wealthy and powerful was especially out of the question, and the poor had little to appropriate. Resentment over taxes, in fact, had touched off the Texas rebellion in the first place.

Foreign interests turned predatory eyes toward the fledgling state of Mexico as it struggled to manage its internal affairs throughout a huge expanse of territory. The French assault on Veracruz and the U.S. acquisition of 890,000 square miles of northern Mexico are examples. In 1861 French, Spanish, and British forces arrived at Veracruz—ostensibly to restore order. Britain and Spain soon gave up the project, but France pursued its attempt to add Mexico as a colony.

The French suffered a resounding defeat at Puebla in 1862, but they returned with reinforcements and eventually occupied Mexico City. Napoleon III installed Maximilian of Hapsburg and his wife Carlota to rule Mexico as emperor and empress in 1863. Their short reign ended in their execution in 1867.

Indigenous Issues and Political Factions

During the early years after independence, "Mexico was not yet a nation of citizens who identified their interests with each other. While calling themselves Mexicans, they had tenuous bonds or none at all" (Ruiz 1992:186). In the political arena, many of those various interests gravitated into the major factions of conservatives and liberals. The conservatives represented the interests of entrenched power—the wealthier landowning *criollos* and *peninsulares* and the upper echelons of the Church. The liberals, for the most part, included the small but growing *criollo* middle class.

By the mid-nineteenth century, many *criollos* were well educated, some with schooling in the United States or Europe. Lawyers, economists, teachers, agronomists, they were increasingly frustrated at their lack of access to positions of wealth and power. For them, political reform was not a matter of profound social restructuring but of access to the power structure.

The numerous political theorists among the liberals became known as the *letrados* ("literati"). From their ranks rose the *científicos*, the intellectual positivists who advocated a "scientific" approach to government. Their assessment of indigenous peoples sprang from post-Enlightenment ideas of cultural evolution and progress, and they would play a major role in Mexican political philosophy during the late nineteenth and early twentieth centuries.

Neither the liberals nor the conservatives generally agonized much over *indios*, though, except when agitation over land or other forms of social unrest drew public attention. The burden of dealing with such disruptions befell whichever faction controlled the government at the moment, while their rivals generally tried to use *indio* unrest to their own advantage.

The problem of dislocated and impoverished indigenous communities continued to be a recurring, if minor, irritant to Mexican governments from independence to the present. Although indigenous peoples accounted for a majority of the Mexican population through the nineteenth century, indigenous uprisings usually were fairly isolated. They created local problems rather than national crises.

The ambivalence of the Mexican state toward its indigenous peoples was evident from the first century of independence. Conservatives, who generally favored separation of *indios*, were not above extolling the glories of the pre-Hispanic past in order to emphasize a unique Mexican identity. Liberals, who favored the assimilation of *indio* populations and promoted the idea of a single Mexican culture, were perhaps even more prone to glorify the indigenous legacy.

Neither faction saw much connection between the indigenous past and the present or had much regard for living indigenous populations. To the extent that *criollo* intellectuals and politicos gloried in pre-Columbian history, they viewed *indios* of the present as lazy, degenerate, apathetic, and a burden on society. Skin color was a major factor in many of these discussions. In the colonial era, the *criollo* scholar don Carlos de Siguenza y Góngora, an avid student of pre-Columbian culture, had asserted that *indios* had no business living near Spaniards (Ruiz 1992:100). In the nineteenth century, only a few voices expressed a more humane view of contemporary indigenous populations or argued that many of their current problems arose from the injustices and loss of lands they had suffered. It was not until the presidency of Lázaro Cárdenas in the 1930s that a Mexican government made concerted efforts to assist indigenous peoples.

The *Reforma*

A major turning point in nineteenth-century Mexican government came with the presidency of Benito Juárez, who enacted changes known collectively as the *reforma*. This was a high point for the liberals. The conservatives had gained office in 1850, but inexplicably, President Lucas

Alamán had given extensive powers to the energetic Santa Anna. So avidly did Santa Anna set about persecuting liberals that he provoked a popular rebellion.

In the aftermath, the liberal Ignacio Comonfort gained the presidency and appointed Benito Juárez as his vice-president. The liberals wrote a new constitution in 1857 imposing democratic reforms that provoked a rebellion among conservatives, who occupied Mexico City. In the ensuing struggles, Comonfort fled the country. Juárez led liberal forces to recapture Mexico City in 1860 and assumed the presidency. The French invasion of 1863 and their installation of Maximilian interrupted Juárez's term and forced him to flee north. In 1867, however, Juárez captured Mexico City and executed the royal couple.

Juárez was a full-blooded Zapotec, but despite that heritage his policies were not particularly beneficial to indigenous peoples. With the Constitution of 1857, the Juárez government called for the breaking up of large landholdings. The *juaristas'* plan supposedly took aim at large *haciendas* in order to promote more individually owned farms, but a consequence was the fragmentation of many indigenous communally held *ejidos*. As a result, *indios* once again lost more land to powerful interests. Many *hacendados*, on the other hand, sidestepped the crisis by assigning subdivisions of their lands to family members. Eric Wolf notes that almost all of the broken-up *ejido* lands in this era ended up in the hands of *hacienda* owners and private land companies (1969:16).

The Church also lost large landholdings during this period. "In the main the Church estates passed in large, unbroken tracts into the hands of the followers of Juárez, and although in this fashion a new landed aristocracy was created, it was nonetheless an aristocracy" (Simpson 1937:24).

The loss of indigenous *ejido* lands was consistent with the liberals' aims, since they favored the merging of *indios* into the wider society. They viewed communal *ejidos* as anachronistic inefficient baggage from the past and obstacles to progress. As we shall see in the next chapter, similar views regarding reservations prevailed in the United States in the 1880s and later.

The reform purported to encourage small individual farms, but for indigenous peoples a major flaw was the need to purchase lands. For *indios* who had lost their *ejido* holdings, this usually was not a possibility.

The *Porfiriato*

After the Juárez presidency, many of his democratic reforms eroded, but succeeding administrations continued to carry out the appropriation of indigenous lands even more intensely. During the long reign of Porfirio Díaz, from 1876 to 1910, *ejidos* lost about two million acres (Phipps 1925:115). The government contracted with private companies to survey lands for redistribution and compensated these firms with title to one-third of the lands involved. Lands given away in this fashion ultimately amounted to one-fifth of Mexico's territory (Wolf 1969:16).

By the end of the Díaz regime in 1910, 99 percent of rural family heads were landless (Hodges and Gandy 1983:4). Díaz upheld the long-standing principle that the government must protect private property at all costs to preserve order. Clearly, the concept of private property did not include *ejido* lands. On this, liberals and conservatives agreed.

By the time of the *porfiriato*, as the Díaz era is known, the Mexican middle class had become much larger and more powerful, although it was hardly monolithic in its concerns. The *porfiriato* was a period when interest groups proliferated and Mexico became inextricably linked to a global economic system. Díaz opened the door to foreign investment, which not only served the interests of a few special constituencies but generated a relationship of dependency that had profound consequences for the mass of the population. Indigenous peoples, with minimal power, bore the heaviest burden of these developments.

Mexico's raw materials—oil, minerals, cotton, henequen twine, cacao, coffee, cochineal dye, and other commodities—were of great interest to industries in the United States, Britain, and various European countries. Copper, which was abundant near the U.S. border, became especially valuable when U.S. electrical industries expanded. Mexico did not have the means to exploit most of these resources without outside investment.

Mexican domestic industries had been slow to develop. In colonial times, the Spanish Crown had outlawed the production of goods such as wine, olive oil, or fine cloth that would have competed with Spanish products. Mines had accounted for a large portion of Mexican production during the seventeenth and eighteenth centuries, but those operations depended heavily on human labor rather than technological innovation or investment in machinery.

During the nineteenth century's series of insurrections and political turmoil, factories and mines had slowed production or become idle. Guerrilla bands and armies had blown up bridges and uprooted railroad tracks, and the scarcity of good roads throughout most of the country made long-distance transportation of goods all but impossible.

Haciendas also were labor-intensive. Despite the common assertion that they were more efficient than *ejidos*, they tended to restrict their production to keep prices high. Other Mexican enterprises included *obrajes,* small sweatshops where poorly paid workers—usually women—labored long hours to produce rough cloth or cigars and cigarettes.

From the eighteenth century on, the majority of these workers were *indios* driven from their lands. They offered abundant, cheap labor. With an ample supply of human energy, none of these industrial operations had stimulated the development of a modernized, sophisticated industrial infrastructure.

Mexico had permitted some foreign operations in earlier periods, particularly in the mining and petroleum industries, but these had tended to become U.S. or British islands in a Mexican sea. To the extent that they used local labor, they generally paid Mexican workers far less than foreign employees—a situation that led to unrest and strikes on several occasions. A major strike erupted at the Cananea copper mine near the Arizona border in 1906, which armed enforcers from the United States helped to put down with violence. In 1907 at Río Blanco, a strike resulted in two hundred deaths and four hundred workers jailed (Wolf 1969:21). These foreign outposts did little to help the Mexican economy, since their profits flowed quickly out of the country.

Some conservatives in the late nineteenth century, notably Lucas Alamán, argued that foreign dependency would keep Mexico impoverished and called for tariffs to protect Mexican goods (Ruiz 1992: 192–194). The prevailing view of the liberal government, however, was that Mexico needed the investment of richer nations. The liberals—and the *científicos* under Díaz—asserted that "trade substitution" of raw materials for imported goods in a free market would benefit the economy.

During the *porfiriato,* foreign capital helped to build an infrastructure to make the extraction of Mexican resources easier. Paved roads, railroad tracks, and electric lines appeared throughout the country. From 1876 to 1910, railroad tracks grew from a total of 666 kilometers throughout the entire nation to 19,280 kilometers (Wolf 1969:20). Most of these ran north to the United States as a means of extracting resources.

Once again the state largely ignored indigenous populations except to preside over the appropriation of their lands. The large *haciendas,* which had always been commercial operations, produced more goods for international export than food for domestic consumption. As the profitability of cash crops increased, *hacendados* seized more *ejido* lands through various means, including raw force. This left the displaced *indios* little choice but to work for low wages as tenant farmers or *peones acasillados* (debt peons) on their former lands or to migrate to cities for other work.

In conjunction with the exuberant profiteering of the economic elite, the disparity grew between the very rich and the very poor. In Yucatán sisal plantations became more important when the invention of the McCormick reaper created a large U.S. market for bailing twine. International Harvester became a major investor in the region. By the close of the *porfiriato*, between one-half and one-third of the Maya population worked on sisal plantations in debt peonage (Wolf 1969:41). A growing mass of desperate people swelled the margins of urban areas, many living in caves and *barrios* around Mexico City.

The economics of the *porfiriato*, based on the principle of export substitution, did much to create Mexico's economic dependency on the global market. Large sectors of the economy became vulnerable to fluctuations in the world market for raw commodities. Domestic manufacturing was weak, and foreign interests controlled most of it. Mexico had become increasingly subject to forces it could not control, and profits from raw material exports fell far short of the costs of imported goods.

Food shortage became a national crisis, since hundreds of thousands of *indios* and other *campesinos* had been driven from their *ranchos* and *ejidos*. During the *porfiriato*, *haciendas* and survey companies acquired at least thirty-eight million hectares of land (Sanderson 1981:211). *Hacendados* were producing coffee, cotton, and henequen fiber rather than corn and beans, and the need for imported food, most of which was beyond the means of the poorest and hungriest, exacerbated the economic tailspin. The price of corn rose while domestic production of corn, chilies, and beans declined.

The Revolution of 1910

The *porfiriato* ended in a revolution comparable to that of 1810 in many respects, but the process in the twentieth century was somewhat more complicated. Indigenous uprisings had occurred sporadically during the Díaz regime—the Yaqui rebelled in 1885 and 1898, for example—but as always these revolts had not spread far enough to become threats to the state's ruling interests.

The increasing disparity of wealth throughout the country, which affected many constituencies besides indigenous communities, did much to produce the revolution. In the north, large *haciendas* drained resources from the countryside to enrich a few families. In Chihuahua seventeen people owned 40 percent of the state (Wolf 1969:33). A small oligarchy controlled other resources as well. In 1908 thirty-six of the largest sixty-six corporations in Mexico had the same thirteen people on their boards of directors (Wolf 1969:13).

The growing middle class was increasingly frustrated at their exclusion from power and the wealth that came with it. The mass of oppressed *campesinos*—both *indio* and *mestizo*—constituted a well of desperation and anger that this restless middle class would ignite, but not easily control (Tannenbaum 1937). When Díaz sought to extend his power beyond the end of his last term in office by naming an unpopular successor, a liberal named Francisco Madero called for revolution.

Madero was hardly a firebrand. In many respects, his views paralleled those of Benito Juárez, both with regard to a wish for democratic reforms and a disregard for the indigenous population. As Daniel Levy and Gabriel Szekely put it, "A form of political liberty, not political equality, and certainly not economic equality, was Madero's guiding principle" (1987:28).

Madero sprang from a wealthy family in the north whose holdings had expanded from *haciendas* to mining and other business enterprises. Like many of their class, the Madero family resented the favorable position that foreign-owned corporations enjoyed under the Díaz regime, such as those that the Rockefeller and Guggenheim families controlled (Hodges and Gandy 1983:12).

The United States had supported Díaz mostly because of his hospitality to foreign investment. The democracy to the north generally had ignored Díaz's authoritarian domestic policies of *pan y palo* ("bread and the stick"). But Díaz had recently irritated powerful U.S. economic interests—Standard Oil in particular—by selling oil to a British rival. At the time, about a third of U.S. overseas investment was in Mexico (Hodges and Gandy 1983:8), and U.S. business interests were in no mood for a capricious Mexican president. Deciding that Díaz had outlived his usefulness, they discretely supported Madero's "democratic reforms." Madero issued his call to arms, the Plan of San Luis Potosí, from sanctuary in the United States.

Díaz resigned in 1911, but he outlived Madero. Soon after Madero assumed the office of president, the conservative General Victoriano Huerta had him shot. The next few decades saw bloody conflict throughout the country as armies and aspirants to power, representing a variety of interests, struggled for position. A few figures played especially important roles.

In the cattle-ranching region of the north, a man of dubious background named Doroteo Arango arose as a highly successful leader of irregular troops. Adopting the name Pancho Villa, he supported the revolution's various factions to the extent that they were compatible with his own interests. Often portrayed as a "social bandit" or a sort of Mexican Robin Hood, Villa on occasion terrorized rural communities with his undisciplined troops.

More significant for indigenous peoples was Emiliano Zapata, a *criollo* landowner from the south in Morelos. Zapata and his followers were concerned with land rights. Like Villa's, Zapata's army became a formidable element in the revolution (see Womack 1968).

Both of these figures were problematic to the people who considered themselves to be in charge of the revolution. The insurgent elite wanted reforms that would open the system to people like themselves, rather than radical changes in the structure of the state. Their interests were profoundly different from Villa's and Zapata's *campesino* followers. Villa's irregulars, for that matter—many of them out-of-work *vaqueros* and occasional bandits—were a different constituency from the sandaled *indios* who followed Zapata in hopes of regaining their farm plots.

Madero had opposed Zapata over the issue of agrarian reforms. "Rural unrest, which proved prolonged and bloody, gave the Revolution its character, so that many historians consider it the first important peasant revolution of the twentieth century. As events proved, however, the agrarian issue was of secondary importance to the question of renovating the Porfirian state" (Ankerson 1984:192).

The short reign of Victoriano Huerta saw the convergence of several independent armies in the north. Venustiano Carranza, a former member of the *porfirista* Senate, had joined the revolution after Díaz turned down his bid to become governor of Coahuila. Backing Madero, he finally attained his governorship. When Huerta had Madero shot, Carranza rose in opposition and declared himself El Jefe Máximo ("the First Chief") of the revolution. In Sonora a rancher named Alvaro Obregón had also supported Madero. After Huerta took office, Obregón allied his forces of Yaqui, industrial workers, and *campesinos* with Carranza. Pancho Villa, calling his forces the *división del norte*, also threw in his lot with El Jefe Máximo.

These armies also drew recruits from various adjacent states, although there remained some pockets of opposition. In the north-central Laguna region, a "pro-Huerta peasant movement arose in reaction to the Madero administration's failure to meet worker and peasant expectations for better wages, improved working conditions, and land" (Meyers 1994:243). Many of the upper classes also supported Huerta in the hope that he would impose order to keep their holdings intact.

United States interests initially had hopes for Huerta, but grew disenchanted when he appeared ready to deal with British oil interests. On balance, the mosaic of opposition against Huerta won out. A United States blockade of Veracruz, which cut off Huerta's supply lines, hastened things to a close.

Following Huerta's resignation, the revolutionary armies occupied Mexico City. Their opposition to Huerta had united the variety of interests, but without that common purpose they tended to diverge. Carranza in victory showed himself to be far less receptive to radical change than he had appeared to be during the campaign. Villa and Zapata soon denounced him as a traitor to the principles of the revolution and took once again to the field.

Obregón, in the meantime, had begun to demonstrate his skills in balancing off various interests and setting them against one another at critical junctures. He urged urban workers to join the movement under Carranza, while talking of the agrarian reform that Madero had opposed. Villa and Zapata, heroes of the revolution, became relatively marginal in the new phase of governance.

By 1915 Villa and Zapata were at war with Obregón, who stood at the head of Carranza's army with battalions of workers. After several massive battles, Obregón pushed Villa's *campesino* forces back to the north. In 1916 Carranza sent an army to Morelos to fight a war of attrition against Zapata's followers.

General unrest and social disorder heightened the demands in 1917 for another convention, which produced a new constitution. The Constitution promised extensive, progressive reforms including land redistribution, the end of debt peonage, the right to unionize and strike, an eight-hour workday, and a minimum wage. It also promised compensation to landowners for their losses through redistribution. It bowed to the old principle of the right to private property, but it also gave the state the right to determine what the acceptable form of that property might be. In short, it gave the centralized government tremendous power. The Constitution also limited the president's term of office, but essentially it allowed the president to *be* the government while in office.

Carranza, with the time remaining to him, continued to assert that power. He launched more attacks on Zapata, until by 1919 half of the population of Morelos had died, including Zapata himself (Hodges and Gandy 1983:26). Zapata's assassination occurred in an ambush on Carranza's orders. By 1920 Villa gave up the struggle in the north.

Obregón was the logical successor to Carranza, but rather than selecting his old supporter, Carranza attempted to name a successor who would amount to his proxy. This would have allowed the old *caudillo* (strong man) to continue ruling Mexico behind the scenes. It was in keeping with a tradition older than Díaz and one that would continue long after him. Carranza was no more successful than Díaz had been, however. Obregón raised an army and advanced on Mexico City as Carranza fled into the mountains, where he soon was shot.

As president, Obregón managed to accommodate and quell or mollify some of the more obstreperous interests competing within the Mexican state. The United States recognized his government in 1923 in exchange for a guarantee that U.S. property interests would be safe in Mexico. Following custom, Obregón named Plutarco Elias Calles to succeed him in office. Calles later returned the favor and Obregón reassumed the presidency, only to be assassinated the same year.

Whether Calles had any role in Obregón's death is unclear. Calles appointed another successor, Emilio Portes Gil, who attempted to carry out some of the reforms the 1917 Constitution had called for. Calles continued in the role of *caudillo*, however, not so far behind the scenes, and opposed many of his successor's reforms. But for the presidential term beginning in 1934, Calles selected Lázaro Cárdenas—a man who would come closer than any other president to bringing about radical change. Before long Cárdenas would dislodge the old *caudillo* himself and send him into exile.

Mexican States Mentioned in Chapter 3

Cárdenas

Calles had run into serious problems trying to balance reforms with the demands of entrenched interests. As Obregón had done, he sought to keep the army acquiescent by winning (or buying) the loyalty of the officer corps. Calles redistributed some land, hoping to quiet the *campesinos*, but alarm among landowners soon dissuaded him. His reversal, in turn, aroused the *campesinos*. When Calles tried to eliminate clerical privileges and redistribute Church lands, he faced the Cristero armed rebellion of Church supporters in 1926. He used harsh and bloody measures to put an end to the Cristeros, but *indio* and *mestizo zapatistas* continued guerrilla warfare in the south long after the death of Zapata. Calles resorted to violence to restore order, but for the next president he chose a reformer—Governor Cárdenas of Michoacán.

Like Madero, Cárdenas sprang from a wealthy middle-class family and had strong concerns about foreign interests that were systematically divesting Mexico of its resources. Unlike Madero or his other predecessors, however, Cárdenas also had a strong sensitivity to the problem of land among rural people, including indigenous communities. Perhaps he had an advantage over Madero in having seen the explosiveness this need had produced over the previous two decades. Cárdenas not only began to return land to indigenous peoples but promoted communal landholdings (see Hamilton 1982).

For decades Mexican governments and other interested parties had argued that *ejido* agriculture, which most indigenous communities practiced, was inefficient compared to *hacienda* production. But indigenous communities with *ejidos* produced food for their own subsistence, selling a few cash crops whenever possible, while *haciendas* typically produced commercial, nonfood crops. We have already seen the problems that arose as a result of this pattern during the *porfiriato* (see Fox 1993, Austin and Esteva 1987).

It is difficult to determine to what extent this assumption of *ejido* inefficiency reflected long-standing axioms inherent in Social Darwinism (or modernization theory, for that matter), which assumed that indigenous practices of any sort were primitive and obstacles to progress. In any case, the assumption ignored many significant factors. For one thing, few indigenous communities had been able to practice their subsistence methods undisturbed. Many of those who retained their lands at all had inadequate plots. The ancient *repartimiento*, levies, and various other means of appropriating labor had undermined their productivity for centuries. As a consequence, many *indios* were fortunate to be able to provide for their own needs, let alone contribute to the national economy.

On the other hand, the record of *hacienda* efficiency was none too convincing. Many business-wise *hacendados* had limited their production of commercial crops in order to influence the market or to wait for more favorable prices. As a consequence, the typical *hacienda* had large areas of land lying fallow at any given time. This produced an incentive for *hacendados* to expand their landholdings to exert more control over local production. The growth of *hacienda* lands generally involved a loss to surrounding *indio* communities.

The growing shortage of food produced in Mexico meant that food imports drained more of the national wealth and that hunger became a chronic feature of Mexican national life except among the wealthy. With these factors in mind, we might well question whether it might have been more efficient for the vast numbers of displaced *indios* and other *campesinos* to have continued producing their own food on a sustainable basis.

Cárdenas tried to promote the viability of *ejidos* by establishing *banco nacional de crédito ejidal* to provide loans for seeds, equipment, and fertilizer. In 1935 he turned over 73 percent of the irrigated lands in the Laguna region of Coahuila to 34,000 *campesinos*. They shared common access to seeds, farming equipment, and profits. He divided another 70,000 hectares in the Laguna area into 150-hectare plots. In Yucatán he turned over 30 percent of the henequen lands to *campesinos* and another 40 percent in 1937 (Ruiz 1992:299). Cárdenas restored 17,000 hectares of irrigated land to the Yaqui people along the Río Yaqui in the north. In Mexicali near the Baja California–United States border, he appropriated the cotton-growing lands of the Colorado River Land Company and converted them to *ejidos*. In 1939 he converted coffee plantations in Chiapas to *ejidos*.

The result was that a million *campesino* families acquired 18.4 million hectares. By 1940 one and a half million *ejidatarios* possessed 47 percent of the arable land in Mexico and accounted for 42 percent of agricultural production (Ruiz 1992:399).

Hacienda owners did not sit quietly as these policies unfolded. They tried to win over conservative army officers to resist, and in many regions they formed their own militias to intimidate the *campesinos*. So-called White Guards, armed militias working for wealthy landowners in southern Mexico, continued to harass indigenous communities for decades. Cárdenas responded by arming sixty thousand *campesinos* to defend their lands (Hodges and Gandy 1983:42).

Unlike his predecessors, Cárdenas was acutely conscious of the importance of a variety of indigenous issues in addition to land. In 1936 he established a Department of Indian Affairs, which devoted much of its resources to addressing problems as indigenous communities perceived them. It sponsored eight Indian Congresses and took action on a few acute regional issues. It undertook projects for the Otomí near the Valley of Mexico, the Yaqui and Tarahumara in the north, and the Chamula in the southeast.

Cárdenas initiated a program to provide schooling that he and his advisers felt would be most appropriate to the needs of *indio* communities. The school system, *escuelas vocacionales para indígenas* ("vocational schools for indigenous people") placed priority on practical strategies for addressing local and regional problems. Primarily this involved vocational training and Spanish-language classes.

Cárdenas did not entirely abandon the idea of assimilation. Perhaps in response to critics, he stated that "our problem is not to preserve the Indian, but to make the Indian Mexican" (quoted in Friedlander 1986:363). In fact, some of his land reforms tended to have this effect. After centuries of beleaguered existence,

> the crucial turning point in Yaqui history occurred with the Cárdenas reforms of 1937. While granting social justice to the Yaqui people, they also laid the groundwork for their integration to the Mexican economic and social system. The principal agent of this directed change was the Banco Ejidal, which, through control of credit, forced the Yaquis to abandon their traditional agriculture, and to replace their independent subsistence farming with commercial or cash-crop cultivation. (Hu-DeHart 1988:174)

Cárdenas's policies were, nonetheless, an important departure from the old liberal approach to indigenous issues that had promoted sporadic, coercive assimilation measures. They promoted communal landholdings that made the survival of indigenous communities more feasible, rather than breaking them up into individualized plots or divesting these communities of land altogether. The *cardenista* education programs, under Narcisco Bassols, recognized the validity of local cultures and emphasized practical training rather than cultural indoctrination.

This era was not to last long, however. Other issues demanded Cárdenas's attention. A prolonged dispute had developed over the desire of foreign petroleum corporations to extract Mexican oil as cheaply as possible and the demands of the Mexican government for fair compensation. Early in the twentieth century, the large oil companies had been paying twenty *centavos* of tax for each ton of oil shipped abroad and sold at immense profit (Ruiz 1992:325). Standard Oil sold Mexican oil more cheaply in the United States than in Mexico (Fehrenbach 1973:472). Cárdenas finally seized the oil facilities and nationalized the industry. Although this move generated popular applause, it created some powerful enemies both within and outside Mexico (see, e.g., Hamilton 1982). Royal Dutch Shell and other industry giants boycotted Mexican oil in retaliation. In nationalizing the petroleum industry and pursuing other programs, Cárdenas provoked the animosity of many Mexican interest groups that had become entrenched during the *porfiriato* and earlier and that had benefited from the status quo. Transnational corporations based in the United States, Britain, and elsewhere took a keen interest in supporting the opposition to this "leftist" government.

Although Cárdenas was not a Marxist, he gave his enemies more reason to accuse him of Marxist sympathies when he offered asylum to Leon Trotsky. Land redistribution to *campesinos* found little favor among the elite, and the Church viewed the secular schools in *indio* communities as antireligious. After Cárdenas left office, things drifted back into the old patterns.

Mexico after Cárdenas

Cárdenas had represented the left wing of the ruling party, the Party of the Mexican Revolution (PRM). His successor, Manuel Avila Camacho, was far more conservative and resumed the long trend of promoting capitalist development (see Cornelius and Craig 1988). In the 1940s, Cárdenas's cabinet-status Department of Indian Affairs disappeared. The Instituto Nacional Indigenista stood in its place, with far less money to spend and a lower status in the structure of government. Writing of the Yaqui situation, Evelyn Hu-DeHart observes that Cárdenas's "successors in the presidency, taking clear advantage of the store of good will and rural stability created by the agrarian reform, redirected the nation's priority toward rapid economic growth at all costs" (1988:169). As Mexico struggled with its financial difficulties, the old ways and old problems continued to beset the countryside. Powerful interests acquired many of the *ejido* lands that Cárdenas had distributed (see Hewitt 1976).

From the 1940s on, Mexican government was in the hands of interests who were eager to strengthen ties with the United States and other foreign powers. Growing foreign loans for "development" increased the national debt. Payment terms depended partly on the political and social stability of the state and the government's congenial stance toward global market interests.

Mexico came to depend more on oil sales as transnationals welcomed it back into the "world economic community," and it enjoyed a flush of prosperity as oil prices rose in the 1970s. This set the stage for disaster when world oil prices dropped in the early 1980s and the government had to declare bankruptcy. Mexico's powerful creditors could demand austerity measures to accommodate burdensome interest payments. Generally this meant decreasing social spending in favor of industrial development, further depriving the poor in favor of transnational corporations and a small Mexican elite.

PRM had become the Institutional Revolutionary Party (PRI) in 1946. PRI has held the dominant center of the arena since that time, with numerous small parties providing token opposition on the left and the more powerful conservative National Action Party (PAN) a somewhat stronger rival on the right. Representation of indigenous interest in the political system has been meager. As has been the case throughout most of Mexican history, indigenous communities have been almost invisible except during episodes of civil disruption. For the most part, indigenous identity in the eyes of the state has been submerged in the more general *campesino* population.

In boom times, the riches accumulated at the upper levels of the social hierarchy. In hard times, the poor suffered the greatest deprivation. Even while outside interests continued to drain resources from Mexico, internal disparity increased between rich and poor, among whom indigenous peoples tended to be the poorest.

The World Bank in 1980 reported that in the previous decade, Mexico had "one of the worst profiles of resource distribution of any nation on earth," with more concentration of income than there had been in 1910, the year of the revolution (Barry 1992:94). In the 1980s, two-thirds of the Mexican population consumed less than the minimal two thousand calories per day (Ruiz 1992:469). The same World Bank in 1986, ironically, recommended that Mexico "produce products of commercial value instead of basic food crops." To this end, it recommended that government "subsidies for fertilizers, fuel, credit, water, seeds, and crop insurance be reduced even more, at a gradual but drastic pace" (quoted in Barry 1992:157; see also Barkin et al. 1990). Tom Barry notes that by 1992 Mexico had become the largest overall recipient of World Bank loans, totaling more than twelve billion dollars (1995:259).

Throughout the 1980s, in the aftermath of the oil bust and during the conservative Reagan-Bush administrations in the United States, Mexico became still more tied to foreign investments. By the 1990s, a thousand or so *maquiladoras*, foreign-owned factories run by U.S., Japanese, or other foreign management dependent upon cheap Mexican labor, lined the United States border. Unlike slavery, the *maquiladora* system had the advantage of using a self-reproducing and inexhaustible supply of labor at minimal cost. While the workers' paltry wages contributed dribbles to the Mexican economy, corporate profits flowed over the border. Many of the consumer goods the Mexican workers were able to buy, moreover, were imported.

As the 1988 elections approached, Cuauhtemoc Cárdenas, son of the former president, led a faction that split from the PRI to form the National Democratic Front (FDN). He ran in opposition to the conservative, Harvard-educated probusiness PRI candidate Carlos Salinas de Gortari. Salinas won in the midst of widespread accusations of election fraud and continued the process of immersing Mexico in the global economy. Salinas's victory, not surprisingly, had the approval of transnational corporations.

Under the banner of "privatization," Salinas pursued a modern version of laissez-faire economics, which in the late 1980s had acquired the name "neoliberal." This was a hostile environment for indigenous communities with *ejidos*. Salinas began breaking them up soon after taking office (see Gates 1993).

During this period, the United States government provided the Mexican government with enhanced means and methods of using force on the population in promoting the "War on Drugs." The issue of illegal drugs crossing the border from Mexico had become a popular theme in the United States. As Beth Sims points out, "Ironically, however, widespread cultivation of Mexican opium poppies—and, to a lesser extent, marijuana—began during World War II, at the request of the U.S. government, which was seeking supplies of pain-reducing medications such as morphine" (1992:330).

Sims adds, "By funding drug control assistance to Mexico's law enforcement agencies and armed forces, the U.S. is strengthening the repressive arms of Mexico's authoritarian regime" (1992:281). By the mid-1990s, ironically, it had become evident that many in the Mexican government were participating in the operations of drug cartels (Reding 1995).

Much of the military equipment supplied for the "War on Drugs" has contributed to the abuse of indigenous populations in particular. Americas Watch referred to Mexico's record on human rights as a "policy of impunity" (Harding 1992:63, 64; see Americas Watch 1990). During the first fifteen months of the Salinas administration, about sixty indigenous leaders were killed in addition to others who died in violence associated with the elections (Harding 1992:67).

In many ways, the Salinas administration was eerily reminiscent of the *porfiriato*. Surrounded by *técnicos* as counterparts to Díaz's *científicos*, Salinas opened Mexico's resources even more to foreign investors, while the gap between the wealthy few and the impoverished masses grew more extreme. The previous president, Miguel de la Madrid, had signed the international GATT treaty, the General Agreement on Tariffs and Trade. Salinas had the historic role of agreeing to a free trade agreement (NAFTA) with the United States and Canada that laid out a banquet of resources for corporate interests (see Barry 1996:65–74).

Indigenous Peoples and Free Trade

In Chiapas, with a large Maya population and by all accounts the poorest state in Mexico, large numbers of *indios* were forced off their lands by coffee growers in the 1990s (see Benjamin 1989). In 1992 the Salinas government pushed an amendment to the Constitution enabling the breakup of *ejido* holdings (Barry 1995:269). Many of these displaced *indios* formed communities of people who spoke different dialects and who previously had felt little in common with one another. Their similar problems, however, led to the development of a broader sense of identity. By 1994 this situation had become the medium for a revolutionary movement that sent alarms to the seat of government in Mexico City and provoked the attention of the world news media.

President Salinas de Gortari's acquiescence to the free trade agreement with the United States and Canada—the North America Free Trade Agreement (NAFTA)—was a precipitating factor. The effect of NAFTA, among other things, would be to open Mexico to unbuttoned exploitation by transnational corporations. For indigenous people and other *campesinos* who hoped to keep their lands, or to retrieve the lands they had lost, this loomed as a disaster (see Harvey 1994, Collier 1994a, Barry 1995).

Many labor groups and other interests in the United States also opposed NAFTA. They feared that dropping protective measures against cheap foreign imports and allowing U.S. corporations to exploit cheaper labor in Mexico would lower their own wages and cost them jobs. In fact, however, NAFTA was largely a formalization of a process already well under way. Many corporate operations in the United States already had moved plants to Mexico for cheaper labor.

In 1987 General Motors had closed eleven plants in the United States and opened twelve in Mexico (Barry 1992:144). The Green Giant company—owned by Pillsbury, which in turn is owned by the British firm Grand Metropolitan—moved one of its broccoli operations from California to Irapuato in Mexico, dropping wages from five dollars to one dollar per hour (Barry 1992:309). These developments have not offered many benefits to Mexican workers either. "The impact of widespread crop substitution and wholesale transfer of technology promoted by transnational processing plants have both reduced the total labor employed and increased the instability of employment through heightened seasonality of labor demand" (Young 1993).

Transnational corporations had long since exceeded the abilities of their home states to control them. NAFTA was an expression by the United States, Canadian, and Mexican states of acquiescence to corporate pressure. Bruce Campbell of the Canadian Labor Congress put the issue succinctly. "The FTA is fundamentally about power. It shifts power from governments (federal and provincial) to the corporate sector. It entrenches that power beyond the reach of future governments. And it limits governmental capacity to define and preserve national developmental goals" (1991:22).

Modern Rebellion

For those in power, stability means business as usual. For those whose situation is unacceptable, stability is not necessarily a virtue. In modern Mexico, short-term stability is crucial for powerful interests to carry out the extraction of resources without interference. This stability has nothing to do with justice.

As economic disparities increase within the population, pressures toward instability seem certain to mount. "The forces of global capitalism give no support to and have little tolerance for nationalist and populist approaches to economic development" (Barry 1992:xvii). Either draconian repression or radical restructuring become inevitable—and as human history has amply shown, one does not preclude the other.

On January 1, 1994, when NAFTA formally went into effect in Mexico, a group who called themselves the Zapatista Army of National Liberation surfaced in Chiapas. Armed and masked, they took control of a few local communities.

As we have seen, indigenous revolt is as old as Mexico itself. The rebellion of local people against oppressive state systems occurred long before the arrival of the Spanish. Rarely, though—except for moments during the long war of independence and a few other instances—have movements spread beyond local regions to threaten the stability of the state (see, e.g., Schreyer 1990, Katz 1988, Campbell et al. 1993, Stanford 1991).

The Mexican government initially reacted to the Zapatista Army of National Liberation with a series of rapidly changing responses. Professing surprise at the uprising that supposedly appeared out of nowhere, it dispatched troops to the region. Soldiers displayed the bodies of Zapatistas for media cameras until officials realized that such photographs did not enhance the image of the Mexican state.

The government then portrayed the rebellion as an isolated incident, most likely the work of outside agitators. The culprits, supposedly, were either radical intellectuals or refugees from neighboring Guatemala. Almost from the outset, however, there was concern that the unrest would spread to other regions of Mexico.

The nature of the movement gave some basis for this fear. Although the Zapatista Army of National Liberation's membership appeared to be mostly Maya, they were not, apparently, from a single locality or dialect group. Moreover, many Maya from the region disavowed ties with the rebels and requested government protection from them. The movement evidently had a far broader base than a single indigenous populace (see Collier 1994a, 1994c, Barry 1995).

To some extent, this broad base was probably a consequence of the massive dislocations in the region. "As Tzeltal, Tzotzil, and other Maya Indians from central Chiapas converged with non-Indian peasants from central and northern Mexico in rapidly shifting frontier settlements, colonists shucked ethnic origins for more generic peasant identities" (Collier 1994c:15).

This process suggests the development of a broad perception of common interest that led to a more encompassing strategy than had characterized resistance in the past. "In a matter of days it became clear that the Ejercito Zapatista de Liberación Nacional (EZLN) was composed of thousands of Mexican Indians (not foreigners), was organized along democratic lines characteristic of other Indian organizations, and had a clearly defined political program for Chiapas and the country" (Nigh 1994:10).

The adoption of Emiliano Zapata as a central symbol seems significant. The numerous earlier movements referring to themselves as Zapatistas long after Zapata's death attest to the power of the image. Zapata was not Maya, nor was he from Chiapas. Zapata was a *criollo* from Morelos whose indigenous followers, for the most part, spoke Nahuatl. The Chiapas rebels' identification with Zapata suggests an appeal to principles and issues that transcend local concerns. There is, no doubt, good reason for the state to fear that such development might not be containable.

A communiqué the Zapatistas issued in February 1994 underscored their appeal to broader principles that were likely to resonate among far-flung indigenous communities. Addressed to "the People of Mexico," the "Peoples and Governments of the World," and "the national and international press," the document evoked the power of indigenous heritage and the principles of "justice, liberty, and democracy." The communiqué stated that these were

> ... barely a dream that the elders of our communities, true guardians of the words of our dead ancestors, had given us in the moment when day gives way to night, when hatred and fear began to grow in our hearts, when there was nothing but desperation; when the times repeated themselves, with no way out, with no door, no tomorrow, when all was injustice, as it was, the true men spoke, the faceless ones, the ones who go by night, the ones who are jungle . . .

It espoused the idea of democratic leadership responsible to the people as an ancient way. "Our path was always that the will of the many be in the hearts of the men and women who command. The will of the majority was the path on which he who commands should walk."

It expressed grievances against the usurpation of power by a small elite:

> And we see that this way of governing that we name is no longer the way for the many, we see that it is the few who now command, and they command without obeying, they lead commanding. And among the few they pass the power of command among themselves, without hearing the many, the few lead commanding, without obeying the command of the many.

It called for the overthrow of the ruling elite and proposed a democratic system that would protect the rights of minorities.

> And we see that those who lead commanding should go far away so that there is reason once again and truth in our land. And we see that there should be change so that those who command obeying lead again and we see that word that comes from afar to name to reason of government, "democracy," is good for the many and for the few. (CCRI-CF del EZLN 1994; quoted in Nigh 1994)

Although the statement evokes indigenous identity, the principles seem likely to appeal to *mestizos* and other disenfranchised constituencies. Whatever the fate of the Ejército Zapatista de Liberación Nacional, its appearance suggests that indigenous self-assertion in Mexico, and perhaps elsewhere, may take a different tack in the future.

The essential difference in this strategy is the attempt to broaden the base of identification—not only beyond local communities and regions, but internationally as well. The skillful use of the mass media will certainly enhance this possibility. As Ronald Nigh comments, "Perhaps no other insurgent movement has provided more information more quickly and effectively to the press—national and international—about its goals and operations" (1994:10). Perhaps one of the most effective tools in the hands of the Zapatistas is electronic mail. This has allowed them to bypass the elite-controlled media and communicate directly over an international network.

With the election of PRI candidate Ernesto Zedillo to the presidency in 1994, following the assassination of Salinas's hand-picked successor, the party's capacity to retain its position seems intact for the moment. Mexico rests upon a tectonic bed of shifting forces, however. The concentration of wealth among the few does not show many signs of reversing and can only build pressure. Thirteen of Mexico's states, as of the 1980 census, were "eminently Indigenous" (Barry 1992:223), and these are among the poorest.

One of the new president's first acts was to "crack down" on the EZLN and arrest purported leaders. After the media displayed a few young people peering through prison bars, however, the government released them. President Zedillo announced a willingness to negotiate, at the same time downplaying the idea that disturbances in other regions had any relationship to the movement in Chiapas.

The process of gathering support beyond the local sphere involves broadening the consciousness of shared issues and concerns among otherwise unconnected communities. In effect, it involves extending the parameters of perceived common interest. If the state is an arena of competing interest groups, the success of indigenous peoples, if not survival itself, depends on the ability to compete effectively.

The ethnographic realities of pre-Columbian Mexico involved highly fragmented indigenous populations with little in common. The Spanish and Mexican states, in promoting the marginalization of indigenous peoples, in effect constructed the broad category of *indio*, only to submerge it again among the rural and urban underclass.

It is ironic, perhaps, that the predominant interests in the Mexican state over the centuries developed the generic senses of *indio* and *campesino*—terms that tended to be pejorative and connote backward, politically troublesome masses. The term *campesino* also blurs any distinction between Indian and *mestizo*. The people to whom these terms refer have not yet been able to utilize such categories fully to their own benefit and to address common issues collectively. The collective implications of this category may offer some promise in the future, however.

Racism, competition among the weak for inadequate resources, language differences, and other factors have inhibited coalescence of these peoples for any common purpose. They will, no doubt, continue to do so in the future. Yet the strategy of coalition building to overcome these divisive factors may become more significant. As the EZLN has demonstrated, access to the global media has changed the situation in important respects.

Beth Sims suggests that the close interaction between Mexico and the United States during the Salinas-Bush years, after decades of inconsistent United States policy toward Mexico, amounted to an alliance of the wealthy in both countries against their general populations (1992:285). Whether or not we accept that analysis, this perspective has gained some credence in United States reactions to the decline in the peso at the beginning of the Zedillo presidency. Billions of dollars have been proffered to "bail out the creditor class" (Todd 1995). Most of the rhetoric justifying this expenditure has involved the safeguarding of investments. There has been little talk of assistance for the impoverished masses.

Despite the continuance of these trends, however, a sense of common cause among the disadvantaged may offer some hope. Although indigenous communities tend to remain locally focused, there are some hints of this. The National Front of Indigenous People and the national Coordination of Indigenous People have been active in several regions in Mexico (Barry 1992:224). There also seems to be a capacity for this sense of common cause to cross international boundaries. Tom Barry notes that several Mixtec organizations, for example, have arisen in California (1992:224).

In later chapters, we shall examine such trends among indigenous peoples in other states. It seems appropriate to turn next to Mexico's ponderous neighbor to the north, the United States.

The United
States

. . . .

4

The white man did not ask anyone for permission to
come upon the land. Maasau spoke to him and said,
"You should ask for permission to enter on this land. If
you wish to come and live according to the way of the
Hopi in this land and never abandon that way, you may.
I will give you this new way of life and some of the
land."

(Andrew Hermequaftewa, Bluebird Chief of
Shungopavi, 1954; quoted in Josephy 1971:4)

When Spain claimed Mexico, it had little competition from other European powers, but the vast region to the north was involved in far
more territorial disputes. France, England, Spain, and the Netherlands
were the main contenders, and there were other minor players as well.
Spain extended claims into what is now western Canada and most of the
southern sector, although there was little attempt to occupy the northern
regions. Hernando de Soto led the first European venture into the Southeast, cutting a destructive path through the area in 1539 (see Kehoe 1992:
179–180). Neither he nor other Europeans met much hostile resistance
from indigenous populations until they had shown their intentions.

Vikings had landed along the North Atlantic Coast as early as the
first millennium A.D., having a few hostile encounters with inhabitants
they called *skraelings*. The identity of the *skraelings* remains uncertain,
but this may have been one of the few cases in which Europeans encountered a hostile reception at the outset.

Long before Columbus set out from Spain looking for India, Basque
fishermen used Newfoundland beaches to dry their codfish for shipping
across the Atlantic. There is little evidence of conflict at that time.

85

European Claims

France staked its claims to the north along the lower reaches of the St. Lawrence River and established fairly congenial relationships with some of the peoples of the area. The inhabitants did take offense, though, when Jacques Cartier erected a large cross and claimed the region for the king of France (Miller 1991:3). Samuel de Champlain complicated matters later when he became involved in a local dispute. Champlain's firearms helped win the day for his Algonkian-speaking companions, but this affront to their enemies, the Hodenosaunee—a people Europeans called Iroquois—helped assure their future animosity toward the French. Much later the French established a base far to the south in New Orleans and acquired the vast area west of the Mississippi from Spain. Napoleon Bonaparte sold his claim to that section of the continent to the United States at the beginning of the nineteenth century, after a slave revolt in the French colony of Haiti that established an independent republic had temporarily altered French plans for a New World empire.

Along the Atlantic Coast, the Dutch established trade relations with Algonkian-speaking communities and carried out a lively commercial enterprise in furs until the British took over. Other foreign initiatives occurred on a smaller scale over the next century or so.

By the nineteenth century, though, most European ventures in eastern North America had left only cultural traces—regional cuisines, place names, architectural remnants, and the surnames of local families. Only England managed to establish and keep a major foothold in the East. English cultural predominance would last long after that foothold had slipped and its thirteen colonies had become independent.

Before things settled down, however, the complex and competitive interaction among European powers was a significant factor affecting the relationships between European and indigenous peoples. For one thing, it tended to inhibit Europeans from unnecessarily alienating local populations that could ally themselves with rival Europeans or cause problems on their own.

The French to the north in what eventually would become Canada were interested in furs. They could acquire these most successfully by negotiating with the people of the region, persuading them to trap and deliver pelts. Forced labor would not have been a practical means of dealing with indigenous people scattered widely throughout a vast wilderness, and attempts to drive them off the land where they trapped the furs would have been self-defeating.

Farther south along the Atlantic Coast, the Dutch followed similar strategies. Dutch traders often established close personal ties with local villages, learning the language and marrying into the community to establish bonds of kinship. The trading relationship was as much a matter of the Dutch adopting to local ways as vice versa, but the process did bring about changes among indigenous populations. Disease depleted many of them, and excessive trapping in some areas altered the local ecology (see Cronon 1983).

Beavers, the prime goal of these transactions, had not been of any special value to indigenous peoples before the trade began. Europeans wanted beaver pelts as a commodity in the European market. The fur went into the production of stylish felt hats that well-dressed people tipped to one another in the narrow cobbled streets of Europe. From indigenous perspectives, other species were much more useful for hides, meat, and other purposes. This may be one reason why indigenous people were willing to trap and offer up the hide of this relatively useless animal for desirable trade items, even if they shrugged at the strange motives of the Europeans.

But beavers are relatively easy to catch compared to most other wild fur-bearers. Like other species, their numbers in any particular region are finite, and they can become depleted rather quickly. As the trade escalated, trappers found it necessary to travel farther afield for pelts, which often led to encroachment into the territories of other indigenous populations. The results were conflicts and in some cases, an altering of roles. Some trappers became middlemen, traveling to distant groups to exchange goods for furs, then taking the furs back to trading posts for a profit. The process became more complex when European traders moved their posts farther inland to bypass old trading partners and when rival trading firms competed for agreements with indigenous trappers (see Hickerson 1962, 1970; see also Ray 1974, Krech 1984).

English Initiatives

The English differed from the other European powers somewhat in their interactions with indigenous peoples. The resources they sought were many and varied. Codfish from the waters off the North Atlantic Coast, white pine tree trunks for masts on the king's vessels, and furs all were important. More than the French and Dutch, though, the English wanted land. Part of the reason for this, as we noted earlier, was to produce commodities such as tobacco and sugar. Much of it, however, was to support an increasing immigrant English population.

Unlike the Spanish who invaded Mexico, many of the English were eager to till the soil. Like Spain, England was a hierarchical, class-structured society, but more of the invading English population arose from the lower ranks of that social order. Many of them were convicts for whom the Crown used North America as a repository. Many were indentured servants who had contracted away their freedom for a few years in order to gain passage to the colonies. In either case, they represented the human consequences of a changing agrarian economy on a land-starved island. Although some looked for a change of political climate, many of them sought the arable land that they could never have had in England.

For these people, indigenous populations were neither a resource nor potential allies but a problem. A few early entrepreneurs who established plantations on the South Atlantic Coast used indigenous people as slaves, but they soon turned to Africans, who had fewer possibilities of escaping and whose trade was part of a larger global system of exchange. The vast majority of English settlers, though, had no particular use for the prior inhabitants of the land. The consequence of these dynamics was a situation of bloody turmoil in the Southeast in which indigenous groups clashed with one another as well as with Europeans (see Perdue 1979, Littlefield 1977).

In Mexico indigenous peoples still vastly outnumbered the few Spanish expatriates and *criollos* even after the devastation of the sixteenth century. The *mestizo* population that began with Cortés's son Martín grew to vast numbers. In the English colonies, though, the indigenous population was smaller and more dispersed to begin with. Their numbers shrank drastically with the first few waves of European disease, as the numbers of English grew and as social boundaries inhibited the development of any large mixed population.

Many of the English came with families. The ratio of men to women was far more balanced in the English colonies than it was in New Spain. The authorities tended to frown upon whatever sexual liaisons occurred between indigenous people and English immigrants, and certainly these were relatively rare compared to relationships in Mexico. The English drew sharp social as well as political borders.

It is intriguing, nonetheless, to note that colonial administrations found it necessary to pass laws forbidding colonists to "run off and join the Indians." On the other hand, the capture of English women by Indians seems to have been the favorite nightmare of the colonies. A feverish "captive literature" involving such tales and personal accounts of varying authenticity remained popular in the United States well into the twentieth century (see Slotkin 1985).

The hierarchical nature of New Spain's indigenous societies had made them vulnerable to labor exploitation by the Spanish, who placed themselves in the upper levels of these hierarchies. To the north, however,

Some Indigenous Groups in the United States

most indigenous societies were far more egalitarian. To impose an authoritarian structure would have been much more difficult. But with relatively tractable indentured servants, small farmers, convict labor, and African slaves, the English had little need for indigenous labor. Relationships with indigenous peoples were more likely to involve displacement, genocide, or at best, attempts to define boundaries between "settled land" and "Indian territory."

Indigenous Peoples

Most of the populations the English encountered south of the St. Lawrence River were Algonkian speakers. North of the agricultural zone, they relied on game, wild plants, fish, and marine animals, usually returning to their village sites on a seasonal basis. From the New England Coast to Florida, people raised crops in addition to collecting wild foods, and their denser populations accommodated more social stratification. Political marriages between high-ranking families linked villages in shifting political alliances. Around the eastern Great Lakes, Iroquoian-speaking peoples had large stockaded villages organized in confederacies, with a central council representing the various communities. Two of these confederacies—those who called themselves Wendat, "People on an Island," and Hodenosaunee, "Longhouse People"—the Europeans called Huron and Iroquois.

Centuries earlier, people in the Southeast and in the Mississippi and Ohio Rivers system had lived in large complex societies and had traded luxury goods over much of the continent, building large earthen mounds and coordinating dense populations (see Fagan 1991:354–408). Smaller villages were more characteristic by the eighteenth century, with governing councils of respected elders or "beloved men" (see Hudson 1976). Many of these communities were linked though a dual division of "red towns" associated symbolically with war and "white towns," associated with peace.

These populations, such as the Cherokee, who spoke an Iroquoian language, and the Muskogean- and Hitchiti-speaking communities whom the English referred to as Creek, relied on a combination of agriculture and hunting. Their use of deer involved a system of game management based on periodic burning of forest, a practice that encouraged new growth to bolster the animals' food supply and vastly increased the wild populations of these animals (see Hudson 1976, Cronon 1983).

Farming villagers occupied the Plains margins along the Mississippi and Missouri Rivers drainage system. These peoples built earth-covered and thatch dwellings and carried on trade and diplomacy between adjacent ecological zones. Far to the west, remote from European settlements, Shoshonian speakers in small family bands combed the deserts of the Great Basin. In the richer Plateau to the north of the Basin, villages relied on game, fish, camas roots, and other wild plants. For inhabitants of northern and central California, acorns provided a food staple for sedentary villages of up to a thousand people.

These scattered examples reflect a universe of cultural systems representing hundreds of languages and varied histories. The people had traded, intermarried, fought, and come to accommodation with one another and their environments over thousands of years.

Changing Modes of Interaction

When they first confronted Europeans, many indigenous people apparently felt little cause for concern. There was no particular reason for them to assume any superiority on the part of the odd-looking and ill-bathed foreigners who often were quite helpless without the assistance of the local inhabitants. Nor could indigenous peoples possibly have predicted the numbers of Europeans who eventually would invade their regions.

In general, too, the assumptions underlying European motivations would have been nonsensical to most indigenous peoples. Exclusive ownership of land, the sale and coercion of labor, and the idea that people's lives were subject to the authority of a distant state would have seemed bizarre to many of them.

The English had honed their methods of dealing with indigenous peoples in areas closer to home when they attacked and subjugated the Celtic tribes in Ireland and Scotland (Bolt 1987:29). Some of the military men who had burned Irish villages later led campaigns against Native Americans in New England. The English destroyed most of the Highland clans in 1765, but as early as the 1600s the British under Cromwell sent eighty thousand Irish to the West Indies as slaves (MacLeod 1967:40). The state forbade the wearing of the traditional kilt and outlawed the bards, poets who were repositories of indigenous history, ethnic identity, and pride. This approach to indigenous peoples in the British Isles would set much of the tone for early policies in the New World.

Some of the first confrontations occurred in New England, where contact was early and land pressure was most intense. Puritans linked aggressive proselytization with their demands for land. They established villages of "praying Indians" who had submitted to baptism and had forsworn such offenses as long hair and "promiscuous behavior." These villages of converts, who were often survivors of disrupted communities, found themselves subject to attack by other indigenous groups who opposed the English presence.

In 1637 a man named Miantonomo tried to unite indigenous groups against the English in what became known as the Pequot War. His movement failed when Uncas, a young relative who had ambitions of his own, murdered him (Burton and Lowenthal 1974). Uncas later achieved fame as a literary character in James Fenimore Cooper's *Last of the Mohicans*.

By the end of the seventeenth century, the indigenous populations of New England had suffered the devastation of wars, disease, and dislocation and had survived in small, scattered enclaves. Many of them took jobs on whaling ships in the nineteenth century. Only in the twentieth century did many of these populations—Pequot, Wampanoag, and others—achieve much success in reasserting their identities.

As the North American colonies became more firmly established, the British government attempted to impose more order on settlers' relations with indigenous peoples. As in Mexico, the colonial situation had involved a proliferation of interest groups. The English elite, like the *peninsulares* in Mexico, tended to link their primary interests with the Crown and often represented its authority. Many of the colonial population, however—including more and more who had been born in North America and had never seen England—found their interests at variance with those of the Crown. This was particularly so when it came to taxation and trade restrictions designed to benefit the mother country. The continued encroachment of settlers on indigenous lands was another point of contention.

Land Appropriations

The demand for land was to be a chronic issue for centuries as the ex-European population of North America continued to grow. The British attitude toward indigenous land ownership, as we noted in the first chapter, was essentially to deny it. The Crown acknowledged prior occupancy, however, and certain rights arising from that occupancy, when situational factors compelled such recognition. The encroachment of settlers on indigenous lands caused problems for the state. It provoked conflicts. With other European powers in North America to worry about, the British state had no wish to provoke animosities that might cause indigenous groups to ally themselves with the French or other parties who could subvert British interests.

The Crown issued a Royal Proclamation in 1763 that defined the bounds of Indian lands and decreed that settlers must not intrude on them without the Crown's authority. As it turned out, however, this was all but impossible to enforce. When the divergent interests of colonists and the British Crown led to revolution a few years later, other concerns predominated.

The Longhouse People

When the American Revolution erupted, indigenous populations such as the Hodenosaunee, or Iroquois, who had retained sovereignty throughout the colonial period, were faced with the choice of which role, if any, they should play in the conflict. The Iroquois had come through the years of English presence largely through their capacity to consider the strategies that best met their own interests and to act upon them collectively. In doing so, they managed to hold their own in an arena of competing French, British, settler, and other indigenous interests.

The Hodenosaunee were a coalition of distinct societies, some of whose languages were not mutually intelligible. They had established a division of complementary responsibility couched in the symbolism of their ancient dwelling, the longhouse. The Seneca and Mohawk were keepers of the western and eastern doors. The Onondaga were keepers of the central fire. Issues of importance to the league came before a council of forty-eight respected men whom the clan mothers from the various member nations had chosen. Their titles had originated with the legendary founding of the league, symbolizing continuity and ancient legitimacy. The league operated by consensus, which often involved lengthy oration and ceremonious protocol. Since the councilors had no real power to impose their will on dissenting minorities, governance rested on persuasion, the moral weight of public opinion, and the general acceptance of collective over specific and local interests.

The stately deliberations involved in this decision-making process sometimes tried the patience of British officials negotiating with the league. The hierarchical structure of British governance bestowed the Crown's authority on designated officials and allowed them to make decisions on the spot. Consensus had little relevance within the British state. The style of the Longhouse People was quite different. Even in relatively small matters, they considered it a breach of etiquette to answer any serious question without sleeping on it first.

The Iroquois had successfully played off French and British interests without losing their independence, effectively using the power of each as a threat to the other in maintaining their own autonomy. They had eliminated the rival Huron confederacy in the 1640s, taking over the fur transport on the St. Lawrence River and its tributaries. In the aftermath, they extended "invitations" to other indigenous peoples to join the league as secondary members. Those who declined were likely to be "knocked on the head," a homely euphemism for war (Trigger 1990, Jennings 1984). Their alliance with the Leni Lenape, or Delaware, to the south involved an agreement that the Delaware would no longer go to war but would carry out diplomacy and rely on the league for protection (Miller 1974). The structure of the league, which was fundamentally a nonaggression pact among member nations, allowed them to present a united front that had formidable war-making capability.

The American Revolution, however, challenged the league's capacity to reach consensus (see Graymount 1972). In the end, they could not agree on a political position. Some argued for neutrality, opting to stay out of a "fight between brothers." The Seneca and Mohawk sided with the British, while the Oneida joined forces with the rebels. The Iroquois could not develop consensus on a common strategy.

Perhaps the vital interests of various groups actually were in conflict. In any case, the Iroquois for a time ceased to operate as an interest group at the maximal political level, and the aftermath of the war left them facing the loss of most of their resources. Opposing forces had burned their fields, ruined their orchards, razed their villages, and left many dead. In negotiating an end to the conflict, the British neglected any provision for their indigenous allies. The Longhouse People faced the mercies of the new American government and its first president, a man they had named "Town Destroyer."

Native Americans after Independence

Treaties established reservations for the various Iroquois groups in New York. The Mohawk under Thayendanagea (Joseph Brant) and other Iroquois moved to reserves the British Crown granted them in Canada. Some left for lands in the West. The Iroquois also consigned the lands of former allies in the Midwest to the United States—an act that annoyed the westerners enough to set off what was called Black Hawk's War against encroaching settlers.

The interests ruling the American state had little sympathy for indigenous peoples, whether they had been enemies or allies in the recent conflict. A major concern of the new state was to balance the demands of the former colonies, regions, and other constituencies. But Britain remained in possession of a large territory north of the border in Canada. The United States was in no position to provoke more conflicts with indigenous peoples at the moment.

The ideological rationale of the American Revolution had involved a renunciation of hereditary privilege in favor of democracy. The American state embraced, albeit selectively, many of the egalitarian principles that sprang from the Enlightenment. From such an intellectual position, flagrant injustices toward indigenous peoples were potentially almost as great an embarrassment as slavery—which many of the political elite continued to practice—and perhaps even more dangerous.

Thomas Jefferson, one of the foremost ideologues of the new state, grappled with these contradictions. A slave owner who disapproved of slavery and fathered children in a long-standing relationship with an African American mistress, Jefferson was an intellectual who believed in equality in principle but who had trouble with its practicalities. He never quite resolved the issue of racial exploitation. As a scholarly Enlightenment dilettante, like many intellectuals in New Spain at the time, he was interested in the archaeological record of the Native American past. But the treatment of living indigenous populations presented more challenges. These contradictions would plague the American state for some time to come. Democratic principles, embedded in the state's rationale for its own existence, offered some possibilities for the weak as well as for the holders of power.

Unlike slaves, most indigenous populations remained outside the American state. The Constitution had recognized the existence of "Indian nations" and empowered Congress to deal with them. In doing so, chief justice of the Supreme Court John Marshall was to rule years later that the Constitution acknowledged their "preconstitutional sovereignty" (Wilkinson 1987:103). It recognized that these nations had existed before the document was written and therefore were not automatically subject to its strictures. In a related decision, Marshall also referred to indigenous peoples as "domestic dependent nations," arguing that conquest had given Congress—though not the individual states—the right to impose laws on indigenous communities. Their preconstitutional sovereignty, however, meant that any rights that Congress had not specifically taken away from them still existed. These rulings were to play a large role in the development of a complex tangle of laws and court decisions affecting indigenous peoples throughout United States history (see, e.g., Cohen 1942, Deloria and Lytle 1983, Williams 1990, Falkowski 1992).

The new government, seeking stability, enacted the Northwest Ordinance in 1789, which acknowledged unconquered indigenous peoples in the regions beyond the thirteen colonies. Like the British Royal Proclamation of 1763, it recognized that indigenous "nations" were sovereign holders of their lands, without disavowing the ultimate right of conquest within the bounds of state hegemony. Put simply, the principle was that only the state itself, not private citizens, had the right to appropriate and dispose of indigenous lands. It also stipulated that indigenous lands could be acquired only through legitimate purchase. The government later tried to bring this sort of transaction under tighter federal control with the Non-Intercourse Acts of 1790. These stated that individuals or states could not carry out land deals with indigenous populations without the approval of Congress. These acts became the basis of many indigenous land claims in the twentieth century.

Indigenous peoples remained a significant political factor in the years following Independence and the consolidation of the American state. Despite the government's prohibition of unauthorized settlement beyond the Appalachian Mountains, settlers continued to push westward. The frontier of expansion exceeded the range of state hegemony, and laws passed by Congress often had little impact on frontier life. This in itself was an attraction to many refugees from the more settled areas of the country. Some members of the government, indeed, were quite in sympathy with the expansion of settlement.

In 1803, when President Jefferson acquired the Louisiana Purchase from France, the United States laid claim to a vast region west of the Mississippi that included the territories of indigenous peoples Americans knew little or nothing about. This abstract transfer of jurisdiction between the United States and a European state over unknown inhabited regions had little to do with the people who had lived there for millennia, except in its consequences.

When Jefferson dispatched Meriwether Lewis and George Rogers Clark to explore the region, they encountered little resistance from indigenous populations, who tended to view the foreigners as curiosities. After extending hospitality, the inhabitants generally went on about their business. Lewis and Clark found many of them willing to trade samples of their tools, weapons, and clothing, which the expedition dutifully took back East. It would be some years before the expansion of United States settlement brought about major intrusions into the region.

Native American Movements to the Plains

Some changes already were occurring west of the Mississippi, however. The fur trade in the western Great Lakes region had led to serious conflicts. While French and British traders competed with one another for agreements with indigenous groups, French traders moving up the Mississippi added still another element to the arena (Hickerson 1962).

Groups of Northern Algonkian speakers, whom the French called Klistinaux and the English referred to as Cree, moved westward into the northern Plains in pursuit of good trading positions. Many struck trading partnerships with the Siouan-speaking Assiniboin. Eventually some of the Cree would commit themselves to hunting buffalo on horseback on the High Plains (Mandelbaum 1979).

The large population of central Algonkian-speaking Anishinabek around the western Great Lakes, whom the English called Ojibwa or Chippewa, competed with the Siouan speakers south of the lakes for a favorable position in the trade. In the course of this conflict, other Siouan speakers would move onto the Plains and become the various bands of Lakota or Teton Sioux, leaving behind their relatives the Dakota or Santee Sioux in the Minnesota region.

The Lewis and Clark Expedition encountered the Lakota near St. Louis, which even then had become a trading center. The Lakota presence at the time turned out to be fortunate for them, since a physician was present offering inoculations for smallpox. The Lakota's early vaccinations gave them some immunity to the later ravages that devastated many of the Plains villagers such as the Mandan and Arikara.

Although most of the indigenous peoples who moved onto the Plains in the late eighteenth and early nineteenth centuries suffered little direct intrusion by European settlers, their lives changed in profound ways. Vast herds of buffalo had grazed over the center of the continent since the ice age. A few hunters had exploited this source of protein on foot, driving herds over cliffs or into arroyos where it was possible to dispatch the large animals with spears or arrows. The appearance of the horse, however, opened new possibilities.

The Spanish had brought good Arabian stock in the sixteenth century, although they had endeavored to keep these animals out of the hands of indigenous peoples. Inevitably, however, people in the northern zone of New Spain managed to steal some. The Apache probably were among the first to acquire them. As horses spread northward, a unique way of life developed based on buffalo hunting and horse raiding.

The horse increased the mobility of Plains peoples and allowed a more efficient culling of the buffalo herds. With horses it was possible to kill the animals one or a few at a time by riding into the herd rather than by painstakingly (and dangerously) coaxing the animals to stampede into traps. The advantages of this, as well as the disruptions associated with the fur trade competition to the east, brought many indigenous populations onto the Plains.

The groups entering the Plains had the internal cohesion of kin ties, common dialect, and shared cultural systems. In the new setting, many of these factors—particularly patterns of social organization—required readjustment. This was especially so among those who made the change from sedentary village agriculture to Plains nomadism. Some, such as the Cheyenne, Arapaho, and Lakota, who formerly had clan systems that were feasible in larger, more sedentary populations, adopted bilateral kinship that incorporated a maximum number of relatives among far-ranging bands (Eggan 1966). Partly in response to the seasonal patterns of the buffalo herds, most replaced older village patterns with large summer encampments that dispersed in the winter when the herds scattered to forage for grass through the snow. Others, such as the Comanche, entered the Plains from the Great Basin area in the West where their previous life had involved desert hunting and foraging. As the general Plains pattern developed, however, the ways of life among all of these groups came to share many similarities.

For a time, the Plains became a competitive arena in its own right (Secoy 1953). The situation placed numerous populations in competition for the same resource—the bison herds—in a circumstance in which few common ground rules applied. They spoke different languages. Territorial boundaries were uncertain, and the buffalo hunt required movement over large areas. Most of them did not breed horses but had to acquire them through trade and raiding. This added another competitive element, since to survive, groups needed to guard their own horses while replenishing their herds from others, all the while maintaining access to hunting territories (see Oliver 1962).

From this situation, a pattern of raiding developed, with a system of social rewards for those who excelled at it. The result was the growth of formidable populations who were well equipped to defend themselves from encroachment, initially, at least.

Other processes came into play on the Plains throughout the nineteenth century. Some of the more powerful groups were able to expand their hunting territories at the expense of the weaker or less numerous. The Lakota, for example, extended their domain westward across the northern Plains at the expense of the Absaroke, or Crow, largely by harassing Crow hunting parties where their territories overlapped. The Lakota power base became stronger when the Cheyenne, Arapaho, Kiowa, and Naishan Dené, or "Kiowa Apache," joined them in a nonaggression pact. The Cheyenne and Lakota developed especially close ties through intermarriage, utilizing the device of kinship for political bonds (see Moore 1987).

It is interesting to speculate how far this process of extending interest group parameters might have gone and what the political results might have been if the buffalo hunting way of life had persisted. As it was, however, the United States sponsored the eradication of the buffalo herds late in the nineteenth century, divesting the Plains nomads of their most essential resource.

Jackson and the Indigenous Peoples of the Southeast

As these events were unfolding west of the Mississippi, various interests in the East vied for control of the American state. In the 1820s, southern interests that sought to acquire the rich farmlands of the indigenous peoples succeeded in placing their man, Andrew Jackson, in the presidency (see Prucha 1964, Satz 1975, Green 1982).

Although Jackson had the Battle of New Orleans against the British to his credit, he had built his career on "Indian fighting," leading troops into Florida in the messy and expensive Seminole Wars. The Seminole, whose English name was a corruption of the Spanish *cimarron* ("renegade"), were mostly displaced Creek who had fled into the recently depopulated Florida region. The Creek, Cherokee, and other southeastern peoples had long been engaged in conflicts involving the British, United States, Spanish, and French. Many had lost lands to settler encroachment.

These populations were divided among themselves to some extent. Many of the pro-U.S. factions had adopted a Euro-American way of living. The Cherokee had developed their own writing system, and some prosperous Cherokee even owned slaves (see Perdue 1979). The Seminole, for the most part, arose from anti-American factions of the Creek.

The territorial conflict between English and Spanish had annihilated the original inhabitants of Florida. The problem with the establishment of a Creek/Seminole population in the Florida wilderness, however, was that slaveholders in the Southeast suspected them of harboring runaway African slaves. Many feared that Florida could be a launching point for a general slave uprising. Regional pressure arose, for that reason, to get rid of the problem.

The fears of the southerners went beyond simple paranoia. The growing dependence of the South on cotton, on which Britain depended for its booming cloth industry, meant that African slaves had come to outnumber Euro-Americans in the deep South by a large proportion. The Seminole did, in fact, give refuge to runaway slaves, who established communities of their own and came to be known as the "Black Seminole" (see Littlefield 1977).

But the series of Seminole Wars was also part of a larger campaign to drive indigenous peoples from the South, and settler interest groups exerted influence on state governments toward this end. In Georgia the legislature made it illegal for an Indian to testify against a white man in court. The effect was to make it all but impossible for an indigenous person to find redress for any offense a citizen might commit, unless another citizen testified on his or her behalf. The legislature later closed this small loophole by making it illegal for a white to testify on behalf of an Indian.

The problem was not merely that Cherokee, Creek, Choctaw, and other southern indigenous groups were culturally distinct. Many Cherokee lived in well-built frame houses with white picket fences and ran farms that others might envy. The problem was that others did envy them. The houses and farms of Cherokee and other indigenous populations often were better than those of other farmers, and they occupied some of the most fertile bottomland in a rather mountainous region.

Jackson pushed for the removal of these peoples to Indian Territory, a dry, flat region across the Mississippi that later became Oklahoma. Chief Justice Marshall ruled that the policy was unconstitutional, but President Jackson defied Marshall to enforce his decision. In the end, troops rounded up thousands of Cherokee, Creek, and other indigenous peoples and forced them to walk to Indian Territory, often in severe weather, bringing only the few belongings they could carry. On this series of journeys that became known as the Trail of Tears, thousands of people died.

A few managed to elude the roundup. Some of their descendants are now the Eastern Cherokee (see Kupferer 1966). Many of the descendants of those who survived the trek to Indian Territory now live in enclaves in Oklahoma.

Jackson's government did not consult the indigenous peoples of the eastern Plains about the establishment of Indian Territory. Indeed, the general feeling in the East was that the region was essentially uninhabited and of no particular value. As it happened, some of the Plains groups took umbrage at the relocation of the southeastern peoples in their territories and added to their harassment. It would have been of no concern to the interests that Jackson represented, though, if Indians killed each other west of the Mississippi.

Westward Expansion of the American State

The dynamics of capitalism and the imperatives of a growing global market increasingly made themselves felt early in the nineteenth century. Even as indigenous peoples perfected the techniques of buffalo hunting for their own subsistence, a market for pemmican and buffalo robes drew many of them into a wider economic system. Pemmican, a portable food made of dried and pulverized meat and fat, was a good trail food for fur traders and middlemen (Ewers 1955; see also Jablow 1951).

In the 1830s, trade between the United States and Mexico opened the Santa Fe Trail, which began in St. Louis and drew traders across the Plains through buffalo-hunting territory. A year after the United States acquired California from Mexico, gold discoveries drew more traffic to the West. Commercial interests within the American state gained more power and influenced policies to extend the national territory.

Texas, as we noted in the last chapter, served as a justification for the United States to contrive a war with Mexico and acquire the northern half of its territory. The Treaty of Guadalupe Hidalgo in 1848 gave the United States more than a vast piece of Mexican territory, however. It also extended U.S. "legal" jurisdiction over the indigenous inhabitants of these regions.

In southern California, the Spanish mission policies of *reducción* had already destroyed many indigenous communities. To the north, however, many people had not yet seen a European. In central California, as in most places, the early years of interaction with Europeans were friendly. This changed by the nineteenth century, when Spanish demands led the local people to withdraw into the mountains, refusing to submit their children to the missions and defending themselves when necessary.

When Mexico secularized its missions in 1830 as a means of weakening the power of the Church, the priests lost much of their authority, and indigenous raids on Spanish settlements increased (Phillips 1993). After the United States invaded California in 1846, however, indigenous peoples in the region became reduced to small pockets in the interior.

The Great Basin had not attracted many outsiders except for a few travelers to California who lost their way. The Plateau was largely undisturbed since Lewis and Clark had ventured into the region, except for a few mountain trappers who established trading relationships with local groups. This would change very soon. But in the area of the Southwest that later became Arizona and New Mexico, the United States acquired a region in which indigenous interaction with Europeans was already three centuries old.

Indigenous Resistance in the Southwest

As we noted in the last chapter, the Spanish had first encountered the Pueblo communities along the Rio Grande in the sixteenth century. A sizable population of *criollos* and *mestizos* had settled in the region since then, and many of their descendants remain there today. Outside the Pueblo area, however, Apache and Comanche kept large areas uninhabitable by outsiders. The road approaching the northern Pueblos from the south had long since acquired the name *jornada del muerto* (the "journey of death").

These mobile groups had been doing what the stable, ordered Pueblo communities had not been able to do: defend their interests by defining relationships on their own terms. The Pueblo communities that survived did so by a judicious combination of apparent accommodation and the erection of barriers to intrusion. Pueblo villages appointed officials whom outsiders took to be leaders, but whose function was essentially to deal with alien authority and protect the internal priestly governance structure. Having nowhere to go, the Pueblo societies crystallized to resist.

The Apache, however, had long made a successful living on wild foods in mountainous areas—a way of life that called for opportunism and mobility. Although they had encountered Spanish by the 1580s, it was not until 1629 that the Apache began carrying out raids—apparently under provocation arising from repeated Spanish slave raids on Apache camps.

In a sense, the Apache had few options but to raid. As the Spanish encroached on their territory, the Apache could not avoid contact without giving up their domain. Spanish actions made reciprocal trade impossible because they refused to deal with the Apache on an equivalent basis. The only other choices for the Apache were nonreciprocal forms of interaction: submission to the Spanish or relationships on their own terms. They chose the latter. They soon perfected the art of raiding and guerrilla warfare.

When the United States acquired jurisdiction over the Southwest after the Mexican War, they inherited abstract claim over Apache territory even though neither the Spanish nor Mexican states had been able to occupy it. The Apache had developed a strong animosity toward the Mexicans of Sonora and Chihuahua, largely because the governors of those states had offered bounties for Apache scalps. Bloodshed had escalated during those years. Some bounty hunters came into the area from the United States, but for some reason the Apache did not extend the same animosity, at first, toward Anglo-Americans.

Many factors probably account for this Apache tendency to make distinctions among foreigners. They gave the benefit of a doubt to those who had not shown themselves to be hostile. This attitude probably arose from the tendency of Apache, like most other people, to project their own social realities onto other groups. The Apache did not consider themselves a collective society. The primary criteria linking people were kinship ties and, to some extent, locality. They seem to have extended this individualistic political model to other peoples as well. They tended to distinguish among Mexicans as individuals and in terms of specific villages, for example, until their experiences led them to categorize all Mexicans as enemies. From this perspective, the Apache had little difficulty placing people from the United States in a different category from Mexicans. U.S. agents may also have supplied guns and ammunition to some Apache bands in their attacks on Mexico. This would not be the last time that other interest groups used the Apache for their own purposes.

Whatever the reasons, the Apache allowed settlers and prospectors from the United States to enter their territory. Despite the Apache reputation for ferocity, they did not drive apparently innocuous strangers out of the territory they had always viewed as a collective resource. This changed when the number of outsiders grew, and a number of incidents provoked hostilities. At first, however, even the formidable Chiricahua Apache under Cochise supplied firewood for and afforded safe journey to passengers and mail of the Butterfield Overland Mail.

Gold prospectors who came into the area, however, were the marginal vanguard of a population in whose culture racism was hardly questioned and in which private property was a semisacred principle. As towns and ranches grew up to supply the miners, the outliers of the American state took root in Apache territory. The Apache themselves showed little evidence of racism in the Euro-American style. No doubt they felt superior to other peoples, but this was largely a matter of foreigners' failure to live up to Apache standards. And since for the Apache, the most significant basis of affiliation was kinship, they often felt little in common beyond the range of kin bonds even with other *nde*, or Apache. This and their high value on personal autonomy made it difficult for them to act in concert as a large collective interest group.

The settlers frequently provoked the Apache. Ranchers drove game off by grazing cattle in hunting areas. "Indian-hunting" expeditions were a favorite sport. In some instances, citizens invited Apache to supposedly peaceful meetings and gave them poisoned food. The escalation of conflict, ironically, led to strident cries among the settlers for army protection. As the number of troops increased, contracting supplies for the army became the basis of the regional economy, and before long an interest group had developed that had a major incentive to keep the "Apache problem" ablaze, at least in the press. To accept Apache overtures for peaceful coexistence would have eliminated the need for troops and ended many lucrative business transactions (see Perry 1993).

The local citizenry effectively derailed efforts at peaceful negotiations, even attacking and slaughtering peaceful Apache living near an army post at Camp Grant in 1871. The perpetrators, who clubbed sleeping Apache to death and sold twenty-seven children into slavery, became local heroes in Tucson. At their trial, the jury acquitted all of them after deliberating for fifteen minutes (Thrapp 1967:182, Perry 1993:109–115).

Apache resistance finally came to an end soon after the Civil War, when industrial interests in the East became aware of the rich copper deposits in Apache territory. In 1871 President Ulysses S. Grant held General George Crook's plans to end the Apache problem through military measures in abeyance for a brief time while he waited for an emissary named Vincent Colyer to negotiate a peaceful solution. Although Colyer found the Apache receptive to peaceful overtures, the local citizens threatened him with death, and he left for the East "followed by the curses of Arizonans" (Wagoner 1970:125–126; see also Perry 1993: 113–115).

Once President Grant gave Crook a free hand, the general announced that any Apache who did not report to the reservation by a given date would be considered hostile. He then proceeded with his winter campaign using Apache scouts, hunting down and killing those who could not elude him. Government officials delineated a reservation on the San

Carlos River in an area that seemed worthless at the time, assuming that this would avoid future conflicts with settlers.

The turning point for the Apache, it seems, was that industrial interests were able to predominate over local citizens in shaping state policies. To appropriate the copper in Apache territory, hostilities had to end. Since local interests had precluded a peaceful solution, which the Apache probably would have accepted, the government had no qualms about escalating the use of force.

Citizen groups continued to harass and threaten the Apache even after the San Carlos Reservation was established in 1872, to the extent that the military had to protect them from mobs of vigilantes as well as supervising them as prisoners. The most drastic policy to eliminate the Apache fell on the Chiricahua, whom the government shipped to a military prison in Florida. The government also sent their children to the Indian boarding school in Carlisle, Pennsylvania, where many of them died within a few years (see Porter 1986:256).

Other Apache populations remained in the Southwest, although the reservation policy was no less a means of divesting them of their resources. When the government discovered that the San Carlos Reservation boundaries had inadvertently encompassed copper-bearing land, President Grant removed those sections and placed them in the public domain. Copper entrepreneurs, some of whom Grant numbered among his close friends, lost little time in seizing the resource, which turned out to contain some of the richest copper ore ever discovered.

Industrial Capitalism and Indigenous Eradication

After the messy business of the Civil War, the American state was ready to expand, and indigenous peoples such as the Apache stood in the way. Neither they nor the local Arizona citizenry were capable of obstructing the wishes of industrial capitalism. Eastern corporate interests had the wherewithal to build smelters, lay railroad tracks, and call upon the war-making machinery of the state to enforce their will.

This process was also manifest on the Plains, where indigenous peoples also found themselves in the way of capitalist enterprise. Railroads, whose aggressive seizures of land and draconian labor practices epitomized the worst stereotypes of the Industrial Revolution, laid tracks across the continent. Many Apache worked in constructing them in the Southwest. In the northern Plains, the railroads used Irish and Chinese labor and killed millions of buffalo to feed them. The government buffalo hunters often used only the tongue, leaving the rest of the carcass to rot in the sun. Beleaguered Plains groups resisted, but the depletion of their food supply undermined their ability to persist. Elimination of the buffalo herds was more than an expedient to feed workers; it was also a military strategy to destroy the indigenous Plains societies.

Commercial buffalo hunting also ravaged the herds. By 1870 industries were using buffalo hides to make conveyor belts for machinery. This opened the buffalo season to summer hunting because the condition of the pelt was irrelevant (Klein 1993:151). Indigenous Plains peoples took part in this trade, but in 1872–1873 they accounted for only 28 percent of the hides sent East (Klein 1993:155). As in the Southwest, the height of this process came in the 1870s, when northern industries boomed and the army, disengaged from the Civil War, was free to direct its attention to the West.

In the Plains, like the Southwest, peaceful camps of indigenous peoples suffered surprise attacks. At Sand Creek in Colorado in 1864, Cheyenne under Black Kettle, who had negotiated for peace in Denver, were asleep when a militia under Colonel John Chivington attacked and slaughtered all they could, regardless of age. Despite national cries of outrage at the atrocity, Chivington ended his days a local hero. An officer who raised public objection to the massacre died of a gunshot wound in the street, apparently a victim of political assassination. Some of the Cheyenne survivors of Sand Creek, including the elderly Black Kettle himself, were camped along the Washita River in 1868, when once again, an army unit attacked and killed all of those who could not escape. This time the troops were under the command of George Armstrong Custer.

The Plains groups had their victories. For a time, the Lakota under Red Cloud managed to close the Bozeman Trail, which had disrupted their buffalo hunting. But in signing the Medicine Creek Lodge treaty— which Red Cloud and other leaders believed to be a nonaggression pact—the Lakota entered the reservation period. The notable episode at the Little Big Horn River in 1876, when Lakota and Cheyenne defending their camp from attack annihilated Custer's Seventh Cavalry, was a Pyrrhic victory. The eastern press treated it as a national catastrophe. The army's fiasco essentially dulled any further objection to the subjugation of the peoples of the Plains.

The Seventh Cavalry took terrible vengeance in 1891, when they shot down over three hundred Minneconjou Lakota at Wounded Knee, South Dakota. The incident occurred in the context of a religious movement, the Ghost Dance, which had promised the return of North America to its indigenous peoples. The movement had not been militant, but the rumor that the Sioux were planning to break out of the reservation provoked panicky demands for military support. When three thousand troops armed with artillery appeared, many of the Lakota fled into the Badlands. The Wounded Knee massacre occurred about six months later, when the last of the fleeing bands was negotiating a surrender. The bodies of fleeing women—many carrying children—lay miles from the "battle" site where troops had chased them down (Mooney 1896, Kehoe 1989:13–26). The army suffered few casualties but won more Congressional Medals of Honor for that action than any other in U.S. history.

Farther west, indigenous resistance to the intrusion of outsiders and their appropriation of land was more sporadic. Many peoples, such as the Washo of the Great Basin, did not encounter settlers until the 1850s. Some of them took jobs on ranches and, to the extent that they were able, attempted peaceful coexistence with the outsiders in their territory.

Reservations

The late nineteenth century was an era in which genocidal policies gradually, if grudgingly, lost favor. The United States had effectively extended its hegemony from coast to coast, and few indigenous peoples continued to offer violent resistance. Elites in the industrial Northeast saw little point or value in continued conflict, and in fact, saw some potential in Native American labor. Some local interests, however—particularly in the western states—continued to push for further removal.

In a sense, the proponents of both views got their way. The reservations became the primary repositories for indigenous populations in out-of-the-way places, thus effectively getting rid of them, and many proponents saw reservations as a means of preparing them to join the larger society. As we saw in the case of the San Carlos Apache, powerful constituencies also succeeded in lopping off large pieces of these reservations when the land turned out to have valuable resources.

Historically, the reservation has been a contradictory phenomenon. In its various manifestations, and in the minds of apologists and critics, the reservation has been prison camp, refuge, schooling institution, and "special treatment." Whatever aspects reservations may have had, however, the concept developed as an alternative to genocide. Put simply, reservations were a means of getting rid of indigenous populations without having to kill them. As a secondary idea, many saw the reservation as a temporary expedient to help indigenous people survive while they learned how to behave like United States citizens. To many this seemed a more humane means of eradication.

The promotion of culture change on reservations—particularly the form that academicians often call assimilation—has been both heavy-handed and narrow in its aims. One heavy-handed aspect has involved such measures as forcibly removing children to boarding schools far from their communities and their elders in order to free the young people from the cultural contamination of old ways. On some reservations in the 1970s, the government also removed elders from the community to rest homes in distant cities, most likely for the same reasons (Perry 1993:202–203).

A narrow aspect is that although reservation officials have tried to promote a transition from indigenous group identity to immersion in the socioeconomic milieu of the state, they have done little to prepare them for positions of power. Assimilation programs most often have emphasized vocational training for relatively low-paying jobs. Indigenous peoples may be encouraged to enter the wider system, but mostly through the lowest door.

Alice Littlefield has documented the historic shifts in government funding for Indian schools corresponding with times of shortages and surpluses of unskilled labor (1989, 1993a, 1993b). At various periods in United States history, corporate and other interest groups have welcomed the presence of a large labor pool, but this market for employment has not been consistent. The Apache of the Southwest, for example, built many highways and harvested countless fields until other populations from Mexico and Eastern Europe entered the region, after which most of the Apache remained on the reservation as a pool of underemployed labor. Divested of most resources, reservation communities have found themselves immersed in a cash economy with little to sell but their labor. They have had few choices but to wait, trying to survive year by year, until that labor comes into demand. As in the *maquiladoras* of Mexico, this source of labor is far cheaper than slavery because the population reproduces itself at no cost to the employers until they need to summon workers.

For many indigenous peoples, though, the reservation, despite its problems, has been an essential base from which they have managed to maintain a collective existence. While this existence often is beset by poverty and all of the social problems that poverty brings, it nonetheless forestalls the dissolution and the scattering of populations who would then be even less able to pursue their collective interests.

The reservation also affords some possibility of protection from competing local interests. In the wake of John Marshall's Cherokee decisions of the early nineteenth century, it has been a legal principle that Congress rather than the states is the arm of government empowered to deal with Native American communities—except on issues in which Congress has given over specific jurisdiction, as it did in the Major Crimes Act. This principle of federal oversight can help override regional attempts to appropriate resources, such as water rights or grazing lands.

Though federal jurisdiction has had its problems, most indigenous leaders would prefer to deal with the federal government rather than to be at the mercy of individual states. More than a century after the massacre at Wounded Knee, the Lakota of Pine Ridge still fly the United States flag. To deal with the local politicians of South Dakota would be far worse (Biolsi 1994).

Reservations and the federal oversight of indigenous communities have nonetheless resulted in exploitation and the appropriation of resources by others—particularly when powerful interests have been able to influence policy in their favor. The Department of Interior, for example, oversees more than the Bureau of Indian Affairs. It also includes the Bureau of Mines, the National Park Service, General Survey, and other agencies representing constituencies whose interests often conflict with those of indigenous communities.

The Department of Interior has ultimate authority to resolve such conflicts. Whoever the secretary may be at a particular moment, however, the office is a matter of political appointment by a president who in turn must answer to the party and constituencies that placed him (someday, perhaps, her) in office.

On the other hand, the very structure that gives the federal government jurisdiction over reservation communities has also allowed reservations to remain a basis for the continued existence of indigenous populations. Despite its problems, the reservation has had some positive effects for peoples whose problems otherwise might have been submerged in the more general affairs of the state. As an Apache man told me in 1970, "The reservation is the Indian's home base."

Second Thoughts about Reservations

Not long after the establishment of most western reservations, their effect of allowing indigenous communities to perpetuate themselves became apparent to many outside interests. Proassimilation observers realized with some alarm that reservations allowed old customs to remain entrenched. In Mexico the major argument against *ejidos* involved their alleged economic inefficiency. In the United States, many concluded that indigenous communal access to land also retarded social and cultural progress. In the late nineteenth century, individual property ownership to many United States residents was a sign of the highest levels of human achievement. If Native Americans were ever to achieve status as full participants in the state, they would have to abandon the primitive habit of sharing their meager resources.

On the face of it, such arguments could sound convincing. There was no doubt that many people in reservation communities were poor and in some cases on the verge of starvation. Nor could anyone deny that many continued to speak indigenous languages, follow their own customs, and honor their kinship obligations. A common conclusion was that their poverty resulted from these customs, which the reservation allowed to persist. This view tended to overlook the recent loss of most of the people's resources as a more obvious reason for their troubles.

It was also clear in the late 1880s that despite the policy of locating reservation lands where intruders would be less likely to disturb and exploit indigenous populations—that is, on lands that no one else wanted—they did turn out to have some resources after all. Many reservations had minerals and petroleum deposits that no one had considered valuable or had even been aware of when government surveyors drew reservation boundaries. Water rights in some areas also became a contentious issue. And with increasing westward population expansion, potential farmland rose in value. There was even some fear that the end of free or cheap western land for expansion could jeopardize the stability of the American state (Wrobel 1993). For these and other reasons, popular pressure grew to separate indigenous peoples from the rest of their lands.

Land Appropriation Strategies

One of the most significant attempts to divest indigenous peoples of their remaining lands came to fruition in the Dawes Act of 1887. Rather than presenting it as a scheme to seize reservation lands, Senator Henry L. Dawes of Massachusetts and his supporters presented the bill as a means of alleviating Native American problems. Resting on assumptions linking progress with individual ownership, the act called for a subdivision of reservation lands by allotting a quarter section of land to each head of household.

When the subdivision was complete, the Bureau of Indian Affairs would sell any remaining lands—which often were considerable—to subsidize farm equipment and seeds. Generally, the government held this money in trust rather than disbursing it to the community. Supposedly the new indigenous landowners would learn to become prosperous farmers and eventually to participate fully in the United States economy, and like any other farmers, they would own their land in fee simple—they could dispose of it as they wished. As it was, many Plains allottees had little or no experience with farming, nor did they usually receive prime land. Already trapped in a cash economy with little or no cash, the overwhelming temptation for many was to sell or lease their land to outsiders.

The demographics of the situation exacerbated this tendency. The allotments failed to allow for the possibility that indigenous populations would increase. To be sure, most of them appeared to be diminishing at the time. When they did begin to grow, it meant that the heirs of an allotment holder would inherit only fractions of the original tract. Many of those who managed to retain their lands long enough to pass on ownership over a few generations left their descendants with tiny, scattered parcels too small to be of any practical use. Sales or long-term leases to outsiders were the obvious, and often the only, solution for many of them.

The Bureau of Indian Affairs supervised much of this process. Officials encouraged many allottees to sell, and they arranged leases at low prices for off-reservation farmers and ranchers. In its capacity as trustee for indigenous peoples, the Bureau of Indian Affairs declared some of those who refused to part with their lands legally incompetent and disposed of the parcels on their behalf. In the same capacity, the bureau also held land sales payments in trust, disbursing the funds gradually as officials saw fit.

The government divided several reservations into allotments before the disastrous consequences became obvious enough to provoke strong objections. Implementation of the act eventually came to a halt, but not before many indigenous groups lost extensive tracts of land. The present Crow reservation in Montana, as an example of the results of this policy, is a checkerboard of small indigenous holdings interspersed with the property of outsiders. But the Dawes Act was far from the last attempt to appropriate indigenous lands on a wholesale basis.

Assimilation and Termination

Efforts at assimilation continued to appear in various forms (see Hoxie 1984). In the aftermath of World War I, when many Native Americans had volunteered and served with distinction, Congress made all Indians citizens of the United States. This angered many who considered themselves members of distinct nations that had acted as allies of the United States in the war effort.

The period between the World Wars, though, saw more explicit acknowledgment of the validity of indigenous communities. This was a central theme of John Collier's term as commissioner of Indian Affairs, which we will discuss more fully below. In pendulum fashion, however, the federal approach to Indian affairs after World War II swung back toward a period more reminiscent of the late nineteenth century.

In the 1950s, when conservative interests held sway in the government and Congress probed for Communists throughout the country, the ideology of the times once again offered a rationale for "freeing" Indian lands. In that climate, powerful interests once again could portray the collective holdings of reservation communities and government oversight as an inappropriate situation for the modern United States. In this case, the objection was not that this way of life was "primitive" but that it reeked of socialism. Congressional orators called for the government to "get out of the Indian business." In 1953 House Resolution 108 provided for the termination of reservations. Like the Dawes Act, it would turn indigenous communities into aggregates of individuals in the political and economic arena, competing on the same basis as other citizens (see Fixico 1986).

The Menomini of Wisconsin had achieved some economic success with a sawmill and other small businesses. Since it appeared that they stood a good chance of surviving termination, they relinquished their reservation status and became "Menominee County." Almost immediately, however, the state of Wisconsin presented them with a staggering tax bill. After struggling to survive in a game in which others had already accumulated most of the points, the Menomini spent the next several years in court seeking a return to reservation status. They succeeded in 1974 (see Kehoe 1992:321–323).

In the meantime, the Klamath of Oregon voted to accept termination and lost their land, which contained valuable timber. The protermination faction received payments for the loss of their resource. Those who had voted against termination refused to accept the payments. Termination, like the Dawes Act, became an obvious disaster for most of those indigenous communities it affected (see Fixico 1986). The government ceased implementing the policy after the first few years, although it remained a law.

President Richard Nixon renounced the policy in the early 1970s. The rationale for termination, however, did not entirely fade. President Ronald Reagan's Secretary of Interior James Watt in the 1980s attributed reservation poverty to the "failure of socialism." President Reagan in a speech in Europe stated that reservations exist "to humor the Indians."

Alternative State Strategies

The policies of the American state toward indigenous peoples have depended on which large interests have had predominant influence at the time. During the Franklin Roosevelt administration of the 1930s, social programs were a major concern. In that era, Commissioner of Indian Affairs John Collier promoted a stance of recognizing the inherent value and legitimacy of Native American cultures.

Congress passed the Wheeler-Howard Bill, often called the Indian Reorganization Act (IRA), in 1934. The thrust of this bill was a departure from aggressive assimilation programs toward more recognition of the continued existence of indigenous societies. It is interesting to note that this period coincided with the progressive reforms of Lázaro Cárdenas in Mexico.

While this shift in policy certainly reflected some genuine goodwill on the part of individuals who happened to be in power at the time, it probably arose in response to the potentially disruptive issues facing United States society. Unemployment affected many in the population. Social and economic problems were rife. Strikes were frequent, and many constituencies were deeply dissatisfied with their economic situations. Both radical socialists and such ultraright groups as the Ku Klux Klan had growing numbers of followers. Racism was rampant. Harsh government measures to keep order could have been dangerously inflammatory.

The government's attention to Native Americans, who constituted a tiny and relatively docile portion of the population, raises obvious questions. Even though Native Americans did not, and do not, constitute a large enough proportion of the population to be a powerful constituency, their symbolic value to the state far outweighs their numbers (Castile 1992). By the 1930s, the abstract concept of the American Indian had become a part of the national mythology. Away from specific reservation communities where local bigotry often was rampant, the popular image of Native Americans was generally sympathetic, if unrealistic. Native Americans afforded the state an inexpensive opportunity to show its goodwill toward minority constituencies in general. By doing something highly visible to address problems of this small group, the government could adopt a posture of fairness and even benevolence toward the weak and disadvantaged.

This position probably also reflected a recognition that despite the assumptions of the nineteenth century, Native American cultures were not about to disappear. By the 1930s, they not only were still around, but many had shown substantial population increases. As George Pierre Castile observes, the general trend since the Roosevelt administration, despite such reversals as the termination era, has been "toward stabilization of the land base of what is left of the reservations, rather than further expropriation, and toward recognizing the permanency of the Indian peoples rather than their assimilation" (1992:273). The effect of the IRA as implemented by Collier was to incorporate these persistent peoples, as Castile refers to them, into the structure of the American state.

One of the act's most significant features was to call for the election of tribal councils on a model of small-town United States democratic process. These councils were to meet periodically and deliberate on reservation issues. Their meetings, however, were to include the reservation superintendent. As representative of the Department of the Interior, the superintendent retained powers to veto major decisions of the council. The superintendent also acted as custodian of tribal records. Clearly, the IRA recognition of reservation autonomy did not extend very far in matters of self-governance. Collier himself referred to this policy as "indirect rule," a term laden with connotations of colonialism (Biolsi 1991; see also Biolsi 1995).

Most indigenous communities had their own long-established systems of internal governance. In some cases, these involved hereditary principles, religious societies, or other factors that did not involve balloting or political campaigns. In some indigenous societies, the very act of seeking political office would tend to disqualify a person because it would suggest an unseemly desire for self-aggrandizement.

Indigenous communities responded to the IRA in various ways. Some found the idea generally acceptable and proceeded to elect their councils. Some merely elected people who already had leadership status. Others saw the model as a contradiction of their established system and refused to vote.

This often gave rise to divisiveness within indigenous communities. In the case of one western Pueblo community, for example, many people who refused to participate considered their action to be a negative vote. Most of those who did vote overwhelmingly supported the new model. This created long-standing tensions over the legitimacy of elected council members as representatives of the community. Conflicts between elected and traditional leadership have troubled many reservation communities ever since. When ratification of the IRA came before a Seminole community of five hundred people and passed 21–0, the courts upheld the validity of the vote (Schwartz 1994).

The IRA also legally reinforced the concept of "tribe." Some indigenous populations instituted tribal constitutions and by-laws. In creating tribal councils as mechanisms firmly articulated to the federal government, the state could give the appearance of participatory democracy and lend legitimacy to various policies, even while placing pressure on the councils and using its power to veto their actions. The Bureau of Indian Affairs worked with tribal councils to negotiate leases for reservation coal, water, grazing land, oil, and other resources. These circumstances do not imply that tribal councils are necessarily illegitimate representatives of many reservation communities. It only means that they have been subject to tremendous pressures from the system that created them. On the other hand, their existence has also afforded their communities some leverage that they might not otherwise have had. The White Mountain Apache trial government, for example, sued the Bureau of Indian Affairs for mismanagement in the 1980s and acquired fuller control over their own resources. Theirs is one of the success stories of Native American development. It seems evident that "relatively successful reservations such as White Mountain (as well as Flathead and Mescalero) are marked by a clear pattern of tribal control of strategic and day-to-day decision-making, with a corresponding subjugation of the role of the BIA" (Cornell and Gil-Swedburg 1990:99).

As many writers have noted, the history of U.S. policies regarding indigenous peoples has been a matter of pendulum swings rather than a linear trajectory. The more accommodating policies of the Collier era arose after the paternalistic interference of the Dawes allotment program and harsh measures to promote assimilation. The termination program of the 1950s followed on the heels of the Collier approach. Some have argued that the failures of Collier's policies helped bring about the termination era (see Schwartz 1994, Philp 1983, Koppes 1977).

We might wonder whether the failures of each of these approaches have pushed the pendulum a bit harder back in the opposite direction. If we pursue that question, however, we might also consider what the term "failure" means. Does it mean failure to empower indigenous communities, or failure to neutralize them in one way or another? As it happens, though, either meaning seems to apply equally well.

In the early 1970s, the conservative Nixon administration, surprisingly, espoused a conciliatory policy of "self-determination" in the period when Native American protesters broke into the Bureau of Indian Affairs headquarters in Washington. Self-determination in practice amounted to little more than the right of tribal governments to opt for or against particular government programs, but its tone, as in the 1930s, reflected acceptance of the permanence of indigenous communities.

The Alaska Native Claims Settlement

The Alaska Native Claims Settlement Act involved an explicit recognition of indigenous rights over their resources. In doing so, however, it placed these populations in jeopardy of losing them through legal means by failing in a game whose rules were new to them and which placed them at a serious disadvantage.

By the late 1960s, the eyes of many interest groups had turned to Alaska. Here was a vast area whose resources had lately, but strikingly, become apparent. Natural gas and petroleum, minerals, and timber were awaiting exploitation. Alaska's Native Peoples, however, unlike the indigenous peoples of the "Lower Forty-eight," had not suffered defeat in wars of conquest, signed treaties, or for the most part, been consigned to reservations.

A few outsiders had been present in Alaska for generations. Whalers in the nineteenth century had contacted people along the coast, and some Inupiat had worked on whaling ships. The Tlingit and other Pacific Coast peoples had confronted Russian explorers and fur traders. Gold prospectors had wandered into the interior and founded a few towns. Missionaries, sport hunters, military personnel, and homesteaders seeking escape from the stresses of urban life all had found their way to Alaska by the mid-twentieth century.

Intrusions into Alaska from the outside had been growing inexorably after midcentury. As the Cold War got under way after World War II, the government placed radar installations in a vast, sparsely inhabited region where Inupiat Eskimos and Dené had hunted for centuries. In one case, the U.S. Air Force decided that the most suitable location for one of its bases would be precisely on the spot where an Inupiat village stood. The Inupiat kept their feelings largely to themselves as they moved to another location (Chance 1990:61–62).

As the number of outsiders grew, many of Alaska's indigenous peoples had found themselves increasingly beleaguered. With the Alaska Highway and improved air travel providing easier access, the northern wilderness had become a commodity. Sport-hunting interests pressured the state to impose game restrictions on indigenous peoples who had hunted for centuries on a sustainable basis. No doubt these trends contributed to Alaska natives' receptivity to some sort of agreement to protect their interests. With the 1970s, however, as talk of pipelines and other development schemes escalated, it became clear that messy and prolonged legal struggles might ensue unless indigenous land rights were clarified. Inevitably, this clarification would mean reduction.

By that time, the old way of appropriating lands through force was less acceptable. It would have been difficult to convince the United States public that marauding Inupiat or Dené hunters posed a threat to civilization. The ends would have to come about through negotiation.

The Alaska Native Claims Settlement Act of 1971 that resulted from these negotiations amounted in many ways to an updated version of the Dawes Act. Rather than individual allotments, indigenous communities acquired designated, bounded territories that they would run as corporations. By the 1970s, the corporation had supplanted the family farm as a United States symbol of economic progress.

Large remaining areas of Alaska became part of the public domain or officially designated wilderness areas that the government would manage for regulated resource extraction. The native corporations would have twenty years to become established and successful, after which they could dispose of their holdings like any other corporation. This model accommodated subsistence hunting and self-sufficiency to the extent that the corporations could show a profit.

Some indigenous groups were well organized to coordinate such efforts and happened to have resources within their territories that they could convert into revenue. Some of these, such as minerals, were not renewable. Others, such as timber, could yield sustainable income only through judicious management. The Tlingit Sealaska corporation opted for short-term profits by clear-cutting much of their forest (Kruger and Etchart 1994). Other indigenous populations had less wherewithal to succeed in the corporate arena. When the economic gloves came off in 1991, several indigenous corporations were bankrupt.

The Alaska Native Claims Settlement Act was more sophisticated than the Dawes Act. It allowed outside interests to benefit from both the successes and the failures of indigenous corporations. The successful ones offered up valuable raw materials. Failed corporations stood to lose their lands.

Indigenous Strategies

Through the vagaries of political and economic circumstances, there has been little question that indigenous people are part of the congeries of interest groups within the American state. Notwithstanding the patronizing tone of the Reagan administration and the "trickle down" economics of the Bush years that gutted social programs that had assisted indigenous peoples, there has been little recent talk of termination or about the "disappearing Indian." President Clinton's conference with Native American leaders in 1993, whatever its substantive results may have been, was at least a recognition of these populations as permanent interest groups within the American state.

One indigenous strategy has been to consolidate and foster cohesion within particular populations—to present a solid front to the outside. Indigenous populations have seized upon indigenous symbols as logos to emphasize their common identity. The Apache of San Carlos, for example, use the image of a *gaan* (mountain spirit dancer) on tribal stationery. While this image has profound meaning for many Apache people, as a tribal emblem it is also a presentation of self (as cohesive group) to an outside audience with no inkling of who or what a *gaan* is, except that it is something Apache.

The issue of consensus has presented problems on reservations where people disagree about vital issues, as they may in any community. It has sometimes been especially difficult when the population that now constitutes a "tribe" has consisted of disparate populations in the past, with little sense of affiliation. The expression of diverse views, which power-holding interest groups would characterize as "lively debate" among themselves, can exacerbate the vulnerability of indigenous communities. Media tend to portray such disagreement as "factionalism" or "bickering," reflecting the dominant group's aspersions that they "can't get their act together." This is another means of implying incompetence. (The United States Congress often faces the same accusation.)

Coalition building has been another strategy of indigenous peoples. If community consolidation is one means to compete, broadening the base of the interest group is another. These may seem to be opposite strategies. Emphasizing tribal identity, which implies exclusivity, may seem conceptually opposed to joining other groups in common cause. But in another sense, they represent different points on a continuum. Coalition building is a means of seeking maximum inclusion and expanding the power base of an interest group. This can occur on the basis of some specific concern without necessarily implying that the interest group be homogeneous in other respects. Both clearly tend to be more effective than total fragmentation, when collectivities dissolve into disunited individuals.

As we have seen, coalitions for common purpose in North America predate the European presence. The confederacies of the Huron and Iroquois are clear examples. During the early phases of colonialism, indigenous populations in many instances combined their efforts in resistance. Miantonomo tried to unite Algonkian communities against the British. The Creek, over a century later, attempted much the same strategy in the Southeast.

Indigenous coalitions have used a range of cohesive tactics. Some, such as the alliance under the Shawnee Tecumseh and his half brother the prophet Tenskwatawa, had religious overtones. Others have used various time-honored ways of creating social bonds. The Mimbres Apache leader Mangas Coloradas built a coalition among disparate Apache groups by marrying his daughters to local leaders. The Lakota and Cheyenne solidified their alliance with intermarriages, as did Cree and Assiniboin. The medium of kinship drew upon a principle that lent internal cohesion to groups but could transcend social boundaries as well as maintain them.

As in Mexico, the generic concept of "Indian" during most of the history of the American state was a relatively meaningless, foreign idea to many indigenous peoples. Members of indigenous communities defined their social universe in terms of kinship and shared realities. They would have felt little or nothing in common with other populations with different languages, cultures, and forms of social organization whom Europeans also called "Indians." This is one reason, no doubt, for the participation of indigenous peoples with Europeans in opposing other Native groups.

"Indian" as a broad "racial" category is a product of European cosmology. Whatever its origins, however, the concept eventually acquired a social and political reality. Many indigenous peoples came to realize that, however dissimilar they may have been, having been treated generically gave them certain common problems and concerns.

The idiom of kinship and intermarriage continues to be a primary means of establishing networks of relationship among Native Americans. This pattern is particularly important in the summer powwow circuit, which provides settings for people throughout wide areas to congregate. It also became more frequent as a result of centralized Indian schools. The early schools prohibited communication between male and female students, but as more young people continued in the institutions through high school and regulations became a bit more humane, many marriages took place among people from different reservations.

Early in the twentieth century, it had become apparent to many indigenous leaders that formal political organizations overriding cultural and historical differences could offer an effective means of pursuing broad policy interests. The National Council of American Indians (NCAI) was one of the earliest. Before long a range of organizations and lobbying groups formed. The American Indian Youth Council formed in the 1960s. Considering the NCAI too conservative, it embraced a more ambitiously progressive agenda. Until the 1960s, however, none of these organizations was particularly radical. All of them tried to operate within the governance structure of the state (see Josephy 1971).

At the same time, the state adopted the stance of listening more respectfully to the concerns of indigenous peoples, even while politicians representing various constituencies carried out sporadic assaults on particular reservations and periodically demanded the abrogation of treaties. In the 1920s, as the American state took a paternalistic stance toward Native Americans in the abstract by bestowing citizenship on them, Congress funded Coolidge Dam, which flooded the best San Carlos Apache farmlands, to supply irrigation water for agribusiness in Arizona (see Perry 1993:147–151). On the Crow reservation in the 1930s, Congress funded the Yellowtail Dam, which also flooded indigenous lands. In the 1950s, New York State seized Tuscarora lands to build a hydroelectric project at Niagara Falls. Bulldozers flattened one woman's house as she was hanging her wash in the yard. In the 1960s, industrialists in Bradford, Pennsylvania, persuaded the Army Corps of Engineers to build the Kinzua Dam, which flooded the Seneca reservation, to lower the Allegheny River (Wilson 1966).

The list of assaults on reservation-held resources during the twentieth century is far too extensive to enumerate. It is amply clear that although political coalition building can be an effective strategy, it may fall short of amassing power sufficient to defeat larger interests, and a focus on general issues may overlook acute local crises that result in further losses.

The late 1960s brought about more activist organizations, the best known of which was the American Indian Movement (AIM). AIM continued the principle of overriding cultural boundaries but took a more active stand in addressing local issues—sometimes forcefully. Much of AIM's leadership involved people with indigenous backgrounds who had not grown up in reservation communities.

In a sense, AIM and other activist groups represent products of the long policies of assimilation and the attempts to fragment indigenous societies. One result was to produce people who continued to identify their interests with Native Americans but who were more conversant with the wider political arena. Such leaders were positioned well to employ many of the strategies that other interests—particularly the Civil Rights and antiwar movements—had developed during that period. Among these strategies were the politics of confrontation and the use of the news media to bring attention to their cause.

In 1973 AIM staged a media event they called the Trail of Broken Treaties. They broke into the offices of the Bureau of Indian Affairs in Washington and emptied file cabinets. They became involved in a conflict at the Pine Ridge Lakota reservation in South Dakota, where the tribal chairman, supported by Bureau of Indian Affairs police and his followers known as the "Goon Squad" (Guardians of the Oglala Nation), had provoked opposition among the community that led to a series of shootings. The federal government reacted with excessive violence. Federal Bureau of Investigation tactical teams created a situation of guerrilla warfare that riveted the attention of the United States public.

Such groups as AIM have not had universal support among indigenous people. Many have considered them too radical and felt that their tactics would do more harm than good. Many felt little or no identification with the rather flamboyant, outspoken leaders. Many—perhaps the vast majority of indigenous people—remained far more concerned with issues affecting their local communities and their kin.

Concurrent with the high visibility of AIM, however, other strategies have continued to develop. The tribal chairs from various reservations meet periodically to discuss common interests. Some of the western groups whose reservations contain energy sources such as coal and oil formed the Council of Energy Resource Tribes (CERT) to exert more collective control over the use of these resources (see Ambler 1990).

Indigenous communities have used the legal system with some success as well. Laws dealing with Native Americans are a tangle of piecemeal legislation and court decisions, much of it arising from particular cases in which outside interests have prevailed over those of indigenous communities. The Supreme Court's *Lone Wolf v. Hitchcock* decision of 1903, for example, held that Congress has the power to override any existing treaties with Native Americans.

Once in place, however, the legal apparatus can afford some foothold for arguments that can assist indigenous interests. Indian preference legislation, as one example, has offered some economic advantage to indigenous communities (Stubben 1994). We have noted the White Mountain Apache's successful suit against the BIA. The San Carlos Apache, after decades of suits, succeeded in restoring a 270,000-acre tract of land to their reservation in the 1980s. In the last decade, many indigenous communities took advantage of John Marshall's Cherokee decision affirming federal jurisdiction to establish gambling casinos on their lands. Since there is no federal law against gambling and state laws do not apply, there was no legal basis for prohibiting gambling.

Gambling proved to be an internally divisive issue on many reservations, but in some communities it brought funding for public works and social improvements. Recently, however, there has been pressure to legalize gambling in many states, or to enact federal legislation to regulate reservation gambling. Either of these would dilute the legal advantage that many indigenous communities have been able to use for a time.

As Critical Legal Studies theorists have long argued, the law develops to favor interests in power, not necessarily to serve an abstract principle of justice (Unger 1986). By no means are indigenous peoples guaranteed a fair and reasonable outcome in the courts. In the 1990s, the San Carlos Apache were unable to prevent a coalition of interests from building a telescope on a sacred site on Mount Graham in Arizona.

The series of land claims cases that many indigenous peoples have won usually have resulted in compensation payments for lands illegally taken, rather than restoration of the land itself. In many cases, the courts have calculated the payments on the basis of land prices at the time the land was taken. When these had occurred in the nineteenth or even the eighteenth century, compensation sometimes amounted to pennies per acre (see Carlson 1985).

The players may adjust their strategies, but fundamentally the game has remained the same in the United States since the inception of the state. Indigenous peoples, as always, face competition for their resources. These competing interests have influenced government policies to promote genocide, assimilation, land allotments, and termination of reservations. Policies have included "employment assistance" or "relocation programs," which encouraged individuals and families to leave for cities. They have utilized the IRA and the idea of self-determination, which recognize indigenous populations—even those the government artificially created by amalgamating different groups on reservations—while subsuming them within the governing apparatus of the American state.

In the decades since President Nixon renounced the termination of reservations and proclaimed the era of self-determination, the state appears to have stepped back and accommodated more autonomy among indigenous communities. This trend, as always, seems to have involved some contradictory aspects.

The tribal college system, for example, was initiated to provide better opportunities for higher education on reservations, preparing young indigenous people to go on as well as helping to affirm their identities. The program for the most part has succeeded despite, not because of, federal involvement, since the Bush administration placed numerous obstacles in its way (Morris 1994). And in an era of cutbacks, tribal governments have been faced with competing with one another in a zero-sum game for government grants, rather than seeking common cause (Barsh 1994). Yet as the development of CERT indicates, there now is more indigenous control over the disposal of their own resources (see Ambler 1990).

This control may also have its dangers. Large corporations, particularly transnationals, are the main customers for the raw materials that lie within the boundaries of many reservations. Appropriation of these resources in the past involved questionable tactics, to say the least. These tactics often raised questions involving contested rights to dispose of resources, unclear title, accusations of government collusion with corporate interests, and so on. In the meantime, many reservation communities languished in the most extreme poverty in the United States. With increased autonomy and the right to dispose of their lands as they see fit, indigenous communities can deal directly with large corporations. From another perspective, however, transnationals now have the opportunity to deal directly with small, impoverished groups without much government intervention. It remains to be seen whether this era marks an upward swing in the fortunes of indigenous communities, or whether it simply amounts to another chapter in the same old story.

At present, reservations not only are targets of interests seeking natural resources. In the postindustrial era, the need grows for places to deposit hazardous wastes. Western reservations, which often include vast tracts of unfarmable land, have attracted attention for this purpose. Communities with unemployment rates of 75 percent and per capita incomes at a tenth of the national average are vulnerable. The temptation to derive income merely for allowing someone to dump waste in an empty area may be difficult to resist.

As of 1992, waste disposal interests had approached over fifty reservations to negotiate dumping permits. At that point, few had agreed. In 1993 a delegation approached the Mohawk of Akwesasne on the United States–Canadian border. The corporate delegates stated that as Native Americans had always been "keepers of the land," they could continue to carry out that honored role by accepting hazardous waste. The Mohawk people of that community had already suffered the ravages of industrial pollution from Reynolds and Alcoa aluminum plants and a General Motors facility. They had been engaged in a decades-long struggle to force a cleanup of the poisons that had killed their cattle and sickened their children. The visitors had prepared a two-hour presentation, but after twenty minutes, according to one Mohawk man, the leaders informed the delegates that they were wasting time and invited them to leave.

In 1993, however, the Mescalero Apache of New Mexico considered accepting nuclear waste on their reservation. The issue divided the community and mobilized people in the nearby off-reservation towns. That issue has yet to reach a conclusion but suggests what many other reservation communities are likely to face in the future.

Transnational corporations in the United States and in Mexico have become important factors in the fortunes of indigenous peoples. Although indigenous accommodations with the American state and the federal government have been complex and evolving, in some ways transnationals represent adversaries of a different magnitude. Many of these corporations originated in the United States, but few of them are particularly concerned about national issues except to the extent that they affect profits (or "earnings," as corporate executives prefer to call them).

Unlike states that need to balance competing interests, corporations are interest groups in themselves and have little inclination to accommodate competitors. Transnationals have exceeded the arenas of the states in which they originated and now compete (and cooperate) with one another on a global scale. To the extent that indigenous peoples must compete as interest groups in their own right, they have much to contend with.

In the next chapter, we shall examine the Canadian state, which exhibits some pride in having been more progressive than the United States in dealing with its indigenous peoples. To some extent, this pride seems justified, although, as we shall see, the historic situation has been quite different.

Canada

. . . .

5

Let us decide what we want taught in our schools. Let us decide how to manage the salmon fishery and the caribou and the forests. Let us set up our own structure where we can help our people to stay out of prison, or can teach our young people that sniffing gasoline is not the answer, a structure of government that's built on our own traditions, where elders are brought back into their rightful place as the real leaders and given the respect that they deserve.

> (Kirk Lethbridge of Labrador testifying before the Royal Commission on Aboriginal Peoples, 1992. Canadian Embassy 1993:13)

The vast region that later became Canada has always been more sparsely populated than the United States or Mexico, even before the appearance of Europeans. The zone in which agriculture is feasible constitutes a small proportion of the southern section. On the West Coast, salmon rivers and rich inlets supported substantial villages. Beyond those areas, expanses of forest, plains, mountain ranges, and tundra extend to the Arctic Archipelago.

European Incursions

Viking and Basque ventures into Canada were brief and had little long-lasting impact on indigenous peoples. The English explorer John Cabot made several attempts to cross the Atlantic beginning in 1480 and landed on the coast of Newfoundland in 1497. English motives at that time had more to do with cod fishing than settlement, however.

The French were the first to make a concerted attempt to explore what later became Lower Canada, when Jacques Cartier sailed up the St. Lawrence River in 1534. He found large villages of Iroquoian speakers near the present sites of Quebec City and Montreal, and his brief visit was a fairly congenial encounter. When several of his men came down with scurvy, his hosts graciously cured them with a cedar bark potion. Cartier abused their hospitality on his next visit, however, when he kidnapped the leader, Donnacona, and several of the villagers and sailed off to show them to the king.

When Champlain led another expedition up the St. Lawrence in 1609, the villages Cartier had visited were gone, and Algonkian speakers occupied the area. By that time, many of the peoples of the region had become involved in the fur trade. This may have exacerbated tensions among indigenous groups, although there is ample evidence that conflict in the area long predated European contact (Dickason 1992:69–70, Trigger 1976).

The primary French interest eventually turned to trade for furs, and many indigenous peoples in the region were willing to participate. In Cartier's first encounter with the Mi'kmaq (Micmac) at the mouth of the St. Lawrence, they waved furs from their canoes and seemed rather put out when he showed little interest in trading for them (Miller 1991: 25–36). French interests in North American furs grew, however, when the Swedish seizure of the Baltic port of Larva in 1583 hampered access to Russian furs and created a greater incentive to seek them elsewhere.

Champlain involved the French in local conflicts by shooting the leaders of a Mohawk war party who confronted his Algonkian companions. Despite (or perhaps partly because of) the strained relationships that developed between the French and the Iroquois in the aftermath of this incident, though, French relations with Wendat (Huron) and Algonkian speakers north of the St. Lawrence remained quite friendly. Champlain, in fact, envisioned extensive intermarriage between the French and indigenous people, especially the Huron, to whom he stated, "Our young men will marry your daughters, and we shall be one people" (quoted in Dickason 1992:167).

Jesuit missionaries to the Huron and the nearby Algonkian peoples encountered some misunderstandings, but the Jesuits had little power to enforce their will on these communities. The Huron tolerated the outsiders and offered them hospitality but were not particularly impressed by them (Trigger 1976). They assumed that the French must have left an impoverished land behind to travel so far. Nor were the Huron above mildly harassing the missionaries on occasion: they delighted in twitting the priests who struggled to learn the language by teaching them obscene phrases (Miller 1991:52).

Some French settlers established farms in Lower Canada, but these operated mainly to support the fur trade. When New France became a

Crown Colony in 1663, there were only a few French towns in the region. North of the St. Lawrence Valley and Huron territory, the growing season was too short for farming, and given the regional political situation, the French were not inclined to contest the powerful, well-organized Huron for their lands.

The Huron had been accomplished traders long before the French arrival. They built their stockaded villages east of Georgian Bay near the northern edge of the agricultural zone with trade routes leading north to the Algonkian hunting territories (Trigger 1976, 1990, Tooker 1964). Their position allowed them to act as middlemen in a trade system that generally ran north and south, linking different ecological regions. They traded tobacco and other agricultural products from the south to the Algonkians in exchange for products of the hunt, such as black squirrel skins (Trigger 1976). They and other peoples of the area were well positioned to enter into trade with the French.

As we noted in the last chapter, it served the French well to leave indigenous peoples in possession of their own lands and to maintain good relationships with them. The main tensions in the region were between French and English. These conflicts eventually drew in the indigenous allies of each—the Huron and Algonkians with French and the Hodenosaunee more tentatively allied with the English.

The Huron had long been at odds with the Iroquois south of Lake Ontario. Similar in language and culture, they had nonetheless carried on sporadic vengeance raids for generations. Perhaps being so much alike, they had little to offer one another compared to the Huron and Algonkians.

Other Iroquoian-speaking groups—the Erie and Susquehannock to the south and the Tionontati and Neutrals on the peninsula north of Lake Erie—had been involved in this conflict to varying degrees. The archaeological record shows fortified villages in the area since at least the thirteenth century (Tuck 1971). The fur trade and competition among European powers, however, intensified the conflict and changed its character.

Early in the seventeenth century, the Iroquois had all but depleted the beaver population in their region. By that time, the English had supplanted the Dutch as the Iroquois's main trading partners. Although English settlers in New England had decimated the coastal Algonkian populations by the mid-1600s, the Iroquois were more formidable. The French presence made it wiser for the British to seek alliance with the Iroquois League than to antagonize it. Realizing this, the Iroquois were able to force important concessions from the British, including demands for guns in exchange for furs.

The French had been reluctant to trade guns to the Huron. As a result, the Iroquois had an arms advantage for a time, despite the larger size of the Huron population. The Huron also lost over half of their population in a measles epidemic between 1634 and 1640. Although the Iroquois also suffered immensely in this epidemic, the Huron appear to have been more seriously weakened. The depletion of beaver caused the Iroquois to look toward the western trade that the Huron controlled, and they began to escalate attacks on Huron canoes carrying furs to Montreal on the St. Lawrence and Ottawa Rivers. The conflict came to a conclusion in 1649 when they attacked and dispersed several Huron villages, decisively nullifying the Huron as a political factor.

The British Acquisition of Canada

A series of wars between France and England, involving many of the indigenous peoples of the region, gradually loosened the French grip on Canada. The French policy of promoting intermarriage between settlers and indigenous peoples had produced many close ties between individual French and local groups, but these did not necessarily result in military alliances. The alliances that did develop were not sufficient to consolidate French holdings.

In the Treaty of Utrecht of 1713, France ceded "Acadia with its ancient limits" to the English—without, however, defining just how far those limits extended beyond eastern Canada. In 1755 the English expelled French settlers from the region, and many of them fled to French territory in Louisiana, where their descendants came to be known as Cajuns (Acadians). In the Peace of Paris of 1763, France relinquished all claims to the northern regions of North America except for a small strip of Newfoundland beach.

The British were more interested than the French in agricultural settlement, but ecological and political conditions inhibited the British from occupying extensive lands at first. For them, like the French, the fur trade not only was a lucrative enterprise but an arena in which economic, social, and political relationships converged. The need to maintain order meant avoiding unnecessary confrontations with indigenous peoples and, if possible, cultivating amicable relations. Iroquois harassment of the French had contributed much to the British success. An Iroquois leader boasted that, as a result of their relentless attacks, for a time French settlers had been afraid to "piss out the door" (Miller 1991:65).

As the vagaries of fashion caused the market for furs to decline and profits to fall, the English found it prudent to maintain trading posts and to continue giving "presents" for furs in order to keep up good relationships with indigenous groups. The decision of British Commander-in-Chief Jeffrey Amherst to cut off the customary "presents" in the late eighteenth century turned out to be unwise and provoked a good deal of resentment. The same Amherst later earned an infamous place in history by distributing the blankets of smallpox victims to indigenous communities, thus becoming one of the few ever to have been scurrilous enough actually to implement germ warfare.

Pontiac's War in 1763 demonstrated the precarious nature of British relationships with indigenous peoples. To some extent, this campaign was an acute expression of anti-British sentiment, although the urgings of the Delaware prophet Neolin, who contributed much of the ideology of the uprising, called for a general expulsion of all Europeans. It represented another early coalition among diverse indigenous peoples for a common purpose. The war erupted among Pontiac's people, the Ottawa, in 1763 but involved numerous groups around the Great Lakes and resulted in the deaths of two thousand settlers.

The Royal Proclamation of 1763, which quickly followed the Peace of Paris, defined the limits of English settlement and proclaimed that usurpation of indigenous lands would evoke His Majesty's displeasure. The proclamation stated that:

> . . . it is just and reasonable, and essential to our Interest, and the Security of our Colonies, that the several Nations or Tribes of Indians with whom We are connected, and who live under our Protection, should not be molested or disturbed in the Possession of such Parts of Our Dominion and Territories as, not having been ceded to Us or purchased by Us, are reserved to them, or any of them, as their Hunting Grounds.

Settler encroachment on arable indigenous land continued, however. The tension between colonists' hunger for these lands and the Crown's attempts to restrain them was one of the issues that led to the American Revolution.

Canada after the American Revolution

The Canadian situation grew more complicated when the Thirteen Colonies rebelled. Many loyalists from the colonies fled north, increasing the English population of Upper and Lower Canada and adding to the pressure for agricultural land. Tension between Canada and the United States remained high in the ensuing years, and the English could not yet afford to antagonize indigenous populations. Despite the British disregard of their Iroquois allies in the Treaty of Paris ending the American

Revolution, the Crown hastily purchased lands in Upper Canada from the Mississauga and offered them to loyalist Mohawk under John Deseronto near Kingston and the followers of Joseph Brant in the Ontario peninsula. These had once been the domain of the Tionontati, Neutrals, and Huron.

The Jay Treaty in 1794 established the eastern boundary between Canada and the United States, although problems between the two countries continued. In the War of 1812, the Shawnee Tecumseh and his half brother, the prophet Tenskwatawa, established a coalition of over thirty indigenous groups. They sided with the British, partly in response to U.S. settler incursions into the Midwest.

After the War of 1812, when the Rush-Bagot agreement banning warships from the Great Lakes firmly settled matters between the United States and Great Britain, the Crown felt less need to accommodate indigenous populations. Canada would continue to be leery of its neighboring state to the south, but it had become firmly established as a state in its own right. Its indigenous peoples were on the way to becoming marginal interest groups within it.

Indigenous Canada

The most intensive early European interactions with indigenous peoples occurred from the mouth of the St. Lawrence to the Great Lakes, but a vast inhabited territory extended thousands of miles to the Pacific in the west and the Arctic Coast to the north. Central Algonkian speakers, Anishinabek, lived in the western Great Lakes area on both sides of the international border. Canadians would refer to them as Ojibwa; Americans, as Chippewa. Primarily hunters and fishers, they also harvested wild rice along the north shore of Lake Superior as an important food staple. Their social organization changed drastically when the fur trade reached them, but in earlier times they lived in scattered semipermanent villages linked by clan ties (Hickerson 1970).

To the west in the prairies that verged onto the Rocky Mountain chain, Algonkian-speaking Blood, Piegan, and Siksika composed the Blackfoot confederacy. Early in the fur trade era, Siouan-speaking Assiniboin and northern Algonkian-speaking Cree also moved onto the northern Plains.

In the Plateau, also straddling what would later become the United States–Canada border, Shuswap, Okanagan, and other villagers lived on wild foods. Beyond the coastal mountain ranges the Tsimshian, Haida, and Kwakwala speakers had large communities of cedar plank houses. A food supply of salmon and marine resources supported a rich ceremonial life, an emphasis on social stratification, and elaborate art forms.

Indian Territory as Defined by the Royal Proclamation of 1763

North of the St. Lawrence, the Cree hunted and fished in the conifer forests and lakes east of Hudson Bay, coalescing in large summer villages and dispersing to hunting camps during the winter. West of Hudson Bay and into the Cordillera, the Athapaskan-speaking Dené followed a similar existence, dispersing in hunting expeditions from base camps. In the barren grounds to the north from Alaska to Labrador, Inuit hunted and fished in some of the most demanding environments on earth.

With the exception of the Pacific Coast peoples, most of these populations were small and widely scattered, exploiting wild foods systematically in sparse regions. Their resources—in the early years at least—were not particularly vulnerable to European appropriation. Europeans, coming from an agrarian economy, were not prepared to thrive in the regions occupied by most indigenous peoples of Canada.

This situation would change when some of the resources of the north became useful to industrial interests. At first, however, the region itself inhibited much hostile confrontation of the sort that occurred in the United States and Mexico. Even now most of the Canadian population has remained concentrated along the southern border, and within much of the rest of Canada's territory, the majority of the population are indigenous peoples.

Consolidation of the Canadian State in the West

As the fur trade extended to the west, the Crown in 1670 granted a trading monopoly over a vast region to a concern that called itself the Company of Adventurers of England. French traders who had aligned their fortunes with Britain, these entrepreneurs founded a powerful interest that eventually became known as the Hudson's Bay Company (HBC). As a private concern with the blessings of the British state, the HBC managed to out-compete rival trading companies and jealously guarded its commercial hegemony. One aspect of such a monopoly was the ability of the company to set the price it paid for furs (see Bishop 1974).

In earlier years, traders had competed with one another as they negotiated for the highest returns from indigenous fur suppliers. Trappers who retained the option of going back to subsistence hunting or taking their pelts elsewhere could exercise some leverage in these transactions. In a few instances, traders had reasoned that by raising the prices they offered for furs, they could induce the indigenous trappers to increase production. On the contrary, though, trappers who received more for their furs simply brought in fewer because they could meet their needs without further effort and devote more time to hunting for food or to other pursuits (Miller 1991:122).

The North West Company, a rival firm of traders from Montreal, extended its activities into the Hudson's Bay Company's domain in the 1790s. The Crown had defined this area to encompass the drainages of all rivers flowing into Hudson Bay, although its distant northern and western boundaries remained unclear. This huge territory, called Rupert's Land, may have been the home of some fifty thousand indigenous people (Miller 1991). The Nor'westers ventured far into its northern and western reaches, establishing relationships with indigenous traders and provoking conflict with the HBC in the process (Abel 1993).

Many traders married into indigenous communities, partly to strengthen business relationships and partly, no doubt, as a normal consequence of close human interaction. British traders referred to the offspring of these unions as "country born." The French traders referred to such liaisons as *mariage a la façon du pays* ("marriage in the fashion of the country") (see Brown 1980, Van Kirk 1983). The Nor'westers, by most accounts, were more inclined than the Hudson's Bay Company traders to enter into such marriages, and as a consequence they became well established in the social as well as the economic network of the region.

Many of these unions were quite stable. Before long a population arising from these marriages between indigenous peoples and French traders in the prairie provinces had grown to become a distinct community known as Métis. In the late nineteenth century, many of these Métis turned to a combination of commercial and subsistence buffalo hunting.

By 1871 the Hudson's Bay Company proved to be more powerful than the North West Company and absorbed it. This effectively marked the end of the Montreal-based fur trade and established the Hudson's Bay Company's monopoly in the region. From the perspective of indigenous peoples and Métis, it meant fixed prices and by many accounts, an increased use of alcohol as an inducement for trade.

Friction arose between Métis and other Plains peoples over competition for the diminishing buffalo herds. As the northern fur trade had expanded, buffalo meat had become commercially important to make pemmican for trail food. As the Métis became more involved in this trade, they took an increasing toll of the herds. Sioux in 1851 attacked a group of Métis at Grand Coteau who were hunting buffalo with wagons, resulting in a major battle. The Métis succeeded in driving them off with substantial Sioux casualties. Competition over hunting also erupted among indigenous peoples. In the 1860s, the Blackfoot had a series of conflicts with Cree who were impinging on their territory from the east, culminating in a major Cree defeat at Belly River in 1870. Although they competed for buffalo, in many respects all these populations had many interests in common. They shared an opposition to the incursion of farmers and ranchers into the buffalo plains.

Canadian government officials in the East had long favored agricultural interests over trapping and had little regard for subsistence hunting. This position owed much to the principle of ownership arising from cultivation, but it also carried connotations of political stability that appealed to ruling interests. Hunters and trappers were difficult to bring within the hegemony of the state, and by the nineteenth century their furs were less important to the national economy. Farmers, however, were more compatible with the English model of the ideal society:

> The ability of many Indians living in Manitoba and the old Northwest Territories to pursue their old form of livelihood, hunting and fishing, was particularly irksome to the government, for it was regarded as a drawback to the Indian's adopting a more settled economic base, farming. (Tobias 1988:48)

The eastern prairies had been marginal for agricultural pursuits until the steel plow was available to rip open the tough sod of the grasslands. This transformation of the land conflicted with the buffalo-hunting way of life that many groups in the region pursued. The situation made friction inevitable. By the early 1800s, settlers moving onto the Plains clashed more frequently with buffalo hunters. Métis attacked and killed twenty settlers at the battle of Seven Oaks in 1816 in what would later be southern Manitoba. But the settlers had the weight of powerful interests behind them. Elites within the Canadian state were eager to extend its hegemony westward.

Prevailing ideology linked the ideals of agriculture and Christianity, generally of the Protestant variety, and church groups mobilized to "civilize" the west. Foremost among them was the British Church Mission Society, an Anglican organization. These emissaries of eastern interests would soon come into conflict with the largely French Catholic population of Métis.

In 1871 the Hudson's Bay Company sold the vast territory that the Crown had granted it decades earlier to the government of Canada. This area, Rupert's Land, encompassed the territories of many indigenous populations that had never negotiated away the rights to their territories. The transactions provoked a response among the local populations and for a time, at least, brought indigenous peoples and Métis together in common cause. The prolonged struggle in the Prairies between the local populations and the Canadian state led to the use of treaties to establish Canada's hegemony over the region.

Treaties

Most early treaties had been used to affirm or formalize relationships. The various HBC agreements with indigenous groups after 1686 had clear commercial implications beyond their rhetoric of friendship. Typically, colonial treaties with indigenous peoples, such as Mascarene's Treaty of 1713, had spoken of "peace and friendship." They often involved the right to travel unmolested or, more important in many cases, the promise to remain neutral in European conflicts.

By the 1830s, however, more treaties also involved the surrender of land. The Selkirk Treaty of 1817 in the Red River region was one of the earliest to include such concessions. In 1837 the governor-general of Canada persuaded some Ojibwa to relinquish claims to their territory and move to Manitoulin Island. The Robinson treaties of 1850, which covered Ojibwa lands north of Lakes Huron and Superior, established more firmly the precedent of treaties extinguishing indigenous territorial claims in return for reserved areas.

Although from the government's perspective, treaties had become a matter of extinguishing indigenous claims, in the view of many indigenous peoples the treaties continued to be agreements establishing formal relationships with the government. In many cases, indigenous groups interpreted them as promises of friendship or protection from further encroachment.

Although indigenous peoples had no doubts about their inherent rights to the territories under agreement, they generally did not share European concepts of absolute ownership. Many had long-established views of group territory, but usually these involved communal or conventionally agreed-upon access to natural resources. The idea of selling lands as if they were private property made little sense to them. In most cases, it seems, they saw treaties as devices for establishing relationships between people rather than between people and land.

Many viewed the treaty process in terms of social or political agreements rather than economic transactions, as agreements to allow others to use the land they had occupied. But they did not necessarily accept the interpretation that they, themselves, could not continue to hunt there or use it in other ways. They tended to interpret the payments they received as "presents" or gifts, tokens of agreement—that is, expressions of social ties—rather than as compensation for relinquishing their lands to others forever.

The Canadian government, perhaps recognizing this perspective, had long since abandoned the earlier negotiations to buy lands outright through payment in full (a practice that seemed to work best with indigenous groups who had recently occupied the lands in question). Instead they offered smaller annual payments and referred to them as presents. The Selkirk Treaty of 1817 with Cree and Ojibwa groups in the Red River area promised that the government would give each band one hundred pounds worth of tobacco each year for several square miles of land. From one perspective, this practice involved payments carried out over time for land sales, but in another sense it suggested the establishment of long-term gift-giving relationships that perpetuated ties between parties rather than abolishing ties to property.

Indigenous groups were not oblivious to the fact that many Canadians conceived of property in an entirely different fashion—not only claiming exclusive rights to their own but sometimes appropriating that of others. This difference in perspective sometimes led to volatile situations. In many cases, too, outsiders violated even the European understandings of indigenous property rights.

The Cree in the Prairie region on one occasion felt compelled to warn squatters not to cut wood on their lands:

> The Roseau River Reserve, south of Winnipeg, had not been surveyed when in March 1872 lumber men started woodcutting operations. The customs officer of Pembina intervened and posted notices forbidding the felling of trees, but as soon as he was gone, the lumberers set to work again, laughing at the Indians' protests yet although the cutting and sale of wood by the Indians was prohibited—the Indians had no means of preventing outsiders from pirating their wood. (Spry 1988:214)

While indigenous peoples may have been aware of the difference in points of view, they were not necessarily inclined to alter their own. Facing more and more encroachment by private individuals, though, some of them were willing to come to terms in the hope that the government's recognition of their rights in treaty would stabilize their situations.

In general, the treaty process failed in that regard—partly because the government often failed to live up to treaty terms, but also because the process of encroachment would have been difficult to contain from Ottawa even if the government had made a serious attempt to do so. The Royal Proclamation and its violations demonstrated the difficulty of enforcing such policies. As it was, though, dominant interests in Ottawa favored promoting agricultural settlement rather than preserving indigenous rights on the frontier.

The encroachment of settlers in 1869, with the impending transfer of Rupert's Land from the Hudson's Bay Company to Canada, finally led to a violent uprising of Métis under Louis Riel. Indigenous and Métis peoples, long-established in the region, had not been consulted when the Crown bestowed the vast tract of land upon the HBC, nor were they involved when the latter decided to dispose of it.

Although tension had grown in the area for some time, the appearance of government surveyors in the Red River region was a precipitating factor. It seemed clear that their activities presaged the division of land into farm plots. Although Métis had inhabited the area for many years, few of them had any deeds to their lands, and the surveyors did not appear to acknowledge existing boundaries. Métis riverfront farms extended back in long, narrow strips, while government officials in Ottawa conceived of farms as square plots. The issue became more inflammatory when the rebels captured a surveying team and executed a young man named Thomas Scott.

The Red River Resistance inflamed another sore spot in the Canadian psyche, since it involved French-speaking Métis executing an English-speaking young man whose death became a cause célèbre in some quarters. In 1870, nonetheless, Parliament offered a measure of self-government in the region by passing the Manitoba Act, which coincided with the wishes of Louis Riel. The prairies continued to be an arena of turmoil, however, and the government established the Northwest Mounted Police in 1873 to keep order in the region.

Riel later became involved in another, more violent uprising in Saskatchewan. The issue was largely a reaction to the government's failure to respond to local Métis grievances. In this case, the government in Ottawa took sterner measures and sent a combined force of eight thousand troops to stop the rebellion. The government tried Riel for treason and executed him in 1885 (see Flanagan 1988, Huel 1988). The trial and execution of Louis Riel had far-reaching associations for many constituencies. "Committed under the juridical patronage of the Queen of England, the hanging of Louis Riel in Regina on 16 November 1885 stands out as the virtual assassination of the Métis canadien" (Morisset 1988:280).

The upshot of this turmoil was the establishment of state hegemony in the prairies. At this juncture, some indigenous populations viewed the appearance of the Northwest Mounted Police with some relief. The region had become dangerous. They and Métis had faced increasing harassment by settlers and other intruders from the east and from the United States.

In this circumstance, treaties offered some groups refuge from encroachment and some possibility of compensation for their lost lands.

The first of the so-called numbered treaties covered the Red River region in southern Manitoba, and by 1877, treaties covered the southern half of the western provinces. The process continued until 1921.

As often seems to be the pattern in such matters, many of the treaty negotiations involved misunderstandings and in some cases, deception by interpreters. Often, too, verbal assurances were not recorded and consequently assumed no legal reality.

> A study of treaty 3 also reveals an insistence by the Indians upon the inclusion of terms not contained in the draft treaty, namely that steps be taken by the government to protect the wildlife, which seemed always to diminish whenever white settlers appeared. There is also evidence to suggest that some Indian bands were shortchanged on the size of their reserves owing to incorrect head counts by government officials. (Stanley 1988:16)

Indigenous negotiators often brought with them individuals whose task it was to remember every word spoken. One government official expressed astonishment at having one of his own statements repeated verbatim at a subsequent meeting two years later (Dickason 1992:276). These recollections, though, had little standing in Canadian courts.

The compensation that many treaties promised, which might have seemed significant in the nineteenth century—a blanket for each band member per year, for example—became little more than symbolic tokens of agreement in later times. Many groups relinquished claims on vast regions of their former domains in return for the promise of peace and quiet, however.

From the British perspective, this was little more than a courtesy extended by the Crown to people who had no rights of ownership in any case. In the St. Catherine's Milling Case of the 1880s, the judge expressed the view that "before the appropriation of reserves the Indians have no claim except upon the bounty and benevolence of the Crown" (quoted in Dickason 1992:342).

Some indigenous groups and their supporters have long argued that the Royal Proclamation of 1763 expressly acknowledged indigenous rights to their lands. In the opinion of some judges, however, it was the proclamation that created those rights in the first place. On the assumption that all lands were the Crown's to begin with, recognition of indigenous rights was a gift of sorts—but a gift that the state could take away at any time. Almost a century after the St. Catherine's Milling Case, Justice Donald Steele in *Attorney-General of Ontario v. Bear Island Foundation* (1984) ruled that "aboriginal rights exist at the pleasure of the Crown, and they can be extinguished by treaty, legislation, or administrative acts" (Dickason 1992:354).

As we discussed earlier, the government applied the principle that indigenous peoples had not cultivated the land and had no true societies, and thus had no claim of territorial ownership. The token payments secured their agreement not to argue in the future that they had such claims. The granting of reserves for the undisturbed occupancy of these "bands" was, in the eyes of the government, an act of largess by the strong toward the weak.

Indian Status

The treaties had another consequence. They legally transformed autonomous populations into "bands" whose existence was a matter of state recognition. The Indian Act of 1867 defined indigenous communities as bands for the first time.

Treaties called for tribal rolls of individual members and designated the boundaries of their domains, and the bands' very existence thus became a matter of official record. Those indigenous populations that had not signed treaties or in some other way been recognized officially were not, in fact, "Indians" in the view of the state. The distinction between "status" and "nonstatus" Indians had the effect of rendering a large part of the indigenous population of Canada bureaucratically invisible.

In Mexico being *indio* was largely a cultural rather than a legal matter. In the United States, an indigenous great-grandparent in some groups was enough to qualify as "Indian." In Canada, however, even people who spoke indigenous languages and by all other criteria were Native Peoples might not have "Indian status" in the eyes of the government. J. S. Frideres (1993) estimates that these nonstatus indigenous people may have amounted to as many as half of all indigenous peoples in Canada.

Status was a problematic issue for the Métis population as well. Although intermarriages between indigenous peoples and Europeans had occurred sporadically throughout most of Canada, in Saskatchewan and Manitoba the resulting population had developed a distinct identity and way of life. Unlike *mestizos* in Mexico, who became the majority, or people of mixed parentage in the United States, who generally have been faced with being either "white" or "Indian," the Métis of the prairie provinces had become a distinct ethnic group in their own right but remained a minority in the Canadian population. The government finally gave them recognition in the Constitution Act of 1982, when it affirmed their "existing rights" along with those of other Native Peoples.

Assimilation Policies

In the late nineteenth century, the state and various interest groups within it gave more attention to assimilating indigenous communities. They were no longer a military factor, but they were economically marginal and, some felt, potentially troublesome. To many it seemed increasingly necessary to absorb them into the general population. As Interior Minister Clifford Sifton remarked to Parliament in 1901:

> The expenditure we are making is large, but it is made in the pursuance of a policy favoured by Parliament for many years based upon a belief that it is better—aside from the justice of the question—to bring the Indians into a state of civilization or comparative civilization, than to take any chance of their becoming a disturbing factor in the community. (quoted in Hall 1988:122)

Sporadic efforts to incorporate indigenous peoples into the Canadian state had been under way for some time. In 1830 the British Crown had shifted responsibility for Indian affairs from the military to the civil administration, reflecting the view that indigenous peoples had become a matter of concern for internal governance rather than independent allies. From the perspective of many interest groups, in fact, their presence had become a domestic problem.

Some observers early in the century had assumed that indigenous peoples would soon disappear. This coincided with the upsurge of Social Darwinism in popular thought. In Mexico during the nineteenth century, *científicos* had argued that *indios* represented a lower stage of human existence and were incapable of civilization. In Canada in 1836, Sir Francis Bond Head, governor-general of Upper Canada, took a similar view.

Arguing that Indians were on the way to extinction—professing sympathy for them at the same time—Bond Head considered reserves and educational programs a waste of resources. He advocated removing Indians to islands where they could die in peace and set about accepting land surrenders from indigenous groups. His extreme measures caused some outcry, but when the policies changed, the land expropriations remained in effect.

The Canadian state would continue to grapple with the issue of indigenous land rights for many years to come. To some extent, it was a matter of reconciling the contradictions between the demands of powerful interests for indigenous resources and the principle of justice, which had implications for the legitimacy of the state. In general, the powerful interest groups succeeded, leaving the state to rationalize the consequences in terms of high principles. During the later nineteenth century, this rationalization took the form of asserting that inducing change was for the good of indigenous peoples, whether they appreciated it or not.

Assimilation policies arose from the recognition that indigenous peoples did not seem to be disappearing very rapidly after all, nor did many of them seem inclined to abandon their ways of life. Although assumptions that they would eventually disappear persisted in many circles, it appeared that something should be done to hasten things along.

The general premise was that indigenous peoples would be better off as participating citizens of the state than as isolated, distinct populations. From this perspective, communal reserve lands appeared to be a deterrent to their progress because they allowed the communities to perpetuate themselves as distinct groups and to continue their old customs. The policy of the day was to rid Canada of "Indians" by converting them to citizens who were interchangeable with the rest of the population.

It would have been difficult to rationalize the overt use of force to bring about this change. Many small acts of violence against individuals continued to occur—most often to children in government schools—but there seemed to be little need or justification for military involvement. Missionaries, teachers, and bureaucrats would carry out the kindly assault.

In the wake of Bond Head's extreme measures, the report of the Bagot Commission in 1842 reaffirmed the idea that the Crown had an obligation to its indigenous peoples. It also stated that these peoples had legitimate claims to compensation for lands they had lost. On the other hand, the report also recommended the promotion of such approved activities as farming and useful crafts rather than hunting, and it favored individual freeholding of lands rather than communal reserves.

The government attempted to link the payment of treaty annuities to census data, which would advance the incorporation of indigenous populations into the state, individual by individual. The census rolls would determine who was eligible for "presents." The state, in the process, would capture indigenous bands on paper, housing their identity in file cabinets in Ottawa.

The Bagot Commission also observed that the day schools that various organizations had established on reserves had been ineffective in bringing about the desired changes. Children returned to their homes at the end of the day to speak in their native languages, to hear the old people tell stories, and to immerse themselves in the old web of kinship ties. Boarding schools, the commissioners felt, would be more successful in keeping children away from these pernicious influences.

Many indigenous parents agreed on the need for more effective schooling. In 1846 band leaders at Orilla pledged one-fourth of their treaty annuities to support the establishment of schools. This support waned quickly, though, when it became apparent that children in these schools often suffered mistreatment.

Some indigenous parents initially saw education as a means of developing the capacity to deal more effectively with the problems facing their communities. The ability to read and write, many felt, was crucial for surviving in their contemporary situation. Their hope was to help their children succeed—as indigenous people—and perhaps to help their communities.

The nonindigenous proponents of the schools, however, tended to see them as mechanisms for helping children get over being Indians. One suggestion of the Bagot Commission, in fact, seemed to assume that education negated Indian identity, since it recommended that educated individuals should no longer be eligible for "presents."

Many also felt that religious training was especially important in altering traditional thinking. The government relied on a number of church organizations to run the schools—partly because of their proclaimed moral standards, but also, no doubt, because church donations helped meet the costs of the schools.

The schools quickly developed a reputation for harsh treatment and outright abuse of children. As in the United States, a major thrust of the Indian education program was to promote proper deportment, including obedience and high moral behavior as the instructors defined it. Missionaries had a large role in running many schools, and the moral tone was often very strict indeed. Like the United States schools, these often relied for discipline on physical punishment. Punishable infractions included speaking in indigenous languages and talking to a child of the opposite sex. Many of these schools continued into the 1960s.

Egerton Ryerson extended these educational measures further by striving to make the schools self-supporting (Miller 1991:107). Children would spend a half day in class and the other half doing some useful work. This vocational training would not only bring income to the school (though presumably not to the laboring children) but would also prepare the students for a life of productive labor.

Unfortunately, many of these children had no opportunity to test the theory, since because of disease and other factors, many of them never reached adulthood. A study in 1909 found that between 1894 and 1908,

28 percent of indigenous children in these schools had died (Dickason 1992:335).

Despite these problems, however, we might almost feel relief at the complaint of one school official that "the most promising pupils are found to have retrograded and to have become leaders in the pagan life of their reserves" (quoted in Dickason 1992:336).

Legislative Incorporation

The assaults on indigenous identity continued in 1850, when the Canadian legislature passed an Act for the Protection of the Indians in Lower Canada. Through this act, the government took upon itself the responsibility of defining who was an Indian. The definition, however, was fairly broad compared to later definitions of indigenous status. It designated as Indians "persons of Indian blood reputed to belong to a particular Body or Tribe" and all persons married to such persons.

The assumption that it was up to the government to define the parameters of indigenous populations—in a fashion that was far less exclusive than the criteria many of them would have used—represented the degree to which the state had begun a concerted effort to incorporate them within its hegemony. The presumption that the government could make such a judgment opened the way for future attempts to define many of them out of existence as Indians after programs to induce change had failed.

The pressure to induce change grew during the latter half of the nineteenth century. In 1857 the Canadian legislature, reflecting the wishes of proassimilation interests, passed an Act for the Gradual Civilization of the Indian Tribes in the Canadas. The aim of this act was to bring about ". . . the gradual removal of all legal distinctions between them and her Majesty's other Canadian subjects" (Milloy 1988:58–59).

The act stipulated the criteria by which indigenous people could attain this lofty status. Paradoxically, however, the requirements that indigenous people would have to meet in order to obtain citizenship were so strict that they constituted a barrier rather than a means of easy access. They required that the candidate, in the judgment of a review board, should be well educated, free of debt, and of good moral character. Many Canadian citizens at the time would have been hard-pressed to meet such standards (Miller 1991:111).

For the successful indigenous candidate for citizenship, the payoff would not only be enfranchisement, but twenty hectares of land—apparently to be excised from communal reserve lands. The Canadian legislature's tampering with indigenous lands was a violation of the Royal

Proclamation of 1763, which held that only the Crown could approve such measures, but as it turned out, that was a rather moot point. Between 1857 and 1876, only one indigenous person went through the process (Miller 1991:114).

There is little reason to suppose that this response on the part of indigenous peoples represented a rejection of participation in the Canadian economy.

> A general Indian position emerged in the 1860's. [Band] Councils across the colony remained pro-development. They wanted education and agricultural and resource development but would not participate in a system designed, as an Oneida petition said, to "separate our people." (Milloy 1988:60)

Violation of the Crown's policy that indigenous peoples "should not be molested or disturbed" in the possession of their lands did not seem to trouble either the Crown or the Canadian government, although indigenous delegates did petition the Prince of Wales for his support when he visited Canada in 1861. In 1867 England passed full responsibility for "Indians and Indian land" to the Canadian government through the British North America Act (Tobias 1988:39).

> In the mid-nineteenth century the Colonial Office bequeathed to the Dominion of Canada the legacy of an Indian policy which was regional in its approach, was characterized by "perpetual compromises between principle and immediate exigency," and which continually vacillated in its purpose and implementation in all parts of British North America. (McNab 1988:100)

Native Peoples after Confederation

Indigenous peoples have continued to seek redress on the basis of the Royal Proclamation, but this became more difficult in 1867, when Confederation diminished the possibility of appeals to the Crown. As in Mexico after independence, whatever disinterested protection indigenous peoples might have had from an overseas monarch all but disappeared, and local or provincial interest groups could operate more freely. Canada became a self-governing dominion of the British Empire in that year and began the process of amalgamating the various separate colonies and territories into a single state from sea to sea.

Upper Canada and Lower Canada had joined under the Unity Act of 1841, later to become the provinces of Ontario and Quebec. The Canadian legislature declared Manitoba a province in 1870. British Columbia joined Canada the same year. In 1871 Canada acquired Rupert's Land and the Northwest Territories, setting off the lengthy treaty process extinguishing indigenous claims to expansive territories.

After the British North America Act established Canadian self-governance, the Canadian state wasted little time in taking steps to link indigenous communities to the structure of the state. The Gradual Enfranchisement Act of 1869 required that all bands elect their own government to manage their local affairs. Band decisions were subject to the veto of the federal government, however, in the person of the minister of Indian Affairs. The act also provided for the governor-in-council to remove from office any elected indigenous leader he deemed unfit because of "dishonesty, intemperance, or immorality" (Milloy 1988:62, Tobias 1988:43).

The act also specified ways by which individuals could lose Indian status. A status woman who married a nonstatus man, for example, would become nonstatus and so would her children. The existence of many indigenous societies that reckoned descent through the mother's line was of little consequence to the legislators. If they considered this practice at all, most would have viewed it as an example of the primitive ways they were trying to eradicate.

Not surprisingly, this plan for furthering the civilization of indigenous peoples met with strong and vocal resistance among them. Not only did it impose a foreign system of governance on groups who had been managing their own affairs for some time, but it created a structure that locked indigenous communities to an intrusive system of federal oversight.

The Indian Act of 1876 continued existing policies, but with some modifications. This act made the election of band councils optional. Subsequent legislation in 1880, however, reimposed the policy when it created the Department of Indian Affairs and provided for that agency to impose the election of councils. The 1876 act focused on status Indians and defined them as wards of the government. The term "wards," with its implication of incompetence, rationalized such protective measures as the prohibition of liquor sales to indigenous peoples and a ban on the presence of non-Indians on reserves after nightfall.

The Indian Act also pursued the policy of breaking reserve lands into individual holdings by dividing them into blocks and issuing "location tickets" to qualified individuals. After a probationary period of three years, during which the ticket holder would demonstrate the ability to live like other rural Canadians, he (rarely she) would obtain full title to the land block and in the process, relinquish Indian status.

Many indigenous peoples had no delusions about this legislative attack on their collective identities and the threat that it posed to their remaining lands. In many ways, it represented a full reversal of the Royal Proclamation's principles. It reflected the immersion of indigenous populations in a state arena in which they carried little competitive weight. Their refusal to acquiesce to many of these initiatives did have some results, though. Very few people opted for enfranchisement over the next several decades—about 250 out of an estimated population of 300,000 or more "status Indians" between 1857 and 1920, or an average of about 4 per year (Miller 1991:190).

Coercive measures intensified over the next few decades. It would be difficult to put it more succinctly than Sir John Macdonald, who in 1887 harumphed in the House of Commons that the "great aim of our legislation has been to do away with the tribal system and assimilate the Indian people in all respects with the inhabitants of the Dominion, as speedily as they are fit for the change" (quoted in Miller 1991:189).

Strategies to accomplish these ends ranged between persuasion and harassment. Edgar Dewdney, as commissioner of Indian Affairs for the Northwest Territory, withheld rations from those who failed or refused to farm—a policy that may have contributed to the Saskatchewan uprising. The Northwest Mounted Police, who originally had enjoyed amicable relationships with many of the Plains groups, now had orders to arrest indigenous people traveling between reserves and to break up meetings. Many of the police were reluctant to carry out these clearly unconstitutional orders (Dickason 1992:314).

The Indian Advancement Act of 1884 reaffirmed the Department of Indian Affairs's power to depose "unfit" band chiefs (Miller 1991:190). In the same year, Parliament outlawed the potlatch of the Pacific Coast peoples and the Sun Dance of the Plains (Miller 1991:191). Both of these ceremonies had been central organizing features of the indigenous societies of their respective regions.

In the following year, the government instituted a pass system that stipulated that band members needed a government official's written permission to leave their reserves. The only thing in favor of this law was that it was so ill conceived and unenforceable that neither indigenous peoples nor the police paid much attention to it. A few reserve agents did use it on a situational basis to harass individuals, however. A major reason for the law apparently was to keep leaders from visiting one another's communities and planning collective strategies. For the same reason, the government refused requests by the Cree leaders Big Bear, Piapot, and Little Pine for adjacent reserves (Tobias 1983:524, 527–528).

As pressures to compel assimilation continued past the turn of the century, many of the contradictions in the state's strategies became more apparent. Policies and legislation had promoted the adoption of agriculture on reserves, but the era of the ox-drawn plow was coming to a close, and farming had become increasingly mechanized. To compete in an agricultural market, it was necessary to have adequate farm machinery. Yet the Indian Act had forbidden mortgages on reserve lands, which meant that indigenous farmers had no credit to invest in equipment. As a consequence, while other Canadian farmers developed commercial enterprises and marketed cash crops, many indigenous farmers could do little more than produce for their own consumption.

Ironically, commercially successful farms might have accomplished much of the assimilation that proponents claimed to desire. When it came right down to it, though, established farmers had no desire for increased competition. As a result, indigenous farmers found themselves in a role more akin to peasantry than participants in agribusiness.

Many indigenous peoples continued to hunt for their own subsistence and trap for a supplemental income. In some areas, this has continued well into the present (see Asch 1988:284–285, Berger 1977). This has been especially true north of the zone in which agriculture is feasible. Even these people, though, found themselves pushed by outside interests. Mineral exploration in the north all but ignored local indigenous populations, and in the 1920s a conservation-minded government created Wood Buffalo National Park south of Great Slave Lake and stopped indigenous peoples from hunting the animals.

In 1895, just a few years after the United States Congress had passed the Dawes Act to break up its reservations, the Canadian government empowered the Department of Indian Affairs to rent out the reserve land plots of individual members at their request without securing band permission. More restraints fell by the wayside in the succeeding years. In 1911 the government made it possible to appropriate reserve lands for roads and other public works. It also empowered the Department of Indian Affairs to relocate indigenous populations from reserves if towns of eight thousand or more grew up on or within their boundaries. Essentially, this made it possible for squatters to commandeer indigenous lands by sheer numbers. The apparent contradiction between promoting assimilation and enforcing segregation does not appear to have bothered many legislators.

The mobilization effort during World War I knocked away still more constraints on reserve land appropriations. Efforts for "greater production" opened the way for taking reserve lands for farming (Dickason 1992:326). After the war, the Soldier Settlement Board confiscated reserve lands for returning veterans (Leslie and Maguire 1978:108–109). The general open season on indigenous lands in this era reflected the

Canada

wish of many Canadians that the Indians should drop their insistence on special identity once and for all and disappear into the general population, preferably leaving their lands behind for the taking. In some respects, land confiscations involved acting on a foregone conclusion.

The social and political assault on indigenous identity continued through the years after World War I. Duncan Campbell Scott, the deputy minister for Indian Affairs, summarized the government's continuing position on indigenous populations in 1920. "Our object is to continue until there is not a single Indian in Canada that has not been absorbed into the body politic, and there is no Indian question, and no Indian Department" (quoted in Leslie and Maguire 1978:114).

Venerable Canadian anthropologist Diamond Jenness observed:

> The Indian administration of that period was a "holding" one, more concerned with preserving the status quo than with improving the economic and social status of the Indians with raising their living standard. The head of the administration [Duncan Campbell Scott] disliked them as a people and gave a cool reception to the delegations that visited him in Ottawa. (1988:161)

In the same year that Scott made his pronouncement, the government passed legislation to divest any indigenous person of status involuntarily if the proper authorities considered him or her "fit" for enfranchisement (Miller 1991:206). The outcry this aroused led to its revocation two years later, but when the conservatives gained office in the early 1930s they once again tried the old strategy of compulsory enfranchisement.

Indigenous Strategies in the Twentieth Century

If World War I served as a justification for land appropriations, it also seems to have been a catalyst for indigenous response. As in the United States, many indigenous peoples had volunteered to serve and had distinguished themselves in service. Many who returned felt strongly that the government owed them more respect and fairer treatment than they had received in the past. Many also, no doubt, had come to view their local issues as aspects of the more general concerns of indigenous peoples throughout Canada. As in the United States, coalition building became an effective strategy.

One of the first examples of coalition building occurred when Frederick O. Loft, a Mohawk war veteran, founded the League of Indians of Canada in 1919. Others followed. The Indian Association of Alberta began in 1939, and the Federation of Saskatchewan Indians, in 1944. One of the most active, however, was the Native Brotherhood of British Columbia, which formed in 1931.

The province of British Columbia had a record of flatly refusing to recognize indigenous land claims. While not inconsistent with the general tenor of Canadian relationships with indigenous peoples, the British Columbia stance was more extreme. British Columbia's early history had involved a relatively dense indigenous population with few settlers until the discovery of gold in the 1860s. The colonial governor in the late 1850s had tried with some success to accommodate indigenous needs for land and pressure from settlers. Joseph W. Trutch, however, who was appointed commissioner of Crown Lands in 1864, held that indigenous peoples had no more land rights "than a panther or a bear" (quoted in Dickason 1992:261).

The late entry of British Columbia into the Canadian state and the relative independence of the Canadian provinces with regard to the federal government, compared to the United States, may have contributed to its recalcitrance in recognizing indigenous rights even after many provinces, which have concentrated and significant local interest groups, had moderated their policies. The relative authority of federal versus provincial governments over indigenous populations has been a crucial and long-standing issue in Canada. In this instance, the British Columbia policies became a provocation for indigenous action.

The indigenous peoples of British Columbia were probably better prepared to mobilize than those of many other regions in Canada. Many of them, especially on the coast, had highly structured stratified societies and relatively dense populations. They were well positioned to exert coordinated pressure on the government.

These various political pressures had some effect. In 1948 the Canadian Parliament revised the Indian Act and dropped some of its more coercive aspects, although the revised act continued to endorse assimilation. In 1951 the government repealed compulsory enfranchisement and dropped the bans on the Sun Dance, the potlatch, and alcohol sales. It continued to espouse assimilation programs but disavowed the use of force, opting instead for "encouragement" (Tobias 1983:52).

The political mobilization of indigenous peoples continued, albeit with difficulties. Canada's Native Peoples included populations who had almost nothing in common with one another, except that they all had to deal with the Canadian state and had been grouped into the same general category *by* that state. At the same time, however, the state's distinction between status and nonstatus people imposed some divergence of interest among them. The question of Inuit and Métis further complicated the situation. Many of these populations had never signed treaties or lost a war with the state. They merely happened to live within a huge territory over which European powers had exchanged jurisdiction on paper. Others had entered into treaties and wished to compel the government to honor the terms of these agreements.

In the mid-twentieth century, indigenous political groups carried on extensive dialogues with the federal government. By the late 1960s, many felt optimistic that the government was receptive to their concerns and needs. In that decade, a commission led by anthropologist Harry B. Hawthorne concluded that the government had indeed violated the rights of indigenous peoples and indicated that their special status was appropriate. The report concluded that indigenous peoples should be considered "citizens plus." Though sympathetic, however, the implication was not greater independence but a more intense incorporation into the state.

The White Paper

In 1969, after extensive consultation with indigenous leaders, the Liberal government under Pierre Elliot Trudeau and Minister for Indian

Affairs Jean Chretien prepared a government position paper. Called the White Paper (perhaps unfortunately), it stated government's views regarding indigenous peoples.

As it happened, indigenous issues were not the most acute problem Trudeau faced. Like any state, Canada involved a nexus of interest groups, and its existence depended upon balancing them. The Province of Quebec had had an ambivalent relationship with the rest of Canada since the eighteenth century, when the British Crown acquired jurisdiction over a French population that had lived there for three centuries. The Louis Riel affair had resonated with this tension. Many Quebecois felt that they had been treated with discrimination throughout Canada's history, and a move for Quebec separatism was growing. In the 1970s, it erupted in violence.

Trudeau, himself a native of Quebec, was concerned with Canadian unity. In that context, the idea of distinct status for indigenous peoples had awkward implications for the Quebec problem. The premiers of some of the western provinces, moreover, who represented constituencies with strong anti-Indian settler traditions, were somewhat testy about indigenous rights at the outset.

For these, and no doubt other reasons, Trudeau had no intention of acknowledging any significant degree of sovereignty for indigenous peoples. The White Paper essentially ignored the issues that indigenous representatives had pushed so consistently in their conferences with government officials and reiterated the old assimilationist position. Trudeau's theme was that "we are all Canadians." It was unthinkable, he asserted, that one group of citizens in a unified state should have treaties with other citizens.

The White Paper proposed the elimination of Indian status and repeal of the Indian Act. It recommended the abolition of the Indian Affairs branch of the Department of Indian Affairs and Northern Development. In its basic position, the White Paper differed little from the pronouncements of Duncan Campbell Scott almost half a century earlier.

Indigenous peoples felt betrayed. To many it seemed that the government was up to its old tricks. The long series of discussions appeared to have been little more than a political charade. The Trudeau government's stand, in the eyes of many, was simply more of the same old thing, though not necessarily for the same reasons. Whereas in the past, the state had followed the will of the most powerful interests at the expense of indigenous peoples, in this case the state was trying to preserve itself through maintaining a precarious balance *among* powerful interests—a balance that the very idea of separatism seemed to threaten. Indigenous peoples lost out in the competitive arena as they so often had before, but in this case they were kicked off to the side in the throes of a struggle among more powerful constituencies.

Reaction to the White Paper was swift and incisive. Harold Cardinal, president of the Indian Association of Alberta, commented wryly that in the view of the Canadian government, "The only good Indian is a non-Indian" (1969:1). Indigenous peoples of Manitoba issued their own "Brown Paper."

In the furor that ensued, the National Indian Brotherhood rose to become one of the most prominent groups confronting the government position. Indigenous groups made it clear that they demanded recognition of treaty rights, existing band rights, and their special status as "First Nations." More specifically, they opposed further reserve land allotments. They asked for a government agency to investigate and prosecute land claims, and they demanded a degree of sovereignty within the Canadian state.

Indigenous peoples had long since recognized that they were involved, like it or not, in a competitive arena in which they could best pursue their common interests by presenting a united front. This strategy would be difficult to maintain at times, but the White Paper served the purpose of galvanizing a broad range of indigenous groups in common opposition.

The Liberal government was somewhat taken aback by the intensity of the indigenous response, and within a year or so it retreated, pointing out that the White Paper had no legislative standing but was merely a set of ideas put forth for discussion.

Indigenous Issues since the White Paper

One result of the response was that, through the media, indigenous issues gained the attention of a public that had little familiarity with them. The public controversy, coupled with the generally sympathetic view the Canadian populace held toward the romanticized, abstract image of Indians, became a political embarrassment to the government. It looked bad to maintain a position that appeared manifestly unfair to people with whom most Canadians had no particular quarrel.

In response to the land claims demands, the government appointed a claims officer in 1969, but this officer had little power to investigate or redress grievances. The move simply inflamed resentment and further unified indigenous political groups. By the 1970s, the government backed down further and empowered the Department of Indian Affairs and Northern Development to fund research on land claims. It also provided funding for the National Indian Brotherhood, which later became the Assembly of First Nations.

Things were far from smooth, however. As Canada embarked on a long discussion to revise its Constitution, a variety of interest groups asserted themselves. A proposed Charter of Rights and Freedoms failed in 1981 when premiers of the western provinces voted against passages safeguarding the rights of indigenous peoples and women.

The western regions historically have had especially troubled relationships with their indigenous populations.

> In 1978, 34 per cent of all inmates admitted into correctional institutions were native. The figure for Saskatchewan is 61 per cent. Similarly, in northwestern Ontario in 1978, native male admissions to provincial jails constituted 24 per cent in Thunder Bay, 32 per cent in Fort Frances, and 48 per cent in Kenora. The percentages are even higher for female offenders. (McCaskill 1988:288)

Trudeau supported the Constitution Act of 1982, which was a bit more congenial to indigenous interests. It affirmed "existing aboriginal and treaty rights" and defined "aboriginal" to include Inuit and Métis. This affirmation of "existing rights" was all very well, but there appeared to be no consensus as to just what these rights might be. This uncertainty also pertained to some treaty interpretations. There was also some doubt as to whether affirmation of existing rights precluded the establishment of new rights in the future. In any case, however, many viewed the act as a step forward.

In 1983 the House of Commons directed Keith Penner to head a special committee to reexamine indigenous affairs in Canada. The Penner Committee endorsed the idea that indigenous people should enjoy more sovereignty over their own affairs. It went so far as to describe indigenous societies as "a distinct order of government in Canada."

When the Conservative government of Brian Mulroney took office in the late 1980s, though, things swung back to the right. Deputy Prime Minister Erik Nielsen led another task force on indigenous affairs that, after deliberating behind closed doors, concluded that government programs had failed to help indigenous populations. The recommendations that sprang from this finding were to cut back on such programs, reduce spending, and shift federal responsibility for indigenous affairs from the federal government to the provinces. The Nielsen recommendations sounded almost like a watered-down version of Bond Head's policies of the 1850s.

Indigenous affairs were no longer at the margins of Canadian consciousness, however. Many of the vast northern regions that had suffered little disturbance up to the mid-twentieth century had come to the attention of large corporate interests. Many of these interests were transnational in their scope and power bases. On the other hand, the public consciousness-raising that had resulted from the activities of the preceding years made it difficult for resource appropriation to take place out of sight. The media and the public had begun to pay more attention to indigenous affairs, and indigenous leaders had learned to use the media more effectively.

One significant development during the 1970s had been the attempt to build a pipeline through the Mackenzie Valley from the Arctic to the south. Proponents considered the area all but unoccupied, implying that the few indigenous people of the region were no longer living like "Indians." The old argument arose once again that they were simply Canadians with no special privileges.

British Columbia Supreme Court Justice Thomas Berger conducted a series of hearings in the affected region, taking testimony from people who explained that they still lived off the land through hunting and trapping. They argued that the pipeline would have deleterious effects on the regional ecology as well as on their lives. The Berger Commission recommended a ten-year delay in construction to hear and settle native claims. Berger's report appeared in book form under the title *Northern Frontier/Northern Homeland* (1977) and quickly sold out in Canadian cities. Another commission examining a pipeline from Alaska through the southern Yukon reached a similar conclusion, arguing for a delay of four years (Miller 1991:255).

Such episodes have not forestalled corporate encroachment on indigenous lands, any more than the government in Ottawa or King George III were able to halt the encroachment of settlers. Scott Rushforth, writing of the Sauhtuot'ine of the Bear Lake region, puts the issue succinctly.

> Northeastern Athapaskans lost economic autonomy when goods acquired through the fur trade became necessities. Dene lost autonomous control of productive resources through treaties with the Canadian government. They lost autonomous control of productive resources as the Canadian government enacted game and fish laws in the Northwest Territories. Tools of western manufacture effectively replaced indigenous material technology. . . . Nonetheless, Sahtuot'ine (and other Dene) still control local knowledge, including primary knowledge of the land and animals that occupy it. (1994:343)

Ultimately, the arguments by interested parties that their gains were for the greater good of society were bound to prevail. Yet during this era, the leverage of indigenous interests continued to grow (see Asch 1989). They might lose their resources, but in some cases, at least, they were able to exact a price.

Localized tragedies continued, however. In the 1960s, the government decided to relocate the Anishinabek community at Grassy Narrows in northwest Ontario to a more compact community—partly, many of them asserted, to free land for the Hudson's Bay Company. The disruption of their residential pattern undermined the social organization, leading to severe social problems including a high rate of gasoline-sniffing and suicide among young people. The community also learned after a few years that their drinking water from the nearby river was polluted with mercury (Shkilnyk 1985). In 1979 the Dunne-Za (Beaver) of British Columbia suffered gas poisoning from an oil well in their territory (Ridington 1990:216–224).

James Bay and the La Grande Complex

Perhaps the best-known issue regarding indigenous resources during this period was the hydroelectric project in Cree and Inuit territory near James Bay. The ancestors of the James Bay Cree may well have been the first human beings ever to occupy those lands, moving into the region when the last glacier receded. Too far north for agriculture, as we noted earlier, the Cree had adopted a seasonal pattern of camping together during the summer on lake shores and dispersing in small groups during the winter months to hunt.

This way of life required the use of large tracts of land, but the sparseness of the environment had kept the Cree relatively free from the encroachment of Europeans. Traders had established posts in the region centuries earlier, but the addition of trapping to the Cree winter hunting activities did not constitute a radical change for most of them. Many of them simply gathered in the summer near the posts rather than their old lakeside encampments. This trading arrangement, while it had some exploitative aspects, had left the people in possession of their territory (see Speck 1977, Tanner 1979, Rogers and Leacock 1981).

The Cree did experience some intrusion from the south in the first half of the twentieth century, generally by sports hunters and commercial trappers when the railroad extended its line northward toward James Bay. Depletion of the beaver in some areas caused the government to impose trapping regulations, which the Cree generally welcomed. They viewed it as the government's recognition of their own game management practices (Feit 1989:189).

The relative isolation of the James Bay Cree changed in the early 1970s, however, when the Province of Quebec decided to construct the world's largest hydroelectric project. This project—the La Grande complex—would dam rivers to flood hundreds of square miles of Cree hunting lands.

The Cree were ill prepared to respond to this situation. Having used large areas of land collectively for centuries, they had developed a system of individual responsibility for particular hunting territories but respected each other's lands as a matter of courtesy and regularly invited others to hunt on them (Leacock 1954). The hunting territories were largely a matter of exercising responsibility for game management rather than ownership (Tanner 1979). The Cree had little experience in guarding their lands from unwanted intruders.

Cree social organization also rested on kin ties among members of local populations. They had no overall political structure that could easily mobilize the entire Cree population. By the time they learned of the project and coordinated their interests under an organization they named the Grand Council of the Cree, the project was well under way.

Inuit to the north would also be affected. The Inuit Taprisat, an elected body that claimed to represent the peoples of the Arctic, joined the Cree in taking the issue to court. They secured an injunction on further construction, but the proponents of the project appealed the decision, and the court ruled that construction could continue while the case was being heard.

The project went on to completion after negotiation of the largest and probably the most complex indigenous treaty in Canadian history up to that time. The Cree and Inuit were to receive $250 million, tracts of land for their exclusive use, additional lands with hunting restrictions pertaining to outsiders, the right to run schools in any language they chose, pensions for elderly hunters, and a range of other considerations (see Price 1979, Feit 1988:199–202). Hundreds of miles of their hunting lands, however, were under water.

The development of the La Grande project revealed once again the complexity of interest group competition within and beyond the Canadian state. It was a matter of provincial rather than federal funding, but the electric power was not merely for the needs of Quebec. One incentive was the sale of power to United States interests, particularly New York State.

The federal government of Canada tended to keep some distance from the issue, even though indigenous affairs had always been a federal rather than a provincial responsibility. Ottawa provided some funding to help indigenous groups attain legal assistance, but otherwise it appeared loath to irritate Quebec. Much of this stance, no doubt, had to do with sensitivities arising from the lurking issue of Quebec separatism.

As has often been the case following treaties, there were problems. By the late 1980s, it had become apparent that many of the rivers were polluted with mercury, although the government argued that this pollution arose from natural rather than industrial sources. On the other hand, government counts of caribou indicate that the herds have increased. The numbers of caribou tend to fluctuate wildly in any case, however, and it is difficult to attribute this with certainty to the effects of the hydroelectric project.

More recently, Hydro-Quebec has begun a second phase on the Great Whale River to the north. This $13 billion project would flood 699 more square miles of land, affecting about twenty-five hundred Inuit and Cree (Bissonnette 1993:7). Environmental and pro-Native groups in Canada and the United States have protested strenuously against this further appropriation. Their greatest victory was to persuade Governor Mario Cuomo of New York to withhold his state's offer to buy power from the project. Despite this setback, however, the project will push on. Industrial interests have considered purchasing hydroelectric power from Quebec, and New York State now has a conservative governor who may be more receptive to the project. Some Canadians, reacting to United States citizens who condemn their treatment of the Cree, have drawn attention to the United States record of dealing with its indigenous peoples.

Modern Indigenous Activism

In the 1980s and 1990s, other incidents served to draw media attention to indigenous peoples. In southern Quebec, the Mohawk community of Kanehsatake near the town of Oka had long been involved in challenges to their land rights. In 1718, the king of France had granted a Sulpician monastery rights to land with the understanding that they were to use it as a mission for the Mohawk living there. Since that time, the rights to the land had been subject to dispute between the monastery and the Mohawk. Matters became worse when the Sulpicians sold off part of the land in question.

The government at one time had offered to buy the land for the Mohawk, who refused. Not only did the purchase not include all of the territory in dispute, but consent would have been tantamount to agreeing that the land had not been theirs to begin with (Druke 1988:318).

The land issue erupted again in 1990 when the town began to construct an eighteen-hole golf course that intruded into lands the Mohawk considered theirs. A Mohawk blockade of the road led to police intervention. The incident escalated to violence when someone shot a police officer in the face. Mohawk argued that a stray bullet from one of the police had killed him, but a police inquiry decided otherwise.

The armed standoff lasted for several weeks and received international media attention. The Quebec Sureté had a long-standing reputation for heavy-handedness in dealing with local indigenous peoples, and the Mohawk asked to deal with some other agency. Quebec Premier Bourassa called for federal troops. Other Mohawk blocked bridges into Montreal in sympathy with the people at Oka and caused havoc with urban commuters. From the Mohawk communities at Kahnawake and Akwesasne, members of a self-proclaimed "warrior society" offered their support.

The incident had many interesting aspects. Members of the Mohawk community did not universally endorse the "warrior society"; the group had formed in the context of internal disputes over the introduction of gambling. The Oka incident, however, with the government's quick resort to force, awakened much of the public to the intensity of native issues.

Many citizens of Quebec—a province that had prided itself on being progressive regarding indigenous peoples—turned out to be capable of vitriolic racism when indigenous protesters disturbed the orderliness of their lives. It took little more than a disruption of rush-hour traffic to evoke calls for genocide. Beyond the local furor, however, the incident at Oka had symbolic import for many. Ironically, it suggested that the Canadian state's relations with indigenous peoples had become more potentially violent late in the twentieth century than it had been for much of the nation's past.

In the wake of the incident at Oka, the Crown tried thirty-three Mohawk protesters for their part in the affair. Presenting their own defense, the Mohawk argued that the incident was part of a long-standing struggle to maintain their rights as a sovereign people. They cited the past use of force against them, the seizure of cultural items under the Indian Act, and the jailing of clan mothers. "All of that, we explained, was designed to destroy our traditional councils and make it possible for the government to install Indian Act councils through elections" (David 1992:12–13).

The judge, rejecting the prosecution's attempt to define the case as a straightforward criminal issue, referred to it as a "dispute between peoples." The jury acquitted all defendants.

The issue continues to simmer, however. The popular media in Quebec were highly critical of the decision. As Joe David, one of the defendants, noted, "For a lot of native groups in Canada, the bottom line is land claims. You can break it up into other categories and call it environment, peace, human rights, and justice, but for us it's all connected" (David 1992:14).

The most dramatic victory for indigenous peoples in those years, though, came about in a peaceful decision by one man in the Manitoba legislature, when Elijah Harper stopped the Meech Lake Accord.

The Meech Lake Accord and the Canadian Constitution

The Meech Lake Accord was the product of lengthy discussion in the 1980s regarding the status of Quebec within the Canadian state. The accord recognized Quebec as a "distinct society" within Canada. These discussions held a bitter irony for indigenous peoples whose comparable demands continued to receive little recognition. The very Mulroney government that pushed for the Quebec special status clause had shown little sympathy for indigenous concerns.

The stipulations of the accord were that it must receive unanimous approval by the provinces by June 23, 1990. Prime Minister Mulroney waited until the final few days to push the agreement though, believing that urgency would add pressure to force its acceptance by reluctant holdouts. When it came before the Manitoba legislature, the speaker called for unanimous consent to proceed quickly on the matter. Elijah Harper, a Cree-Ojibwa member, said no, and the Meech Lake Accord was dead.

Harper later explained his position.

> We blocked the accord because it posed a threat to aboriginal people. Aboriginal people have no quarrel with Quebec. But we're a distinct society too, and we've fought for many years for the basic rights that Quebec takes for granted, such as participating in constitutional talks. (quoted in Miller 1991:302)

Developing Land Issues

Other developments have suggested the direction indigenous peoples' fortunes may take in Canada. In the 1970s, a case regarding the Nishga of British Columbia left the panel of judges split as to whether they had constituted a society with rights of ownership to land. While the Nishga lost the case, the judges' disagreement left an opening to challenge the hoary principle that had denied the basis of numerous indigenous land claims.

On the other hand, the long-standing assumption has been persistent. In a 1989 claims case involving the Gitksan and Wet'suwet'en of British

Columbia, the attorney general of Canada stated, "If the plaintiffs ever had sovereignty, it was extinguished completely by Great Britain" (quoted in Asch 1993:34). In 1991 the British Columbia Supreme Court denied the existence of aboriginal land rights and stated that "the discovery and occupation of this continent by European nations, or occupation and settlement gave rise to a right of sovereignty" (quoted in Menzies 1994:785).

As of 1990, five hundred claims cases remained unresolved, with only forty-five settled since 1973 (Dickason 1992:392–393). Since the late 1980s, though, indigenous people have pushed a few claims with some success.

Perhaps the most spectacular development has been the approval of territorial status for Nunavut, a region carved out of the Northwest Territories that amounts to a fifth of Canada's land area. Though Nunavut is by no means independent of Canada, the vast majority of its population are Inuit, which gives them de facto self-rule in territorial matters. A more ominous note, perhaps, is the glee with which multinational corporations greeted the move. The ground rules for Nunavut may provide for political self-governance, but the federal government retains subsurface mineral rights over most of the territory. The trade-off for political sovereignty is the extinguishment of claims to minerals in an area that includes the Arctic Archipelago—a region where surface resources have been insufficient even to support the Inuit.

It may be significant that the Dené, who constitute a minority in Nunavut, voted against its establishment in a referendum. Clearly, indigenous solidarity is not absolute. Attempts to establish Denendeh, a region with a Dené majority, ran into more problems. While many argued against the government's demands that they relinquish treaty rights in return for the settlement, some groups broke ranks and accepted separate deals (Dickason 1992:414). As always, it appears that while coalitions tend to be the most effective means of achieving common goals, they tend to be fragile.

The Canadian state continues to struggle with the issue of indigenous rights. In 1992 various constituencies developed a compromise plan for the shape of their new constitution. Known as the Charlottetown Accord, it included specific support for Aboriginal rights to self-government. As it turned out, however, native peoples divided on the issue.

The Inuit had different interests from Métis and Indian peoples below the 60th parallel. Métis had different demands than Indians. Aboriginal peoples in cities had different needs than those on reserves. Treaty Indians (granted particular rights by the

Canadian government) saw things differently than non-treaty Indians. And self-government means little to those chiefs whose priority was resolving land titles. (May 1993:11)

When it came to a vote, the accord failed in all but a few provinces.

Canada has settled several major land claims since 1975, including the James Bay and Northern Quebec settlement involving Inuit, Cree, and Naskapi, and the Inuvialut Final Agreement, covering 25,000 square miles of Arctic land. The Gwich'in of the Mackenzie River Delta acquired 8,700 square miles with 3,000 square miles of subsurface rights (Bissonnette 1993:8). Other agreements involve the 135,000 square miles of the Nunavut settlement and 16,000 square miles for the Yukon First Nations.

Canadians have been justifiably proud of their relatively nonviolent relationships with indigenous peoples. Atrocities such as the Sand Creek massacre in Colorado, the Camp Grant massacre in Arizona, or Wounded Knee in South Dakota do not mar Canada's history. Even the Cypress Hills massacre of Assiniboin, which took place on Canadian soil, was committed by United States citizens who crossed the border (Allen 1988). But the assault of powerful Canadian interest groups on indigenous peoples and their resources has been relentless, nonetheless.

In the absence of excessive violence, there has been oppression of children in government schools, the poisoning of water systems with mercury, the confiscation of lands, and the chronic assault on indigenous identity through legislation. Canada has not been a violent state compared to others. But it has nonetheless been a state, which means that it has balanced off the interests of the powerful at the expense of the weak.

Unlike Mexico, Canada's politics and the periodic transfer of power have been peaceful and ceremonious. It has not been subject to violent shifts in policy. But it has also been unlike Mexico in having had a power structure to which indigenous peoples, until recently, have had little hope of access. Unlike Mexico, the possibility of an indigenous head of state in Canada would be unthinkable. In this respect, Canada resembles the United States and Australia. It is interesting that indigenous peoples of Australia have begun to confer often with indigenous peoples in Canada. We shall turn our attention to Australia in the next chapter.

Australia

· · · · · · · · ·

6

You decided to clean the people out from their own
country. *Ngumpin* never went to kill you there longa
England. He never made a big war longa you there,
finish you there. No! You did the wrong thing,
finishing up *ngumpin*. Like that now, no good that
game. Well, you made it very hard.

(Aboriginal man at Victoria River Downs, Northern
Territory; quoted by Deborah Bird Rose 1991:265)

W hen the British laid claim to the southeastern coast of Australia in
1788, they were not seeking the resources that had impelled European colonialism in North and South America. They sought another
goal—a place to get rid of some of their own excess populace.

The English population had increased rapidly in that century, and the
surplus humanity had caused growing problems. The English economy
could not begin to absorb them all into the labor force, despite the Industrial Revolution's need for labor. The enclosure of common pasture lands
by individual property owners had driven many people from the countryside into the cities. English disruption of Scotland and Ireland had
also resulted in displaced, often desperate people struggling to survive.

One of the few alternatives for many of them was crime, as the English state broadly defined it. The Crown took a dim view of this disorderly behavior, and Parliament enacted stern measures. An increasing
number of offenses called for the death penalty. As Robert Hughes notes,
most of these misdeeds—poaching game, burning haystacks, or picking
pockets—were crimes involving property rather than human life
(1986:171–173).

Despite the numerous public hangings, however, there was a limit to how much this carnage could alleviate the problem. With the existing prisons crowded to capacity, the British government began holding prisoners in converted ships moored in the Thames. The dark hulks laden with convicts loomed offshore as a grim reminder of the majesty of the law.

Another solution, preferable to many, was to send shiploads of prisoners to the colonies where they would carry out "useful labor" under compulsion. Tens of thousands of English and Irish prisoners crossed the Atlantic to work in the Thirteen Colonies and the Caribbean islands.

The practice of using British subjects as slaves in all but name caused uneasiness in some quarters. Generally, though, there was more approval than not. The elite viewed these miscreants of the lower classes as unredeemable, although Jeremy Bentham noted that transport to the colonies was an "experiment" that might very well result in some rehabilitation. Eric Williams observed that although African slavery already had a long history as a mainstay of the English economy, race was no barrier when it came to compulsory servitude (1984:101). Britain's own poor could serve as well. The elite in England—many of whom had strong interests in American and Caribbean plantations—felt little in common with the lower economic classes. This was especially so with regard to the dispossessed Irish, whom many considered little better than savages.

The promising solution of transport ran into problems in the late eighteenth century. Although England's urban population had continued to grow, Britain lost its thirteen North American colonies in the American Revolution. Canada offered no real answer. There were no large tobacco or sugar plantations there, and the fur trade did not call for much European labor. By the 1780s, however, the huge land mass of Australia—literally on the other side of the world—offered another possibility.

A few Dutch explorers had ventured to the Australian coast in the 1600s. Abel Tasman had sailed around the southeast point of the continent. The English buccaneer William Dampier had stopped on the west coast of Australia in the course of his adventures in 1699, departing with a decidedly negative opinion of the inhabitants he encountered.

Captain James Cook landed briefly on the southeastern coast of Australia in 1770 at a place that the English would later call Botany Bay. One of Cook's party, a naturalist named Sir Joseph Bank, collected a few samples of the flora and fauna including a small wallaby, whose pelt he took back to England for taxidermy. Cook soon sailed on to other waters, though, and few in England paid much attention to Australia's existence until the idea arose that it might offer a possible repository for convicts. In 1787 the Crown sent a fleet of ships to establish a penal colony. They arrived in January 1788.

English Incursions

The English outpost on the southeastern coast of Australia had rough going at first. The local food supply—or at least, that portion of it accessible to the English—was meager. Supplies dwindled before gardens could replenish them, and the British government seemed rather absentminded about sending more. That the convicts should suffer was to be expected. They were there, after all, for punishment. But the detachment of Royal Marines who guarded them and the handful of administrators began to starve as well.

Discipline was harsh, and the British state relied heavily on violence to maintain order in this remote outpost. Since the convicts already were prisoners, flogging was the main method of applying punishment. A few lashes with the "cat," a whip with knots tied at the ends of its several cords and stiffened in seawater, laid flesh open to the bone. A dozen strokes could be fatal. For relatively minor infractions, the marines, who were subject to eighteenth-century military discipline, suffered punishments as severe as those the convicts had to endure.

The new colony's administration paid little attention to the indigenous occupants of the region. These local inhabitants approached from time to time in small numbers to view the bizarre arrivals and to engage in brief attempts to communicate, but for the most part they soon left to go on about their business. As the colony eventually became better established, local officials concluded that the inhabitants were essentially harmless and largely irrelevant to the business at hand. Indigenous peoples had no apparent resources that would interest the colony, and there was little need for their labor; the convicts supplied that. And because it was a penal colony, there was no particular incentive to encompass more territory for the time being.

This situation would change before many years had passed, but in the early phases British authorities had all they could do to keep order among their prisoners. They had no wish to provoke trouble with the local populace, which could only have complicated their task for no useful reason.

The British did, however, use indigenous people to track down the occasional escaped convict. The local people, with their intimate knowledge of the land, had little difficulty in leading detachments of marines to convicts who had fled blindly into the vast interior with no knowledge of where they were going. This role as convict hunters, and the obvious freedom with which the indigenous people could come and go, nurtured a long-standing animosity that would trouble Australia's history for many generations.

The Indigenous Population

At the time of the British arrival, Australia probably had a population of at least 300,000 people—comparable to Canada's, with a somewhat smaller land area. More recent estimates have revised that figure upward, however, to 750,000 (Mulvaney and White 1987:115–117) or even a million (Butlin 1983). Scholars estimate that they comprised about seven hundred distinct groups who spoke about as many languages and dialects (Berndt and Berndt 1992).

Much of the continent, west of the mountain chain running along the east coast, was a vast dry region of desert and scattered grassland. Northern areas toward the Equator had a moist tropical climate where temperatures often exceeded 100 degrees Fahrenheit. The southern coast was temperate, and on rare occasions the temperature could fall to zero Fahrenheit.

People had lived on this continent for at least forty thousand years with little outside contact except for brief encounters in the north, with peoples of the Malaysian Archipelago and islands off southern New Guinea (see Swain 1993). None of them practiced agriculture, although in richer areas some, such as the Tiwi, had relatively settled communities (Goodale 1971, Hart and Pilling 1960). But their ancient adaptations had led them to develop complex systems of relationship to the land and its resources that were fundamental bases of their social organization as well.

For many, social identity, in addition to the bonds of marriage and descent, derived from the spiritual essence people shared with the supernatural beings associated with sacred sites and features of the country. The intimacy of the inhabitants' relations to the land far exceeded European concepts of property ownership. They rested on a sense of intensely personal resonances with the focal points of a sacred landscape where the activities of ancestral beings—timeless, in being both ancient and immediate—transcended European concepts of past and present. Rather than defining land as the property of particular persons or groups, many of them perceived of humans as an aspect of the land—or more properly, of the entire multidimensional reality of the place, including its water and air (see Goodale 1982).

The implications of this view were not only that particular individuals had ties to specific areas. It also, in many cases, involved cross-cutting linkages through which an individual had bonds with various sites by different criteria—the place at which a spirit entered the mother's body at conception, the place where birth occurred, the place where the father's people lived, and so on (see Tonkinson 1991, Goodale 1971, Hiatt 1989, Myers 1986, Rumsey 1989).

This array of linkages meant that no two individuals would be likely to have identical ties (see Burridge 1973:133, Munn 1973). Each would share one or more in common with many others in a network of bonds that extended throughout a region (see, e.g., Myers 1986). The dynamics that tied people to the land also linked individuals. Tonkinson and others have referred to this as the "estate," meaning the "heartland of a local group and the locus of its members' attachment to territory" (1991:195). He contrasts this with a group's range, "the area over which a band normally hunts and gathers in the course of its yearly travels" (1991:196; see also Stanner 1965).

In most areas, the social order restrained people from entering territory in which they had no connection to sacred sites. Far worse, desecration of sites could lead to violence. But even though the various constellations of spiritual ties would bind local groups to particular regions, intermarriage and the cross-cutting nature of these relationships ensured that boundaries were permeable. It was not a matter of exclusive territorial ownership, but responsibility for the land's well-being. Sacred sites rather than lineal boundaries were the focal points (Berndt and Berndt 1992:40, Tonkinson 1991, Swain 1993).

Over thousands of years, this view of human relationships to land had accommodated a sustainable harvest of natural foods and maintained an intimate knowledge of them. One aspect of this adaptation—particularly in such sparse areas as the great interior desert—was the movement of small populations over large areas to take advantage of fluctuating seasonal opportunities. This mode of living that was developed over many centuries made it difficult for people to mount concentrated defense against the new experience of persistent foreign encroachment (see, e.g., Altman 1987, Hamilton 1980, Meggitt 1962, Stanner 1965, Turner 1980).

The intricate identification of people with various localities coordinated an effective population dispersal over a broad resource base, but it also militated against a sense of broad, common interests among indigenous populations. Although the idea of spiritual identities linked to the land created regional affiliations, it also connoted profound differentiation beyond the sphere of those linkages. As Ronald and Catherine Berndt have noted, the kin ties and the shared spiritual essence that they involved defined the realm of interaction, which normally encompassed all known individuals. Beyond this range, there were few mutually understood ground rules (Berndt and Berndt 1992:68).

When faced with the encroachment of outsiders in their territories, most of these groups were perfectly capable of responding with force (see, e.g., Warner 1937). Rarely, however, did this involve the mobilization of numbers beyond small, local populations.

The Beginnings of the Australian State

In the first few years after the penal colony of New South Wales's inception, the essential dynamic was not only the growing number of transported prisoners but the growing number whose terms had ended. Freed convicts began to form a sizable component of the colony's population. In many respects, they began to constitute a major interest group. There was also a significant number of government functionaries and their families, from the governor on down. Most of these placed themselves in an entirely different social category from the convict population, whether the convict status was current or former.

As the colony expanded, a small number of displaced indigenous peoples also became a part of this cosmopolitan population (see, e.g., Elkin 1951). These included people who visited the towns occasionally but spent most of their time in the countryside on their own business, although a few became persistent local characters begging for food, tobacco, and money. Some of them became an annoyance to colonial town dwellers, prompting irritable letters to the local press by the early nineteenth century.

Expansion into Tasmania

With an increasing immigrant population, the colony extended southward. Another penal colony opened in Van Diemen's Land, later renamed Tasmania, and more confrontations occurred between indigenous peoples and the colonists. The English were concerned about French ships in the area and considered it wise to establish a presence on the southeast point of land. The French threat turned out to be a false alarm, but there were still a few United States ships in the vicinity. English settlement of the "unclaimed lands" seemed a prudent course of action.

In 1803 the first English force—a small combined expedition of free settlers and convicts—ventured along the coast of Van Diemen's Land but found the inhabitants of the north coast of the island to be rather unfriendly. The expedition continued south to set up an outpost on the southern tip, where the indigenous population seemed more congenial—possibly because they had less knowledge of the strangers with whom they were dealing.

As in the earlier days of the penal colony at Sydney, the post on Van Diemen's Land was hard-pressed for food. The settlers found that the island had a plentiful kangaroo population, though, and their primary subsistence activities turned to hunting rather than farming. The settlers had none of the indigenous people's regard for the local ecology, however. While the game had remained plentiful after tens of thousands of years of indigenous hunting, the settlers soon depleted the local regions. Hunger forced them farther inland, and by this time habit had made them loath to farm. More and more, they came into confrontations with the indigenous population.

The quest for food had persuaded the administrators of the settlement to allow convicts to use guns—a policy much at variance with practice on the mainland. The settlers themselves were not predisposed to establish congenial relationships with the indigenous people, whom they despised as savages. This attitude and the many guns in their hands led to tragic consequences.

Before long the English population of Van Diemen's Land was engaged in a campaign to eliminate the indigenous people (see Bonwick 1970, Turnbull 1974). They were

> ... shot like kangaroos and poisoned like dogs, ravaged by European diseases and addictions, hunted by laymen and pestered by missionaries, "brought in" from their ancestral territories to languish in camps. It took less than seventy-five years of white settlement to wipe out most of the people who had occupied Tasmania for some thirty thousand years. (Hughes 1986:120)

Tasmania represents an extreme case, in the sense that the entire population of an island died as a result of genocide. But by the time this had gotten well under way in Van Diemen's Land, similar processes were developing elsewhere on the mainland.

Settlers

Like the United States and Canada, Australia is a settler society—a state in which the predominant population arises from immigrants and the indigenous population has become a displaced minority (see Denoon 1983). "The settler society reached its apogee in the period preceding the First World War, between 1906–1914" (Alexander 1989:51). Australian history involved the extension of frontier settlement from the early years of the penal colonies through the mid-twentieth century.

Most freed convicts were in no position to return to England, nor would most of them have found a welcome if they did. Some, to be sure, had been unjustly taken from their families and longed to return to them. But many others had cut their ties to their homeland, and they ventured inland to seek their fortunes. Some prospected for gold. Some established farms and tried to raise sheep and cattle. Many of these activities brought them into confrontations with the people who already inhabited the land and who felt intimately connected with it.

In many cases, indigenous populations at first tolerated the presence of settlers in their territories. In general, they were prepared to give them the benefit of a doubt, particularly when settlers were willing to exchange gifts and engage in other modes of friendly interaction. For most indigenous people, marriage was a complex relationship involving linkages among members of appropriate categories of kin, but short-term sexual exchange was a common means of establishing human bonds. Since European women constituted a minority of the convict population—albeit a sizable one—many settlers were happy to engage in sexual liaisons with indigenous women. The meaning they placed on this relationship, however, certainly differed from that of their hosts.

In some cases, too, settlers had periodic need for labor. For those near the coast with well-established stations, convict labor was available until the end of the 1840s. Farther in the interior, though, many settlers sought indigenous people to help them in their operations.

Usually this involved offering food or other small items for short-term work. Indigenous groups would stay a short time and then leave to resume their normal subsistence activities in other parts of their territory, returning later in the year for another brief visit. These "walkabouts" for "bush tucker" became an established pattern in the relationships between indigenous peoples and settlers. It allowed station managers to tap cheap labor when they needed it without having to worry about sustaining the labor force. They could let the people worry about their own survival.

The situation was not entirely stable, though. As the number of settlers increased, they took over more and more land. Contact with settlers introduced new diseases to indigenous peoples. When ranchers became dependent on indigenous laborers, some used coercion to bring them in. Livestock drove out the game, and in some cases, settlers intentionally killed off the game to make way for their stock. When indigenous groups took livestock to eat in lieu of wild animals, ranchers retaliated with "punitive expeditions" that sometimes resulted in the

slaughter of entire camps. As Deborah Bird Rose puts it, "The first settlers established a political economy of terror" (1991:24).

State Hegemony and the Frontier

Indigenous groups retaliated, sometimes spearing an individual stock-
man and, more rarely, confronting settlers in larger numbers. The situation developed into an arena in which the control of the state was
minimal, and violence was endemic (see Reynolds 1982).

The history of the colony fed this violence. Most of the settlers shared
a long-standing animosity toward indigenous peoples who had enjoyed
the freedom that was beyond their reach as convicts and who had worked
for the authorities to track them down. But the disdain for the local
populations ran deeper, drawing on the racism that would trouble Australia throughout its history.

The elite were not necessarily more sympathetic to indigenous
peoples—nor, for that matter, did they have much more regard for
the freed convicts. Most of those in positions of power at the time were
English expatriates who had never been convicts themselves and felt
little in common with those who had. The class distinctions the population brought with them from England became more extreme in
Australia (see Hughes 1986). As time went on, these distinctions became overlain with a dichotomy between the self-consciously urbane
dwellers of the colonial cities and the shirt-sleeved stockmen of the
Outback.

But the government was in no position to exert much control over
the interior even if officials had tried. In the early nineteenth century,
the small European population of freed convicts and their convict workers in the hinterland were not limited to the roles of prospectors and
stock raisers. Police, militia members, and the other agents to enforce
the laws of the state were little different from the settlers and mostly in
sympathy with them.

The few who were not had reason to fear for their safety. The reminiscences of one traveler in the Northern Territory early in this century
reveal the social pressures that helped perpetuate the violence.

> The Lads, being young and new to the North, were secretly a
> little upset over this state of affairs, but it seemed that one
> could easily make themselves unpopular by remonstrating
> against the prevailing customs. . . . nobody was expected to have
> any feelings but contempt for the niggers. (Quoted in Rose
> 1991:22)

The wishes of the colonial elite who shaped government policy in Sydney amounted to a faint voice in the interior regions. By the 1830s, though, escalating violence forced the state to direct its attention to the issue. It had long been an assumption that the indigenous peoples of Australia would soon disappear (see, e.g., Stevens 1972:111, Reynolds 1987:109–123). We have seen that the same Social Darwinist perspective predominated at about the same period in Mexico, the United States, and Canada. The Australian version involved the assumption that no real Aboriginal policy was necessary because the problem could only be temporary. Some even feared that programs to assist indigenous peoples would only put off the inevitable and prolong the problem. But it soon became apparent that the situation, whether temporary or not, had become disruptive.

If a state is to exist in the balancing of competitive interests, it must maintain some degree of internal order. Barring the resort to oppressive rule, which might not be feasible, it must maintain a semblance of justice that does not drastically contradict the ideology of fair treatment of its constituents. By the 1830s, violence between settlers and indigenous peoples had become disorderly enough to come to the attention of the British Parliament.

Concerns for Order

In the 1820s, George Augustus Robinson had traveled among indigenous groups unarmed and found them willing to discuss the issues peacefully (Rowley 1970:47). In 1830, however, the settlers of Tasmania carried out a "Black drive," establishing a line of dogs and men who moved from one end of the island to the other in an attempt to eliminate the indigenous people once and for all. Most of the Tasmanians somehow managed to elude this drive, although it was only a temporary reprieve. The last indigenous Tasmanian, an elderly woman, died well before the end of the nineteenth century, not too long after the death of the last Beothuk in Newfoundland.

In the southern section of New South Wales, which would become the Colony of Victoria in 1851, between two and three thousand indigenous peoples died from 1835 to 1839. The Battle of Pinjara in the Western Desert took more lives in 1835 (Berndt and Berndt 1992:505).

In 1838 a group of settlers at Myall Creek in New South Wales accused a local indigenous group of stealing livestock and stampeding cattle, causing the animals to lose weight. The accused people had long been associated with the station and had maintained friendly relationships with the settlers. Settlers forced the people, including women and children, into a corral and murdered them. In an apparent effort to destroy the evidence, they chopped the bodies into pieces and burned them. In another instance, settlers found a group of indigenous people

> upon the Orara camped in great numbers. A cordon was formed during the night, hemming the camp in with the river behind it. At a given signal at daybreak men, women and children were shot down indiscriminately. Some took to the river, and were shot as they swam. Their dead bodies subsequently floated down past the settlement. (Quoted in Rowley 1970:113)

Such incidents are reminiscent of those that occurred in the American West at about the same time. General Crook's slaughter of a group of Apache trapped in a rock shelter at Salt Rock Cave in 1871 seems especially comparable to the Orara incident (see Perry 1993:104). In the United States, however, it was government troops as well as settlers who carried out many of the atrocities.

Indigenous peoples tried to resist as best they could, but their numbers, their decreasing sources of food, and the settlers' weaponry imposed serious disadvantages. In 1843, however, a large group of indigenous people drove settlers from a station near the Mooney River. Indigenous raiders, in various instances, speared stockmen and drove off cattle and sheep. Some acquired guns and carried out guerrilla warfare on vulnerable stations and settlements. The settler press depicted indigenous peoples as rapacious savages terrorizing the countryside and called for drastic measures.

Explanation of indigenous reactions hardly required the assumption of an implacable savage nature, though. The game that they depended on for food became critically scarce in many regions. Settlers shot kangaroos as pests, and cattle fouled the waterholes game needed to survive. Settlers also left poisoned food for local groups to find, just as their counterparts did in the U.S. Southwest.

In many places, indigenous peoples had no choice, eventually, but to come to terms with the invaders (see, e.g., Broome 1982). Although they resisted as long as they could, eventually the level of violence made the retention of their autonomy impossible.

The Extension of Law

As the increasing violence became difficult for the public to ignore, revulsion and political embarrassment stirred the government to take some action. It became apparent to many that the remedy for lawlessness in the rural areas was to extend the authority of the legal system throughout the colonial realm.

In the 1830s, a Crown commission on the state of aboriginal peoples in all of the British colonies painted a stark picture of injustice. Parliament in 1837 received a report on the situation of indigenous peoples in its colonies in South Africa, North America, and Australia that emphasized the rights of indigenous peoples to their own soil.

The British Parliament had ruled in 1836 that the indigenous peoples of Australia were Crown subjects entitled to the protection of British law. Governor George Bourke declared that the killing of Aboriginals demanded legal inquiries (see Armitage 1995:189). As one result of this policy, the alleged perpetrators of a massacre at a place called Port Fairy came to trial.

As it happened, though, justice still was far from certain. When the judge began to summarize the case of three men tried for this "punitive expedition":

> The foreman of the jury informed him that they would not trouble His Honor to read over the notice of evidence, as they had made up their minds to the verdict the jury then returned a verdict of Not Guilty against each of the prisoners, which was received with applause from a very numerous audience.
> (Portland Messenger–Normanby Advertiser 23 August 1843; quoted in Reece 1974:192)

The similarity of the Port Fairy trial to the one that followed the Camp Grant massacre in Arizona, which would occur almost forty years later, is striking. A similar verdict followed the Myall Creek massacre, although a second trial led to the hanging of four of the twelve defendants.

The settler press did its utmost to portray indigenous peoples as irredeemable savages who threatened the lives of decent folk. Settlers in 1830 compiled a list of outrages that indigenous groups supposedly had committed against peaceful settlers. Citizens of Arizona submitted a similar affidavit to their government regarding the Apache in 1871 (Arizona Territorial Legislature 1871). Among other misdeeds, Australian settlers accused the indigenous peoples of cannibalism—a tale that rested largely on the aspersions enemy groups leveled at one another, if not on settlers' overheated imaginations.

The Myall Creek trial became a divisive issue between those who felt that the slaughter of helpless people was not appropriate to a civilized society and those who felt that the perpetrators had performed a public service. Some politicians began to consider the idea of reserved areas for indigenous peoples to put an end to the confrontations. This had little support among the settlers and their allies, however. The *Sydney Herald* editorialized in 1838 that indigenous people's "ownership, their right, was nothing more than the Emu or the Kangaroo" (Reece 1974:170). We might recall Canadian Lands Commissioner Trutch's late comment drawing a similar analogy to "a panther or a bear" (Dickason 1992:261).

Governor George Gipps approved a plan for reserves in 1848. Gipps's attempts to calm matters were not entirely successful, however. From the perspective of indigenous peoples, relocation away from their lands was not a solution. But many Australians objected even to this accommodation.

> A governor who saw him [the Aboriginal] as having something of his own to contribute, or as entitled to use his land in his own way, might just as well have abdicated his main responsibilities, among which Aboriginal rights were hardly in the first order of priority. Even the effort to establish and protect minimum rights to life itself could lead, as Gipps learned, to hysterical enmity from settlers. (Rowley 1970:123)

Determining Indigenous Status

The government's policies often coincided with settlers' views regarding the appropriate treatment of indigenous peoples. Until the 1840s, indigenous peoples could not give testimony in court. The reasoning was that as non-Christians, they could not take a valid oath (Little 1972:81). Whatever the logical intricacies of this reasoning, in its net result it was reminiscent of the Georgia legislation aimed at Native Americans in the early nineteenth century. A further argument that some Australians voiced in the early 1800s was that since accused indigenous persons could not participate in their own trials, they should be punished summarily (Reece 1974:108).

As various interest groups had their effects on policy in Australia and England, contradictory postures continued to develop. As in Canada, the United States, and Mexico, some of the most palpable tensions arose between the need to incorporate indigenous peoples into the state and the desire to exclude them from any significant participation. To incorporate them as individuals would permit the appropriation of their lands. To allow them too much participation within the state, however, could empower them to resist those appropriations.

One strategy was to impose state power by making the indigenous group leadership responsible to the government. Governor Lachlan Maquarie, second governor of the colony, tried to co-opt indigenous leaders by giving them brass plates as badges of government authority "to create an Aboriginal political hierarchy responsible for the behavior of their race" (Reece 1974:47).

In Mexico the Spanish had propped up indigenous *caciques* for much the same purpose. In the United States and Canada during the same era, the English also appointed indigenous leaders. The Spanish had more success, since they were dealing with societies that to one degree or another were hierarchical to begin with. To most Australian peoples, however, the idea of "chiefs" made little sense.

Through the 1940s, however, some pastoral stations bestowed crescent-shaped brass plates on Aboriginal men they designated "kings" (Trigger 1992:51). These people supposedly were responsible for keeping the workforce in line, and to the local people they often represented station authority. In some cases, they operated as brokers or mediators between the two, although there are also instances of such individuals apparently abusing their power (Trigger 1992:52).

Development of the Australian State

The extension and consolidation of the Australian state in some ways paralleled Canada's, since it involved the eventual unification of several distinct and mutually independent British colonies. After the founding of New South Wales in 1788, Western Australia became another colony with an economy based on convict labor in 1829. South Australia was established in 1836 on the same basis. Transport of convicts to New South Wales ended in 1840 but continued in the west.

In 1851 the British Parliament passed an Act for the Better Government of Her Majesty's Australian Colonies, creating the new Colony of Victoria from the Port Phillip District of New South Wales. The Moreton Bay District became the Colony of Queensland in 1859. By that time, all of the colonies had their own legislatures comprised of a combination of elected and appointed members.

By the late nineteenth century, support grew for a more independent status for the continent, and in 1901 Britain passed the Commonwealth of Australia Act as a basis for the federation of Australian states. Many interests saw an advantage in greater solidarity among the states, both as a means of easing trade barriers among them and of suppressing the demands of labor for better conditions (Head 1989:276).

Although the transition to independence was more peaceful in Australia than in Mexico or the United States, the dynamics arising among

Indian Ocean

Darwin

NORTHERN
TERRITORY

Coral Sea

QUEENSLAND

WESTERN
AUSTRALIA

SOUTH
AUSTRALIA

Perth

NEW SOUTH
WALES

Indian Ocean

Canberra

Sydney

VICTORIA

Melbourne

TASMANIA

Australia with Aboriginal Reserves

Hobart

dominant interests in Australia seem reminiscent of Mexico, in particular. "The debate on the Constitution was conducted mainly by 'men of property' or bourgeois politicians concerned to entrench the influence of political and economic elites in their own colonies" (Head 1989:279). There was strong sentiment to retain a close relationship with Britain, however. "The maintenance of close ties with 'British civilization' helped to exclude Aboriginals and other non-Europeans from the conception of Australian citizenship" (Head 1989:276).

Many factors contributed to this desire for their exclusion. Immigrant labor from Asia and the Pacific Islands had aroused some concerns, and Australia's history as a settler society (see Denoon 1983) gave these sentiments a particular character. Among the dominant sectors of the Australian population in the nineteenth century, a division arose between those who identified strongly with Britain and those who envisioned a new social order on the United States model. "Both groups, however, were obsessed by fantasies of racial superiority promoted by Social Darwinism" (Alexander 1989:50).

In the succeeding decades, political parties traded places in office, but the transition of power was peaceful compared to Mexico. As in Canada and the United States, the dominant interests that alternated in the seat of government had much in common. Other constituencies whose interests conflicted radically with those of the elites had little access to positions of power. Throughout most of this period, the individual states in Australia, unlike those in Mexico or the United States or the provinces of Canada, remained autonomous with regard to policies and legislation dealing with indigenous peoples, who were not citizens. As we shall see, it was only in the late twentieth century that the federal government took on greater responsibility for the fortunes of Aboriginal populations.

Early Positions on Land Rights

The legal rationale for the British position on Aboriginals required some dexterous logical exercises. The Crown had never forcibly seized Australia by conquest, nor had it acquired the territory through purchase or treaty. Britain had simply treated the continent as if it were uninhabited terrain, despite the obvious presence of human beings (Frost 1981). "Colonization was thus seen as a process of settlement, not invasion. This remained the accepted view of the course of Aboriginal-white contact until the 1960s" (Garton 1989:195).

As in other colonies, the Crown applied the principle that ownership of land required modifying it or "subduing it" through labor. If such ownership did exist, according to British legal tenets, it would manifest itself in such aspects of common law as the right to exclude others from that property, and so on. In a later court case, a lack of evidence to show the rigorous exclusion of others from territory demonstrated a lack of indigenous ownership (Williams 1986).

If one accepted the criterion of cultivation as a prerequisite for ownership, the principle was somewhat easier to apply in Australia than in North America, where many indigenous groups had cultivated the land extensively, in some cases for well over a thousand years. In Australia all indigenous peoples relied on wild foods. Techniques of game management, such as periodic burning of grasslands, did not qualify in the British view as an equivalent to yeoman farming. Nor, as a judge in Arnhem Land ruled in the 1970s, did the complex indigenous social rules regulating land use, access, and responsibility amount to ownership in a fashion that English law would accommodate (Williams 1986).

The indigenous peoples of Australia, it seemed, were simply there. Not having disappeared as expected, and clearly human beings despite the aspersions of some settlers, they became a problem the government could no longer ignore. They lived within territory that Britain claimed, but they were not citizens of the state. But neither were they immigrant foreigners. The only obvious solution was to dub them British subjects by decree, which therefore rendered them deserving of the protection of the Crown. That "protection" offered a rationale for special measures and restrictions that did not apply to other subjects who qualified as full citizens. Indigenous peoples, after all, were not even counted in the national census until the late 1960s. These protective measures included attempts to manipulate them under the rubric of education programs and other initiatives.

In the late 1830s, the colonial government in Australia issued a manifesto reminiscent of the North American Royal Proclamation of 1763. There were to be no new territories. No one could purchase land from the Natives without permission of Her Majesty's Executive, nor could other parties make treaties with them. In 1835 settlers had negotiated with an indigenous group to persuade them to accept payment for a large block of land, a transaction that tested this principle. The courts ruled that the agreement, known as "Batman's Treaty," was illegal and had no standing (Williams 1986:127).

Government Oversight

The Australian government took a paternalistic turn in urging the "utmost indulgence" for indigenous people who violated British law—perhaps a tacit acknowledgment that the state had imposed this legal system without their acquiescence or in some cases, for that matter, without their knowledge. By the same token, it encouraged indigenous groups to turn over offenders among them for British justice. This was an interesting feature, considering that until the 1940s indigenous people in rural areas who found themselves in custody generally had to walk to jail in a neck brace and chain alongside a mounted officer. Legal authorities' treatment of indigenous people has continued to be a serious problem up the present (see Eggleston 1975, Tobin 1992). The government in the 1990s found it advisable to appoint a commission to look into the issue of Aboriginal deaths in custody (see Coombs 1994).

As in Canada and the United States at various periods, the law forbade the sale of liquor to indigenous people. It restricted labor contracts to twelve-month terms with the intent of limiting some of the most egregious abuses. It also called on missionaries to work among indigenous populations to bring about social and moral improvement.

Even if these policies conflicted with the views of Australian citizens, they reflect a position of the British state that as an aspect of its hegemony over the region in question, it had responsibilities to the Aboriginal inhabitants. To ignore them totally, in effect, would face the state with the unacceptable alternatives of being unjust by permitting disorder or of allowing indigenous peoples de facto independence. To maintain stability, the British state could afford neither of these options.

A clear alternative was to incorporate indigenous peoples as subjects under the protection of the Crown without allowing them to pose a serious threat to more powerful constituencies. This required balancing many contradictory factors. As a result, the gap between benevolent rhetoric and political expedience was often extremely wide, and the role of indigenous peoples within the state remained problematic.

Canada had indigenous populations that could enter into profitable trade and offer leverage against competing European states. The United States had indigenous peoples who could become a surplus pool of labor after other interests took their lands. Mexico had a huge indigenous population whose labor and lands constituted resources for centuries. But Australia merely had a small population of indigenous people who refused to die out, no matter how gently anyone smoothed the dying pillow. Their use as labor was marginal except in a few regions. They had no valuable furs or other commodities to trade. Once settlers had pushed them out of the rich areas, their remaining land, sparsely inhabited, was vast and arid. There was no need to cultivate them as allies against competing nations. The greatest threat they posed, in fact, was to the conscience of the state. For many decades, this was very slight, but it was enough to rankle.

Since they would not disappear of their own volition, and settler advocacy of genocide was neither palatable nor feasible, the alternative strategy, as in other states, was to nullify them by converting them into undifferentiated citizens of the Australian state. Assimilationist programs, led by missionaries there as in the other states, got under way in earnest in the late nineteenth century.

Assimilation Programs

The entrenched racism of many of the Australian citizenry posed a problem. Indigenous peoples, whatever their acquaintance with English custom, looked very different from Europeans. These physical features constituted a criterion that even the most miserable convicts could summon as a basis for claiming their own superiority.

It had not been in the interests of penal authorities to pay much attention to animosity between convicts and indigenous people. Any collusion among them, unlikely as that was, would have been a problem for the authorities. And there is no doubt that the elite shared many of the same attitudes toward indigenous inhabitants that the convicts did. Racism served the interests of various constituencies in many ways.

But it also posed a barrier to full assimilation. Some felt that it would be enough to Christianize indigenous peoples and persuade them to live peacefully as farmers and menial laborers in their own separate communities. But the long intermingling of settlers with indigenous populations, however hostile it often was, had also produced another result. In many areas, there were growing populations of mixed parentage.

"The pastoral frontier was male-dominated. Hartwig gives the ratio of one white woman to ten white men in the last quarter of the [nineteenth] century" (Bell 1993:65). There was much ambivalence surrounding this situation. Dr. C. E. Cook, medical officer-in-chief in the Northern Territory from 1927 to 1938, "feared the emergence of a coloured group outnumbering the whites, which if living in depressed conditions, would be 'revolutionary' in outlook" and which would present an "incalculable future menace to purity of race in Tropical Australia" (quoted in Stevens 1972:117).

The offspring of settlers and indigenous women often lived as full members of indigenous societies. In many cases, though, they had been raised without becoming fully immersed in the social order of either their indigenous mothers or their settler fathers (which was by far the most frequent parental combination). Indigenous women who cohabited with settlers often became separated from their people for long periods. Yet it was a rare settler who would treat his mixed children as he would his full heirs. Many of these children became socially marginal, far from their ancestral lands, and settled near towns where the citizens viewed them with misgivings.

A few assimilation strategies, though, focused most intensely on these populations. In 1837 the Report of the British Parliament's Select Commission had noted that reaching children offered the best hope of changing Aboriginal populations (Armitage 1995:204). In keeping with the classic model of biological racism, some theorists argued that children with some "white blood" would be more capable of learning European ways. The "full bloods," many assumed, were beyond help. All investment in education and training would be more wisely spent on those with mixed background.

This became associated with another idea—that this population mixture could eventually result in the disappearance of indigenous populations. As in the other states, it had become clear that genocide was costly, messy, disruptive, and usually failed anyway. Theorists still assumed that indigenous populations who remained intact would eventually die out, but they were taking their own sweet time to do it. It would be possible to hasten the process along, some argued, by encouraging the admixture of settlers and indigenous people, gradually absorbing the latter into the general mass of lower classes.

One government official saw this policy as a means of achieving the "ultimate absorption."

> To achieve this end, we must have charge of the children at the age of six years; it is useless to wait till they are twelve or thirteen years of age. In western Australia we have the power under the act to take any child from its mother at any age of its life, no matter whether the mother is legally married or not. (Quoted in Armitage 1995:44)

This offers still another interesting contrast with the ways in which other states have dealt with the process of admixture. *Mestizos* in Mexico came to predominate in the population, despite the elite *criollos'* adamant construction of their own social distinctness and their retention of power within the state. Métis in Canada became a recognized population in their own right, albeit a minority, whom the state eventually relegated to a status comparable to other indigenous groups. In the United States, people of mixed indigenous and European parentage formed no highly visible "mixed" group, but generally either merged into indigenous communities or into the general "non-Indian" population. Mixtures with other populations complicated the U.S. situation further.

In Australia, the United States, and Canada, the concept of "blood quantum" became significant. It is interesting to note that in the United States the legal definition of "Indian" for most groups is often one-eighth "Indian blood" or even less. A single indigenous great-grandparent could qualify one to be "Indian" in the eyes of the government. One European and seven indigenous great-grandparents generally would not, however, suffice to classify a person as "white." United States society tended to reinforce boundaries rather than obliterate them, and passage between social categories was far easier in one direction than in the other.

The strategy of promoting admixture between populations in Australia might seem anomalous, considering the construction of social boundaries there and in other British-derived states. The difference, perhaps, was in the relationship among interest groups in Australia. Although

English class distinctions had tended to wane in the United States, they became still more acute in the Australian penal colonies, where the convict and ex-convict population occupied a social realm far from that of the elites.

The most powerful interest groups in Australia tended to see the settler population as only slightly higher in status than the indigenous people and at a vast social distance from themselves. The fact that the origins of most convicts were English was less important than the fact that they were "criminal types" of the lowest classes. Irish convicts were even more marginal. From the view of the ruling elite, the mixture of these lowest classes with indigenous people offered the possibility of creating a large, docile class of laborers and food producers who would be more educable and tractable than either "full blood" Aboriginals or obstreperous freed convicts.

This idea did not sit well universally, however. For many, the barriers of race were too significant to encourage such liaisons. E. W. P. Chinnery, the first director of Native Affairs, strongly opposed such "familiarities" and favored strict segregation policies (Stevens 1972:117). The social elites, although they held a great deal of power, were outnumbered by the lower and middle classes who did not share their views on such issues. From 1790 to 1860, in fact, the population of Australia grew from 2,056 to 1,145,585, and the bulk of the increase was a result of free immigration. This had some democratizing effect on the politics of the Australian state, at least among the European-derived population. Freed convicts and their offspring, aspiring to the middle class, saw far more difference between themselves and indigenous peoples than their "social superiors" did. It seems quite likely that this did much to foster popular racism as a distancing mechanism.

The fact remained, however, that the population of mixed parentage had become a part of Australian life. They seemed even less likely than the remaining indigenous peoples to disappear very soon. These individuals continued to receive special attention in assimilation programs well into the twentieth century, and generally this attention was rather forceful. "Welfare personnel removed children from homes they deemed unsuitable, and placed them in 'good' white homes. Part-Aboriginal children were forcibly removed from their parents and placed in institutions or with 'good' white families" (Bell 1993:292).

Mission Stations

Many Aboriginal populations, forced off their lands by settlers and increasingly by such industrial enterprises as mining, had little choice but to gather near mission stations, where the staff exercised stern supervision of their lives. Many in government viewed Church organizations as especially suited to bringing about civilization among indigenous peoples, and it was all to the good that they were less expensive than government agencies would have been (Armitage 1995:35).

For many indigenous groups, the effect of missions was disastrous. Alienated from their lands, Aboriginals were no longer able to carry out initiation rituals that gave young men the knowledge and authority to guide the people as elders. The missionaries, in any case, actively discouraged such customs and prohibited them when possible.

While many early missionaries seem to have had reasonably good relationships with the people, the subsequent mode of interaction came to be more authoritarian. "Particular aspects of such control were the routinization of Aboriginal daily life, the institutionalization of children and young adults in dormitories, and the opposition to significant parts of Aboriginal tradition" (Trigger 1992:293; see also Swain and Rose 1988). E. A. Wells also comments that "Aboriginals being regarded as indispensable in Australian frontier conditions and even on mission stations, the racist attitude governs what it is permissible for them to possess by way of a possible educational adaptation" (1972:245).

Children growing up around mission stations also were less likely to learn the practical skills they needed for survival in the old ways. Many groups attempted to maintain their seasonal subsistence rounds and left the missions periodically for walkabouts, but often they suffered harassment and restrictions on their movements.

Relocated indigenous peoples were no longer in their own territories, and customary restrictions on entering the lands of others hampered them in their movements. Many people suffered nutritional deficiencies from the interference in their food-getting activities and the inadequacy of the mission station diets. Diseases made matters worse. Remaining in one place created hygiene problems they had not encountered as mobile hunters and foragers. Crowded living conditions increased the likelihood of contagion.

In many groups, the birth rate—both in terms of conception and live births—fell drastically, and infant mortality rose. This was not a cause of universal concern among most of the Australian citizenry, however. To some extent, it seemed to confirm the assumptions that these people were unable to survive in the modern world. As the bishop of Adelaide had declared to the legislature in 1860, "I would rather they die Christians than drag out a miserable existence as heathens" (SAPP 1860 no. 65—Report of the Select Committee of the Legislative Council on the Aborigines; quoted in Rowley 1970:104–105).

Pastoral Stations

If life in mission stations was harsh, the situation of indigenous groups on cattle and sheep stations could be worse. In the north, particularly, as stock operations pushed people from their lands and cattle replaced game, many had no choice but to offer their labor for subsistence. Displacement of indigenous people in the northern part of the continent was often violent. One Aboriginal man at Victoria River Downs recalled:

> Old people got shot. Why? By land. Just stealing the land. The white man been coming here stealing the land from blackfellows. Just from land. Wasting blackfellows, shooting blackfellows from land. "Don't worry about blackfellows. [We] want to finish [them] off for this country." (Quoted in Rose 1991:21)

The reminiscences of one G. W. Broughton who came north early in the twentieth century seem to agree.

> Native life was held cheap, and a freemasonry of silence among the white men, including often the bush police, helped keep it that way. . . . if the wild blacks got in the way, or in other words speared men and killed or harassed cattle, they would be relentlessly shot down. It was as simple and brutal as that. (Quoted in Rose 1991:21)

As Deborah Bird Rose puts it, "There were few choices. In the early years, people worked for Europeans, or resisted. Those who resisted, or were simply in the way, were shot, beaten to death, poisoned" (1991:46).

The "extension of civilization" into the northwest involved not only punitive expeditions but also the calculated murder of apparently "cooperative" indigenous groups. Another Aboriginal man in the 1980s recalled a time when he was a child at a place called Pigeon Hole and a cook at one of the stations offered some food to an Aboriginal work crew.

> He made a big stew for those boys, in the big oven. And he put a strychnine. And that's why they called it Poison Creek. That's the place. Fancy putting strychnine in the big oven, for the boys [who] were working. Poor buggers, eh? (Quoted in Rose 1991:45)

Rose summarizes the early years of European settlement in Victoria succinctly.

> Europeans bought and sold human beings; children were captured and raised as household adjuncts; women were captured, raped, and used to track their relations; . . . Aboriginal people were treated like game to be hunted, like vermin to be

exterminated, as slaves of sexual and murderous violence. (1991:47)

After at least one massacre of Aboriginal people, perpetrators collected the skulls and other bones of some individuals. A few of these found their way to museums as scientific specimens. At least one skull, however, became a spittoon (Rose 1991:31).

In the Northern Territory, the 1911 census counted seventeen hundred "whites" in the area (Powell 1988:62). Recent explorations had determined that the area was better suited to cattle raising than had previously been thought. A third of the land was under pastoral leases and permits before World War II (Berndt and Berndt 1987:5). The promotion of a pastoral economy began well before that, however, and involved some competition between pastoral and mining interests.

The government favored the extension of pastoral enterprises, although mining would grow to be an important industry in the area. Although a "grotesque jumble of land laws . . . had given the advantage to the speculator over the genuine settler" (Powell 1988:62), there was little legal concern for the land rights of the indigenous inhabitants.

When small operations had a rough go of it, the Labor government planned a meat-freezing operation at Darwin to boost the industry:

> Its Liberal successors preferred private enterprise and commissioned a British-based transnational group, Vestey, which spent almost £1 million on the big meatworks. Moving quickly, Vestey's consolidated its hold by acquiring Wave Hill Station (6,000 square miles, 15,500 sq. km); by 1916 it controlled almost 28,000 square miles (over 72,000 sq. km) in the Territory and 8,400 square miles (c. 21,750 sq. km) in Western Australia's Kimberlys. (Powell 1988:63)

Vestey was at one time a subsidiary of Hooker, the chemical corporation that earned fame in North America in the 1970s by releasing cyanide into the Niagara River. Vestey's and the British firm Bovril became the major pastoral interests in the region.

Stock enterprises ignored indigenous territories, but the importance of indigenous labor for stock work grew in the north during this period despite the common complaints that Aboriginal labor was unreliable. "The whole population of Aboriginals within the domain of the stations was transformed into a working class and the original war between Aboriginals and settlers has continued within the framework of class conflict" (Avery 1983:62). Stock stations depended almost entirely on indigenous labor—generally people who had lost possession of their lands. Stock managers made it difficult, if not impossible, for indigenous workers to seek better terms at other stations, using police unofficially to arrest and bring back people who had left their "home" stations. In some cases, stockowners captured indigenous people from distant areas and brought them to work at their stations, knowing that the Aboriginals would be afraid to travel through the lands of other groups to return home.

Stations often paid indigenous workers in food rather than wages. The food often consisted of entrails from slaughtered cattle (see Rose 1991:206). Living conditions were dismal. Sewage polluted drinking water. Although stock managers tended to refer to indigenous men of any age as "boys," many did prefer to use young boys, apparently because they considered them more tractable and easier to train. These conditions persisted in many areas well past the 1940s (Berndt and Berndt 1987). Colonial labor practices persisted in Queensland and the Northern Territory until the late 1960s (Trigger 1992:44) and perhaps later. A letter from one Northern Territory schoolteacher to the *Katherine Times* in 1987 offers a more recent glimpse:

> Where I live, within the Katherine region, Aboriginal workers have their meals dished out to them on tin plates to eat outside whilst workers of European origin serve themselves on crockery and eat inside. Only two weeks ago Aboriginal people had to buy a raffle ticket in aid of a whites only institution as a condition of cashing their cheques. (Quoted in Rose 1991:246)

Indigenous workers did not compete with white Australians for employment. Few, if any, nonindigenous people would have been willing to labor under such conditions for payment that often consisted of offal from slaughtered cattle. More desirable jobs usually were not available to indigenous workers. The dairy industry was off limits to them, since by the early twentieth century, popular racist concepts had fostered the idea that they were too "dirty" to work with milk (Morris 1989:45)—an interesting case of symbolic connotations associated with "black" and "white."

Despite high mortality and low birth rates, indigenous peoples continued to offer a self-reproducing, cheap labor force. The apparent decline in numbers under station conditions, however, did cause concern among cattle companies in the 1930s. We can detect some of the ambivalence, if we can call it that, in the comments of one H. V. Miller in his letter to a newspaper in 1927.

The Northern Territory Aborigines are the Territory's biggest problem. They are a menace in many ways. They are gradually dying out. They might be better away, but at present they cannot be done without. (Quoted in Rose 1991:299)

Vestey's requested a government research team to find ways of alleviating this threat to the industry (Berndt and Berndt 1987). The stock industry's concern for the Aboriginal population decline was a case of one elite interest group experiencing a concern that other elites, who had little use for Aboriginal labor, did not necessarily share.

Managers often found that employing indigenous workers on the basis of task completion rather than time spent was the most efficient, since it required less supervision and minimal record keeping. On the other hand, on many cattle and mission stations, the administrators maintained an authoritarian regime. The state reinforced this pattern with the establishment of the Aboriginal Protection Board in the early twentieth century.

The Aboriginal Protection Board

The Aboriginal Protection Act provided for more official supervision of the lives of indigenous groups—what Barry Morris calls "bureaucratic custodianship" (1989:105). Station managers had the power to enter indigenous dwellings at any time without warning. Officials removed children—especially "half castes"—and sent them to rigidly run schools. Matrons inspected indigenous homes twice a week to ensure that they were tidy. Managers also tried to undermine whatever group solidarity might exist in these aggregates, even to the extent of interfering with gatherings around campfires where people shared food.

Some indigenous people fled the stations to escape the oppressive life that prevailed there. The removal of children was especially onerous. The schools established for such children removed them from the influence of their elders and, as in Canada and the United States, rigidly segregated the children by sex. By the 1930s, many Aboriginal leaders were vigorously protesting the board's policies, referring to it as the "Aboriginal Persecution Board" (Morris 1989:116).

The Aboriginal Protection Board (APB) had emphasized paternalistic supervision over a dying race who were presumed to be incompetent to run their own affairs. "Protectors of the Aborigines" in various states had wide-ranging powers over indigenous peoples, including such things as the power to designate where they could live, to control employment by permit, to approve marriages, to make local regulations, and to manage reserves and lands. Perhaps one of the most chilling powers, however, was legal guardianship of all Aboriginal children, which superseded that of their parents (Armitage 1995:35). The removal of as many as 40 percent of their children during the height of this era contributed greatly to the impression that Aboriginal communities were disappearing (Armitage 1995:40, 189).

Like comparable bureaucracies in the United States and Canada, the APB pursued the idea of molding indigenous peoples into a more acceptable identity, and they assumed that this could occur most easily on an individual basis. The ideological link between hard labor and character building was an old one, particularly when the elite applied it to those who were less powerful. In the 1930s, the APB adopted a policy of issuing certificates of "progress." Though this did not go quite as far as the Canadian policies of enfranchisement, it exempted some individuals from the restrictions of the Aboriginal Protection Act.

Yet acceptable progress had its limits. Earlier in the 1880s, the APB had established small, scattered reserves to facilitate the supervision of indigenous groups, and in the interest of promoting their progress, the APB had encouraged them to establish small farms. As it happened, some of them did so and were quite successful. In 1925, though, "the islands that [indigenous] farmers had transformed from bush into profitable farm land in the 1880s were handed over to the Lands Department to be sold off" (Morris 1989:119). Apparently such individual successes were not to be carried too far.

The posture of the state during these decades went through interesting transformations (Morris 1989). In the early nineteenth century, a prevailing intellectual view of Aboriginals was that they had been geographically and historically disadvantaged. The corollary was that with proper exposure to civilization, many could become productive members of the state—albeit in the lower echelons.

Most assumed that this effort must focus on the young and those of mixed parentage, since the older "full bloods" were too committed to old ways. Prevailing ideas held that group segregation and supervision were appropriate. Indigenous collectivities, as such, were not acceptable as active constituencies of the state. The reserves would function as expedient repositories in which the elders could die away, but qualified young individuals would be better off away from these settings.

This led to many tragic and widespread consequences. We might look again at the figures indicating that during the period when authorities implemented this policy most aggressively, the government or its agents in Australia (and in Canada) essentially kidnapped up to four hundred per one thousand indigenous children (Armitage 1995:189). Rose indicates that this may have involved forty thousand children in New South Wales alone (1991:170). The simple comments of a police officer at Wave Hill in 1950 suggests the nightmarish quality of such policies.

> Despite my efforts to assuage the fears of both mothers and children, the final attempt at separation was accompanied by such heart-rending scenes that I officially refused to continue to obey such future instructions. (Quoted in Armitage 1995:59)

Whatever the shortcomings of this policy, these assimilation measures did not necessarily rest on assumptions of inherent biological inferiority, although it did not rule them out. Concomitant perspectives, though, grew through the late nineteenth and early twentieth centuries, when many intellectuals embraced a popular version of "scientific racism." As in other states, notions of biological inferiority implied a fundamental deficiency on the part of indigenous peoples. As this view became more predominant, assimilation policies lost some ground to an emphasis on stricter segregation.

At the same time, an increase in effective indigenous resistance apparently led the state to exert more oppressive measures. In keeping with its focus on individual rather than group efforts, by the 1930s the APB was keeping detailed records on individuals it considered troublemakers. Indigenous protests eventually did have some effect, though, and the legislature finally abolished the Aboriginal Protection Board in 1940. In its place, a more centralized agency assumed responsibility for overseeing indigenous affairs and served to curtail some of the autonomous power that local managers and protectors held over indigenous communities.

In the 1940s, perhaps in reaction to the horrifying consequences of racist philosophy in Nazi Germany, government policies retreated from overt segregation. Bureaucratic emphasis swung toward the idea of development through education. Liberal intellectuals disavowed racism, though for the most part they were still unwilling to entertain the possibility that indigenous cultures and forms of social organization were viable and valid in their own right.

The emphasis on dealing with individuals rather than groups, and policies to compel change on that basis, continued. Under the Social Services Act of 1959, "An Aboriginal native of Australia who follows a way of life that is, in the opinion of the Director-General, nomadic or primitive is not entitled to a pension, allowance, endowment, or benefit under this Act" (quoted in Armitage 1995:24). The alternative to racism, in that view, was the ideal of individual equality. Aboriginal peoples as individuals should be invited and encouraged to take their place one day as full Australian citizens. But such a view was not compatible with the retention of distinct indigenous group identity.

Mining Interests

Mining enterprises became more predominant at midcentury in the Northern Territory and Western Australia, although gold prospecting already had a long history in Australia. In the Northern Territory, mining interests had been excluded from Aboriginal reserves until 1950 (Altman 1983). Bauxite deposits were discovered there in 1949, however, and pressure grew to open the reserves to mining "for the national interest."

The concern for opening these resources for exploitation coincided with the growth of a greater concern for assimilation. In 1951 the First Native Welfare Conference in Canberra had a decidedly assimilationist emphasis (Altman 1983). By 1952 the Northern Territory Department of Mines and Native Affairs (whose title suggests a certain juxtaposition, if not conflict, of interests) conferred with the Commonwealth Department of Territories about the negotiation of mineral royalties with indigenous peoples. The issue of mineral rights in Australia differed somewhat from the situation in the United States or Canada, since the Crown had long assumed rights to subsurface resources (Libby 1989).

Like pastoral operations, mining created still another arena in which indigenous people confronted a range of competing interests. Non-indigenous people in local towns often saw mining as a potential source of jobs and income. Mining interests tended to portray indigenous peoples as obstacles to progress and prosperity. Although the perceptions of local benefits to accrue from mining were exaggerated, H. C. Coombs notes that "they add to the public conviction that only Aboriginal recalcitrance stands in the way of El Dorado" (1994:51).

As it turned out, according to one study of mining effects on local prosperity, "the only significant benefit to that economy came from the expenditure by Aboriginals and their organizations of the money paid to them by mining companies under the terms of the Commonwealth land rights legislation" (Coombs 1994:105). The mining corporation's profits, on the other hand, flowed out of the region and to a great extent out of the country to the profit of transnational firms and stockholders.

Mining has had deleterious effects on the environment as well. Although the state has supposedly overseen such operations, as in so many other cases, the corporate interests have exerted considerable influence. "It is apparent that environmental and related concerns have been overridden in government and private sector zeal to fast-track the process (a euphemism for ignoring all considerations other than those raised by the mining company)" (Coombs 1994:112).

Changes in Indigenous Strategies

The decades of the mid-twentieth century not only affected indigenous peoples' circumstances but saw the development of new responses on their part. The physical resistance of the earlier nineteenth century had not been particularly successful for them, although some of the more moderate state policies developed where resistance was strongest (Rowley 1970:151). By 1900, however, indigenous peoples were vastly outnumbered. Australia's nonindigenous population had reached almost 4 million, while the original indigenous population of 300,000 had dropped precipitously.

In some regions such as the Western Desert, there were still some indigenous peoples who had been relatively undisturbed, having the advantage of living in lands for which other interests had little use. They accounted for a vast geographic area, but they constituted a minority of the total Aboriginal population. In most instances, however, it was only a matter of time before they too confronted intrusions. The Pitjandjatjara of the Western Desert saw few outsiders until the 1930s, when a mission appeared in their territory. They had ceased many of their former activities by the 1970s after the government relocated them because of atomic weapons testing (Wallace 1990:83). Soon they suffered from the same problems as Aboriginal communities elsewhere, including a high rate of alcohol abuse and violence among themselves (Wallace 1990). They had, in effect, begun manifesting many of the symptoms of social breakdown, poverty, and oppression that had long afflicted reservations and reserves in the United States and Canada.

Many groups had lost possession of their lands far earlier, and in some cases the populations of reserves and stations consisted of aggregate communities with people from various localities. This was one consequence of state policies that favored the desires of outside interests to appropriate indigenous lands. The problems in these communities underscored the importance of indigenous social organization in providing security and regulating behavior—a casualty of the state's emphasis on individual rather than group identity.

In many instances, gathering people from different indigenous groups exacerbated their material deprivation with social problems. In some cases, though, it also gave rise to a different political consciousness that transcended the older group affiliations. Just as in Mexico, where the collection of displaced indigenous people in common villages generated a broader sense of common "Indian" issues, some displaced people in Australia came to perceive problems they shared with other "Aboriginals."

One result was the establishment of the Australian Aboriginal Progressive Association, which organized protests over government policies. Its base was in New South Wales, but its focus was pan-Aboriginal. Ironically, it seems, the state had succeeded in obliterating the boundaries of indigenous local group identity only to foster a larger sense of indigenous common interest, rather than the dispersion of individuals into the general populace.

It is ironic too, perhaps, that in expressing Aboriginal interests, the organization appealed to the government's own stated ideals regarding equal rights rather than stressing the maintenance of indigenous patterns as such. Equal rights and freedoms would, of course, have important implications for the maintenance of distinctive indigenous ways of life. But in this arena, it may well have been more effective for the organization to point out some of the contradictions between the rhetoric of state ideology and its own practices (Morris 1989:120–121). It seems to be a strategy of using "the politics of embarrassment."

Various other forms of activism developed during the century, some involving strikes and walk-outs in the pastoral areas (see, e.g., Wilson 1980, Rose 1991:225–236). Aboriginal groups in the 1960s also adopted strategies such as "freedom rides" that had played a prominent role in the U.S. civil rights movement. It may be significant that these efforts involved significant numbers of non-Aboriginal Australians in support.

Assimilation through "Equality"

At the same time, though, many aspects of Australian state policies of the 1960s paralleled the termination efforts in the United States a decade earlier. Many officials, still embracing an assimilationist position, held that reserves had failed and should be abolished. Pointing to continued poverty and social problems in reserve communities, they argued that government programs to assist indigenous peoples had kept the people from standing on their own. The Australian rhetoric anticipated Canadian Prime Minister Trudeau's White Paper of 1969, taking the position that legal differentiation of groups within a democratic state was unacceptable. It also paralleled the Mulroney government's Nielsen report blaming social assistance for social problems.

In 1967 a government official stated that "in due course all Aboriginal reserves should disappear" (Morris 1989:168). A proposal to bring that about failed in the legislature. At the same time, 87 percent of voters in a general referendum favored the incorporation of Aboriginals into the national census.

It is worth noting that the proposal for inclusion did poorly in rural areas. The 150-year-old urban/settler distinction had not, apparently, faded entirely. One might also draw parallels with the United States and Canada, where policies toward indigenous populations in the western states and provinces, which had more recent settler histories, continue to be less sympathetic than in the East, where the "frontier" situation has faded more deeply into the past.

The 1967 referendum appears to have represented a popular sentiment favoring Aboriginal inclusion as an alternative to the racial separatism of the past, but we could also regard it as an expression of opposition to sovereign status. Although this shift to inclusion rather than marginalization as an ideal had much in its favor, in some respects the shift was merely a matter of placing a more benign face on an old position. As in Canada, the United States, and Mexico, the philosophy of equality under the law converted easily into an argument against special or distinct status for indigenous peoples within the state. In its extreme version, it would eliminate indigenous populations as interest groups altogether.

Understandably, indigenous peoples in all four states have viewed this approach with deep misgivings. For many, the demand for equal rights included the right to autonomy, to the redress of unjust resource appropriations, and to the freedom to maintain the way of life of their own choosing, not homogenization into the national populace.

Popularizing Aboriginality

The government's political concerns with indigenous peoples in the 1960s involved an interesting ideological development in Australian national culture as well. Symbols of Aboriginal culture became popular. As the media and schools promoted respect for indigenous peoples as the "First Australians," the icon of Aboriginal culture was relegated to the hushed, remote aura of museum displays—held at a distance, but at the same time incorporated into the ideological property of the state. Aboriginal culture became a part of "Australia's heritage." Generalized portrayals of indigenous culture washed over local and regional distinctions. Aboriginal artifacts became commodities in a market in which indigenous peoples had little involvement (see also Myers 1994).

Just as in the United States, where the Plains feathered headdress became a generic symbol of the "First Americans," or in Mexico, where symbols of Aztec grandeur decorate government buildings, the Australian state co-opted the didgeridoo and the boomerang as distinctive symbols of the state almost on a par with Quantas Airlines' koala bear. Considering the situations of indigenous peoples in all three states, these developments in some respects are more evocative of trophy collections than evidence of shared national pride.

In the United States, the process went farther, with numerous nonindigenous peoples building sweat lodges and commoditizing sacred ceremonies to exploit the search of a gullible public for a taste of "Indian spirituality." In Australia guided tours and school field trips to Aboriginal demonstration sites increased in popularity. At the same time, the Australian public has grappled with its own historic relationship with indigenous peoples. Australia has sought political and economic relationships with many former colonies. "To speak of Australia as a settler society in this context is to draw attention to our history as a frontier of European imperialism, to emphasize Europeans' displacement of indigenous peoples and their appropriation of global resources to feed Europe's industrialization" (Alexander 1989:50).

Such Australian films as *Backwoods* and *Where the Green Ants Dream* have dealt with the situation of indigenous peoples and attempted to come to grips with the issue of racial relationships. "Many of these have been produced by a troubled white liberal conscience and they tend to see racism as phenomenal and inexplicable rather than being linked to power relations such as class and gender" (Moran 1989:190).

Indigenous peoples have resisted the development of culture-as-commodity as a ransacking and lampooning of their customs, but in some cases the process has accompanied a resurgence of indigenous practices that had lapsed. The new public appreciation for things indigenous, however selective and naive it has been, has made the active repression of indigenous identity less politically acceptable than it was in the past. In 1985 the Dhan-Gadi of New South Wales held an initiation for the first time in half a century (Morris 1989).

The Move toward Self-Determination

The political shift in Australia, as in Canada after the White Paper and the United States in the 1970s, has been toward more indigenous "self-determination." The appearance of this phrase in government discussions, however, did not mean a cessation of attempts to draw indigenous populations into the state through dissolution of their societies. The establishment of Aboriginal voting rights in all states by 1965, and the 1967 referendum to include them in the national census, were not moves toward acknowledging their special status but were moves further incorporating them into the state.

The election of local indigenous councils was one example of this. As in the United States and Canada, elected councils resonated well with the state's governance structure, although such councils were generally at variance with existing modes of governance in indigenous communities. The councils were articulated to the government in ways that local elders,who were responsible only to their own people and lands, were not.

In 1967 the federal Labor government under Harold Holt took on concurrent responsibility for Aboriginal affairs with the states. Prime Minister Holt introduced the Constitution Alteration (Aboriginals) Bill, stating that its purpose was

> . . . the removal of the existing restriction on the power of
> the Commonwealth to make special laws for the people of the
> Aboriginal race in any State if the Parliament considers it
> necessary. As the Constitution stands at present, the Common-
> wealth has no power, except in the Territories, to legislate with
> respect to people of the Aboriginal race as such. (Quoted in
> Morse 1984:23. Parl. of the C. of Aus., Two Years later . . . Report
> by the Senate Standing Committee on Constitutional and
> Legal Affairs on the Feasibility of a Compact or "Makarrata"
> Between the Commonwealth and Aboriginal People. Canberra
> 1983, art. 81)

The bill passed by a wide margin.

The Labor government under Gough Whitlam came into office in 1972 and adopted self-determination as a policy. The intent of the phrase "self-determination" was "assertively non-colonial" (Palmer 1990:165). The phrase rankled conservatives, however, since it suggested an unacceptable degree of autonomy that could strengthen demands for special status. "Self-management," which replaced the earlier term, implied keeping indigenous peoples cozily within the Australian state while allowing for some responsibility for their local affairs.

Up to this time, the autonomy of the Australian states had resulted in significant variation in Aboriginal policies, though few of these were favorable to indigenous people. Like Canada, Australia consisted of formerly distinct British colonies that had long traditions of relative autonomy from any central government, including their policies toward Aboriginal peoples (see, e.g., Doobov 1972).

As a result of Holt's bill, indigenous affairs became involved in the wider issue of centralized versus federalized distribution of power within

Australia. From the perspective of indigenous peoples, one aspect of federal involvement was the possibility of achieving some relief from the intensity of conflicts with local interests in the smaller arenas of the individual states and territories.

The issue of indigenous land rights received national attention in 1971, when the Yolngu in Arnhem Land pressed a land claim against the Nabalco corporation. Widely known as the Yirkalla Case (*Milirrpum v. Nabalco Pty*, supra), the suit failed because the court did not accept indigenous ownership of the land in question. The presiding judge of the Northern Territory Supreme Court ruled that the Yolngu did not have recognizable proprietary interest in the land because they had no recognizable form of government (Williams 1986:112).

The implications of federal involvement came to the forefront when the Whitlam government commissioned an inquiry into Aboriginal land rights in Northern Territory, partly in reaction to the case. In 1972 the prime minister had stated, "We will legislate to give Aborigines land rights—not just because their case is beyond argument, but because all of us Australians are diminished while the Aborigines are denied their rightful place in this nation" (quoted in Morse 1984:39).

The Labor government created a Department of Aboriginal Affairs in 1972 with a minister in charge and a National Aboriginal Consultation Council as an advisory body with forty-one elected Aboriginal members. In 1976 this disbanded, and a smaller, weaker National Aboriginal Conference (NAC) took its place (Weaver 1993:56). Its thirty-five members were elected in 1977, but after suffering credibility problems for several years, the NAC disbanded in 1985.

The House of Representatives passed the Aboriginal Land Rights (Northern Territory) Act in 1976. The act defined indigenous land rights in a manner that attempted to accommodate indigenous principles to Australian law. Section 3 of that act defined Aboriginal owners as

> a local descent group of Aboriginals who (a) have common spiritual affiliations to a site on the land, being affiliations that place the group under a primary spiritual responsibility for that site and for the land; and (b) are entitled by Aboriginal tradition to forage as of right over that land. (Quoted in Williams 1989:204)

Aboriginal and Other Interests

Land claims proceeded more successfully after the early 1970s than they had in the past (see Maddock 1980, Neate 1989, Peterson and Langton 1983). Several states passed legislation defining and thereby acknowledging some degree of indigenous land rights. In 1966 South Australia had already begun to transfer mission and reserve lands to an Aboriginal Lands Trust that had full indigenous membership. The trust had the power, with the oversight of a nonvoting government official, to dispose of lands in order to benefit Aboriginal people. Many of its transactions have been to grant or sell individual landholdings in fee simple, however, rather than to designate them for collective use by indigenous groups.

Victoria, New South Wales, and Western Australia also created land trusts, although some critics have alleged that these trusts have been subjected to heavy government influence. One aspect of land grants and leases has also been to expand mining operations. Land rights have also been bogged down in procedure. "Under the guise of accountability, Aboriginal communities and groups have been flooded with bureaucratic procedures, intrusive inquiries and guidelines for viability, until the purposes of their initiatives have been denied and their autonomy undermined" (Coombs 1994:72).

The interplay between Aboriginal and other interests continues to evolve in a shifting arena. Ronald Libby, discussing the interplay between Aboriginal and mining interests in Western Australia, notes that when the Labor Party was relatively unified in supporting indigenous rights against mining interests, the mining corporations stood in firm opposition to the party. As various constituencies in Western Australia exerted pressure on the Labor Party to modify its stand on Aboriginal rights, however, party opinion split on the issue. When the Labor Party opinion split, mining interests quieted down and even lent some support to those Labor members whose views they found more congenial (Libby 1989).

One strategy the mining corporations used was to inflame racist propensities among the public through a media campaign. While we might well see this as a negative development, it does offer another example of coalition building to strengthen and expand the parameters of an interest group. Aboriginal peoples have also built coalitions with some success, although the diversity of indigenous populations has made concerted action difficult.

One interesting case was the Pitjandjatjara Land Council, which formed in 1971. It consisted of a range of different local groups "who were insistent that this jointly-based Council had no role in the domestic affairs of those separate peoples, but for this specific purpose. It existed solely for the purpose of negotiating a united basis for land rights and their development into a functioning system" (Coombs 1994:175). In the course of these developments, there has been a growing tendency for some indigenous peoples to return to their lands as they become accessible. It remains to be seen how extensive and significant this "homeland movement" may turn out to be.

Despite extensive attempts by recent Australian governments to reform and improve the situation of indigenous peoples, the goal of incorporating them into the state seems to have continued, regardless of shifts in public rhetoric or innovative phraseology. In 1987 Aboriginal Affairs Minister Gerry Hand expressed the goal of reaching the day when indigenous peoples "can take their rightful place as full and equal participants in the richness and diversity of this nation" (quoted in Tonkinson and Howard 1990:68).

As Tonkinson and Howard observe, "Rhetoric emphasizing the term 'Aboriginal nation' is . . . viewed as threatening the notion of a united, homogeneous Australia and as taking autonomy too far" (1990:69–70). The conservative position opposing indigenous special status resounds with a noble ring in the slogan "one land, one law."

The Labor government promised a "new deal" in 1989 and created the Aboriginal and Torres Strait Islander Commission (ATSIC) to take over many of the responsibilities of former government agencies. The substance of the government's position, though, appeared to have changed very little.

> If the language of assimilation actually concealed a discourse aimed at the "proletarianization" of Aborigines, the language of "self-determination" may be discovered as concealing a discourse aimed at drawing them inexorably into the corporate state— either directly by recruiting Aborigines *qua* Aborigines into the bureaucracy, or by means of a more indirect process, mainly by the creation of "Aboriginal" organizations which are required or demanded or are invited to participate in government decision-making. (Von Sturmer 1985:48; quoted in Tonkinson and Howard 1990:71)

A significant development occurred in 1992, however, which could prove to be a turning point in Aboriginal affairs. In what has become known as the Mabo Case, a group of Torres Straits Islanders brought suit against the federal government and the State of Queensland, claiming ownership of their lands. In its decision, the court essentially overruled the long-standing principle by which the British had denied indigenous land rights for centuries. "The High Court eliminated *terra nullius* from Australian common law and affirmed land titles based on traditional Aboriginal possession" (Tonkinson and Tonkinson 1993:35).

Essentially, the ruling abrogated the presumption that Australia had been unoccupied at the time of the British arrival. While this may seem to be a matter of formalizing the obvious, it had tremendous implications. Since the state must therefore recognize the prior existence of indigenous peoples, it follows that they had prior rights arising from their occupancy. The sense of the decision was that even though Crown's rights over the land remain valid, these do not preclude the continuance of Aboriginal rights.

The logic of this derived from the idea that the Crown preserves the rights of its subjects. As in several rulings of the Canadian courts, the concept was that title "was derived from the Crown and the Crown was committed to protect it" (Coombs 1994:202). This concept has a range of likely implications for future claims.

> At the same time, opposition is rising, particularly from conservative politicians, pastoralists, and mining companies, whose pronouncements often feature gross exaggeration and scaremongering. In the past, mining giants in particular have orchestrated highly effective and frequently racist campaigns against Aboriginal interests. Already, some media commentators have inflamed existing anti-Aboriginal sentiments. (Tonkinson and Tonkinson 1993:35)

Like Canada, the United States, and Mexico, the Australian state continues to balance indigenous interests with those of other constituencies. Will the recent tendency toward increased sovereignty and land restoration turn out to be a lasting shift, or is it one of the pendulum swings that eventually will reverse direction?

In the next chapter, we shall look briefly at several other states and consider whether the patterns we have seen in Australia, Canada, the United States, and Mexico appear elsewhere. The final chapter will explore some of the conclusions we might draw from these cases.

Comparisons

. . . .

III

Other States and Indigenous Peoples

· · · · · · · · ·

7

I was a hunted man. I remained in my country for
seven months, sleeping in different houses every night
or in the jungle. Any one of the people who gave me
shelter could have betrayed me, but no one did. This is
proof, I believe, of the effectiveness of the resistance in
East Timor.

(Constancio Pinto, Timorese activist; quoted in
Donovan 1993:4)

The indigenous populations of Australia, the United States, Canada, and Mexico offer extreme variations in indigenous culture and social organization. The purposes of European invasions also varied, ranging from gold to furs to agricultural land to dumping grounds for convicts. Cortés met armed resistance in Mexico. In Canada the French met people willing to trade. In Australia the British met people who viewed them with mild curiosity and left.

In North America and Australia, the sheer numbers of Europeans eventually overwhelmed the indigenous peoples. The ravages of disease and warfare exacerbated this disparity, and indigenous people came to constitute a tiny proportion of the population. In those three cases, the social boundaries between indigenous and nonindigenous people were sharp, and an ideology of racism reinforced them. In Mexico, with a much larger indigenous population to begin with, the number of Spanish who actually immigrated and settled was small. As late as 1570, half a century after the Conquest, people with indigenous ancestry outnumbered the Spanish-born population of Mexico by almost a hundred to one. The rigid hierarchy of the Spanish state allowed the few elite to impose their regime on the populace, but by the twentieth century the vast majority of Mexico's population still had at least some indigenous ancestry. Even though the percentage of those still categorized as *indios* had dwindled, indigenous people remained a far larger proportion of the population than in the other states. Racism played a significant role in Mexico, but the social boundaries between *indio* and *mestizo* were far more permeable than in the other cases, except in parts of Canada.

As we have seen, the four states are also similar in many ways. Prolonged contact led to more concerted indigenous resistance in all of them, although the form it took varied a great deal depending on the circumstances. Rarely did indigenous peoples see the situation initially in terms of European versus "Aboriginal," although pan-indigenous coalitions developed sooner or later in all of the states. People defined the situations within the framework of their own precepts, according to their own experiences, and in terms of the parameters of their perceived interest groups. Indigenous peoples at first defined their identities in local terms and reacted to the invasions situationally. Their responses reflected the diversity of local populations rather than some common identity that Europeans implied in categorizing them generically as *indios*, "Indians," or "Aborigines."

Where local animosities existed, indigenous groups sometimes welcomed European alliances to strengthen their own positions with regard to rival peoples. We can see this in the St. Lawrence River area, where the Huron and Algonkian were receptive to a French alliance against the Iroquois confederacy. We can also see it in Mexico, where indigenous people formed the bulk of Cortés's army in his campaign against the Aztec cities.

In areas where trading relationships extended among local groups, the participation of Europeans often was merely an additional element. In some cases, as in Australia, the mere presence of Europeans at first had little significance except as an anomaly in the normal course of events. In a well-ordered, intellectually coherent universe, strangers with no connection to the land or to the past had little relevance until they began to disrupt peoples' lives.

Only later—often much later—did this aspect of European thought begin to reflect political reality. Usually a sense of common purpose arising from having been the original inhabitants took some time to develop beyond local regions. Much of this amounted to a response to a shared experience of having to deal with the state. One might say that while the Gardujarra or the Dené had some prior social reality, the state created the "Aboriginal" and the "Indian."

Although we have seen some common patterns among the four states, the question remains whether these apply to all, to most, or, for that matter, to any other states. The four we have discussed up to this point have much history in common. It is difficult for that reason to determine whether the patterns we have noted here are characteristic of state systems in general or happen to be peculiar to those historic cases.

Even if we accept as a fundamental principle that interest groups compete within and between states, this does not necessarily predetermine what those interests might be. Perhaps we should not assume that the motivations of powerful constituencies are necessarily destructive to indigenous populations, however frequently they have been in the four examples. To explore these and other issues, we might glance briefly at a few other states with different histories and still other indigenous populations ranging from southern Africa to Siberia. We can begin with Indonesia, an expansionist state outside the European arena.

Indonesia

Indonesia acquired most of its holdings when the Netherlands, itself a colonizing state, granted it independence in 1949 after four years of war. The Dutch had occupied the island of Java in 1750 and continued to conquer the outer islands well into the twentieth century, establishing sovereignty over most of the area that later became Indonesian territory. As a result, Indonesia inherited jurisdiction over many indigenous peoples in the southeast Asian archipelago.

Indonesia incorporates a more diverse range of peoples than most states within a relatively restricted area. With 735,268 square miles of territory, its population in 1991 was an estimated 193 million, or about 262 people per square mile. Perhaps for this reason, the Indonesian state has followed an aggressive policy of political integration and often has used force to compel acquiescence among its indigenous peoples.

Many so-called Third World states, which themselves had experienced colonization, seem to repeat the actions of earlier European states in their own policies toward indigenous peoples.

> What is called "economic development" is the annexation at gun point of other people's economies. What is called "nation-building" is actually state expansion by [indigenous] *nation-destroying*. Territorial consolidation, national integration, the imperatives of population growth, and economic development are phrases used by Third World states to cover up the killing of indigenous nations and peoples. (Nietschmann 1989:192)

South China Sea

Sulu Sea

Pacific Ocean

MALAYA

SABAH

Celebes
Sea

SARAWAK

PAPUA
NEW
GUINEA

KALIMANTAN

SUMATRA

IRIAN
JAYA

Jakarta Java Sea

CELEBES

Banda Sea

JAVA

TIMOR

AUSTRALIA

Indian Ocean

Timor Sea

Indonesia

Many of Indonesia's policies of relocating populations and disrupting cultural patterns have had clear economic motives. Indigenous peoples have lost extensive lands to timber-cutting enterprises, for example.

Coercive programs to assimilate islanders and induce conformity with the predominant Javanese population have extended to suppression of local religious practices, forced relocation to centralized villages, and such apparently trivial issues as compulsory haircuts. As innocuous as hair styles may seem, we have seen in other states, such as New Spain and Puritan New England, that such cultural features have often been subject to attack as powerful symbols of distinct identity.

Indonesia's actions on the island of Timor have been drastic enough to arouse world outrage but little action. Indonesia seized the eastern half of Timor in 1975 with little objection from the Portuguese, who had granted East Timor self-government the week before. Since that time, the Indonesian military has waged a war of attrition against the Timorese people. As many as 200,000 Timorese—about a third of the population—died between 1975 and 1990 (Donovan 1993:4). Despite Indonesia's persistent assaults on the Timorese, the United Nations removed the Timor problem from its agenda in 1985. At the time, Indonesia held a seat on the U.N.'s Human Rights Committee.

The issue regained prominence in 1991, however, when the Indonesian military attacked a large Timorese funeral procession in the capital city of Dili in full view of a British television crew. In the aftermath of the Dili attack, the United States House of Representatives voted unanimously to cut off military aid to Indonesia. Most of the world's states, though, sat back once again when the Indonesian government agreed to appoint its own commission to investigate the incident.

Australia continued its military aid to Indonesia and retained a congenial relationship with its neighbor. An agreement known as the Timor Gap Treaty provides for joint oil ventures between the two states.

Indonesia's policies in Irian Jaya, the western section of the island of New Guinea, have also been aggressive. The Dutch in the nineteenth century had claimed the region and retained possession after Indonesian independence, but eventually they relinquished it when the Indonesian government exerted pressure by seizing Dutch property. The United Nations, after mediation, turned over the region to Indonesia in 1963 on condition that a plebiscite allow the local people to express their choice of national affiliation or independence.

Irian Jaya had an indigenous population of up to a million people, most of them living in villages and hamlets linked by ties of trade, ceremonial exchange, marriage, and intermittent small-scale conflicts. They subsisted on horticulture and pig raising with little hunting, although fish and other marine food sources were important in coastal areas. Their population consisted of hundreds of distinct societies and languages. They had no history of any large-scale overall political organization that united more than a few groups. Although they were capable of defending territory against encroachment by their neighbors, their spears, clubs, and arrows did not equip them to resist a force the size of the Indonesian military with its modern weapons.

The Irian Jaya plebiscite took place in 1969. Despite wide protest among the people, local leaders voted to remain a part of Indonesia. By all accounts, however, it was not a particularly free election. Of an estimated population of 800,000, 1,025 voted (Nietschmann 1988:197). An Indonesian army major put the matter simply when he announced to those about to vote, "I am drawing the line frankly and clearly. I say I will protect and guarantee the safety of everyone who is for Indonesia. I will shoot dead anyone who is against us—and all his followers" (TAPOL 1984:31; quoted in Nietschmann 1989:197).

Indonesian Brigadier General Ali Murtopo warned local representatives that Indonesia had made great sacrifices to acquire Irian Jaya,

and they would not therefore allow their national aspirations to be crossed by a handful of Papuans. Short shrift would be made of those who voted against Indonesia. Their accursed tongues would be torn out, their full mouths would be wrenched open.

Upon them would fall the vengeance . . . of the Indonesian people, among them General Murtopo who would himself shoot the people on the spot. (TAPOL 1984:31–32; quoted in Nietschmann 1988:198)

The Indonesian state has continued to rule Irian Jaya with a consistent philosophy, relocating East Timorese as settlers on indigenous lands and seizing territory for mineral exploitation. To cite one example of the ways in which the Indonesian state has dealt with resistance: "After Amungme in the southern Akimuga villages ejected two Indonesian policemen, the Indonesian military retaliated by strafing the area on the 22nd of July, 1977, from two Bronko OV-10s until they ran out of ammunition" (Hyndman 1988:286). The local people in that case retaliated by blowing up a copper slurry pipe. The Indonesian government responded with *Operasi Tumpas* ("Operation Annihilation"). "The Indonesian military destroyed Amungme gardens, burned down houses and churches, and tortured and killed men, women, and children. The OPM believes thousands of Me, Dani, and Amungme were killed in 1977, although Indonesia claims it was far less, only about 900" (Hyndman 1988:286).

Because of the authoritarian control of the area, recent information regarding the circumstances of the population is difficult to acquire. It seems that these events have not had much effect on public opinion in the rest of the world, however. In May 1995, an article in the Travel Section of the Sunday *New York Times* gushed excitedly over the improvements the Indonesians had made in Irian Jaya, describing it as a delightful place for tourists. The article noted that while Indonesians occupy most of the government positions and own most businesses, the indigenous Dani hold menial jobs. The author conveys a sense of thrill, however, at being able to walk across a bridge into the "Stone Age" (Howe 1995).

Papua New Guinea

Papua New Guinea, the eastern section of the island, also has a long history of colonial occupation. Britain claimed the southern region in 1884 and transferred jurisdiction to Australia in 1905. Germany claimed the northern half in 1884, but lost it to Australia in World War I. The League of Nations, and later the United Nations, granted Australia administrative authority over the area, which it exercised until Papua New Guinea became an independent nation in 1975.

Before independence, the colonial government's attempts to extend hegemony over eastern New Guinea were most intensive near the coast. Outsiders knew little about the interior until the 1930s, when the search for gold drew prospecting expeditions into the region. The first of these to penetrate the interior set out in 1929 (Connolly and Anderson 1987).

The Australian colonial government in New Guinea pursued a policy of ending intergroup warfare, enforcing pacification by establishing a monopoly on the use of violence. Patrols carried out punitive expeditions and, in many cases, summarily shot offenders.

The Australian administration recruited labor from indigenous populations by imposing a head tax payable in Australian currency. Penalties for failure to pay the tax involved jail time. For most indigenous people, the only way to obtain this currency was to enlist for plantation labor, often on distant islands. This policy depleted many local communities of young men, who spent years on plantations to pay their communities' taxes.

The Australian administration also appointed indigenous police to represent the authority of the state in remote areas. These were called *luluais* in the Mandated Territory and village constables in Papua to the south. The government also appointed *tultuls*, who were not necessarily people with local leadership status, and later, village councilors. Often candidates were those who appeared cooperative and could speak English or Pidgin and who therefore were sometimes marginal to the communities. By appointing indigenous officers from outside the community, the administration could also exploit preexisting social and political divisions among regional populations.

Resistance flared up sporadically, although after the ineffectiveness of armed revolt became apparent it often took the form of movements Europeans referred to as "cargo cults" or "millenarian movements." Typically, these were attempts by indigenous peoples to explain and exert some control over the colonial predicament and to offer hope of a new age (Burridge 1960, Worsley 1968, Lawrence 1964, Cochrane 1970). Among populations who believed that ancestors looked after the well-being of the living, such movements often promised the ancestors' assistance, and sometimes their return with wealth (hence, "cargo"), and the departure of the invaders in one way or another. In some cases, movements promised a reversal in the relative status and power between European and indigenous people. When these events failed to occur, most of these movements waned, although some adapted through time and became more distinctly secular and political.

The colonial period had important consequences for the population of Papua New Guinea. It did diminish intergroup fights for a time. It introduced material items and equipment, much of which indigenous peoples incorporated into their lives without radical change. It also led to the development of a lingua franca that involved a blending of several European and indigenous languages—Tok Pisin—which became one of the three official languages of Papua New Guinea. For all of that, however, Australian rule did little to unify the internally diverse population. To promote the political unity of millions of colonized people would not have been in the best interests of the administration.

With independence Papua New Guinea adopted a parliamentary system of government, but internal order remains a chronic problem. Some old animosities broke out in the 1970s between groups with long-standing grievances (see, e.g., Brown 1982). More recently, violent crime has become endemic, often involving criminals ("raskols") who are no longer closely associated with indigenous societies.

The end of formal colonialism in Papua New Guinea did not mean economic independence. In some ways, economic dominance may be as oppressive as outright violence—although the two are not mutually exclusive. It often amounts to the dominance of indigenous populations by outside interest groups through other means. As we have seen in all of the examples, though, violence tends to remain at least a potential factor.

Cash cropping of coffee, coconuts, and other commodities that began during the colonial era in Papua New Guinea place local producers at the mercy of world prices they cannot control. Timber cutting by transnational corporations has denuded many regions, causing local and regional ecological disasters. A logging company called Japan and New Guinea Timbers (JANT), for example, a subsidiary of the transnational corporation Honshu Paper, negotiated a contract with the Australian administration a few years before independence to cut on the north coast. Their operation led to local complaints regarding the loss of arable land and game, small royalty payments, and a general indifference to local concerns (De'Ath and Michalenko 1988). Peter King of the Sydney University Peace and Conflict Studies Centre stated in 1992, "It is PNG's politicians and bureaucrats who profit when foreign companies exploit PNG's forests for timber, whatever the impact on local communities and the ecology" (Robie 1992:7).

The same observations might apply to mining, a form of economic development that often has had troublesome consequences. In 1981 the government of Papua New Guinea entered an agreement with Amoco, BHP, and a German consortium to mine gold on the Ok Tedi River in the Central Highlands. The government's share was 20 percent.

In January 1984 a 50-million tonne, one-kilometre-long landslide on the Ok Ma [River] destroyed all prospects of a permanent tailings dam as a solution to pollution problems and threatened closure of the project. In June 1984 a barge overturned in the Fly River estuary, loosing 2700 sixty-litre drums of cyanide, and a bypass valve left open at the mine released 1000 cubic metres of highly concentrated cyanide waste into the Ok Tedi. (Hyndman 1988:290)

The river is now officially dead.

The Ok Tedi operation has produced great wealth for a few in the 1990s, although it is questionable whether most of the population has benefited. In the glow of its financial successes, OK Tedi Mining ran a full-page advertisement in the 1992 *Pacific Islands Monthly* supporting the Ninth South Pacific Games that year and proclaiming that the athletes' gold medals came from its operations. The ad noted that they were "Medals symbolizing OK Tedi's contributions to the promotion of sports, education, training, health, and overall economic development" (*Pacific Islands Monthly* 62[9]:12).

Australia, in its attempts to maintain profitable economic relationships in the Pacific region, has applied pressure on Papua New Guinea to maintain order and to assure the safety of investments. When protesters shut down a mining operation at gunpoint in the highlands, investors were disturbed. Australian Foreign Affairs Minister Senator Gareth Evans stated that "the recent, well-organized attack on the Mount Kare mine gives added urgency to the need for the PNG government to act on law and order" (Hlambohn and Cook 1992:89). To this end, Australia has given military support to the Papua New Guinea government, including four U.S.-made military helicopters (Hogan 1992).

The Papua New Guinea case represents a dilemma that confronts many former colonial states. Unlike Australia, Canada, and the United States, Papua New Guinea is not a settler society. No large invading population immigrated or remained there after independence. Papua New Guinea returned to the possession of its indigenous peoples, but many economic structures from the colonial era remain. These structures and institutions have continued to develop along their own trajectories, posing some new and many old problems for the population.

The resources of Papua New Guinea remain subject to appropriation by outside interests. The crises that have arisen as a result of drops in the world market prices for such products as copra and coffee, provoking scrambles to offer other commodities such as tropical hardwoods, underscore this economic vulnerability. Papua New Guinea is immersed in a global economy, and transnational corporations have replaced the colonial state in affecting and restricting the people's options.

Papua New Guinea is a state with great internal diversity but little history of attempts to expand and conquer colonies of its own. Perhaps this is partly because its internal problems continue to be a more acute concern and because it remains surrounded by more powerful neighbors. On the other hand, Papua New Guinea's behavior toward Bougainville indicates that this state, too, is capable of aggressive measures toward indigenous peoples. Despite its internal problems, Papua New Guinea may well be following patterns of other states we have examined.

The British occupied Bougainville in the Solomon Islands and traded it to Germany for German Samoa in the nineteenth century. In World War I, Australia captured Bougainville from Germany and held it until Papua New Guinea gained independence, whereupon Bougainville became a province of Papua New Guinea.

Bougainville, like most of the rest of the Solomon Islands, had been the home of several distinct societies organized on the basis of matrilineal kinship and sustaining themselves through horticulture and pig raising. Men rose to prominence through hard work, judicious marriages, skillful politicking, and success in war (a Melanesian pattern not unknown to European societies). Matrilineal clans owned the land corporately, and each person had access to garden plots by birthright and marriage (see Oliver 1955).

The Solomons had been subject to chronic onslaughts by outsiders. One of the most egregious phenomena was the practice of "blackbirding," capturing people to work on plantations on distant islands. Australian taxation later continued much the same tradition through other means. Until the early twentieth century, however, most of the Solomon Islands people remained in possession of their ancestral lands. For most of the population, clan rights to land and group integrity remained intact (see Keesing 1983).

In the 1970s, however, a company called Conzinc Riotinto of Australia (CRA) negotiated the rights to mine copper in the territory of one of these groups, the Nasioi. The negotiations were mainly with one man who, according to later accounts, had no authority to dispose of land rights—particularly since matrilineal clans held corporate rights to land (Robie 1989:14). Nonetheless, the mining operations went forward over local protests.

By 1985 the open pit Pangura mine and extension operations covered 1,210 hectares (1 hectare equals 2.471 acres). Waste rock dumps extended over 300 hectares. Deposits of mine tailings covered 3,000 hectares, and mine refuse polluted the nearby Kawerong and Jaba Rivers. At the point where these rivers flow into Princess Augusta Bay, the tailings formed a delta of 900 hectares (Robie 1989:16). "In its initial proposal, the company had argued that dumping the tailings into the river would cause broad-scale land loss. Later, however, it decided to dump the tailings in the Kawerong and Jaba Rivers after all because it was cheaper" (Robie 1989:16).

The Papua New Guinea government supported the mining operations in the province of Bougainville and in 1988 received 58 percent of the profits, 1 percent of which went to the displaced landowners—mostly Nasioi—who had lost most of their land base.

The mine employed about 1,000 Solomon Islanders and Bougainvilleans out of 3,550 workers. (The population of Bougainville in 1992 was about 140,000). By local accounts, the living conditions of workers were deplorable, and working conditions were dangerous. In 1988 rebels shut down the mine by dynamiting a power pylon.

Papua New Guinea sent troops to quash the revolt. The resistance, calling themselves the Bougainville Liberation Army, presented explicit terms. They demanded secession from Papua New Guinea, the closure of the Pangura mine, and 10 billion *kina* in compensation for land lost and the destruction of the environment (1.3 *kina* are roughly equivalent to a U.S. dollar).

Some observers in the ensuing months noted that a major basis for the revolt had been the corporation's failure to recognize the special Melanesian perspective toward the land. Some pointed out that the displaced landowners, like other Melanesians, held the land sacred and felt that their connection to it extended below the surface as well as to the space above.

We might wonder whether the Nasioi reaction represents a peculiarity of Melanesian thought, however. The idea of a connection between humans and the land that supports them seems far more common among indigenous peoples globally than does the industrial perspective, in which the land is an inanimate resource to plunder. In any case, allusion to some peculiar Melanesian worldview hardly seems necessary to account for Bougainvilleans' resentment at having the gaping chasm of an open pit mine where their land used to be, with little compensation.

In addition to sending troops, the Papua New Guinea government placed a bounty of 200,000 *kina* on the heads of the purported ringleaders. The Bougainville Liberation Army established an insurgent government in hiding, and the occupying Papua New Guinea army carried out guerrilla warfare against the rebels. The PNG government relocated local populations from "free fire" zones, declaring anyone remaining to be hostile and subject to attack. They closed off outside communication from Bougainville and used the helicopters they had acquired from Australia to carry out attacks.

The helicopters were U.S.-made Bell-212 ships, ironically named "Iroquois" (Hogan 1992:10). In the agreement to supply them, Australia had stipulated that the helicopters should not have guns mounted on them, but this did not prevent the PNG army from suspending automatic weapons from ropes inside the cabins and firing through the doorways.

The world community averted its gaze from the affair. At the Pacific Forum in Honiara in 1992, the delegates refused to hear representatives from Bougainville "on the grounds that it was an internal affair of PNG" (Williams 1992a:15). Later that year, Mike Forster, representing the International Work Group for Indigenous Affairs, told the United Nations that

> the PNG blockade had imposed two years of detention on the whole people of the island. "The people were being held for ransom because of their desire for self determination." He went on to accuse PNG forces of imprisonment and execution without trial and alleged the "care centres" were in fact concentration camps. (Williams 1992a:15)

The United Nations was not prepared to take action, however. As it happened, the chair of the Special Commission on Decolonization was Papua New Guinea's ambassador.

Australia and international conglomerates continued to play a prominent role in these affairs. CRA, the major Australian corporation involved in mining in Bougainville, Papua New Guinea, and elsewhere, is a subsidiary of Rio Tinto Zinc, a British-based firm that currently is the largest and most diversified mining transnational in the world. Rio Tinto Zinc has some fifty-two mines in forty different countries (Sharma 1992:13). As we have seen, states—or the prevailing interest groups that steer the policies of states—tend to be responsive to such global economic powers.

Perhaps it is not surprising that Papua New Guinea should behave as it does. When hundreds of diverse constituencies compete without any of them predominating, the people who occupy the government offices may well become a predominant interest group in their own right within the state. We have seen this in Mexico and, to some extent, within the United States. Such interest groups, particularly if their positions are precarious, make likely allies (or tools) for transnationals.

States such as Papua New Guinea have also been affected by a shift in power strategies that developed in the 1970s, when OPEC nations caused some concern among transnationals and industrialized states by raising oil prices. In 1975 delegates to the Conference for International Economic Co-operation in Paris urged policies that ultimately would weaken the economic independence—and hence the political sovereignty—of the Third World states of the Southern Hemisphere. The strategy involved the pressing of development loans on poorer states by such organizations as the World Bank and the International Monetary Fund (IMF).

The result was the creation of large foreign debts that in many cases crippled the abilities of these poorer states to address domestic needs. As in Mexico and elsewhere, the creditor status of the IMF and other agencies allowed them to impose austerity programs to enforce the payment of debt service.

Many Third World governments have acquiesced to the demands of development agencies in order to forestall economic disaster, while allowing social conditions to worsen and exacerbating the possibility of social unrest. At the same time, they felt the need to accept still more loans to improve their situation and imposed more stringent domestic measures to keep order among their own increasingly impoverished populations. The downward spiral of this process often made the need for faster development seem all the more desperate, even as its pursuit made matters worse.

Southern Africa

Africa offers many examples of state-indigenous interaction. The continent's complexities defy any general discussion in a book this size, but southern Africa invites some special attention. This is an area in which a widespread population known by several names—San, Basarwa, "Bushmen," or Ju/'hoansi—have lived for many centuries (see Lee 1984). There is some debate among scholars as to whether these people represent a hunting and gathering way of life that has existed virtually unchanged in the region for tens of thousands of years, or whether they arise from refugee populations whom other groups displaced from their lands. For the purposes of this discussion, however, their remote past is less significant than their more recent interactions with state systems.

The territory of these populations lies mostly within three states—Botswana, the Republic of South Africa, and Namibia. The Ju/'hoansi have exploited the Kalahari Desert region, which overlaps these state boundaries, for many generations—partly because they have had the skills to glean a living from the arid lands and partly because other peoples burdened with livestock or dependent on agriculture have had little reason to displace them from their dry habitat. The Ju/'hoansi have traded and worked for various peoples in the area, although for the most part

Namibia, Botswana, South Africa, Tanzania, and Kenya

they have been able to retain some degree of autonomy in their movements and activities in the desert until the past few decades.

Europeans beleaguered them in some of the richer areas from the eighteenth century, when settlers tried to use them as menial labor or displace them altogether. Although the Ju/'hoansi often were able to avoid the most abusive assaults, there were many "punitive expeditions," as in Australia and the United States, in which settlers massacred small camps of indigenous people. As a further Australian parallel, the Ju/'hoansi acquired a reputation as a menace to civilized society when they carried out retaliatory raids or stole cattle for food (see Gordon 1992).

By the 1950s and 1960s, the process of global politics had encroached more intensively into the region. As the racial policies of the Republic of South Africa grew still more extreme under the Verwoerd government, that state derived some advantage from the Cold War situation. The United States and other "Free World" powers, as they liked to call themselves, saw Botswana as a left-leaning nation and considered South Africa strategically important, in addition to its economic value as a source of gold, diamonds, and many other minerals.

Namibia, as a possession of the Republic of South Africa, was subject to that state's racial policies. Germany had claimed Namibia in 1890 and named it South-West Africa. South Africa seized it from Germany in World War I, and the League of Nations approved South Africa's mandate over the region in 1920. In 1966 the South-West Africa People's Organization (SWAPO) began a war of independence from South Africa, which it finally achieved in 1990 after a long guerrilla struggle.

South Africa's withdrawal from the British Commonwealth had left it a state ruled by a small population whose livelihood depended on the labor and suppression of millions of indigenous people. It shared a border with Botswana, whose population and governing elite were indigenous Africans.

Botswana had become the British protectorate of Bechuanaland in 1886. After independence in 1966, when it became Botswana, it had no large European settler population remaining as a major constituency. The Tswana, the predominant group in the state, had experienced intense missionizing and European influence. But they had also had a history of reciprocal relationships with the Ju/'hoansi people—not always necessarily cordial, but usually peaceful, nonetheless.

Namibia to the west, with its own diverse population of Ovambo, Kavango, Herero, Damara, and Ju/'hoansi, became more problematic for South Africa. Botswana had important trade relationships with South Africa, but its border with Namibia became more rigid. This created barriers to the movements of the scattered, mobile Ju/'hoansi peoples and inhibited their subsistence activities.

By the 1970s, Ju/'hoansi on the Namibia side under the hegemony of South Africa were living in small government-administered camps. Unable to carry out their hunting and foraging practices, they subsisted on meager government rations. Old methods of resolving and avoiding conflict, which often had merely involved moving to other areas, had become impracticable. Under conditions of nutritional deprivation and political oppression, the ethic of cooperation and sharing faltered. Social disruptions flared among the people. In effect, the South African government in Namibia relegated the Ju/'hoansi to small rural slums that developed many of the social problems common to such aggregates elsewhere.

The South African state used Namibia as a corridor for raids into Angola in its campaign against SWAPO, carrying out military recruitment in the Ju/'hoansi camps and drawing the people into wider conflict. Angola, a former Portuguese colony with a socialist government and Cuban military assistance, was a Cold War target. South Africa, in the ironic role of representing the capitalist "Free World" in the southern African region, received the support of the United States and other powers in its military campaigns despite several United Nations resolutions that rejected its dominance of Namibia.

With Namibian independence and free elections in 1990, the new state drafted a constitution stressing human rights and full democratic participation for its various populations. With this development, the situation for the Ju/'hoansi people seems likely to improve, although too little time has passed to be certain (see Gordon 1989). The Namibian state encompasses diverse populations. The Ovambo are far more numerous than the others, amounting to about half of the population. It remains to be seen whether this imbalance will result in a predominant interest group acquiring undue influence over state policy.

The Botswana state developed far more humane policies toward the Ju/'hoansi than South Africa had. The government has initiated programs for education and encouraged culture change, but its tactics have been far less coercive than comparable programs in many states. The Remote Area Dwellers Office of the Botswana government has worked to identify and address the needs of Ju/'hoansi populations (Lee 1984:306).

The effect of global economics remains a question, however. To the extent that Botswana needs to accept foreign aid and World Bank loans for development, it may experience pressure to adopt more energetic programs and to utilize lands in possession of the Ju/'hoansi. International development organizations heavily favor cash cropping over hunting and foraging or pastoralism, despite mounting evidence that in some regions long-standing indigenous subsistence patterns are far more sustainable. The Botswana state so far, however, seems to have been more successful than many in balancing the interests of its various constituencies without resorting to oppressive measures.

East Africa

In East Africa, Kenya offers another example of a postcolonial state whose remaining settler population, though economically powerful, is a relatively minor constituency. Kenya's diversity results from the inclusion of numerous ethnic populations within its former colonial boundaries and from its earlier history of population movements from the coast.

Kenya gained independence in 1963 following years of resistance by the Mau Mau movement, which was predominantly Kikuyu (see Edgerton 1989). The large Kikuyu population of farmers had expanded throughout the rich Central Highlands, only to be displaced by British settlers. The Kikuyu themselves had spread at the expense of Maa-speaking pastoral peoples such as the Maasai and Samburu.

To the north of the cool Central Highlands most of Kenya's land is too dry for reliable agriculture, and peoples such as the Turkana, Gabbra, Boran, Pokot, and Samburu have relied mostly on livestock herds to survive. Agriculture is more feasible to the south and east of the Central Highlands. The Bantu-speaking Kamba and Taita farm steep, green hillsides to the southeast. On the coast of the Indian Ocean, populations in the old cities of Mombasa, Malindi, and Lamu show a strong Arab influence.

During the first years after independence, President Jomo Kenyatta, a Kikuyu, managed to balance these various interests despite the deep misgivings of other groups about Kikuyu power. After his death, President Daniel Arap Moi, whose heritage is among the Kalenjin herding peoples of the west, has ruled with a strong hand to the extent that international funding agencies withheld aid in the early 1990s until the human rights situation improved.

Although the Kenyatta government had attempted to unify Kenya and downplay ethnic identities, the Moi government in the mid-1990s began discussing a policy of *majimbo* ("states") drawn on ethnic lines. This has led to some redistribution of lands and dislocation of peoples and resulted in several violent clashes. The president himself has kept some distance from the policy, and it remains to be seen whether this will develop further as a "divide and rule" strategy.

Like many states, Kenya has been receptive to development funds from outside. Most of these appear to be aimed at the drier regions, where agro-pastoral peoples have achieved some success in balancing stock raising with supplemental farming in the few localities where the erratic rainfall permits. This generally takes the forms of seasonal activity or the trade of animal for vegetable products with sedentary peoples.

Reflecting the First World's bias toward agriculture, however—and perhaps the uneasiness with which most states regard nomads—numerous projects have promoted irrigation, often at the expense of pastoral activities. With a few possible exceptions, none of these appear to have been sustainable.

As one example, an Italian company called Lodagri established an irrigation project among a Pokot population who had been doing fine without it. As the manager stated with some frustration, there seems to be no doubt that the project will collapse when the company pulls out (personal communication). The beneficiaries, however, were the government of Kenya and the company itself—which received a subsidy from the Italian government—rather than the local Pokot. It seems evident that the West Pokot project was essentially a means of transferring wealth from the Italian government to a transnational corporation under the guise of foreign aid.

In Turkana District, a French corporation has built a dam on the Turkwell River to produce hydroelectric power and control the river's seasonal flow. The Turkwell, flowing from the mountains through a desert, is dry for much of the year. The river overflows periodically, though, to support a strip of riverine forest on which many of the local people and their animals depend. Stabilizing the river's flow will have profound effects on the ecosystem.

Once again, however, the beneficiaries of the development will not be the local population. The power lines lead out of the district to the south, and the French company which built the complex did so at approximately twice the price that it would have cost if it had been submitted to open international bidding.

Tanzania offers another East African case of some interest. Comprising the former British protectorates of Tanganyika and Zanzibar, it incorporates numerous diverse populations and many languages, although the government has been successful in establishing Swahili as a national language. After years of internal conflict and disruption, Tanzania united in 1977 under Julius Nyerere.

Unlike many other former colonies, Tanzania does not incorporate any single predominant ethnic group but hundreds of small ones. The government under Nyerere tried to develop the idea that the total population constitutes a single interest group. Nyerere introduced an extensive program of practical education throughout the countryside, and under the concept of *ujamaa* ("family") he relocated populations into village cooperatives. The program met many obstacles, but little civil disruption has occurred. One significant factor may have been Nyerere's frequent military actions against Uganda, which during the 1980s directed much of the state's energies to a common cause. Tanzania now has embarked on a multiparty system. With Nyerere having retired from government and with relatively peaceful relationships with Uganda, the success of his policy of *ujamaa* remains to the seen.

Siberia

As a final example, we might look northward to Siberia and note briefly the experience of the hunters and herders of northeast Asia within the Russian and Soviet states. The people of that region, which extends some two thousand miles from the Taimyr to the Chukchi peninsulas, lived for centuries as hunters and herders of reindeer. The Russian "Small Peoples of the North" include some twenty-six distinct groups who speak a range of languages, including Samoyedic, Chukchi, and Tungus (see Czaplicka 1914). In the 1960s, the non-Russian indigenous population of Siberia was about 800,000 (Levin and Potapov 1964).

Russian expansion into northeastern Siberia in the late sixteenth century followed many of the same patterns we have seen elsewhere. Cossacks in the service of the czar arrived to conscript the local population as fur producers. Unlike the French in Canada, the Russians were more inclined toward coercion than negotiation of trade relationships. The north was attractive because the furs were thicker than they were in the south, while the populations were smaller and less able to resist (Slezkine 1994:14).

The Russian state did not necessarily promote harshness as a policy for its own sake, however. Orders from Moscow urged peaceful initiatives in drawing northern peoples into the state's hegemony to exact *iasak* ("fur tribute"). "And the iasak for the sovereign should be taken with kindness and not with cruelty and the people of those lands should be placed, from now on, under the czar's exalted hand in direct slavery as iasak people for ever and ever" (quoted in Slezkine 1994:14).

Despite Russian incursions into the region, there was no large-scale invasion. "The natural and man-made conditions in the Russian Arctic were not conducive to interventionism. Agriculture was not feasible; most industries were unprofitable" (Slezkine 1994:392). As in Canada, the fur trade prevailed as the main link with the state. "In Siberia as in Canada, it relied on a continuation of the hunting and trapping economy, discouraged incursions by non-natives (other than as trading intermediaries), and usually demanded a greater adaptive effort from southern settlers than from northern trappers" (Slezkine 1994:392).

State intervention escalated after the Russian Revolution, when the government made efforts to incorporate the peoples of Siberia, creating a series of "autonomous" regions roughly corresponding with ethnic populations.

> The creation of these autonomies facilitated the organization and activization of the backward peoples, mobilized them to carry out the most important political, economic and cultural tasks, promoted friendship between them and the Russian people, and contributed to the strengthening of the Soviet state. (Sergeyev 1964:488)

The Soviets set up schools in remote areas in an attempt to wean children from the old ways. The reformers made a special target of shamans, indigenous specialists in the spiritual realm, defining them as exploiters of the people. The indigenous population, they assumed, labored under primitive superstition that had no place in the enlightened and highly secular Soviet state. "As the meaning of most 'superstitions' remained obscure, the struggle was waged primarily against symbols: braids, tattoos, and amulets" (Slezkine 1994:241).

The Soviet attitude toward indigenous populations differed little from those in other states.

> The material culture of the small peoples was distinguished by its high degree of adaptation to the severe conditions of life in the North. Nevertheless, in spite of the value of many of the cultural achievements of the backward peoples, their way of life was wretched, primitive and dangerous to health. (Sergeyev 1964:489)

Special instructors visited the regions through the Red Tent program to enlighten the people about the oppression of the masses by capitalists. These volunteers, many of them young people from urban backgrounds, ventured into the tundra to enlighten the local inhabitants. "They covered every aspect of life, from looking after children to the campaign against witchcraft" (Sergeyev 1964:199). One teacher in Chukotka wrote:

> I managed to teach the children the very beginnings of class consciousness and an understanding of the nature of the exploitation of the poor by the rich. It may sound strange but at that particular moment in time the children did not have such

notions at all. Therefore the schoolteachers have to work very hard, particularly considering the poor knowledge of the Chukchi language, in order to instill in the children the feeling of hatred towards shamanism and exploitation. (Quoted in Slezkine 1994:242)

Apparently some Red Tent instructors, unlike their counterparts in the United States and Canada during the same period, tried to use indigenous languages to teach the children, though rarely with much success. The populace showed considerable resistance. A Khanty woman in the 1930s berated a young volunteer, asking:

Why are you Russians trying to prevent us from living our way? Why do they take our children to school and teach them to forget and to break up our Khanty way? You like children, for example, so how would you feel if they took away your children and taught them to despise everything about the way you live? (Quoted in Slezkine 1994:237)

Some parents resisted with threats of violence, but much of the resistance was relatively passive. A Koriak man stated simply, "We obey the authorities but we aren't sending our kids to no schools" (Slezkine 1994:238). People refused to help set up the Red Tent operations, "refused to give reindeer for the red tents and sometimes left particularly persistent 'red tenters' to freeze in the tundra" (Slezkine 1994:230).

The children, for their part, resisted in small but effective ways through creative misbehavior—missing classes, refusing to do schoolwork, boycotting strange foods, and spitting on the floors (Slezkine 1994: 244). By the 1960s, however, the schools and programs had had an effect. Northern peoples had abandoned many of their old ways, and children in schools had failed to learn the skills they would have needed to continue living as their grandparents had.

As minerals in the region became more important and outside labor moved into the area, the indigenous people of the region became less a matter of concern for the state. With this marginality, however, popular interest and curiosity grew about the peoples of northern Siberia— even a tendency to romanticize the simple, pure life they supposedly led. We have seen such developments in other states with the intensification of industrial development and the social stresses that came with it. Urban intellectuals in twentieth-century Mexico, the United States, Canada, and Australia have all found a deep appeal in the images of the indigenous cultures that their forebears had displaced.

With *perestroika* under the Gorbachev administration, it became apparent that earlier programs intended to bring modern prosperity to Siberian populations had failed. Many of the indigenous people were living in impoverished conditions. They had, however, abandoned or been unable to continue their old ways of living and had entered the global economy mainly in the sense that they required cash and had little of it. They had become poor.

Some northern people argued that they could resolve many of their problems if they gained control over the resources that other interests were extracting from their lands. A Nenets journalist wrote:

> . . . what is a Nenets supposed to feel if he knows that every year, every month, every day millions of tons of oil and billions of cubic meters of gas are being pumped out of his native soil? What is a Khanty supposed to think, if he knows that under different circumstances this oil and this gas could drastically change the life of his people? (Quoted in Slezkine 1994:379)

As in other states, however, the return of resources to the indigenous people did not strike many of those in power as a practical solution. There was more concern for "protecting" the remaining populations. "The idea was to preserve a *way of life,* and like so many *perestroika-*related ideas, it led one to the West or back to the 1920s—that is to say, to reservations, otherwise known as ethnic territories, reserves, zones for the preferential development of traditional economies, nature and culture parks, and even 'ethnoecopolises'" (Slezkine 1994:379).

There was a problem with preserving ways of life that in many cases had long since disappeared. "Thousands of young northerners were said to have lost their ethnic identity along with their mother tongue and traditional skills" (Slezkine 1994:383). There was, however, much interest in restoring the indigenous traditions that the Red Tent programs had tried so persistently to uproot only a few decades earlier. In some areas, classes endeavored to teach indigenous children the languages they had never learned in their homes.

With the changes taking place since the end of the former Soviet Union, it is difficult to discern a trajectory. Despite the Soviet breakup, most of the region remains within the Russian state. That state, however, now confronts serious problems in maintaining order within its most populous regions. It may be some time before the "Small Peoples of the North" draw much attention again.

The examples of these various states show a range of differences, but at this point many patterned similarities seem apparent. In the concluding chapter, we shall examine some of their dynamics.

Conclusions from
Cases Compared

. . . .

8

A t this juncture, we can return to a few basic questions. Why do states act as they do with regard to indigenous peoples? What can indigenous peoples do to pursue their own interests most effectively? Surely this is not the place to offer advice, but we can look at the history of these interactions and consider which have been more or less successful.

To understand why states do what they do, it is necessary to keep in mind that states per se are not the main players. Interest groups of various sorts divert, nudge, or deflect their actions. We noted at the beginning that states are more than their governments, but they do inevitably have an apparatus of government, including enforcement mechanisms. In some cases, interests may gain control of this governing apparatus and direct it for their own benefit. In Mexico the ruling party has occupied the central government for more than seventy years. In most cases, though, this governing apparatus remains contested territory among multiple constituencies.

More and more during recent decades, the most powerful interests, such as transnational corporations, have operated across states as well as within them. Many have been very successful in seeing that those in positions of government, through threats or rewards, respond to their concerns. The recent enactment of various interstate free trade agreements such as NAFTA is an example.

This application of pressure on the state suggests an approach to the second question. Whatever strategies indigenous peoples adopt within state arenas, they have little choice but to compete *as* interest groups among a field of many others. To this end, expanding the parameters of their own interest groups would seem to confer some advantage. Some of the most effective indigenous strategies, at least for brief periods, have involved coalitions.

The use of coalitions does not does not necessarily mean assimilating indigenous peoples into a greater, more massive constituency. There is no prima facie reason why constituencies that are profoundly different in most ways cannot work toward a specific, focused common purpose without relinquishing their identities. Many such coalitions, ranging from Pontiac's uprising to the Pitjandjatjara Land Council, have achieved at least some short-lived success while preserving diversity under a common cause. On the other hand, the ideal of preserving local indigenous cultures as pristine, unchanged entities seems overly romantic and historically naive. Not only do all indigenous societies have long histories of change, but adaptation is their best hope of continuing to exist.

Many observers and indigenous spokespeople have lamented the loss of indigenous knowledge by younger people at the hands of the state. Their failure to undergo initiations, to learn the sacred lore of their people, or even to gain fluency in the languages of their parents is indeed regrettable. Often, this amounts to the loss of irreplaceable knowledge, concepts, and varieties of human experience. Many individuals have suffered personal tragedies in the process. Yet much of the leadership representing indigenous interests within and among states has arisen from among these apparently marginalized people.

The elder generation of indigenous leaders, though they may be custodians of the ancient ways, often are ill equipped to deal effectively within a state arena. Often the ground rules of behavior and underlying assumptions are alien to them. Not only are their interests in conflict with those of other constituencies, but the understandings that frame the nature of the discourse are no longer mutual. If they retain a sense of identity with their people, individuals who have experience in the wider milieu may be more effective.

There are many likely obstacles to this, including the question of such people's legitimacy in the eyes of indigenous groups. But of the tens of thousands whose lives have become marginal in the process of incorporation by state systems, a few have arisen to effect positive change. There are many cases in all states in which vocal proponents of indigenous rights have been people who attended boarding schools away from their communities, or who grew up in aggregate communities of displaced indigenous survivors, or who have spent most of their lives in urban areas. Strengths may arise from these traumas.

This by no means dismisses the value or significance of indigenous culture or the extent to which it affects the choices of action. We have discussed many cases in which culture has had a major effect on the ways in which indigenous peoples have initially confronted state systems. As Alice Pomponio (1992) has shown in the society of the Mandok of Papua New Guinea, for example, the people's image of themselves as seafaring traders led them to resist the adoption of agriculture.

Cultural symbols, moreover, may be important devices for affirming identity. And culture is a means of survival. However successful any cultural system may or may not be in resolving common human problems, it must provide for the continued existence of the people who create and maintain it within a particular context. Incorporation within a state is a context radically different from the circumstances of autonomous populations. When the very survival of the people is at stake, preservation of orthodox cultural forms may be a secondary concern.

Forms of Resistance

In the early years of state expansion, violent resistance was more frequent and sometimes quite effective. Pontiac and Tecumseh, for example, gave ruling interests of the British and American states much cause for concern. With the consolidation of state hegemony, though, violence usually has become less feasible. Mature states claim a monopoly on the use of force and invariably amass a disproportionate amount of power to carry it out.

But state consolidation also offers opportunities. Some of these have to do with the state's need for legitimacy as a means of maintaining order and balancing the interests of its constituencies. The legal system may offer short-term options. As Critical Legal Studies theorists have noted, the laws of the state tend to safeguard dominant interests and maintain the status quo, but their effectiveness in doing so requires a degree of consistency in their application. This can provide the possibility of some redress. This is particularly so when state ideology stresses universal participation, which is another side of the coin of assimilation policies.

General Conclusions

Let us consider what we can glean from the cases we have examined. Many of these conclusions may appear obvious, but their implications are worth exploring. With regard to the states, we can conclude that:

1. States have been far more likely to expand than smaller nonstate, autonomous societies have.

2. The early stages of state expansion have usually involved violence.

3. After initial expansion, states have attempted to consolidate their holdings, both externally and internally.

4. Internal consolidation has often involved attempts to eradicate indigenous populations.

5. Early attempts at indigenous eradication have involved genocidal policies.

6. Genocide has usually failed, and efforts at assimilation have followed, often coupled with displacement or relegation to reserved areas.

7. Assimilation policies in turn have usually failed. States eventually, if grudgingly, have come to accept the continued existence of indigenous populations and often to permit some degree of indigenous self-determination.

We can also summarize the ways in which indigenous peoples have reacted to these initiatives.

1. Indigenous peoples have often met intrusions without violence, except where violence among indigenous groups has been endemic.

2. Violent indigenous resistance has generally ensued after more aggressive intrusions, though usually this has been limited to the parameters of existing indigenous affiliations.

3. Coalitions for violent resistance that transcend these local allegiances have arisen sporadically among indigenous people during the process of state expansion.

4. After the consolidation of states, many indigenous peoples have sought to retrench, entering into treaties or seeking refuge.

5. Many indigenous peoples have sought participation in the state's

economic system, particularly when the permeability or inadequacy of refuges has become apparent.

6. Facing lack of access to the rewards of the economic system, some indigenous peoples have sought political solutions, including attempts to initiate pan-indigenous movements of various sorts.

We can elaborate on each of these points in turn. With regard to state actions, the tendency to expand is worth some discussion because it sets state systems apart from nonstate societies. Certainly there are important examples of nonstate societies, such as the Turkana of Kenya or the Lakota of the U.S. Plains, expanding territories at the expense of their neighbors. Usually these cases have involved a quest for more resources, such as grazing lands and cattle in the Turkana case or buffalo-hunting territory for the Lakota. But such motivations are far more typical of states.

State Expansion

The ruling interests within most of the expanding states that we have discussed have followed comparable patterns in dealing with indigenous peoples. All, in one way or another, have involved the acquisition of resources in the possession of indigenous peoples. The degree to which the quest for resources has driven colonial state policies sets these systems apart from the indigenous societies they incorporated.

In states that have not expanded—many of them former colonies—domestic and transnational interests have competed for indigenous resources within state boundaries. Many former colonial states, such as Kenya, encompass numerous indigenous populations as a result of previous state expansion during the colonial period. State dynamics in that case are more consistent with the later phase of consolidation. As the example of Indonesia shows, however, these states, too, can be capable of further expansion.

Indigenous peoples in all of the colonized areas had engaged for centuries in complex interactions and population movements and even in some competition over resources. But in general, these indigenous societies had been far more self-sustaining than the states that eventually incorporated them. The European-derived states had outgrown their own resources and developed the need to appropriate those in other parts of the world. Indonesia, more recently, seems to be following the same pattern.

As Andre Gunder Frank, Immanuel Wallerstein, Fernand Braudel, and others have pointed out (see Chapter 2), an important aspect of European expansion involved the dawning of a capitalist economy whose dynamics went far beyond the simple needs of subsistence. It was not merely that Europe was becoming crowded. At the time of the early explorations, in fact, the population was small compared to what it became a couple of centuries later.

But the distribution of wealth and power had diverged widely, and the possibility of accumulation among the upper echelons had become open-ended in a way that would not have been possible in a subsistence economy. Historical details aside, this factor meant that inevitably the powerful interests that drove these states would confront indigenous peoples beyond the states' boundaries to appropriate their land, labor, minerals, or whatever else of value they had.

This quest for resources has also been manifest in the case of Indonesia and, to a lesser extent, Papua New Guinea. Most theorists might not consider the Soviet expansion in Siberia to be a matter of capitalist enterprise, but the quest for resources—furs, in this case—provided comparable motivations for incorporating indigenous peoples.

As we have seen, interest group motivations have commonly involved resource appropriation and the acquisition of the power to do so. This arises at least partially from the fact that states, unlike many other forms of human association, involve open-ended forms of wealth that lead them to exceed the more stable, sustainable resource needs of smaller autonomous societies.

If apparent differentiation in wealth exists in smaller societies, it usually amounts to perishable goods or intangible values such as status or ritual knowledge. Although status and knowledge may be socially real, ultimately, they exist only in people's minds. They are replicable and are not depleted through consumption. They do not necessarily lead to rampant expansionism or to growing economic disparities. If a hierarchical structure exists at all in such societies, one of the primary measures by which elites maintain their status is by giving tangible or consumable resources away in feasts or other social mechanisms for redistribution.

The perishability and consumption value of food resources, which usually constitute the bulk of material wealth in smaller societies, places a limit on the amount that one can sensibly accumulate. Where imperishable forms of wealth occur—shell money, iron bars, or whatever— these generally are meaningful only in being given in such transactions as marriages, feasts, and competitive exchanges. Their value is usually social rather than intrinsic in the material itself.

Within the larger populations of state systems, however, wealth and power are more likely to accumulate at the top of the social hierarchy.

The elite are more distant from the general populace, and they can accumulate wealth in the form of luxury items or other nonutilitarian goods. Generally, too, the use or threat of force, rather than reciprocity, redistribution, or negotiation, comes to predominate as a means of maintaining their position.

The Aztec state, which had barely established itself along these lines, had already begun to incorporate neighboring peoples when the Spanish interrupted the process. Unlike many others, the Aztec state was not particularly interested in assimilating the peoples it confronted but directed its energies more toward acquiring their resources (although to some degree this included people for sacrifice). The incorporation of other populations took the form of extending tribute channels rather than amalgamation.

Like the French and Dutch seeking furs in North America, the Aztec had no incentive to remove the producers from their lands. Unlike the European fur traders, however, the Aztec were in a position to extract resources by coercion as well as by negotiation. The Inca in the Andes to the south also developed an expansionist state, as had many earlier populations in what was to become Latin America.

As the Aztec, Inca, Indonesian, and Papua New Guinea examples show, some of the underlying features we have observed in Australia, Canada, Mexico, and the United States have not been unique to European colonial states. We might also have included many West African examples. The ways in which these principles have manifested themselves in particular historic circumstances has varied, but the principles themselves seem consistent. The development of capitalism may have imbued European state actions with unique dynamics (except for the Soviet example), but the quest for resources—whether through trade, tribute, or enslavement—underlay the processes in all cases.

State Violence

The tendency of state expansion to involve violence may seem too obvious to require comment, but its causes are worth considering if only because it does not seem to be an inevitable aspect of contact. In many cases, as we have seen, indigenous populations have met initial incursions with little or no violent reaction. This has even been so in some cases in which they had histories of violent interactions among themselves, as in the St. Lawrence Valley.

In a few instances of state intrusion, also, state violence was minimal. The French incursion into Canada, for example, generally was peaceful with regard to the Huron and Algonkian, even though the

French came into conflict with the Iroquois to the south. Australia, too, involved little violent conflict at first. Violence often appears to have grown out of the subsequent dynamics of interaction—usually involving resource appropriation.

It seems significant that since French demands in Lower Canada did not entail the forcible seizure of indigenous resources, and since the British presence constrained French behavior, relatively stable coexistence was possible. Most commonly, though, the state apparatus has acted as a vehicle for powerful interests—whether trading companies, plantation investors, or the Church—to confront indigenous peoples over their resources or to co-opt their labor. These factors were far more likely to produce conflict.

One might suspect that the use of violence in the expansion of the Australian, Mexican, Canadian, and American states was partly a function of the earlier historic period. Indonesia, however, offers a modern version of state expansion that seems to follow the same pattern that Britain and Spain did centuries before.

State Consolidation

State consolidation also follows discernible patterns. Where state territories abut indigenous populations who retain at least de facto autonomy, the state may enact treaties with them. This was the case in Canada and the United States, but not in Australia or Mexico. In British North America, the size and power of indigenous populations compelled the British state to bestow some recognition of their sovereignty, even though Crown legal theory tended to minimize or deny it. The overriding interest was the security of the state.

In Mexico, where the Spanish state and many indigenous societies were more hierarchical to begin with, most agreements were between elites and more typically were personalized understandings rather than legalistic pacts between polities. Spain often recognized, supported, and co-opted local leaders in such societies, practicing an early version of indirect rule. In Australia, where indigenous populations posed little threat to the security of the state, the British did not recognize their sovereignty and made few attempts to deal with them on a basis of parity.

The treaties of Canada and the United States tended to falter when further European immigration and the decline of indigenous populations through disease and displacement changed the balance of power. In 1906 the United States Supreme Court, in the *Lone Wolf v. Hitchcock* decision, ruled that Congress could abrogate any and all treaties with Native

Americans (see Deloria 1985:109). United States officials had ceased writing them in 1871, in any case. Canadian Prime Minister Trudeau, as late as 1969, held that treaties with indigenous peoples were incompatible with a democratic state.

Genocide

Attempts at genocide, whether sporadic or concerted and whether official or vigilante, characterized all of these states at one time or another as a means of eliminating indigenous interest groups from the field of competition. Indonesia seems to be the most recent of the states discussed here to pursue such a policy, in East Timor and Irian Jaya. Competing interests within states have had no wish to allow the development of increased rivalry. Not only have the resources that indigenous peoples held been a matter of contention, but in all cases other constituencies have sought to nullify these populations in one way or another as competing entities.

Genocide succeeded in a few cases, such as in Tasmania and Newfoundland, but for the most part such measures were unacceptable to state ideology except as an aspect of warfare on expanding frontiers. Mexican policies of offering bounties for Apache scalps in the 1840s only escalated conflict in the area (see Griffen 1988, Bancroft 1962). As states consolidated, genocidal policies would have tended to threaten political stability, opening the possibility of eventual threats to other vulnerable constituencies. Where such constituencies are scattered, as in the Indonesian Archipelago, this may not be as great a problem.

Attempts toward the physical destruction of rival constituencies even within established states certainly has occurred in some instances. If one interest predominates in directing the policies of the state, though—as in the former Soviet Union before the 1990s—such measures as genocide may provoke unrest among other small interests, unless the state can portray the victimized constituency as an enemy to the others. The most notorious example was Nazi Germany.

The maintenance of stability in balancing the interests of constituents has been a central problem in each of these states. Canada has had its French-English and provincial-federal issues. The United States has had its Civil War and continuing racial tensions. Mexico has had its regional, class, rural-urban, Church-secular, and many other competitive struggles that have led to sporadic uprisings and a history of political assassination. Australia has had rural-urban, regional, and class conflicts. In the interstices of these dynamics, indigenous peoples have pressed their cases and tried to hold their ground.

If the state involves numerous interests with none having overwhelming power, as in Papua New Guinea, the governing apparatus may have greater independence but usually no need to eliminate any of the competing constituencies. The United States, Australia, and Canada during most of their histories seem to have fit this model. In such cases, the most drastic conflicts may take place among the constituencies themselves, whether through vigilante violence or the development of racist or otherwise bigoted popular ideology to place competitive interest groups at a disadvantage. In many states, including the United States, the most vitriolic racism often occurs at the grass-roots level where the most disadvantaged among the competing interests vie for small rewards. This may become disruptive if the state loses centralized power, as we have seen recently in the former Yugoslavia and in the various regions of the former Soviet Union.

Eradication by Bureaucratic Means

Short of genocide, states have employed other means of suppressing the presence of indigenous interest groups. In some cases, exploitative and dangerous labor practices have constituted physical assaults on indigenous populations. The use of Navajo workers in uranium mines without safety precautions, despite federal oversight, is one stark example (see Eichstaedt 1994).

Throughout these dynamics of interaction, a central imperative, clearly, has been to diminish indigenous populations. Scattering them among the general population was one way. Changing them into something else on an individual basis was another. Pretending that they were fewer through undercounting the population was another. Still another was to depress their reproductive rate.

The United States Public Health Service in the 1970s carried out the sterilization of thousands of indigenous women without their knowledge and, obviously, without their consent. The same thing happened in Australia. In Mexico there is little evidence of such government practices, although the infant mortality rate in many indigenous communities is extremely high in any case. Such practices, as one might expect, have made indigenous peoples in many areas extremely distrustful of birth control programs, however well intended these programs may be.

Many states have also taken indigenous children from their natal communities. In the United States, Canada, and Australia, as we have noted, social agencies regularly took children away from their families and turned them over to foster homes or to boarding schools. Loss of their children in this fashion was a major issue among indigenous people in

Australia in the early twentieth century. In the United States, social workers often entered reservation communities and removed children on the basis of local housing codes, claiming that their living conditions were inadequate. The Indian Child Welfare Act made this removal illegal after 1967. In Canada compulsory education laws provided a legal rationale for similar seizures of children from their families in remote areas. One consequence of the boarding schools, in addition to their stated purpose of eradicating indigenous identities of children, was that many children simply died there before growing up.

Indigenous education has been a prime mechanism for inducing change. In all states, education has been a hallmark of the elite, associated with power, success, and access to the rewards of the economic system. The concept of education has had a benevolent ring. Education for indigenous peoples, however, has generally been another matter. In substance it has been quite different from the education to which the more powerful interests have had access. On the other hand, education has been a useful tool in inducing change by its very nature as a process that supposedly alters the ways in which people think.

Mexico under various regimes pushed to establish schools in small indigenous villages. The major emphasis in most cases was to teach Spanish, making it possible for indigenous people to deal more successfully with the wider society and to incorporate them more fully into it. Educational philosophies have varied in different political climates, though.

Under conservative governments early in the century, some *científicos* argued that indigenous peoples were incapable of benefiting from formal education. Cárdenas in the 1930s instituted an extensive system of schools for indigenous communities, stressing not only Spanish but vocational and practical training that addressed many of their most immediate problems—agriculture, health, and so on. He also linked educational programs with government-sponsored congresses of indigenous people that identified acute issues facing specific populations. These waned after Cárdenas left office and a less sympathetic regime took over.

Indigenous education in the United States took a different form. Rather than being community based, it focused on separating children from their homes and collecting them in boarding schools. The policy of separation went beyond physical removal and involved attempts to eradicate even so fundamental an aspect of cultural identity as language. The content of school curricula often ignored or, in many cases, denigrated indigenous culture in the attempt to reorient children's sense of identity.

The curricula of Indian schools did not focus on what educators now would call "college track," or the liberal arts. They generally stressed what the instructors deemed to be useful skills and personal discipline.

Unlike the community-based education programs of Cárdenas in Mexico, which also stressed vocational training, the idea was not to help indigenous communities prosper but to dissolve them and provide labor for the wider market. The correspondence between levels of government funding for Indian education and the national market for cheap labor seems to reflect this practice (Littlefield 1993b).

We have discussed many of these patterns in earlier chapters. The intended effect was not only to remove children from their cultural setting but to instill "high moral character" and a work ethic. One additional aspect, however, was that in creating aggregates of children from different communities and treating them collectively as a special category of being, the schools probably helped foster a sense of "Indian" or "Aboriginal" identity. Many of these children became politically active as adults in addressing indigenous issues.

Political activism was not the intent of the programs, whose aims were to create a compliant, menial workforce. During summer vacation, many of the indigenous students at the Carlisle Indian School in Pennsylvania did not return home but spent the months in the homes of nonindigenous people where they worked as servants. By no means was the boarding school experience uniformly negative, however. Schools and instructors varied, and by the nineteenth century some indigenous communities were so disrupted and impoverished that children welcomed a chance to have food and clothing.

In Canada the government experimented in the nineteenth century with a few schools located in reserve communities, but officials concluded, as did their counterparts in the United States, that they were ineffective because they did not sufficiently protect children from home influences. The state subsequently tried "residential," "vocational," and boarding schools that accomplished that goal. During the height of the assimilationist period, the Canadian legislature required passes for indigenous people to leave reserves, largely with the intent of keeping parents from visiting their children in the schools. As in the United States, the curricula seemed largely to be aimed at eradicating indigenous identity, with severe punishment for speaking indigenous languages. As we noted above, the Canadian boarding school system continued well into the 1960s. Its philosophy was hardly different from the system in the United States and apparently borrowed many ideas from the neighbor to the south.

Australia also instituted boarding schools for indigenous children, and in the nineteenth century some proponents were explicit about their function as training grounds for menial laborers. Edward Willson Landor, in his account of life in Australia in 1847, wrote that

Considerable pains have been bestowed (especially by Wesleyans) upon the native children, many of whom are educated in schools at Perth, Fremantle, and other places, in the hope of making them eventually useful servants to the settlers. Most of these, however, betake themselves to the bush, and resume their hereditary pursuits, just at the age when it is hoped they will become useful. (Quoted in Williams 1986:239)

Apparently some people at the time found it puzzling that indigenous people would fail to take the opportunity to serve settlers.

Like the schools in the United States and Canada, but unlike most in Mexico, the Australian institutions involved rigid sexual segregation as well. This may have been a strategy to depress the birth rate as well as to build moral fiber (Morris 1989:110).

We might note that with regard to another side of education—that is, educating the population of the state about indigenous peoples— Cárdenas's regime in Mexico also surpassed the others, at least in its intent. Many politicians in Mexico had embraced the abstract concept of *indigenismo*. But Cárdenas encouraged the recognition of living indigenous cultures as having validity in their own right. This, however, was a brief aberration in a more general trend.

In the United States, the Bureau of Indian Affairs under John Collier also acknowledged the validity of indigenous cultural heritage, even while articulating their communities to the federal government through the provisions of the Wheeler-Howard bill calling for elected councils. But well into the 1990s, the general mass of U.S. schoolchildren knew little about indigenous peoples. In the earlier twentieth century, school history textbooks had discussed the "winning of the West" as the march of civilization through the wilderness. A more benign approach in the 1980s stressed the contributions of indigenous peoples to U.S. society. Sometimes these went beyond accounts of Indians showing Pilgrims how to grow corn. A few texts reveal that such groups as the Iroquois had complex social systems. But the quantity and quality of this education about indigenous history and culture generally have been slight, and usually it has emphasized what these people had "given" to U.S. life rather than discussing them as societies in their own right.

A similar trend was manifest in Australia, although there the Aboriginal peoples remained far in the background, with less of the romanticizing that Native American cultures underwent. In the 1950s, it was still possible to publish a scholarly history of Australia in Canberra without the words "Aboriginal" or "indigenous" appearing in the index (see, e.g., Greenwood 1959).

States have also artificially reduced the number of indigenous peoples through bureaucratic sleight of hand and legal sophistry. In the United States, reservation censuses have chronically undercounted populations, although some of the reason certainly arises from logistic difficulties in reaching all members of dispersed communities. Nor have people on reservations always been inclined to welcome government census takers.

In the 1950s and 1960s, the United States government initiated programs to get people off reservations with the inducement of job opportunities or vocational training. In some cases, the government offered enrollment in college—although the BIA "colleges" often turned out to be vocational training facilities. Government agencies also have removed elderly people from reservations and placed them in rest homes in distant cities. This policy, however, probably has had less to do with simple population decrease than a strategy representing a counterpart to the boarding school plan. The elderly rest home program separated children from their elders—in this case by removing the old people rather than removing the children.

In Canada the legal category of "Indian status" eliminated approximately half of the indigenous population from recognition by the state. From the government's point of view, the nonstatus people, whatever the realities of their lives, did not exist except as undifferentiated citizens of Canada. The Canadian legislature also had a chronic habit of periodically bestowing enfranchisement by decree, either on a case-by-case basis or, at times, in sweeping legislation. "The acceptance and denial of Native difference works to determine the scope of federal and provincial sovereignty over Native People and to maintain a hierarchical relationship between Native people and the Canadian state" (Macklem 1993:15).

The precise number of Aboriginal people in Australia has never been certain, although when the government finally included them in the census of 1967, the count was well over 200,000 (Tonkinson and Howard 1990). As we noted earlier, there had been attempts to place people of mixed ancestry into a separate category and to promote the disappearance of indigenous populations through admixture. The prevailing assumption throughout most of Australia's history until recently, though, had been that indigenous peoples were on the verge of extinction anyway.

In Mexico the definition of indigenous peoples rested more on such cultural criteria as language, clothing style, and membership in indigenous communities. Identity as *indio* generally carried significant social and economic disadvantage but no particular benefits through government recognition compared to Canada or the United States, where some treaties had promised various forms of compensation. Because of the relatively easy transition from *indio* to *mestizo*, Mexico has probably succeeded more than the other states in reducing the proportion of its population who maintain an explicit indigenous identity. Despite this process, though, indigenous communities persist in many regions of Mexico, particularly in the geographic peripheries of the state.

In most of the states we have considered, assimilation policies gained momentum after the failure of attempts to ignore indigenous populations altogether or to eliminate them physically. Assimilation was a matter of eradication by other means.

Assimilation

Assimilation policies to some extent were a manifestation of early nineteenth-century assumptions about the inevitable demise of these populations. The ideological justification for such policies was that they were a means of helping along a process that would continue anyway. Some states allocated reserves as temporary, expedient holding areas where the people could survive as they progressed toward assimilation, or die off, if need be.

In Mexico the process of directed assimilation began early, when Spanish priests collected indigenous people around missions and compelled them to cut their hair, wear clothing, and accept Christianity. We have seen that assaults on the symbols of indigenous identity have usually been an aspect of state incorporation. As in the other states, the entry of these people into the society of New Spain was to be at the lowest social and economic strata as Christianized rural or domestic labor.

In the United States, the heyday of assimilation programs was from the mid nineteenth century through the 1960s. Two centuries earlier, the New England Puritans had established villages of "Praying Indians" whose experience was comparable to that of their Roman Catholic counterparts in Mexico. Short hair, modest clothing, and moral rigor all were part of the package of Christianity. But the presence of relatively intact indigenous societies until well into the nineteenth century from the Great Lakes southward along the Appalachian chain inhibited the process of coercive assimilation in those regions.

Throughout this period, indigenous peoples did change their ways of life independently of assimilation programs. The Iroquois had freely adopted aspects of European culture they considered useful. By the end of the seventeenth century, they were using metal pots, iron-tipped arrows, firearms, factory-made cloth, and an array of other introduced items. To the south, the Cherokee, Choctaw, Creek, and others established farms that compared favorably with those of Europeans. But these changes arose from autonomous choice and did little to undermine the collective identity of these groups. When the Cherokee developed a writing system, it was in their own language, not in English.

Quakers and other missionaries worked among these groups, but they had little leverage beyond the concepts of heaven and hell and the degree to which they could maintain congenial relationships with their indigenous hosts. It was not until settler interests induced the state to remove these populations and confiscate their lands that they became targets of more aggressive programs to induce change.

Jesuits in Canada had established early relationships with indigenous people north of the Great Lakes and the St. Lawrence Valley, but here, too, the missionaries were in no position to force their agendas on the people. The indigenous populations tolerated them as part of their alliance with the French, but not without dealing with them on their own terms. Some of the Jesuits, after living immersed in the lively, smoky sociability of Huron longhouses, opted for the relative privacy of separate quarters. They continued to complain, however, that people thought nothing of dropping in and annoying them at all hours.

In Canada, as in the United States, concerted assimilation efforts got under way in the nineteenth century when Protestant missionaries were able to apply pressure on reserve communities that had already lost possession of much of their land. By this time, the power balance had shifted, and these missionaries had the backing of an established state.

In Australia the model was comparable, with some differences in the forms of confrontation. By the mid nineteenth century, endemic violence in the rural areas had left many indigenous groups in remnant reserve areas and around mission and stock stations with a diminished capacity to resist. In Australia, as elsewhere, missionaries played a leading role in implementing the state's interests, although the effects of their ideological suasions seem often to have been rather slight. Stockmen's interactions with indigenous groups, when peaceful, had been to recruit them for periodic labor rather than to promote cultural change. Missionaries had the charge of changing their way of life in a fashion that would make them more amenable to absorption within the state.

Reserves

The United States, Canada, and Australia used reserves to remove indigenous populations from desired areas even while state rhetoric emphasized the protective aspects of these policies. Mexico was somewhat different, in that regional and other interests were powerful enough to pose chronic threats of destabilization. The number of indigenous people in Mexico also meant that from the perspective of many constituencies, recognition of reserved lands sufficient for their needs would have been too large to be acceptable to local interests. Such a policy would also have tended to crystallize the official sanction of separate indigenous status to a degree that was incompatible with Mexican political ideology.

As we have noted, nineteenth-century Mexican liberals and conservatives differed mainly on whether indigenous peoples should merge with the general population or remain separate to die out on their own. Until the Cárdenas government, there was little feeling that they should receive special consideration. To the extent that Mexican governments did concern themselves with the rural populace—usually in times of disruption—they tended to merge both *indios* and *mestizos* generically as *campesinos* or peasants.

The Spanish in the eighteenth and early nineteenth centuries had designated *establicimientos de paz* ("regions of peace") for recalcitrant indigenous peoples such as the Apache in the northern regions, apparently on the model of their *moros de paz* ("peaceful Moors") program in North Africa (John 1989:7). These were not particularly successful, however, partly because they were usually created by decree rather than negotiation. In their various North American colonies, the Spanish designated *reservas* or *parcialidades* as special regions for indigenous populations (Beltrán 1979:96).

After independence, Mexico established "indigenous zones" (Hill 1991:76). President Cárdenas established a *zona indígena* for the Yaqui in Sonora in the 1930s. Such zones have been notoriously insecure, however, and generally have not had a formal structure comparable to reserves or reservations in the other states. The reservation system that the British-derived states found appropriate, with its sharp social and political boundaries, was not a predominant Mexican solution. Overt protection of indigenous holdings in most times and localities would have been a dangerous policy for the state.

During most of Mexican history, the central government did little to prevent the direct usurpation of indigenous lands. Indigenous communities remained or precipitated into areas that other groups had not appropriated, or where landowners allowed them to remain in order to exact their labor. Although the federal government under Cárdenas restored many of these lands, subsequent administrations allowed outsiders to retake most of them.

State policies of incorporation have involved serious internal contradictions. Assimilation has most often been a matter of attempting to render indigenous peoples harmless within the larger arena rather than to allow them access to positions of power. The few cases in which indigenous persons such as Benito Juárez in Mexico have come to high office have been consistent with this pattern. Despite Juárez's personal background, his policies toward indigenous peoples were no more favorable than those of earlier or later leaders. Indeed, they were considerably less so than those of Cárdenas.

Although states have attempted to prevent indigenous groups from achieving positions from which they could compete effectively with more powerful constituencies, government rhetoric has generally disguised this intent and cited humanitarian principles. Appeals to democracy, equality under the law, supremacy of the individual, and so on, have served as overt rationales for policies aimed toward group dissolution.

The cant of inclusion, however, has consistently come up against the reality of exclusion. Racism and similar rationales for discrimination have functioned to deny access to the upper levels of the state. In many cases, this discrimination, rather than a simple aversion to change on the part of indigenous peoples, has fostered resistance to assimilation. In the states we have considered, indigenous peoples have tried to participate in the larger economic, social, and political structure. In all states, they have been frustrated in their attempts.

Dispersal of Indigenous Populations

When populations on reserves failed to change rapidly enough, critics in the United States and Canada declared the reserve or reservation system a failure and moved to abolish it, arguing that it had inhibited change. From the perspective of indigenous peoples, retaining a land base was a crucial aspect of retaining their political integrity. Eventually realizing this need, interests within the United States and Canada abandoned the idea that reserves would act as temporary repositories from which indigenous peoples would eventually disappear and instead made persistent attempts to dismantle them. In the United States, the Dawes Act of 1887 was an attempt to break up reservations into individual land plots. The termination policy of the 1950s was directed at abolishing reservations by decree.

In Canada, Bond Head began removing indigenous populations from their lands in the 1830s. He turned out to be ahead of his time, and the government temporarily abandoned his policies. Subsequent politicians called for the enfranchisement of indigenous peoples and the subdivision of reserves into individual plots, generally in the face of band opposition and in some instances without the consent of the individuals involved. The process came to a head in Trudeau's White Paper of 1969, which spoke against special indigenous status or treaty rights.

In Mexico, where reserves never became the major means of dealing with indigenous peoples, and Australia, where they appeared rather late and tentatively, there was also, nonetheless, a concern about the slow pace of assimilation. In the Soviet Union and Australia, ironically, the reserve concept came into vogue later as a means of helping to preserve indigenous identity that seemed to be disappearing. At that juncture, indigenous peoples in those states had little but sentimental relevance to predominant interests and, to some extent, had even become emblems of state identity. They posed no threat, and there was little need for their labor.

In Australia the vastness of many indigenous areas that few outsiders coveted tempered the process somewhat. There was also strong support among many Australian citizens for keeping indigenous populations out of sight. Up through the 1960s, mission stations rather than reserves predominated in most areas as agencies to promote assimilation. The main exceptions were cases in which indigenous groups did hold valuable land, as in 1925, when the Aboriginal Protection Board consigned indigenous farms for sale to the public. Details aside, the general process in all four states was almost monotonously comparable.

Social Manipulation

Indigenous social organization has been a prime target of assimilation initiatives. We have already noted the imposition of elected councils on indigenous systems of governance. In the United States, the Bureau of Indian Affairs in the 1960s and 1970s attempted to undermine extended family and clan structures on some reservations by providing assistance for new housing, with the stipulation that the houses be arranged as nuclear family units along roads rather than clustered in larger kinship units.

Government recognition of family structure also frequently assumed male-headed nuclear families, which in many cases—particularly in matrilineal and matrilocal societies—had little to do with social reality. In Canada a woman of "Indian status" who married a nonstatus man was no longer "Indian" in the eyes of the law, nor were her children. In the United States, the economic needs for government assistance that arose from the loss of resources and exclusion from labor opportunities also undermined existing social structures in matrilineal communities. Assistance checks generally went to the male "head of household." As early as the nineteenth century, the Dawes Act emphasized household allotments on the same basis.

In Canada, the United States, and Australia, the late 1960s turned out to be a transitional period in state strategies. An escalation of indigenous political activity and an insistence on negotiation had already led governments to back away from most of the coercive measures of the past.

Politicians made a last try at offering assimilation in the guise of equality within the state, attacking special status from the position of appeals to national unity. Mexico, struggling with internal economic problems, gave little attention to indigenous social organization except for supporting local progovernment political leaders, although the political intent there was comparable. Dislocations and land loss in many regions, often for commercial agriculture, had more devastating effects on the social order.

Self-Determination

The negative reactions of indigenous peoples to the neo-assimilationist position in Australia, Canada, and the United States, though they varied in intensity, led to an era of "self-determination." The outcome of this development is not yet clear, but it seems likely to represent a shift in strategy rather than a nullification of the principles that have operated in the past. The relaxation of state responsibility for indigenous peoples at this juncture may involve some old dangers in new guise.

Although the circumstances of indigenous peoples in all states differ in important ways, most have lost economic self-sufficiency. Under state oversight, they have become impoverished. One cannot help but wonder why the states should offer them more latitude now to dispose of their remaining resources.

Perhaps one clue lies in the large number of tribal councils in the United States that have received proposals for hazardous waste dumps. Immersed in a cash economy with few sources of income, many indigenous communities will be sorely tempted by this apparently easy revenue. The new policies of self-determination restrict the extent to which the government is able or willing to intervene. Still in a highly competitive arena, these populations—many of them staggered and largely disarmed by their recent history—are now left to make do on their own.

Indigenous communities may well be able to meet this situation successfully. It may work to their benefit. But transnational corporations now are freer to bypass the state and deal directly with small, often desperate populations. This presents grave dangers. Although for much of their history these states have balanced many interest groups with none predominating, it may now be that the growth of transnational corporations has produced a situation in which one or a few interests are able to have their way and to influence states to reflect their special concerns.

The recent passage of the North American Free Trade Agreement, which divests member states of much of their power to regulate industrial enterprises, may be an ominous sign.

> . . . NAFTA fails to preserve the basic rights for indigenous peoples granted by these national governments. NAFTA ignores the unique legal status of indigenous tribes and fails to recognize tribal governance or reservations. . . . NAFTA will probably affect the right of a tribe to regulate the sale of privately-held lands within reservation boundaries if such regulation attempts to keep Canadian or Mexican investors out. (Forbes 1994:3)

Indigenous Strategies

Indigenous peoples for their part have continued energetically to resist land usurpation. In Mexico demands for the restoration of lands was probably the most basic and consistent reason for indigenous uprisings throughout the history of the state. Emiliano Zapata's cry *tierra y libertad* ("land and liberty") continued to resonate with the Zapatista Army of National Liberation in Chiapas in 1995 and no doubt will, in other regions if not there, for some time to come.

In most cases, however, physical resistance has failed as an indigenous strategy, although it has often been temporarily effective. The Apache of the southwestern United States managed to hold off the expansion of the Spanish, Mexican, and American states for three centuries. In Quebec the resistance at Oka in 1990 helped mobilize political strategies and may yet prove to have significant effects. In general, however, resistance shifted toward political tactics other than the use of force.

In recent years, many indigenous groups in the United States have attempted to take control of their own educational systems. Tribal colleges to prepare young people for further education have developed on many reservations. Their purpose has not been to wean students from the communities as government and missionary schools generally did, but to equip them to operate more effectively as members of those communities. It is interesting that despite the documented success of these initiatives and the government's proclaimed support of education, the Reagan and Bush administrations consistently placed bureaucratic obstacles in the way of the Tribal College program (Morris 1994).

The pattern among all of these states is clear enough without a more lengthy reiteration of policies, programs, and initiatives. States have tended to deal with indigenous peoples in accord with the wishes of the states' most powerful constituencies. With surprising consistency, however, those indigenous peoples who survived the early direct attempts to eliminate them have shown great persistence. Their reactions to assimilation programs have ranged from subtle resistance to explicit rejection.

Despite some assumptions to the contrary, it is clear that indigenous resistance has not necessarily arisen from a conservative clinging to old ways. We have seen many examples of indigenous people having sought access to the economic and political systems of their respective states. Allusions to "knee-jerk traditionalism" are among the aspersions the elites have often cast to discredit indigenous self-assertion. Often, though, indigenous resistance has involved the perception that assimilation generally means relegation to a disadvantaged position within the state and that the best chance for self-preservation is in collective action.

National and Local Arenas

We might suppose that for indigenous peoples, a relatively non-hierarchical state with many competing interests is often preferable to states in which a single interest predominates and can have its way with fewer constraints. Neither of these alternatives is comparable to autonomy, but in a state with many competing interests, the concern for order and the need to balance these interests may be more likely to lead to negotiated solutions. Heavy-handed policies are less likely in such a situation, though not impossible.

Small constituencies in competitive state arenas are in great danger. The state's need to keep order may offer some protection. If one especially powerful and aggressive interest steers state policies at the expense of the rest, however, the situation of indigenous populations is likely to be far more precarious. This is one reason why many indigenous people have preferred a larger national or even imperial authority to state or local jurisdiction. The larger state widens the arena of competitive interests, decreasing the likelihood that any one interest group will dominate. When Mexico separated from Spain, indigenous peoples lost some of the Crown's protection and found themselves more vulnerable to immediate local interests. Much the same result occurred with American and Canadian independence when the Royal Proclamation of 1763 fell by the wayside.

In subsequent decades, indigenous peoples in the United States and Canada have found federal oversight problematic but, nonetheless, have preferred it to state or provincial jurisdiction that would leave them to face more direct competition from local interests. In Australia many indigenous peoples welcomed the federal government's assumption of concurrent responsibility for Aboriginal affairs as a relief of sorts from the vagaries of policy within the individual states.

Coalitions

Walker Connor (1973), in an influential article, notes that "in a world consisting of thousands of distinct ethnic groups and only some one hundred and thirty-five states, the revolutionary potential inherent in self-determination is quite apparent." While this may be true, the multitude of ethnicity also represents a serious weakness in the position of indigenous peoples. The fact that they constitute thousands of small, distinct populations does not offer them much leverage. Indigenous peoples represent only a tiny proportion of the world's population. Simple population increase is one logical option, though not often practical.

Population size alone does not necessarily mean power. The Navajo in the twentieth century have increased dramatically to well over 200,000 people from a population of little more than 10,000 in 1864, but they remain severely disadvantaged.

Some of the greatest successes involved the expansion of interest group parameters through forming coalitions. Indigenous peoples in many cases have been able to transcend earlier social boundaries based on restricted, relatively autonomous local or regional identities.

Local patterns of group definition, usually based on kinship ties, had developed as efficient means of regulating interactions among people and distributing populations over their resource bases. In some instances, coalition building has meant overcoming old animosities. Some animosities also have arisen through the manipulations of outside interests, as in the Navajo-Hopi land dispute in the U.S. Southwest (see Brugge 1994). More frequently, it has meant developing the idea that people who have felt nothing in common in the past, or perhaps even have been unaware of each other's existence, now share at least some common concerns.

The tendency of ruling elites to group all indigenous populations into a single category inadvertently fostered this idea. In the early phases of state encroachment, the single category served the purposes of social and economic exclusion. Within an established state, however, the submersion of differences to emphasize common concerns can afford some increased leverage.

During the early phases of invasion, some states tried to prevent indigenous political coalitions from forming, somewhat in contradiction to the generic indigenous categories that operated at the level of social interaction. In the north of Mexico, the Spanish cultivated animosity between the O'Odham and the Apache, for example. England, in the southern colonies, carried out aggressive diplomacy to keep the Cherokee from joining the Creek uprising in the eighteenth century.

But many coalitions did form. Indigenous coalition building began early, in some cases developing on precontact relationships. At one point, the Iroquois constructed a powerful, if brief, alliance involving groups from the Gaspé Peninsula to the Ohio Valley. In Mexico the Mixtón Wars around Zacatecas in the 1500s involved numerous regional populations that gave the Spanish difficulties for a time. The Ghost Dance religious movement on the Plains in the late nineteenth century transcended group boundaries, though it never became a basis for a political coalition, despite the fears of some government officials that it might.

In more recent times, as we have seen, Australian indigenous people have formed pan-Aboriginal political organizations and regional coalitions such as the Pitjandjatjara Land Council that have operated with some success in land rights cases. In Canada the Grand Council of the Cree in collaboration with the Inuit Tapirisat and other native organizations was able to exert some pressure in negotiating the appropriation of their lands, though unable to prevent it. The sense of indigenous unity expressed in the Assembly of First Nations reflects this trend. In the actions of Elijah Harper in defeating the Meech Lake Accord, indigenous people have insisted that their interests within the Canadian state are on a par with those of the Province of Quebec.

The dynamic of interest groups competing within and beyond state arenas is a simple principle. But then, so is the force of gravity. The effects of gravity involve interesting and complex results, in phenomena ranging from architecture to flight to the aging human body. We have seen many similarities in the actions of state systems—some of them strikingly parallel despite the differences in the populations involved. In case after case, we have seen that constituencies within states have operated according to the single guiding principle of their own advantage. The ways in which powerful interests have dealt with indigenous peoples have reflected this principle, according to varying historical circumstances.

Ultimately, many factors that we would expect to be significant have made little difference. It does not seem to matter whether indigenous populations have been large or small, densely settled or scattered. It does not seem to matter in the long run whether they have met intrusions peacefully or with violent resistance. It does not even seem to matter whether they have possessed resources of apparent value. Indigenous Hawaiians lost a sacred island, Ka'o'olawe, for U.S. Navy bombing practice. Innu territory in northeastern Canada has been used for NATO supersonic aircraft maneuvers. Bikini, Kwajalein, and Muruoa atolls in the Pacific became sites for nuclear bomb tests. Hazardous waste disposal companies have approached many Native American reservations in the United States.

The Marshall Islands, where the United States conducted sixty-seven atmospheric nuclear tests during the 1940s and 1950s, experienced severe contamination. "In 1994, releases of classified information about the test programme in the Marshalls, confirmed that not only has the United States been lying for 40 years about the extent of the contamination but that the US deliberately exposed the Marshallese people to radiation as part of a medical experiment code-named 'Project 4.1'" (Rashid 1995:15). Ironically, the Republic of Marshall Islands government now has offered the islands to store nuclear waste.

At present, however, France seems to lead the world in the abuse of Pacific island indigenous populations through nuclear testing. France has conducted approximately 130 atmospheric and underground nuclear tests in French Polynesia since 1966. In 1985, as the Greenpeace protesters' ship *Rainbow Warrior* stood in New Zealand's Auckland harbor, French commandos sank it, killing a photographer on board. On July 9, 1995, the *Rainbow Warrior II* sailed into the territorial waters of French Polynesia to protest a nuclear test on Muruoa Atoll, 650 miles east of Tahiti. French commandos assaulted the ship with tear gas and boarded it, arresting eleven protesters.

Although former French President François Mitterrand had suspended nuclear testing in 1992, newly elected President Jacques Chirac announced that he would resume them. Fifteen Pacific island nations protested, and Australia and New Zealand suspended military cooperation with France. President Chirac, nonetheless, remained adamant in his intention to carry on eight more nuclear tests during the coming year.

Perhaps the most significant issue affecting the fortunes of indigenous peoples has been the extent to which their continued existence has been useful to larger interests. The particular histories or cultures of the groups involved does not seem to have made much difference except to the extent that they have developed the ability to link their interests with those of other constituencies.

Are They Us?

We should note that individuals within the most powerful constituencies have often protested against oppressive tactics. Alexander Wollaston (1988), explorer, adventurer, and honorary secretary of the Royal Geographic Society of London, argued strenuously in 1920 that Europeans should leave the interior of New Guinea untouched. In the United States in 1871, Vincent Colyer (1971) urged humane policies toward the Apache.

As it happens, however, such voices usually have not affected policy in any significant way. Wollaston appears as an interesting historical aberration. As to his ideas, "The president of the Royal Society brushed them aside by suggesting that Britain really needed all of the land, labor, and natural resources it could get" (Bodley 1988:359). Colyer, called a "black dog" in local newspaper editorials that called for his murder, barely escaped the wrath of local Arizona citizens with his life.

Individuals in key positions have played prominent roles in the process, to be sure. Heads of state and other high officials have been able to enact programs and set policies. But such people usually occupy pivotal positions in the first place because they represent the interests of powerful constituencies. To the extent that they fail to do so, they rarely occupy those positions for very long.

Lázaro Cárdenas in Mexico served out his term as president, but after he left office his successors dismantled most of what he had accomplished on behalf of indigenous peoples. Even the Spanish monarchs were unable to carry out reforms that conflicted with some of the most powerful interest groups within their state, such as the Church.

The process has clearly been a matter of collective dynamics rather than individual decision. Major changes have occurred only when the interests of constituencies and the parameters of the interest groups themselves have changed. Thus, in Mexico and the United States, historic processes led to a critical divergence of interests between the colonial populations and their respective Crowns, culminating in revolution. For some brief periods in Mexico, *criollos* and *indios* acted in concert through their common interest in overcoming the power of *gachupines*. But this common interest proved fleeting when competition for land set these populations against one another.

If there is much reason for optimism in this rather discouraging model, it may lie in the fluidity of interest group parameters. We have seen that changes have come about when interest group concerns and power bases have shifted.

Such change may not necessarily bring relief to weaker constituencies. In some cases, powerful elites who oppress indigenous peoples have recruited the support of masses whose interests, by most objective measures, have not coincided with those in power. Racism has been a useful means of dividing the weak.

Having examined these various cases and histories, we have seen what has happened to indigenous peoples at the hands of more powerful interests. But neither the author nor most readers, probably, are members of indigenous populations. Do we share anything with them besides our general humane concerns for other human beings?

Indigenous peoples now are seeking common cause and devising strategies more frequently on a global scale. In some cases, collaborative efforts have transcended the "indigenous/nonindigenous" categories. It seems evident that indigenous peoples share overlapping concerns with a vastly larger proportion of the world's people.

As trade barriers continue to fall and transnational corporations use states as stepping stones for global enterprises, much of the world's population has become less relevant to the elites. Small numbers of the extremely powerful continue to extract resources at an increasing rate, while improved technology results in worsening global unemployment and plummeting wages. The *New York Times* reports that United States Labor Department figures in 1995 "are particularly striking because they suggest that wage problems in the work force do not just reflect a widening gap between high-paid workers and low-paid workers. People who rely on paychecks also appear to be losing ground to people with dividends and investment gains" (Bradsher 1994:4). Even in the old First World states, a growing proportion of the population are unneeded for labor and too poor to be of much interest as consumers.

The number of people that this process places at a disadvantage is growing. Despite their geographic and cultural diversity, millions suffer in common from the widening disparity in wealth and the environmental degradation of corporate operations. Perhaps this will become a principle for the formation of a larger and more effective transnational interest group.

There are some indications of this, albeit on a small scale. In Australia, Australian National Parks and the Anangu people have collaborated in the joint management of Ulura–Kata Tjuta National Park. The park includes Uluru (Ayers Rock), a sacred site that the Australian government returned to the Anangu people (see Wittaker 1994). A particular concern of the indigenous population and the park scientists has been the protection of endangered species in the area. "Anangu readily showed scientists where to find endangered species and taught them tracking skills which helped them locate animals they had been struggling to record" (Thompson 1992:38). Parks in other areas have addressed the protection of indigenous rights as well as the environment and endangered species (see Clad 1988).

There are many pitfalls and problems with such ventures, which to a great extent depend on genuine collaboration and the reconciliation of divergent concerns, like the need of indigenous peoples to hunt for subsistence. Nor can parks offer solutions to many of the array of other problems that confront indigenous populations. In some African game parks, the exclusion of pastoral peoples with their herds has resulted in ecological changes from grassland to shrub growth that has caused much of the game to leave.

The potential significance of park initiatives, however, lies more importantly in the coalescence of interests that otherwise would have little in common in a shared effort to oppose environmental and social destruction. Much about this collaboration is new, although in some ways it amounts to a contemporary version of an old pattern. We have seen coalitions in the past. We have also seen that as the political landscape develops, indigenous interests have sometimes been able to use mechanisms of the state, such as the legal system, to some advantage, even though such structures had developed initially to serve the interests of the elite.

In contemporary times, the global communications media may offer greater opportunities. Mass public opinion, though often muted and manipulated, can be effective in opposing corporate initiatives. There may be some opportunities for raising the consciousness of the public regarding the extent to which its interests and those of indigenous peoples coincide. Strategies utilizing the "politics of embarrassment" may illuminate some of the more outrageous aspects of corporate and state collusion. Consumer boycotts can change corporate policy, particularly if they mobilize populations on which transnationals rely for markets. Increasing public awareness of ecological and social rapine may have some role to play in the future.

Perhaps placing hope in this development is overly optimistic, but it could not have happened in earlier times. It is naive to hope that human beings will cease acting to their own advantage, but perhaps many may come to perceive their interests in a broader way. The possibility that a wide spectrum of humanity will perceive a common interest in time to take effective action may be our best hope for survival.

From the perspective of the interest group model we have employed here, it seems that most of us who are not members of the small political and economic elite do, indeed, share some of the interests of these populations. During the past few decades, as Richard Barrett and John Cavanaugh (1994) and others have pointed out, the increasing global disparities in wealth and the decreasing need for labor has made much of the world's population less relevant to the most powerful global interests. In effect, larger segments of the world's population have been relegated to many of the circumstances that had mainly been the lot of indigenous peoples.

We might consider that many policies toward indigenous peoples derived not merely from the fact that they were indigenous. That identity often became an ideological rationale, but these policies arose more importantly from their having been relegated *as* indigenous populations into the role of weak interest groups in a competitive arena.

In many states now, including the United States, the nonindigenous poor and disadvantaged hold a comparable status. To an increasing degree, they are experiencing many of the same politically oppressive measures that states have directed at indigenous populations.

In late 1994, members of the conservative majority in the United States Congress proposed taking children from mothers on welfare and placing them in institutions. As we recall, similar measures separated tens of thousands of indigenous children from their families in Australia, Canada, the United States, and Mexico. Katha Politt (1994), writing in *The Nation*, points out that to relegate such children to orphanages would hardly be an economic saving, but this factor did not stop the process in the past. Other recent measures have involved the elimination of school lunch subsidies for poor children, a proposal to eliminate support for medical treatment for impoverished disabled children, and other "reforms" in the same vein.

In June 1995, President Bill Clinton, addressing a conference of state governors, warned that such measures harmed a constituency that had little voice, but who would end up "on their doorstep." A commentator on National Public Radio, however, stated that the governors were fed up with assistance programs that had not been effective. They would, he believed, insist on "mandatory work" for aid. In the present context of widespread job elimination and the devaluation of labor, we can only guess at what form this mandatory work might take and what its level of compensation might be.

The trend seems clear. The mass of the indigent populations of states are tending to become "indigenized" regardless of their ethnic heritage. The most powerful interests are shaping state policies in ways that tend to blur the difference between the indigenous and nonindigenous weaker constituencies. Those in power have found it easy to see the disadvantaged as a generic "other," particularly when there has not been any particular use for them at the time.

Clearly, racism has been a predominant aspect of this economic division of resources in all the states we have considered. But to a greater extent than before, the disadvantaged have come to share many common interests in opposition to the small elite who control most of the wealth and exercise most of the power in modern postindustrial states—partly because they have become less useful to those interests. As the problems of this mass of the world populations grow, the disadvantaged will become less and less convenient.

Greater perception of these shared concerns might help. Coalitions, as we have seen, have often been effective in the past. Whether effective coalitions embracing the indigenous, the disenfranchised, and the concerned can develop in the future remains to be seen.

References
Cited

· · · · · · · · ·

Abel, Kerry
  1993 *Drum Songs: Glimpses of Dene History*. Montreal and Kingston: McGill-Queens University Press.

Alexander, Malcolm
  1989 "Australia: A Settler Society in a Changing World." In *Australian Studies: A Survey*. Ed. James Walter. New York: Oxford University Press. Pp. 49–69.

Allen, Robert S.
  1988 "A Witness to Murder: The Cypress Hill Massacre and the Conflict of Attitudes toward Native People of the Canadian-American West during the 1870's." In *As Long as the Sun Shines and Water Flows: A Reader in Canadian Native Studies*. Ed. Ian A. L. Getty and Antoine Lussier. Vancouver: University of British Columbia Press. Pp. 229–246.

Altman, J. C.
  1983 *Aborigines and Mining Royalties in the Northern Territory*. Canberra: Australian Institute of Aboriginal Studies.
  1987 *Hunter-Gatherers Today: An Aboriginal Economy in North Australia*. Canberra: Australian Institute of Aboriginal Studies.

Althusser, Louis
  1971 *Lenin and Philosophy and Other Essays*. London: New Left.

253

Ambler, Marjane
   1990 *Breaking the Iron Bonds: Indian Control of Energy Development.*
         Lawrence: University Press of Kansas.

Americas Watch
   1990 *Human Rights in Mexico. A Policy of Impunity.* Americas Watch Re-
         port. New York: Human Rights Watch.

Anderson, Benedict
   1983 *Imagined Communities: Reflections on the Origin and Spread of Na-
         tionalism.* New York: Verso.

Ankerson, Dudley
   1984 *Agrarian Warlord: Saturnino Cedillo and the Mexican Revolution in
         San Luis Potosi.* DeKalb: Northern Illinois University Press.

Arizona Territorial Legislature
   1871 *Memorial and Affidavits Showing Outrages Perpetrated by Apache
         Indians, in the Territory of Arizona, During the Years 1869 and 1870.*
         San Francisco: Francis and Valentine, Printers.

Armitage, Andrew
   1995 *Comparing the Policy of Aboriginal Assimilation: Australia, Canada,
         and New Zealand.* Vancouver: University of British Columbia Press.

Asch, Michael
   1984 *Home and Native Land: Aboriginal Rights and the Canadian Consti-
         tution.* Toronto: Methuen.
   1988 "The Slavey Indians: The Relevance of Ethnohistory to Develop-
         ment." In *Native Peoples: The Canadian Experience.* Ed. R. Bruce
         Morrison and C. Roderick Wilson. Toronto: McClelland and Stewart.
         Pp. 271–296.
   1989 "To Negotiate into Confederation: Canadian Aboriginal Views on
         Their Political Rights." In *We Are Here: Politics of Aboriginal Land
         Tenure.* Ed. Edwin N. Wilsem. Berkeley: University of California Press.
         Pp. 118–137.
   1993 "Aboriginal Self-Government and Canadian Identity: Building Recon-
         ciliation." In *Ethnicity and Aboriginality: Case Studies in Ethno-
         nationalism.* Ed. Michael Levin. Toronto: University of Toronto Press.
         Pp. 29–52.

Austin, James E., and Gustavo Esteva, eds.
   1987 *Food Policy in Mexico: The Search for Self-Sufficiency.* Ithaca: Cornell
         University Press.

Avery, John
   1983 "The Recent History of the Boroloolu Aboriginal People and Their
         Struggle for Land Rights." In *We Are Bosses Ourselves: The Status and
         Role of Aboriginal Women Today.* Canberra: Australian Institute of
         Aboriginal Studies. Pp. 62–65.

Bancroft, Hubert Howe
   1962 *History of Arizona and New Mexico, 1530–1888.* Albuquerque: Horn
         and Wallace.

Barkin, David, Rosemary L. Batt, and Billie R. DeWalt
1990   *Food Crops vs. Feed Crops: The Global Substitution of Grains in Production.* Boulder, CO: Lynne Reiner.

Barret, Richard J., and John Cavanaugh
1994   *Global Dreams: Imperial Corporations and the New World Order.* New York: Simon and Schuster.

Barry, Tom
1992   *Mexico: A Country Guide.* Albuquerque: Inter-Hemispheric Education Resource Center.
1995   *Zapata's Revenge: Free Trade and the Farm Crisis in Mexico.* Boston: South End Press.

Barsh, Russel Lawrence
1994   "Indian Policy at the Beginning of the 1990s: The Trivialization of Struggle." In *American Indian Policy: Self-Governance and Economic Development.* Ed. Lyman H. Legters and Fremont J. Lyden. Westport, CT: Greenwood. Pp. 54–70.

Bell, Diane
1993   *Daughters of the Dreaming.* Minneapolis: University of Minnesota Press.

Beltrán, Aguirre Gonzalo
1979   *Regions of Refuge.* Society for Applied Anthropology Monograph Series 12. Washington, DC: Society for Applied Anthropology.

Benjamin, Thomas
1989   *A Rich Land, a Poor People: Politics and Society in Modern Chiapas.* Albuquerque: University of New Mexico Press.

Berdan, Frances E.
1982   *The Aztecs of Central Mexico: An Imperial Society.* New York: Holt, Rinehart and Winston.

Berger, Thomas R.
1977   *Northern Frontier, Northern Homeland: The Report of the Mackenzie Valley Pipeline Inquiry.* Ottawa: Minister of Supply and Services Canada.

Berndt, Ronald M., and Catherine H. Berndt
1987   *The End of an Era: Aboriginal Labor in the Northern Territory.* Canberra: Australian Institute of Aboriginal Studies.
1992   *The World of the First Australians: Aboriginal Traditional Life: Past and Present.* Canberra: Aboriginal Studies Press.

Biolsi, Thomas
1991   "Indian Self-Government as a Technique of Domination." *American Indian Quarterly* 15(1):23–28.
1994   "The Political Economy of Lakota Consciousness." In *The Political Economy of North American Indians.* Ed. John H. Moore. Norman: University of Oklahoma Press. Pp. 20–42.
1995   "The Birth of the Reservation: Making the Modern Individual among the Lakota." *American Ethnologist* 22(1):28–53.

Bishop, Charles
  1974   *The Northern Ojibwa and the Fur Trade.* Toronto: Holt, Rinehart and Winston of Canada.

Bissonnette, John
  1993   "Aboriginal Land Claim Agreements and Self-Government." *Canada Today/Canada d'Aujourd'hui* 23(1):6–9.

Bodley, John H.
  1982   *Victims of Progress.* Palo Alto: Mayfield.
  1988   *Tribal Peoples and Development Issues: A Global Overview.* Mountain View, CA: Mayfield.

Bolt, Christine
  1987   *American Indian Policy and American Reform: Case Studies of the Campaign to Assimilate the American Indian.* London: Allen and Unwin.

Bolton, Herbert E.
  1916   *Spanish Explorations in the Southwest, 1542–1706.* New York: Charles Scribner's Sons.

Bonwick, J.
  1970   *The Last of the Tasmanians; or, The Black War of Van Diemen's Land.* New York: Johnson Reprint.

Boserup, Ester
  1965   *The Conditions of Agricultural Growth.* Chicago: Aldine.

Bradsher, Keith
  1995   "Productivity Is All, but It Doesn't Pay Well." *New York Times* Sunday, June 25, "Week in Review": 4.

Braudel, Fernand
  1979   *The Perspective of the World.* Vol. III of *Civilization and Capitalism.* New York: Harper and Row.

Brinton, Daniel G.
  1896   "The Aims of Anthropology." *Proceedings of the 44th Meeting of the American Association of the Advancement of Science*, pp. 1–17.

Broome, R.
  1982   *Aboriginal Australians: Black Response to White Dominance, 1788–1980.* Sydney: George Allen and Unwin.

Brown, Jennifer S. H.
  1980   *Strangers in Blood: Fur Trade Company Families in Indian Country.* Vancouver: University of British Columbia Press.

Brown, Paula
  1982   "Chimbu Disorder: Tribal Fighting in Newly Independent PNG." *Pacific Viewpoint* 23:1–21.

Brugge, David M.
  1994   *The Navajo-Hopi Land Dispute.* Albuquerque: University of New Mexico Press.

Bukharin, Nikolai I.
[1925] 1961 *Historical Materialism: A System of Sociology.* Ann Arbor: University of Michigan Press.

Burawoy, Michael
1976 "The Functions and Reproduction of Migrant Labor: Comparative Material from Southern Africa and the United States." *American Journal of Sociology* 81:1050–1087.

Burridge, Kenelm
1960 *Mambu: A Study of Melanesian Cargo Movements and Their Social and Ideological Background.* New York: Harper Torchbooks.
1973 *Encountering Aborigines: A Case Study: Anthropology and the Australian Aboriginal.* New York: Pergamon.

Burton, William, and Richard Lowenthal
1974 "The First of the Mohicans." *American Ethnologist* 1(4):589–599.

Butlin, N. G.
1983 *Our Original Aggression: Aboriginal Populations of Southeastern Australia, 1788–1850.* Sydney: George Allen and Unwin.

Campbell, Bruce
1991 "Beggar Thy Neighbor." *NACLA Report on the Americas* May 1991: 22.

Campbell, Howard, Leigh Binford, Miguel Bartolome, and Alicia Barabos, eds.
1993 *Zapotec Struggles.* Washington, DC: Smithsonian Institution.

Canadian Embassy
1993 "Framing the Issues: The Royal Commission on Aboriginal Peoples." *Canada Today/Canada d'Aujourd'hui* 23(1):12–14.

Cardinal, Harold
1969 *The Unjust Society: The Tragedy of Canada's Indians.* Edmonton: Hurtig.

Carlson, Leonard A.
1985 "What Was It Worth? Economic and Historical Aspects of Determining Awards in Indian Land Claims Cases." In *Irredeemable America: The Indians' Estate and Land Claims.* Ed. Imre Sutton. Albuquerque: University of New Mexico Press. Pp. 87–109.

Castile, George Pierre
1992 "Indian Sign: Hegemony and Symbolism in Federal Policy." In *State and Reservation: New Perspectives on Federal Indian Policy.* Ed. George Pierre Castile and Robert L. Bee. Tucson: University of Arizona Press. Pp. 165–186.

Chance, John K.
1989 *Conquest of the Sierra: Spaniards and Indians in Colonial Oaxaca.* Norman: University of Oklahoma Press.

Chance, Norman A.
1990 *The Inupiat and Arctic Alaska: An Ethnography of Development.* New York: Holt, Rinehart and Winston.

Childe, V. Gordon
  1942 *What Happened in History.* New York: Pelican.

Clad, James C.
  1988 "Conservation and Indigenous Peoples: A Study of Convergent Interests." In *Tribal Peoples and Development Issues: A Global Overview.* Ed. John H. Bodley. Mountain View, CA: Mayfield. Pp. 320–333.

Claessen, Henri J. M., and Peter Skalnik, eds.
  1978 *The Early State.* The Hague: Mouton.

Claessen, Henri J. M., and Pieter van de Velde, eds.
  1991 *Early State Economics.* New Brunswick: Transaction.

Coatsworth, John H.
  1988 "Patterns of Rural Rebellion in Latin America: Mexico in Comparative Perspective." In *Riot, Rebellion, and Revolution: Rural Social Conflict in Mexico.* Ed. Friedrich Katz. Princeton: Princeton University Press. Pp. 21–62.

Cochrane, D. Glynn
  1970 *Big Men and Cargo Cults.* Oxford: Clarendon Press.

Cohen, Felix
  1942 *Handbook of Federal Indian Law.* Albuquerque: University of New Mexico Press.

Cohen, Ronald, and Elman R. Service
  1978 *Origins of the State: The Anthropology of Political Evolution.* Philadelphia: Institute for the Study of Human Issues.

Collier, George
  1994a *Basta! Land and the Zapatista Rebellion in Chiapas.* Oakland: Institute for Food and Development Policy.
  1994b "The New Politics of Exclusion: Antecedents to the Rebellion in Mexico." *Dialectical Anthropology* 19(1):1–44.
  1994c "The Roots of the Rebellion in Chiapas." *Cultural Survival Quarterly* 18(1):14–18.

Colyer, Vincent
  1971 *Peace with the Apaches of New Mexico and Arizona: Report of Vincent Colyer, Member of Board of Indian Commissioners.* Freeport, NY: Books for Libraries Press.

Connolly, Bob, and Robin Anderson
  1987 *First Contact.* New York: Viking.

Connor, Walker
  1973 "The Politics of Ethnonationalism." *Journal of International Affairs* 27(1):1–21.

Coombs, Herbert Cole
  1994 *Aboriginal Autonomy: Issues and Strategies.* Cambridge: Cambridge University Press.

Cornelius, Wayne, and Ann Craig

1988 *Politics in Mexico: An Introduction and Overview.* San Diego: Center for U.S.-Mexican Studies.

Cornell, Stephen, and Marta C. Gil-Swedburg

1990 "Sociohistorical Factors in American Indian Economic Development: A Comparison of Three Apache Cases." *Harvard Project on American Indian Economic Development.* Project Report Series, John F. Kennedy School of Government. Cambridge: Harvard University.

Cortés, José

1989 *Views from the Apache Frontier: Report on the Northern Provinces of New Spain.* Ed. Elizabeth A. H. John. Norman: University of Oklahoma Press.

Cowling, K., and R. Sigden

1987 "Market Exchange and the Concept of a Transnational Corporation." *British Review of Economic Issues* 9:57–68.

Cronon, William

1983 *Changes in the Land: Indians, Colonists, and the Ecology of New England.* New York: Hill and Wang.

Czaplicka, M. A.

1914 *Siberia: A Study in Social Anthropology.* Oxford: Clarendon Press.

Darnell, Regna

1974 *Readings in the History of Anthropology.* New York: Harper and Row.

David, Joe

1992 "A Two-Row Violation: Mohawks on Trial in Quebec Turned the Courtroom into a Vehicle for Arising Issues of Sovereignty." *Cultural Survival Quarterly* 16(3):12–14.

De'Ath, Colin, and Gregory Michalenko

1988 "High Technology and Original Peoples: The Case of Deforestation in Papua New Guinea and Canada." In *Tribal Peoples and Development Issues: A Global Overview.* Ed. John H. Bodley. Mountain View, CA: Mayfield. Pp. 166–180.

Deloria, Vine, Jr.

1985 *Behind the Trail of Broken Treaties: An Indian Declaration of Independence.* Austin: University of Texas Press.

Deloria, Vine, Jr., and Clifford M. Lytle

1983 *American Indians, American Justice.* Austin: University of Texas Press.

Denoon, Donald

1983 *Settler Capitalism: The Dynamics of Dependent Development in the Southern Hemisphere.* New York: Oxford University Press.

Dickason, Olive Patricia

1992 *Canada's First Nations: A History of Founding Peoples from Earliest Times.* Toronto: McClelland and Stewart.

Dicken, Peter
1994   "The Roephe Lecture in Economic Geography—Local Tensions: Firms and States in the Global Space-Economy." *Economic Geography* 70:101–128.

Dobyns, Henry F.
1966   "An Appraisal of Techniques with a New Hemispheric Estimate." *Current Anthropology* 7:395–416.
1983   *Their Number Become Thinned: Native American Population Dynamics in Eastern North America.* Knoxville: University of Tennessee Press.

Donovan, Colleen M.
1993   "East Timor Activists Tour North America." *Action for Cultural Survival* No. 10, June 1, 1993.

Doobov, A., and R. Doobov
1972   "Queensland: Australia's Deep South." In *Racism: The Australian Experience.* Ed. F. S. Stevens. Vol. 2. *Black versus White.* New York: Taplinger. Pp. 159–170.

Druke, Mary A.
1988   "Iroquois and Iroquoian in Canada." In *Native Peoples: The Canadian Experience.* Ed. R. Bruce Morrison and C. Roderick Wilson. Toronto: McClelland and Stewart. Pp. 302–323.

Edgerton, Robert B.
1989   *Mau Mau: An African Crucible.* New York: Ballantine.
1992   *Sick Societies: Challenging the Myth of Primitive Harmony.* New York: Free Press.

Eggan, Fred
1966   *The American Indian: Perspectives for the Study of Social Change.* Chicago: Aldine.

Eggleston, Elizabeth
1975   *Fear, Favour, or Affection. Aborigines and the Criminal Law in Victoria, South Australia, and Western Australia.* Canberra: Australian National University Press.

Eichstaedt, Peter H.
1994   *If You Poison Us: Uranium and Native Americans.* Santa Fe: Red Crane Books.

Elkin, A. P.
1951   "Reaction and Interaction: A Food-Gathering People and European Settlement in Australia." *American Anthropologist* 53:184–186.

Erasmus, Charles
1961   *Man Takes Control.* Minneapolis: University of Minnesota Press.

Ewers, John C.
1955   *The Horse in Blackfoot Indian Culture.* Bureau of American Ethnology Bulletin 159. Washington, DC: Smithsonian Institution.

Fagan, Brian M.
1991   *Ancient North America: The Archaeology of a Continent.* London: Thames and Hudson.

Falkowski, James E.
  1992 *Indian Law/Race Law: A Five-Hundred-Year History.* New York: Praeger.

Farriss, Nancy
  1983 "Indians in Colonial Yucatán: Three Perspectives." In *Spaniards and Indians in Colonial Mesoamerica: Essays in the History of Ethnic Relations.* Ed. Murdo MacLeod and Robert Wasserman. Lincoln: University of Nebraska Press. Pp. 1–39.

Fehrenbach, T. R.
  1973 *Fire and Blood: A History of Mexico.* New York: Bonanza Books.

Feit, Harvey A.
  1988 "Hunting and the Quest for Power: The James Bay Cree and Whitemen in the Twentieth Century." In *Native Peoples: The Canadian Experience.* Ed. R. Bruce Morrison and C. Roderick Wilson. Toronto: McClelland and Stewart. Pp. 271–307.
  1989 "James Bay Cree Self-Governance and Land Management." In *We Are Here: Politics of Aboriginal Land Tenure.* Ed. Edwin N. Wilmsen. Berkeley: University of California Press. Pp. 68–98.

Fixico, Donald L.
  1986 *Termination and Relocation: Federal Indian Policy, 1945–1960.* Albuquerque: University of New Mexico Press.

Flanagan, Thomas
  1988 "Louis Riel and Aboriginal Rights." In *As Long as the Sun Shines and Water Flows: A Reader in Canadian Native Studies.* Ed. Ian A. L. Getty and Antoine S. Lussier. Vancouver: University of British Columbia Press. Pp. 247–262.

Forbes, Jack D.
  1960 *Apache, Navaho, and Spaniard.* Norman: University of Oklahoma Press.
  1994 "A Native American Perspective on NAFTA." *Cultural Survival Quarterly* 17(4):3.

Fox, Jonathan
  1993 *The Politics of Food in Mexico: State Power and Social Mobilization.* Ithaca: Cornell University Press.

Fowler, Melvin L.
  1975 *Perspectives in Cahokia Archaeology.* Bulletin 10. Springfield: Illinois Archaeological Survey.

Frank, Andre Gunder
  1972 "Introduction." In *Dependence and Underdevelopment: Latin America's Political Economy.* Ed. James D. Cockroft, Andre G. Frank, and Dale L. Johnson. Garden City, NY: Doubleday. Pp. ix–xxix.
  1975 *On Capitalist Underdevelopment.* Bombay: Oxford University Press.

Frideres, J. S.
  1993 "The Quest for Indian Development in Canada: Contrasts and Contradictions." In *American Indian Political Economy.* Ed. John H. Moore. Norman: University of Oklahoma Press. Pp. 161–183.

Fried, Morton H.
   1967   *The Evolution of Political Society.* New York: Random House.
   1968a *On the Evolution of Stratification and the State.* New York: Random House.
   1968b "State." In *International Encyclopedia of the Social Sciences.* New York: Macmillan and Free Press. Vol. 15. Pp. 143–150.

Friedlander, Judith
   1986   "The National Indigenist Institute of Mexico Reinvents the Indian: The Pame Example." *American Ethnologist* 13:363–367.

Frost, A.
   1981   "New South Wales as Terra Nullius: The British Denial of Aboriginal Land Rights." *Historical Studies* 19:77.

Galtung, Johan
   1983   *Self-Reliance: Beitrage zu einer alternativen Entwicklungsstrategie.* München: Minerva.

Garton, Stephen
   1989   "Aboriginal History." In *Australian Studies: A Survey.* Ed. James Walter. New York: Oxford University Press. Pp. 189–215.

Gates, Marylin
   1993   *In Default: Peasants, the Debt Crisis, and the Agricultural Challenge.* Boulder, CO: Westview.

Goodale, Jane C.
   1971   *Tiwi Wives: A Study of the Women of Melville Island, North Australia.* Seattle: University of Washington Press.
   1982   "Production and Reproduction of Key Resources among the Tiwi of North Australia." In *Resource Managers: North American and Australian Hunter-Gatherers.* Ed. Nancy M. Williams and E. S. Hunn. Boulder, CO: Westview. Pp. 197–210.

Gordon, Robert J.
   1989   "Can Namibian San Stop Dispossession of Their Land?" In *We Are Here: Politics of Aboriginal Land Tenure.* Ed. Edwin N. Wilmsen. Berkeley: University of California Press. Pp. 138–154.
   1992   *The Bushman Myth: The Making of a Namibian Underclass.* Boulder, CO: Westview.

Gould, Stephen Jay
   1981   *The Mismeasure of Man.* New York: Norton.

Gramsci, Antonio
   1971   *Selections from the Prison Notebooks.* New York: International Publishers.

Graymount, Barbara
   1972   *The Iroquois in the American Revolution.* Syracuse: Syracuse University Press.

Green, L. C., and Olive Dickason
   1989   *The Law of Nations and the New World.* Edmonton: University of Alberta Press.

Green, Michael D.
1982 *The Politics of Indian Removal.* Lincoln: University of Nebraska Press.

Green, Stanley C.
1987 *The Mexican Republic: The First Decade, 1823–1832.* Pittsburgh: University of Pittsburgh Press.

Greenwood, Gordon, ed.
1959 *Australia: A Social and Political History.* Sydney: Angus and Robertson.

Griffen, William B.
1988 *Utmost Good Faith: Patterns of Apache-Mexican Hostilities in Northern Chihuahua Warfare, 1821–1848.* Albuquerque: University of New Mexico Press.

Hale, Charles A.
1989 *The Transformation of Liberalism in Late Nineteenth-Century Mexico.* Princeton: Princeton University Press.

Hall, David J.
1983 "Clifford Sifton and Canadian Indian Administration, 1896–1905." In *As Long as the Sun Shines and Water Flows: A Reader in Canadian Native Studies.* Ed. Ian A. L. Getty and Antoine S. Lussier. Vancouver: University of British Columbia Press. Pp. 120–144.

Hamilton, Annette
1980 "Dual Social Systems: Labour and Women's Secret Rites in the Eastern Western Desert of Australia." *Oceania* 51(1):4–19.

Hamilton, Nora
1982 *The Limits of State Autonomy: Post-Revolutionary Mexico.* Princeton: Princeton University Press.

Harding, Erika
1992 "Human Rights." In *Mexico: A Country Guide.* Ed. Tom Barry. Albuquerque: Inter-Hemispheric Education Resource Center.

Harris, Marvin
1968 *The Rise of Anthropological Theory.* New York: Thomas Y. Crowell.

Hart, C. W. M., and A. R. Pilling
1960 *The Tiwi of North Australia.* New York: Holt, Rinehart and Winston.

Harvey, Neil
1994 *Rebellion in Chiapas: Rural Reforms, Campesino Radicalism, and the Limits to Salinismo.* San Diego: Center for U.S.-Mexican Studies.

Head, Brian
1989 "Political Ideas and Institutions." In *Australian Studies: A Survey.* New York: Oxford University Press.

Heider, Karl
1991 *Grand Valley Dani: Peaceful Warriors.* New York: Holt, Rinehart and Winston.

Hewitt de Alcántara, Cynthia
1976 *Modernizing Mexican Agriculture: Socioeconomic Implications of a*

Technological Change, 1940–1970. Geneva: United Nations Research Institute for Social Development.

Hiatt, L. R.
  1989   "Aboriginal Land Tenure and Contemporary Claims in Australia." In *We Are Here: Politics of Aboriginal Land Tenure.* Ed. Edwin N. Wilmsen. Berkeley: University of California Press. Pp. 99–117.

Hickerson, Harold
  1962   *The Southwestern Chippewa: An Ethnohistorical Study.* Memoir 92. American Anthropological Association.
  1970   *The Chippewa and Their Neighbors: A Study in Ethnohistory.* New York: Holt, Rinehart and Winston.

Higgott, Richard A.
  1983   *Political Development Theory: The Contemporary Debate.* London: Croom Helm.

Hill, Jane H.
  1991   "In Neca Gobierno de Puebla: Mexicano Penetrations of the Mexican State." In *Nation-States and Indians in Latin America.* Ed. Greg Urgan and Joel Sherzer. Austin: University of Texas Press. Pp. 72–94.

Hlambohn, Wally, and Beryl Cook
  1992   "PNG Emphasis on Internal Security." *Pacific Islands Monthly* 62(3):8–9.

Hobsbawm, Eric
  1989   *Politics for a Rational Left: Political Writings, 1977–1988.* New York: Verso.

Hodges, Donald, and Ross Gandy
  1983   *Mexico, 1910–1982: Reform or Revolution?* London: Zed.

Hogan, Evelyn
  1992   "Iago's the Name, but What's the Game?" *Pacific Islands Monthly* 62(9):10.

Hout, Wil
  1993   *Capitalism and the Third World: Development, Dependence and the World System.* Brookfield, VT: Edward Elgar.

Howe, Marvine
  1995   "A Stone Age Corner of Indonesia." *New York Times* Sunday, April 23, Travel section.

Hoxie, Frederick E.
  1984   *A Final Promise: The Campaign to Assimilate the Indians, 1880–1920.* Lincoln: University of Nebraska Press.

Hu-DeHart, Evelyn
  1988   "Peasant Rebellion in the Northwest: The Yaqui Indians of Sonora, 1740–1976." In *Riot, Rebellion, and Revolution: Rural Social Conflict in Mexico.* Ed. Friedrich Katz. Princeton: Princeton University Press. Pp. 141–175.

Hudson, Charles M.
  1976   *The Southeastern Indians.* Knoxville: University of Tennessee Press.

Huel, Raymond
  1988   "A Parting of the Ways: Louis Schmidt's Account of Louis Riel and the Metis Rebellion." In *As Long as the Sun Shines and Water Flows: A Reader in Canadian Native Studies.* Ed. Ian A. L. Getty and Antoine S. Lussier. Vancouver: University of British Columbia Press. Pp. 263–279.

Hughes, Robert
  1986   *The Fatal Shore: The Epic of Australia's Founding.* New York: Vintage Books.

Hyndman, David
  1988   "Melanesian Resistance to Ecocide and Ethnocide: Transnational Mining Projects and the Fourth World on the Island of New Guinea." In *Tribal Peoples and Development Issues: A Global Overview.* Ed. John H. Bodley. Mountain View, CA: Mayfield. Pp. 281–298.

Jablow, Joseph
  1951   *The Cheyenne in Plains Indian Trade Relations, 1795–1840.* New York: J. J. Augustin.

Jenness, Diamond
  1988   "Canada's Indians Yesterday. What of Today?" In *As Long as the Sun Shines and Water Flows: A Reader in Canadian Native Studies.* Ed. Ian A. L. Getty and Antoine S. Lussier. Vancouver: University of British Columbia Press. Pp. 158–163.

Jennings, Francis
  1984   *The Ambiguous Iroquois Empire.* New York: Norton.

John, Elizabeth A. H., ed.
  1989   "Editor's Introduction." In *Views from the Apache Frontier: Report on the Northern Provinces of New Spain by José Cortés.* Trans. John Wheat. Norman: University of Oklahoma Press. Pp. 3–13.

Josephy, Alvin M., Jr.
  1971   *Red Power: The American Indian's Fight for Freedom.* New York: McGraw-Hill.

Kairys, David, ed.
  1982   *The Politics of Law: A Progressive Critique.* New York: Pantheon Books.

Katz, Friedrich, ed.
  1988   *Riot, Rebellion, and Revolution: Rural Social Conflict in Mexico.* Princeton: Princeton University Press.

Keesing, Roger M.
  1983   *Elota's Story: The Life and Times of a Solomon Islands Big Man.* New York: Holt, Rinehart and Winston.

Kehoe, Alice B.
  1989   *The Ghost Dance: Ethnohistory and Revitalization.* New York: Holt, Rinehart and Winston.

1992 *North American Indians: A Comprehensive Account.* Englewood Cliffs, NJ: Prentice-Hall.

Klein, Alan M.
1993 "Political Economy of the Buffalo Hide Trade: Race and Class on the Plains." In *American Indian Political Economy.* Ed. John H. Moore. Norman: University of Oklahoma Press. Pp. 133–160.

Koppes, Clayton R.
1977 "From the New Deal to Termination: Liberalism and Indian Policy, 1933–1953." *Pacific Historical Review* 46:543–566.

Krech, Shepard, III
1984 *The Subarctic Fur Trade: Native Social and Economic Adaptations.* Vancouver: University of British Columbia Press.

Kruger, Linda, and Graciela Etchart
1994 "Forest-Based Economic Development in Native American Lands: Two Case Studies." In *American Indian Policy: Self-Governance and Economic Development.* Ed. Lyman H. Legters and Fremont J. Lyden. Westport, CT: Greenwood. Pp. 191–216.

Kupferer, Harriet Jane
1966 *The "Principal People," 1960: A Study of Cultural and Social Groups of the Eastern Cherokee.* Bureau of American Ethnography Bulletin 196, Anthropological Paper 78. Washington, DC: Smithsonian Institution.

Laclau, Ernesto
1979 *Politics and Ideology in Marxist Theory: Capitalism, Fascism, Populism.* London: New Left.

Lamphere, Louise
1976 "The Internal Colonization of the Navajo People." *Southwest Economy and Society* 1(1):6–13.

Lawrence, Peter
1964 *Road Belong Cargo: A Study of the Cargo Movement in the Southern Madang District.* New York: Humanities Press.

Leacock, Eleanor
1954 "The Montagnais 'Hunting Territory' and the Fur Trade." *American Anthropologist* 56(5). Memoir 78.

Lee, Richard B.
1984 *The Dobe !Kung.* New York: Holt, Rinehart and Winston.

León-Portilla, Miguel
1963 *Aztec Thought and Culture.* Norman: University of Oklahoma Press.

Lerner, David
1964 *The Passing of Traditional Society: Modernizing the Middle East.* New York: Free Press.

Leslie, John F., and Ron Maguire, eds.
1978 *The Historical Development of the Indian Act.* Ottawa: Indian and Northern Affairs.

Levin, M. G., and L. P. Potapov, eds.
1964   *The Peoples of Siberia*. Chicago: University of Chicago Press.

Levy, Daniel, and Gabriel Szekely
1987   *Mexico: Paradoxes of Stability and Change*. Boulder, CO: Westview.

Lewis, I. M.
1968   "Tribal Society." In *International Encyclopedia of the Social Sciences*. New York: Macmillan and Free Press. Vol. 16. Pp. 146–151.

Libby, Ronald T.
1989   *Hawke's Law: The Politics of Mining and Aboriginal Land Rights in Australia*. University Park: Pennsylvania State University Press.

Little, J.
1972   "Legal Status of Aboriginal Peoples: Slaves or Citizens?" In *Racism: The Australian Experience*. Ed. F. S. Stevens. Vol. 2. *Black versus White*. New York: Taplinger. Pp. 77–87.

Littlefield, Alice
1989   "The B.I.A. Boarding School: Theories of Resistance and Social Reproduction." *Humanity and Society* 13:428–441.
1993a "Learning to Labor: Native American Education in the United States, 1880–1930." In *American Indian Political Economy*. Ed. John H. Moore. Norman: University of Oklahoma Press. Pp. 43–59.
1993b "Native American Labor and Public Policy in the United States." In *Marxist Approaches in Economic Anthropology*. Ed. Alice Littlefield and Hill Gates. Monographs in Economic Anthropology 9. New York: University Press of America. Pp. 219–232.

Littlefield, Daniel F., Jr.
1977   *Africans and Seminoles*. Westport, CT: Greenwood.

Macklem, Patrick
1993   "Ethnonationalism, Aboriginal Identities, and the Law." In *Ethnicity and Aboriginality: Case Studies in Ethnonationalism*. Ed. Michael Levin. Toronto: University of Toronto Press. Pp. 9–28.

MacLeod, William Christie
1967   "Celt and Indian: Britain's Old World Frontier in Relation to the New." In *Beyond the Frontier: Social Process and Cultural Change*. Ed. Paul Bohannan and Fred Plog. Garden City, NY: Natural History Press. Pp. 25–41.

Maddock, Kenneth
1980   *Anthropology, Law, and the Definition of Australian Aboriginal Rights to Land*. Nijmegan, Neth.: Catholic University.

Mandelbaum, David G.
1979   *The Plains Cree*. Regina: Canadian Plains Research Centre.

May, Elizabeth
1993   "Canada's Constitutional Referendum: A Defeat for Aboriginal Rights?" *Cultural Survival Quarterly* 17(1):10–11.

McCaskill, Don
1988   "Native People and the Justice System." In *As Long as the Sun Shines and Water Flows: A Reader in Canadian Native Studies*. Ed. Ian A. L. Getty and Antoine S. Lussier. Vancouver: University of British Columbia Press. Pp. 288–298.

McClelland, David C.
1961   *The Achieving Society*. Princeton, NJ: Van Nostrand.

McNab, David T.
1988   "The Administration of Treaty 3: The Location of the Boundaries of Treaty 3 Indian Reserves in Ontario, 1873–1915." In *As Long as the Sun Shines and Water Flows: A Reader in Canadian Native Studies*. Ed. Ian A. L. Getty and Antoine S. Lussier. Vancouver: University of British Columbia Press. Pp. 145–157.

Meggitt, M. J.
1962   *The Desert People*. Sydney: Angus and Robertson.

Menzies, Charles R.
1994   "Stories from Home: First Nations, Land Claims, and Euro-Canadians." *American Ethnologist* 21(4):776–791.

Meyers, William K.
1994   *Forge of Progress, Crucible of Revolt: Origins of the Mexican Revolution in La Comarca Laguna, 1880–1911*. Albuquerque: University of New Mexico Press.

Michels, R.
1948   *Political Parties*. Glencoe, IL: Free Press.

Miller, J. R.
1989 (rev. ed. 1991)   *Skyscrapers Hide the Heavens: A History of Indian-White Relations in Canada*. Toronto: University of Toronto Press.

Miller, Jay
1974   "The Delaware as Women." *American Ethnologist* 1(4):507–514.

Millon, Rene F.
1967   "Teotihuacan." *Scientific American* 216:38–48.

Milloy, John S.
1988   "The Early Indian Acts: Developmental Strategy and Constitutional Change." In *As Long as the Sun Shines and Water Flows: A Reader in Canadian Native Studies*. Ed. Ian A. L. Getty and Antoine S. Lussier. Vancouver: University of British Columbia Press. Pp. 56–64.

Mills, C. Wright
1956   *The Power Elite*. New York: Oxford University Press.

Mooney, James
1896   *The Ghost-Dance Religion and Wounded Knee*. New York: Dover.

Moore, John H.
1987   *The Cheyenne Nation*. Lincoln: University of Nebraska Press.

Moran, Albert
 1989 "Australian Film and Television." In *Australian Studies: A Survey*. Ed. James Walter. New York: Oxford University Press. Pp. 156–174.

Morisset, Jean
 1988 "La Conquete du Nord-Ouest, 1885–1895, or the Imperial Quest of British North America." In *As Long as the Sun Shines and Water Flows: A Reader in Canadian Native Studies*. Ed. Ian A. L. Getty and Antoine S. Lussier. Vancouver: University of British Columbia Press. Pp. 280–287.

Morris, Barry
 1989 *Domesticating Resistance: The Dhan-Gadi Aborigines and the Australian State*. New York: Berg.

Morris, C. Patrick
 1994 "Indian Self-Determination and the Tribal College Movement: A Good Idea That Not Even the Government Can Kill." In *American Indian Policy: Self-Governance and Economic Development*. Ed. Lyman H. Legters and Fremont J. Lyden. Westport, CT: Greenwood. Pp. 71–90.

Morse, Bradford W.
 1984 *Aboriginal Self-Government in Australia and Canada*. Background Paper 4. Institute of Intergovernment Relations. Kingston, Ont.: Queens University.

Mosca, Gaetano
 1939 *The Ruling Class*. New York: McGraw-Hill.

Mulvaney, D. J., and J. Peter White, eds.
 1987 *Australians to 1788*. Sydney: Fairfax, Syme and Weldon Associates.

Munn, Nancy
 1973 *Walbiri Iconography: Graphic Representation and Cultural Symbolism in a Central Australian Society*. Ithaca: Cornell University Press.

Murray, Charles A., and Richard J. Herrnstein
 1994 *The Bell Curve: Intelligence and Class Structure in American Life*. New York: Free Press.

Myers, Fred
 1986 *Pintupi Country, Pintupi Self: Sentiment, Place, and Politics among Western Desert Aborigines*. Washington, DC: Smithsonian Institution.
 1989 "Burning the Truck and Holding the Country: Pintupi Forms of Property and Identity." In *We Are Here: Politics of Aboriginal Land Tenure*. Ed. Edwin N. Wilmsen. Berkeley: University of California Press. Pp. 15–42.
 1994 "Culture-Making: Performing Aboriginality at the Asia Society Gallery." *American Ethnologist* 21(4):679–699.

Neate, Graeme
 1989 *Aboriginal Land Rights Law in the Northern Territory*. Vol. 1. Sydney: Alternative Publishing Cooperative.

Nietschmann, Bernard
 1988 "Third World Colonial Expansion: Indonesia, Disguised Invasion of

Indigenous Nations." In *Tribal Peoples and Development Issues: A Global Overview.* Ed. John H. Bodley. Mountain View, CA: Mayfield. Pp. 191–208.

Nigh, Ronald
1994 "Zapata Rose in 1994: The Indian Rebellion in Chiapas." *Cultural Survival Quarterly* 18(1):9–13.

Oliver, Douglas
1955 *A Solomon Island Society: Kinship and Leadership among the Siuai of Bougainville.* Cambridge: Harvard University Press.

Oliver, Symmes C.
1962 "Ecology and Cultural Continuity as Contributing Factors in the Social Organization of the Plains Indians." *University of California Publications in American Archaeology and Ethnology* 48(1):13–68.

Palmer, Kingsley
1990 "Government Policy and Aboriginal Aspirations: Self-Management at Yalata." In *Going It Alone? Prospects for Aboriginal Autonomy.* Ed. Robert Tonkinson and Michael Howard. Canberra: Aboriginal Studies Press. Pp. 165–183.

Perdue, Theda
1979 *Slavery and the Evolution of Cherokee Society, 1540–1866.* Knoxville: University of Tennessee Press.

Perry, Richard J.
1993 *Apache Reservation: Indigenous Peoples and the American State.* Austin: University of Texas Press.

Peterson, Nicolas, and Marcia Langton, eds.
1983 *Aborigines, Land, and Land Rights.* Canberra: Australian Institute of Aboriginal Studies.

Phillips, George Harwood
1993 *Indians and Intruders in Central California, 1769–1849.* Norman: University of Oklahoma Press.

Philp, Kenneth R.
1983 "Termination: A Legacy of the Indian New Deal." *Western Historical Quarterly* 14:166–179.

Phipps, Helen
1925 *Some Aspects of the Agrarian Revolution in Mexico: A Historical Study.* Austin: University of Texas Press.

Pollitt, Katha
1995 "Subject to Debate." *Nation* 260(6):192.

Pomponio, Alice
1992 *Seagulls Don't Fly into the Bush: Cultural Identity and Development in Melanesia.* Belmont, CA: Wadsworth.

Porter, Joseph C.
1986 *Paper Medicine Man.* Norman: University of Oklahoma Press.

Poulantzas, Nikos
1980   *State, Power, Socialism.* London: Verso.

Povinelli, Elizabeth A.
1993   *Labor's Lot: The Power, History, and Culture of Aboriginal Action.* Chicago: University of Chicago Press.

Powell, J. M.
1988   *An Historical Geography of Modern Australia: The Restive Fringe.* Cambridge: Cambridge University Press.

Price, John
1979   *Indians of Canada: Cultural Dynamics.* Scarborough, Ont.: Prentice-Hall.

Prucha, Paul
1964   "Andrew Jackson's Indian Policy: A Reassessment." *Journal of American History* 56:527–539.

Rashid, Yanus
1995   "Commercial Sense or Sheer Madness." *Pacific Islands Monthly* 65(6): 15–16.

Ray, Arthur J.
1974   *Indians in the Fur Trade.* Toronto: University of Toronto Press.

Reding, Andrew
1995   "Web of Corruption: Narco-Politics in Mexico." *Nation* 261(2):50–54.

Reece, R. H. W.
1974   *Aborigines and Colonists: Aborigines and Colonial Society in New South Wales in the 1830s and 1840s.* Sydney: Sydney University Press.

Reff, Daniel T.
1995   "The 'Predicament of Culture' and Spanish Missionary Accounts of the Tepehuan and Pueblo Revolts." *Ethnohistory* 42(1):63–90.

Reynolds, Henry
1982   *The Other Side of the Frontier: Aboriginal Resistance to the European Invasion of Australia.* Ringwood, Austral.: Penguin.
1987   *Frontier: Aborigines, Settlers, and Land.* Sydney: George Allen and Unwin.

Riding, Alan
1985   *Distant Neighbors: A Portrait of the Mexicans.* New York: Vintage Books.

Ridington, Robin
1990   *Little Bit Know Something: Stories in a Language of Anthropology.* Iowa City: University of Iowa Press.

Robie, David
1989   "Bougainville One Year Later." *Pacific Islands Monthly* 59(22):10–18.
1992   "Diplomacy, or Turning a Blind Eye?" *Pacific Islands Monthly* 62(3):9.

Rogers, Edward S., and Eleanor Leacock
1981   "Montagnais-Naskapai." In *Handbook of North American Indians.* Vol.

15. *Subarctic*. Ed. June Helm. Washington, DC: Smithsonian Institution. Pp. 169–189.

Rose, Deborah Bird
  1991 *Hidden Histories: Black Stories from Victoria River Downs, Humber River, and Wave Hill Stations*. Canberra: Aboriginal Studies Press.

Rowley, C. D.
  1970 *The Destruction of Aboriginal Society: Aboriginal Policy and Practice*. Vol. 1. Canberra: Australian National University.

Ruiz, Ramon Eduardo
  1992 *Triumphs and Tragedy: A History of the Mexican People*. New York: Norton.

Rumsey, Alan
  1989 "Language Groups in Australian Land Claims." *Anthropological Forum* 6(1):69–79.

Rus, Jan
  1983 "Whose Caste War? Indians, Ladinos, and the Chiapas 'Caste War' of 1869." In *Spaniards and Indians in Southeastern Mesoamerica: Essays on the History of Ethnic Relationships*. Lincoln: University of Nebraska Press.

Rushforth, Scott
  1994 "Political Resistance in a Contemporary Hunter-Gatherer Society: More about Bearlake Athapaskan Knowledge and Authority." *American Ethnologist* 21(2):335–352.

Rustow, Dankwart A.
  1968 "Nation." In *International Encyclopedia of the Social Sciences*. New York: Macmillan and Free Press. Vol. 11. Pp. 7–14.

Said, Edward W.
  1993 *Culture and Imperialism*. New York: Knopf.

Sanderson, Steven
  1981 *Agrarian Populism and the Mexican State*. Berkeley: University of California Press.

Satz, Ronald N.
  1975 *American Indian Policy in the Jacksonian Era*. Lincoln: University of Nebraska Press.

Schreyer, Frans J.
  1990 *Ethnicity and Class Conflict in Rural Mexico*. Princeton: Princeton University Press.

Schwartz, E. A.
  1994 "Red Atlantis Revisited: Community and Culture in the Writing of John Collier." *American Indian Quarterly* 18(4):507–531.

Secoy, Frank R.
  1953 *Changing Military Patterns on the Great Plains*. Monographs of the American Ethnological Society 21. New York: J. J. Augustin.

Sergeyev, M. A.
1964 "The Building of Socialism among the Peoples of Northern Siberia and the Soviet Far East." In *The Peoples of Siberia*. Ed. M. G. Levin and L. P. Potapov. Chicago: University of Chicago Press. Pp. 487–510.

Service, Elman R.
1975 *Origins of the State and Civilization: The Process of Cultural Evolution*. New York: Norton.

Sharma, Davandra
1992 "Where the Money Goes." *Pacific Islands Monthly* 62(9):13.

Shenon, Philip
1994 "In Isolation, Papua New Guinea Falls Prey to Foreign Bulldozers." *New York Times* Sunday, June 5, p. 1.

Shkilnyk, Anastasia M.
1985 *A Poison Stronger Than Love: The Destruction of an Ojibwa Community*. New Haven: Yale University Press.

Simpson, Eyles
1937 *The Ejido*. Chapel Hill: University of North Carolina Press.

Sims, Beth
1992a "U.S. Foreign Policy." In *Mexico: A Country Guide*. Ed. Tom Barry. Albuquerque: Inter-Hemispheric Education Resource Center. Pp. 281–288.
1992b "U.S. Security Assistance." In *Mexico: A Country Guide*. Ed. Tom Barry. Albuquerque: Inter-Hemispheric Education Resource Center. Pp. 329–336.

Slezkine, Yuri
1994 *Arctic Mirrors: Russia and the Small Peoples of the North*. Ithaca: Cornell University Press.

Slotkin, Richard
1985 *The Fatal Environment: The Myth of the Frontier in the Age of Industrialization, 1800–1890*. Middletown, CT: Wesleyan University Press.

Smith, Marvin T.
1990 *The Mississippian Emergence*. Washington, DC: Smithsonian Institution.

Speck, Frank
1977 *Naskapi: The Savage Hunters of the Labrador Peninsula*. Norman: University of Oklahoma Press.

Spencer, Herbert
1896 *Principles of Sociology*. New York: D. Appleton.

Spicer, Edward H.
1967 *Cycles of Conquest: The Impact of Spain, Mexico, and the United States on the Indians of the Southwest, 1533–1960*. Tucson: University of Arizona Press.
1980 *The Yaquis: A Cultural History*. Tucson: University of Arizona Press.

Spry, Irene M.
  1988 "The Tragedy of the Loss of the Commons in Western Canada." In *As Long as the Sun Shines and Water Flows: A Reader in Canadian Native Studies*. Ed. Ian A. L. Getty and Antoine S. Lussier. Vancouver: University of British Columbia Press. Pp. 203–228.

Stanford, Lois
  1991 "Peasant Resistance in the International Economy: Theory and Practice in Michoacan, Mexico." *Research in Economic Anthropology* 13:69–101.

Stanley, George F. G.
  1988 "As Long as the Sun Shines and Water Flows: An Historical Comment." In *As Long as the Sun Shines and Water Flows: A Reader in Canadian Native Studies*. Ed. Ian A. L. Getty and Antoine S. Lussier. Vancouver: University of British Columbia Press. Pp. 1–28.

Stanner, W. E. H.
  1965 "Aboriginal Territorial Organization: Estate, Range, Domain, and Regime." *Oceania* 36(1):1–26.

Stanton, William
  1960 *The Leopard's Spots: Scientific Attitudes toward Race in America, 1815–1859*. Chicago: University of Chicago Press.

Stevens, F. S.
  1972 "Parliamentary Attitudes to Aboriginal Affairs." In *Racism: The Australian Experience*. Ed. F. S. Stevens. Vol. 2. *Black versus White*. New York: Taplinger. Pp. 110–149.

Steward, Julian H.
  1955 *Theory of Culture Change: The Methodology of Multilinear Evolution*. Urbana: University of Illinois Press.

Stubben, Jerry D.
  1994 "Indian Preference: Racial Discrimination or a Political Right?" In *American Indian Policy: Self-Governance and Economic Development*. Ed. Lyman H. Legters and Fremont J. Lyden. Westport, CT: Greenwood. Pp. 103–118.

Swain, Tony
  1993 *A Place for Strangers: Towards a History of Australian Aboriginal Being*. Cambridge: Cambridge University Press.

Swain, Tony, and Deborah B. Rose
  1988 *Aboriginal Australians and Christian Missions*. Adelaide: Australian Association for the Study of Religion.

Tannenbaum, Frank
  1937 *Peace by Revolution: An Interpretation of Mexico*. New York: Columbia University Press.

Tanner, Adrian
  1979 *Bringing Home Animals*. New York: St. Martin's Press.

Thompson, Liz
    1992   "Caring for the Country: A New Dimension." *Pacific Islands Monthly*
            62(10):38–39.

Thrapp, Dan
    1967   *The Conquest of Apacheria*. Norman: University of Oklahoma Press.

Tobias, John L.
    1983   "The Subjugation of the Plains Cree, 1879–1885." *Canadian Histori-
            cal Review* 54(4):519–548.
    1988   "Protection, Civilization, Assimilation: An Outline History of
            Canada's Indian Policy." In *As Long as the Sun Shines and Water
            Flows: A Reader in Canadian Native Studies*. Ed. Ian A. L. Getty and
            Antoine S. Lussier. Vancouver: University of British Columbia Press.
            Pp. 39–55.

Tobin, P.
    1972   "Aborigines and the Political System." In *Racism: The Australian Ex-
            perience*. Ed. F. S. Stevens. Vol. 2. *Black versus White*. New York:
            Taplinger. Pp. 65–76.

Todd, Walker F.
    1995   "Bailing Out the Creditor Class." *Nation* 260(6):193–194.

Todorov, Tzvetan
    1984   *The Conquest of America: The Question of the Other*. New York:
            Harper and Row.

Tonkinson, Robert
    1991   *The Mardu Aborigines*. New York: Holt, Rinehart and Winston.

Tonkinson, Robert, and Michael Howard
    1990   "Aboriginal Autonomy in Policy and Practice: An Introduction." In
            Going It Alone? Prospects for Aboriginal Autonomy. Ed. Robert
            Tonkinson and Michael Howard. Canberra: Aboriginal Studies Press.
            Pp. 67–81.

Tonkinson, Robert, and Myrna Tonkinson
    1993   "Aborigines of Australia." *Cultural Survival Quarterly* 17(3):35.

Tooker, Elisabeth
    1964   *An Ethnography of the Huron Indians, 1615–1649*. Bureau of Ameri-
            can Ethnology Bulletin 190. Washington, DC: Smithsonian Institution.

Trigger, Bruce G.
    1976   *The Children of Aataentsic I: A History of the Huron People to 1660*.
            Montreal: McGill-Queens University Press.
    1990   *The Huron*. Fort Worth: Holt, Rinehart and Winston.

Trigger, David S.
    1992   *Whitefella Comin': Aboriginal Responses to Colonialism in North Aus-
            tralia*. New York: Cambridge University Press.

Tuck, James A.
    1971   *Onondaga Iroquois Prehistory*. Syracuse: Syracuse University Press.

Turnbull, Clive
1974   *Black War: The Extermination of the Tasmanian Aborigines.* Melbourne: Sun Books.

Turner, D. H.
1980   *Aboriginal Social Organization.* Atlantic Highlands, NJ: Humanities Press.

Unger, Robert Mangabeira
1986   *The Critical Legal Studies Movement.* Cambridge: Harvard University Press.

Van Kirk, Sylvia
1983   *Many Tender Ties: Women and Fur-Trade Society, 1670–1870.* Norman: University of Oklahoma Press.

Von Sturmer, J. R.
1985   In "On the Notion of Aboriginality. A Discussion." *Mankind* 15(1): 45–49.

Wagoner, Jay
1970   *Arizona Territory, 1863–1912: A Political History.* Tucson: University of Arizona Press.

Wallace, Noel M.
1990   "European Domination and Cultural Confusion: Forced Change among the Pitjantjatjara." In *Going It Alone? Prospects of Aboriginal Autonomy.* Ed. Robert Tonkinson and Michael Howard. Canberra: Aboriginal Studies Press. Pp. 83–97.

Wallerstein, Immanuel
1974   *The Modern World-System: Capitalist Agriculture and the Origins of the European World-Economy in the Sixteenth Century.* New York: Academic Press.
1984   *The Politics of the World-Economy: The States, the Movements, and the Civilizations.* Cambridge: Cambridge University Press.
1986   "Walter Rodney: The Historian as Spokesman for Historical Forces." *American Ethnologist* 13:330–337.

Warner, W. Lloyd
1937   *A Black Civilization: A Study of an Australian Tribe.* New York: Harper and Row.

Warren, J. Benedict
1985   *The Conquest of Michoacan: The Spanish Domination of the Tarascan Kingdom in Western Mexico, 1521–1530.* Norman: University of Oklahoma Press.

Wasserstrom, Robert
1983   "Spaniards and Indians in Colonial Chiapas, 1528–1790." In *Spaniards and Indians in Colonial Mesoamerica: Essays on the History of Ethnic Relations.* Ed. Murdo MacLeod and Robert Wasserstrom. Lincoln: University of Nebraska Press. Pp. 92–126.

Weaver, Sally M.
   1993   "Self-Determination, National Pressure Groups, and Australian Ab-
          origines: The National Aboriginal Conference, 1983–1985." In *Ethnicity
          and Aboriginality: Case Studies in Ethnonationalism.* Ed. Michael
          Levin. Toronto: University of Toronto Press. Pp. 53–74.

Weber, Max
   1949   "Power." In *Max Weber: Essays in Sociology.* New York: Oxford Uni-
          versity Press. Pp. 159–264.

Wells, E. A.
   1972   "The Mission and Race Prejudice." In *Racism: The Australian Experi-
          ence.* Ed. F. S. Stevens. Vol. 2. *Black versus White.* New York: Taplinger.
          Pp. 243–249.

White, Richard
   1983   *The Roots of Dependency.* Lincoln: University of Nebraska Press.

Wilkinson, Charles F.
   1987   *American Indians, Time, and the Law.* New Haven: Yale University
          Press.

Williams, Eric
   1984   *From Columbus to Castro: The History of the Caribbean, 1492–1969.*
          New York: Vintage Books.

Williams, Ian
   1992a "Bougainville on the Agenda." *Pacific Islands Monthly* 62(10):15.
   1992b "The East Timor Dilemma." *Pacific Islands Monthly* 62(10):13.

Williams, Nancy
   1986   *The Yolngu and Their Land: A System of Land Tenure and the Fight
          for Its Recognition.* Stanford: Stanford University Press.

Williams, Robert A., Jr.
   1990   *The American Indian in Western Legal Thought.* New York: Oxford
          University Press.

Wilmsen, Edwin N., ed.
   1989   *We Are Here: Politics of Aboriginal Land Tenure.* Berkeley: University
          of California Press.

Wilson, John
   1980   "The Pilbara Aboriginal Social Movement: An Outline of Its Background
          and Significance." In *Aborigines of the West: Their Past and Present.*
          Ed. R. M. Berndt and C. H. Berndt. Perth: University of Western Aus-
          tralia Press. Pp. 51–158.

Wilson, Edmund
   1966   *Apologies to the Iroquois.* New York: Vintage Books.

Wittaker, Elvi
   1994   "Public Discourse on Sacredness: The Transfer of Ayers Rock to Ab-
          original Ownership." *American Ethnologist* 21(2):310–334.

Wittfogel, Karl A.
1957   *Oriental Despotism: A Comparative Study of Total Power.* New Haven: Yale University Press.

Wollaston, A. F. R.
1988   "Remarks on 'Opening of New Territories in Papua.'" In *Tribal Peoples and Development Issues: A Global Overview.* Ed. John H. Bodley. Mountain View, CA: Mayfield. Pp. 359–360.

Wolf, Eric R.
1969   *Peasant Wars of the Twentieth Century.* New York: Doubleday.
1983   *Europe and the People without History.* Berkeley: University of California Press.
1986   "The Vicissitudes of the Closed Corporate Peasant Community." *American Ethnologist* 13:325–329.

Womack, John, Jr.
1968   *Zapata and the Mexican Revolution.* New York: Random House.

Worsley, Peter
1968   *The Trumpet Shall Sound: A Study of "Cargo" Cults in Melanesia.* New York: Schocken.
1984   *The Three Worlds: Culture and World Development.* Chicago: University of Chicago Press.

Wrobel, David M.
1993   *The End of American Exceptionalism: Frontier Anxiety from the Old West to the New Deal.* Lawrence: University Press of Kansas.

Young, Linda Wilcox
1993   "Labor Demand and Agricultural Development: The Evidence from Mexico." *Journal of Development Studies* 30(1):168–189.

Recommended Sources on Indigenous Groups

. . . .

Some of these are relatively new; others are classics that may be available only in libraries.

Mexico

Chiñas, Beverly
   1973   *The Isthmus Zapotecs: Women's Roles in Cultural Context.* Prospect Heights, IL: Waveland.

Berdan, Frances
   1982   *The Aztecs of Central Mexico: An Imperial Society.* New York: Holt, Rinehart and Winston.

Friedlander, Judith
   1976   *Being Indian in Hueyapan: A Study of Forced Identity in Contemporary Mexico.* New York: St. Martin's Press.

Spicer, Edward H.
   1980   *The Yaqui: A Cultural History.* Tucson: University of Arizona Press.

Turner, Paul
   1972   *The Highland Chontol.* Fort Worth: Holt, Rinehart and Winston.

United States

Chance, Norman A.
  1990 *The Iñupiat and Arctic Alaska: An Ethnography.* Fort Worth: Holt, Rinehart and Winston.

Garbarino, Merwyn S.
  1972 *Big Cypress: A Changing Seminole Community.* Prospect Heights, IL: Waveland.

Hoebel, E. Adamson
  1960 *The Cheyennes: Indians of the Great Plains.* New York: Holt, Rinehart and Winston.

Opler, Morris E.
  1941 *An Apache Life-Way: The Economic, Social, and Religious Institutions of the Chiricahua Indians.* Chicago: University of Chicago Press.

Wallace, Anthony F. C.
  1969 *The Death and Rebirth of the Seneca.* New York: Random House.

Canada

Brody, Hugh
  1981 *Maps and Dreams.* Vancouver: Douglas and McIntyre.

Mandelbaum, David G.
  1940 *The Plains Cree.* Anthropological Papers 37, pt. 2. New York: American Museum of Natural History.

Ridington, Robin
  1988 *Trail to Heaven: Knowledge and Narrative in a Northern Native Community.* Iowa City: University of Iowa Press.

Rohner, Ronald P., and Evelyn C. Rohner
  1970 *The Kwakiutl Indians of British Columbia.* New York: Holt, Rinehart and Winston.

Trigger, Bruce G.
  1969 *The Huron: Farmers of the North.* New York: Holt, Rinehart and Winston.

Australia

Bell, Diane
  1993 *Daughters of the Dreaming.* Minneapolis: University of Minnesota Press.

Hart, C. W. M., Arnold R. Pilling, and Jane C. Goodale
  1988 *The Tiwi of North Australia.* 3d ed. New York: Holt, Rinehart and Winston.

Meggitt, M. G.
1962 *The Desert People*. Sydney: Angus and Robertson.

Rose, Deborah Bird
1992 *Dingo Makes Us Human: Life and Land in an Australian Aboriginal Culture*. New York: Cambridge University Press.

Tonkinson, Robert
1991 *The Mardu Aborigines*. New York: Holt, Rinehart and Winston.

Index

Abel, Kerry, 132
Aboriginal and Torres Straits
  Islanders Commission
  (ATSIC), 197
Aboriginal Land Rights (Northern
  Territory) Act, 195
Aboriginal Protection Board,
  186–187, 241
Absaroke, 98. *See also* Crow
Acadia, 127
Acoma, 54
Act for the Better Government of Her
  Majesty's Australian Colonies, 174
Act for the Gradual Civilization
  of the Indian Tribes in the
  Canadas, 142
Act for the Protection of the Indians
  in Lower Canada, 142
Age of Discovery, 15
AIM: 119,120
Air Force, U.S., 115

Akimuga, 206
Akwesasne, 122, 157
Alamán, Lucas, 58, 64–65, 67
Álamo, El, 62
Alaska, 114–116, 130, 153
Alaska Highway, 115
Alaska Native Claims Settlement
  Act, 114–116
Alcoa corporation, 122
Alexander, Malcolm, 42, 167, 176,
  193
Algonkian speakers, 86, 89, 96, 117,
  125, 126, 129, 202, 229. *See also*
  Anishinabek, Arapaho, Blackfoot,
  Blood, Cheyenne, Chippewa, Cree,
  Mi'kmaq, Mississauga, Ojibwa,
  Ottawa, Piegan
Allegheny River, 119
Allen, Robert S., 160
Althusser, Louis, 7
Altman, J.C., 165, 189

Ambler, Marjane, 120, 121
American Indian Movement (AIM), 119, 120
American Indian Youth Council, 118
Americas Watch, 78
Amherst, Jeffrey, 128
Amoco, 208
Amungme, 206
Anangu, 249
Andalucia, 46
Anderson, Benedict, 12
Anderson, Robin, 207
Andes, 229
Angola, 216
Anishinabek, 96, 129, 154. See also Chippewa, Ojibwa
Ankerson, Dudley, 70
Apache, xiii, 11, 12, 20, 51, 54, 97, 101–104, 107, 108, 114, 116, 122, 171, 172, 239, 243, 246, 248. See also Chiricahua Apache, Mescalero Apache, Mimbres Apache, San Carlos Apache, White Mountain Apache
Appalachian Mountains, 95, 237
Aragon, 45
Arango, Doroteo. See Villa, Pancho
Arapaho, 97, 98
Arctic, 153, 155, 160, 219
Arctic Archipelago, 124, 159
Arikara, 96
Arizona, 51, 101–105, 118, 160, 172, 248
Armitage, Andrew, xiii, 172, 179, 180, 182, 187, 188
Army Corps of Engineers, 119
Arnhem Land, Australia, 176, 195
Asch, Michael, 11, 146, 154, 159
Assembly of First Nations, 151, 246
assimilation, 17, 61, 75, 106–108, 110, 112, 119, 121, 139–142, 144–148, 150, 153, 177–181, 186–189, 191–192, 197, 204, 220, 224, 225, 226, 229, 232–242, 244
Assiniboin, 23, 96, 117, 129, 160
Athapaskan speakers, 131, 153. See also Apache, Dunne-Za, Dené
Atlantic Coast, 20, 85–88
ATSIC: 197

Attorney-General of Ontario v. Bear Island Foundation, 137
Auckland, 247
Augustinians, 46
Austin, James E., 73
Australia, 160, 161–198, 241, 247, 249; assumptions about indigenous disappearance, 13, 178, 179–180, 182, 187, 236; as colonies, 10, 161–164; compared to other states, 167, 170, 171–178, 180, 186, 190–194, 198, 201, 229–233; conservatives in, 194, 197, 198; convicts in, 13, 14, 16, 162–164, 166, 168, 169, 174, 179, 181; co-optation of indigenous leadership, 173–174, 194; displacement of indigenous people, 170–173; immigrant labor in, 175; indigenous birth rates in, 182, 185, 235; indigenous labor in, 181–187, 235, 238; indigenous land use in, 13, 19, 164–165, 167, 176, 195, 196, 197–198; indigenous populations of, xv, 10, 16, 164–166, 180, 181, 184, 190, 236; indigenous reactions to Europeans in, 163, 167, 168; indigenous resistance in, 20, 23, 165, 166, 169, 170, 171, 246; indigenous territories in, 19, 164–165, 182, 185; interest groups in, 166, 170, 173, 175–176, 180–181, 189, 195–196, 198, 231; Labor government in, 184, 194, 195, 196, 197; liberals in, 184, 188, 193; livestock stations in, 23, 183–186, 238; mining in, 23, 181, 184, 188–190, 196, 198; missions in, 23, 178, 180–182, 190, 241; penal colonies in, 163, 166–168, 181; policies toward indigenous peoples in, 166, 170–174, 176–181, 186–187, 189–192, 194, 196–198; precontact population size, 10, 16; punitive expeditions in, 168–172; reasons for colonization, 13, 161; relations with Indonesia, 205; relations with Papua New Guinea, 206–207, 209, 210, 211–212;

removal of indigenous children in, 181, 186–188; reserves in, 172–173, 187, 190, 191, 241; sacred sites in, 19, 249; settlers in, 23, 166–173, 175, 177–181, 184, 192, 193, 235; treaties in, 177; use of indigenous labor in, 20; use of term "Aboriginal" in, 13
Australian Aboriginal Protection Association, 191
Australian National Parks, 249
autonomous societies, 7; defined, 3
Avery, John, 184
Ayers Rock, 249
Aztec, 19, 45, 48–50, 58, 193, 202, 229; city-states, 47; as cultural theme in Mexico, 58, 64; as hierarchical state, 50; intermarriage with Spanish, 27; reaction to horses, 49. *See also* México

Bagot Commission, 140, 141
banco nacional de credito ejidal, 74, 75
Bancroft, Hubert Howe, 231
band: as concept, 12, 18; in Canada, 143, 144, 145
Bank, Sir Joseph, 162
Bantu speakers, 217. *See also* Kamba, Kikuyu, Taita
Barabos, Alicia, 80
Barkin, David, 77
Barrett, Richard J., 39, 250
Barry, Tom, 77, 79, 80, 81, 83, 84
Barsh, Russel Lawrence, 121
Bartolome, Miguel, 80
Basarwa. *See* Ju/'hoansi
Basques, 85, 124
Bassols, Narcisco, 75
Batman's Treaty, 177
Batt, Rosemary L., 77
Battle of Pinjara, 170
Bear Lake, 153
Beaver, 154
Bechuanaland, British Protectorate of, 215
Belize, 7
Bell, Diane, 179, 181
Belly River, Australia, 132

Beltran, Aguirre Gonzalo, 239
Benavides, Fray Alonso de, 11
Benjamin, Thomas, 79
Bentham, Jeremy, 162
Beothuk, 170
Berdan, Frances E., 47
Berger Commission, 153
Berger, Thomas R., 146, 153
Berndt, Catherine H., 13, 164, 165, 166, 170, 184, 185, 186
Berndt, Ronald M., 13, 164, 165, 166, 170, 184, 185, 186
BHP corporation, 208
BIA. *See* Bureau of Indian Affairs
Big Bear, 145
Binford, Leigh, 80
Biolsi, Thomas, 108, 113
Bishop, Charles, 130
bison. *See* buffalo
Bissonnette, John, 156, 160
blackbirding, 210
Blackfoot, 129, 132. *See also* Blood, Piegan, Siksika
Black Hawk, 23, 94
Black Hawk's War, 94
Black Kettle, 105
Blood, 129. *See also* Blackfoot
blood quantum, 180
boarding schools, 18, 104, 106–107, 118, 140–142, 177, 179, 182, 187, 232–234, 236, 243
Bodley, John H., 34, 248
Bolt, Christine, 91
Bolton, Herbert E., 11
Bond Head, Sir Francis, 139, 140, 152, 240
Bonwick, J., 167
Boran, 217
Boserup, Ester, 5
Botany Bay, 162
Botswana, 213–217
Bougainville, 210–213
Bougainville Liberation Army, 211
Bourke, George, 172
Bovril corporation, 184
Bozeman Trail, 105
Bradsher, Keith, 249
Brant, Joseph, 94, 129. *See also* Thayendanagea

Braudel, Fernand, 14, 227–228
Brinton, Daniel G., 31
British: in Africa, 215, 217; in Australia, 161–164, 166–167, 172–174, 176–177; the church in, 28; in New Guinea, 206; in North America, 11, 39, 63, 67, 70, 85–89, 91–92, 126–129, 134–137, 139–140, 142–144; policies toward Celtic tribes, 91; position on indigenous land rights, 15, 92, 137; reasons for state expansion, 13–14, 28, 85–86; the slave trade in, 31–32
British Church Mission Society, 133
British Columbia, 143–144, 148–149, 153, 154, 158–159
British North America Act, 143, 144
Broome, R., 171
Broughton, G. W., 183
Brown, Jennifer S. H., 132
Brown, Paula, 208
Brugge, David M., 245
buffalo, 97, 100, 104–105, 132, 133, 146, 227
Bukharin, Nikolai, 6
Burawoy, Michael, 18
Bureau of Indian Affairs (BIA), 108, 110, ,113–114, 119, 120, 235, 241
Bureau of Mines, 108
Burridge, Kenelm, 165, 207
Burton, William, 91
Bush, George H. W., 77, 84, 116, 121, 243
Bushmen. See Ju/'hoansi
Butlin, N. G., 164
Butterfield Overland Mail, 102

Cabot, John, 124
cacao, 54, 66
caciques, 18, 53
Cajuns, 127
California, 90, 100–101
Calles, Plutarco Elias, 72–73
Camacho, Manuel Avila, 76
Campbell, Bruce, 80
Campbell, Howard, 80
campesinos, 68, 69, 70, 73, 74, 76, 77, 79, 83, 239
Camp Grant massacre, 103, 160, 172
Canada, 124–160, 162, 232, 238;

assimilationist policies in, 139–142; as colonies, 10, 85, 86; compared with other states, 123, 138, 141, 146, 148, 160; confederation of, 143; conservatives in, 148, 152; Constitution of, 152, 158; French Canadians, 125–126, 150; French interests in, 85–86, 124–127, 231, 238; imposition of band governments by, 18, 143, 144, 145; indigenous coalitions in, 23, 90, 93, 246; indigenous labor in, 21; indigenous population of, 124, 130, 148, 149; interest groups in, 139–140, 143, 146, 150, 160, 231; liberals in, 149–151; provincial autonomy in, 148–149, 150, 155; relations with the United States, 128–129, 136, 156; reserves in, 134, 138, 140, 142, 144–146, 151, 234, 240; status of indigenous people in, 137–138, 142, 144, 145, 147–149, 152, 158, 159–160, 180, 236, 240–241; treaties in, 133–138, 140, 144, 149, 150, 151, 152, 153, 155–156, 159–160; use of "band" in, 12, 143; White Paper, 149–151
Canadian Embassy, 124
Canadian Labor Congress, 80
Cananea copper strike, 67
Canberra, 235
Cancuc, 54
capitalism, 35, 36, 37, 228, 229
Cárdenas, Cuauhtemac, 78
Cárdenas, Lázaro, 64, 72–76, 112, 233–234, 235, 239, 240, 248
Cardinal, Harold, 151
cargadores, 21
cargo cults, 207
Caribbean, 14, 161
Carlisle Indian School, 104, 234
Carlson, Leonard A., 121
Carranza, Venustiano, 70–71
Cartier, Jacques, 29, 86, 124–125
Caste Wars, 23, 58
Castile, 45, 46
Castile, George Pierre, 112
cattle stations, Australia, 23, 168, 183–186
Cavanaugh, John, 39, 250

Celtic tribes, 91
CERT, 120, 121
Chalco, 49
Champlain, Samuel de, 86, 125
Chamula, 75
Chance, John K., 21, 51, 52, 53, 59
Chance, Norman A., 115
Charles V, King of Spain, 51
Charlottetown Accord, 159–160
Charter of Rights and Freedoms, 152
Cherokee, 23, 90, 98–100, 238, 246
Cherokee Nation decisions, 12, 120
Cheyenne, 97, 98, 105, 117
Chiapas, 18, 23, 52, 54, 74, 79,
    80–83, 243
Chichimec, 48
Chihuahua, 54, 68, 102
Childe, V. Gordon, 5
Chinnery, E. W. F., 181
Chippewa, 96, 129. *See also*
    Anishinabek, Ojibwa
Chirac, Jacques, 247
Chiricahua Apache, 102, 104. *See
    also* Apache
Chivington, Colonel John, 105
Choctaw, 99, 238
Christianity: role of, in Australia,
    179, 182; in ideology of Mexican
    conquest, 49; in New England, 91;
    in state expansion, 13, 26–27, 133.
    See also Church, missionaries,
    missions, Puritans
Chukchi, 219, 221
Chukchi Peninsula, 219
Chukotka, 220
Church: in Australia, 182; in Canada,
    141; in the Enlightenment, 29; as
    interest group, 46, 51, 230, 248; in
    Mexican state, 57, 60–61, 65, 73,
    76, 101, 231; roles in Spanish and
    British colonies compared, 28; in
    Spanish Conquest, 27; use of
    indigenous labor in New Spain by,
    50–51; in war against Moors, 49
científicos, 12, 13, 63–64, 67, 78,
    139, 233
civil rights movement, 191
Clad, James C., 249
Claessen, Henri J. M., 4
Clark, George Rogers, 96, 101

Clinton, Bill, 116, 251
Coahuila, 70, 74
coal, 113, 120
coalitions, 22–24, 39, 83–84, 98,
    117–119, 128, 129, 133, 148, 151,
    156, 159, 190–191, 196, 224, 226,
    245–252
Coatsworth, John H., 57
cochineal, 52, 66
Cochise, 102
Cochrane, D. Glynn, 207
coconuts, 208
Cody, Buffalo Bill, 29
coffee, 66, 68, 74, 79, 208, 209
Cohen, Felix, 95
Cohen, Ronald, 4
Cold War, 115, 214, 216
Collier, George, 79, 81
Collier, John, 110, 111, 113, 114, 235
Colorado, 160
Colorado River Land Company, 74
Columbus, Christopher, 27, 29, 45,
    47, 85
Colyer, Vincent, 103, 248
Comanche, 97, 101
Commonwealth Department of
    Territories, 189
Commonwealth of Australia Act, 174
Comonfort, Ignacio, 65
Company of Adventurers of England,
    130. *See also* Hudson's Bay
    Company
competition: in development models,
    34; in 19th-century thought, 30
Conference for International
    Economic Co-operation, 213
Connolly, Bob, 207
Connor, Walker, 245
conquistadores, 45, 50
Constitution Act of 1982 (Canada),
    138, 152
Constitution Alteration (Aboriginals)
    Bill, 194
Constitution of Cádiz, 56
convicts: in Australia, 13, 14, 16,
    162–164, 166, 168, 169, 174, 179,
    181; in North America, 88, 89
Conzinc Riotinto of Australia (CRA),
    210, 212
Cook, Beryl, 209

Cook, C. E., 179
Cook, Captain James, 162
Coolidge Dam, 118
Coombs, Herbert Cole, 177, 189, 190, 196, 198
Cooper, James Fenimore, 91
Coordination of Indigenous People, 84
copper, 66, 67, 103–104, 210
Cornelius, Wayne, 76
Cornell, Stephen, 114
Coronado, Francisco Vásquez de, 51
Cortés, Hernando, 19, 42, 45, 47, 48, 49, 50, 51, 52, 54, 88, 201, 202
Cossacks, 219
Costilla, Father Miguel Hidalgo y, 56
cotton, 31, 32, 52, 54, 66, 68, 74, 99
Council of Energy Resource Tribes (CERT), 120, 121
Council of the Indies, 51
Cowling, K., 40
CRA, 210, 212
Craig, Ann, 76
Cree, 20, 23, 96, 117, 129, 130, 132, 135, 145, 154–156, 160
Creek, 22, 90, 98, 99, 117, 238, 246
criollos, 47, 52, 53, 55, 56, 58, 59, 60, 63, 88, 101, 180, 248
Cristeros, 73
Critical Legal Studies, 120, 225
Cromwell, Oliver, 91
Cronon, William, 87, 90
Crook, General George, 103, 171
Crow, 98, 110, 118. *See also* Absaroke
Cuomo, Mario, 156
Custer, George Armstrong, 105
Cypress Hills massacre, 160
Czaplicka, M. A., 219

Dakota, 96. *See also* Santee Sioux
Damara, 215
Dampier, William, 162
Dani, 5, 206
Danish interests, 14
Darnell, Regna, 29
Darwin, Australia, 184
David, Joe, 157–158
Dawes, Senator Henry L., 109
Dawes Act, 109, 110, 111, 114, 115, 116, 146, 240, 242
De'Ath, Colin, 208

debt peonage, 21
Delaware, 93, 128. *See also* Leni Lenape
Deloria, Vine, Jr., 95, 231
Dené, 115, 153, 159
Denendeh, 159
Denoon, Donald, 42, 167, 175
Denver, 105
Department of Aboriginal Affairs, 195
Department of Indian Affairs (Canada), 144, 145, 146
Department of Indian Affairs and Northern Development (Canada), 150, 151
Department of Indian Affairs (Mexico), 75, 76
Department of Interior (U.S.), 108, 113
dependency theory, 35–38
Deseronto, John, 129
development. *See* underdevelopment
DeWalt, Billie R., 77
Dewdney, Edgar, 145
Dhan-Gadi, 193
DIAND. *See* Department of Indian Affairs and Northern Development
Díaz, Porfirio, 66–69, 70
Dickason, Olive Patricia, 15, 125, 137, 138, 142, 145, 146, 148, 159, 173
Dicken, Peter, 40
Dili, East Timor, 204–205
disease, 20, 48, 49, 51, 52, 87, 88, 91, 96, 127, 128, 141–142, 168, 182, 185, 201, 230
Dobyns, Henry F., 48
"domestic dependent nations," 95
Dominicans, 46, 51
Donnacona, 125
Donovan, Colleen M., 201, 204
Doobov, A., 194
Doobov, R., 194
Druke, Mary A., 156
Dunne-Za, 154. *See also* Athapaskan, Dené
Dutch interests, 14, 86–87, 126, 162, 202, 205, 229
East Africa, 217–219. *See also* Kenya, Tanzania

East Timor, 201, 203, 231
Edgerton, Robert B., 34, 217
education: for indigenous peoples, 18–19
Eggan, Fred, 97
Eggleston, Elizabeth, 177
ejidos, 58, 59, 65, 66, 67, 68, 73, 74, 76, 78, 79, 108; defined, 58
Eichstaedt, Peter H., 232
elites, 228–229, 230, 233, 245, 248–251; defined, 6; in Africa, 215; in Australia, 162, 166, 169, 170, 175, 176, 179–181, 186, in Canada, 133; in Mexico, 57, 60, 65, 67, 68, 77, 84, 92, 202; in United States, 92, 106
Elkin, A. P., 166
El Salvador, 7
encomenderos, 14
encomiendas, 15, 21, 50
England, 14, 28, 85, 87–89, 98, 99, 127, 161–162, 246. See also British
Enlightenment, 11, 29–30, 32, 94
Erasmus, Charles, 34
Erie, 126
establicimientos de paz, 239
Esteva, Gustavo, 73
Estremadura, 45
Etchart, Graciela, 116
Evans, Gareth, 209
Ewers, John C., 100
exclusion policies, 17
EZLN. *See* Zapatista Army of National Liberation

Fagan, Brian M., 90
Falkowsli, James E., 95
Farriss, Nancy, 55
FBI. *See* Federal Bureau of Investigation (U.S.)
FDN. *See* National Democratic Front
Federal Bureau of Investigation (U.S.), 119
Federation of Saskatchewan Indians, 148
Fehrenbach, T. R., 76
Feit, Harvey A., 154, 155
Ferdinand VII of Spain, 45, 55–56
First Native Welfare Conference (Australia), 189

fish: as motive for state expansion, 14, 28, 87
fishing industries, 21, 85, 124
Fixico, Donald L., 111
Flanagan, Thomas, 136
Flathead, 114
Florida, 89, 99, 104
Fly River, 208
Forbes, Jack D., 50, 54, 243
Forster, Mike, 212
Fort Frances, Ontario, 152
Fowler, Melvin L., 11
Fox, Jonathan, 73
France, 29, 62, 65, 85, 86, 126, 247. *See also* French interests
Franciscans, 46, 51, 54
Frank, Andre Gunder, 10, 35, 36, 37, 227–228
Freemantle, Australia, 235
French interests, 14, 87, 93, 96, 124–127, 166, 229, 230
French Polynesia, 247
Frideres, J. S., 138
Fried, Morton H., 4
Friedlander, Judith, 75
Frost, A., 176
Fula, 36
furs, 14, 17, 28, 87, 133, 201, 219–220, 228, 229
fur trade, 21, 86–87, 93, 96, 100, 125–127, 129–132, 154

Gabbra, 217
gachupines, 53, 56, 248
Galtung, Johan, 37, 38
gambling, 120
Gandy, Ross, 66, 69, 71, 74
Garton, Stephen, 176
Gaspé Peninsula, 246
Gates, Marylin, 78
GATT Treaty. *See* General Agreement on Tariffs and Trade
General Agreement on Tariffs and Trade, 79
General Motors, 79, 122
General Survey, 108
genocide, 9, 17, 89, 103, 106, 121, 157, 167, 170, 177, 180, 183, 226, 231–232
George III, King of England, 153

Georgia, State of, 99, 173
Georgian Bay, 126
German Samoa, 210
Germany, 206, 210, 215, 231
Ghost Dance, 105, 246
Gil, Emilio Portes, 72
Gil-Swedburg, Marta C., 114
Gipps, George, 173
Gitksan, 158
gold, 13, 27, 28, 51, 100, 102, 115, 148, 168, 189, 201, 206, 208–209, 215
Goodale, Jane C., 164, 165
GOON squad. *See* Guardians of the Oglala Nation
Gorbachev, Nikolai, 221
Gordon, Robert J., 215, 216
Gortari, Carlos Salinas de. *See* Salinas de Gortari, Carlos
Gould, Stephen Jay, 31
government: as aspect of states, 11; used by interest groups, 9
Gradual Enfranchisement Act, 144
Gramsci, Antonio, 9
Grand Coteau, 132
Grand Council of the Cree, 155, 246
Grand Metropolitan, 79
Grant, Ulysses S., 103, 104
Grassy Narrows, Ontario, 154
Graymount, Barbara, 93
Great Basin, 20, 90, 97, 101, 106
Great Lakes, 20, 89, 96, 128, 129, 237, 238
Great Plains, 96–98, 100, 104–106, 109, 129, 133, 145, 227, 246
Great Slave Lake, 146
Great Whale River, Quebec, 156
Green, L. C., 15
Green, Michael D., 98
Green, Stanley C., 57
Green Giant corporation, 79
Greenpeace, 247
Greenwood, Gordon, 235
Griffen, William B., 54, 231
grito of Dolores, 56
Guardians of the Oglala Nation, 119
Guatemala, 7, 81
guerra de los pasteles, la, 62
Guerrero, Vicente, 57
Guggenheim corporations, 69

Gwich'in, 160. *See also* Athapaskan, Dené

haciendas, 21, 52, 60, 65, 66, 67, 68, 69, 73, 74
Haida, 129
Haiti, 86
Hale, Charles A., 61
Hall, David J., 139
Hamilton, Annette, 73, 165
Hamilton, Nora, 76
Hand, Gerry, 197
Harding, Erika, 78
Harper, Elijah, 158, 246
Harris, Marvin, 30
Hart, C. W. M., 164
Harvey, Neil, 79
Hawaiians, 23
Hawthorne, Harry B., 149
hazardous wastes, 122, 208–211, 242, 247
Head, Brian, 174, 175
hegemony, 9, 17, 53, 58, 61, 95, 106, 133, 136, 142, 144, 169, 178, 207, 216, 225; defined, 9
Heider, Karl, 5
henequen, 21, 66, 68, 74
Herero, 215
Hermequaftewa, Andrew, 85
Herrnstein, Richard A., 32
Hewitt de Alcantara, Cynthia, 76
Hiatt, L. R., 165
Hickerson, Harold, 87, 96, 129
Higgott, Richard A., 38
Hitchiti, 90
Hlambohn, Wally, 209
Hobsbawm, Eric, 11
Hodenosaunee, 86, 90, 92–94, 126. *See also* Iroquois
Hodges, Donald, 66, 69, 71, 74
Hogan, Evelyn, 209, 212
Holt, Harold, 195
Honduras, 7
Honiara, 212
Honshu Paper corporation, 208
Hooker corporation, 184
Hopi, 85, 245
horde: as term used in Australia, 13
House Resolution 108, 111

Houston, Sam, 62
Hout, Wil, 35, 36, 38
Howard, Michael, 197, 236
Howe, Marvine, 33, 206
Hoxie, Frederick E., 110
Hu-DeHart, Evelyn, 75, 76
Hudson, Charles M., 90
Hudson Bay, 130, 132
Hudson's Bay Company, 39,
    130–136, 154
Huel, Raymond, 136
Huerta, Victoriano, 69, 70
Hughes, Robert, 16, 161, 167, 169
hunting territories, 20
Huron, 90, 93, 117, 125, 126, 127,
    128, 202, 229, 238
Hydro-Quebec, 156
Hyndman, David, 206, 208–209

iasak, 219
ideology, 7, 25–42; colonialist, 25–31;
    in the United States, 94
Iguala, Plan of, 57
imagined communities, 12
imperialism, 37
Inca, 229
indentured servants, 88, 89
Indian Act of 1867 (Canada), 138
Indian Act of 1876 (Canada), 144, 145,
    149, 150, 157
Indian Advancement Act (Canada), 145
Indian Association of Alberta, 148, 151
Indian Child Welfare Act, 233
Indian preference legislation, 120
Indian Reorganization Act (IRA). *See*
    Wheeler-Howard Bill
Indian Territory, 99–100
indigenous peoples: coalitions among,
    22, 89–90, 91, 92–93, 98, 117–119,
    128, 129, 133, 148, 151, 156, 159,
    190–191, 196, 224, 227, 245–247;
    concepts of ownership among, 16,
    154–155, 164–165; conflicts
    among, 87, 88, 91, 97–98, 125–127,
    132, 202, 208, 217, 229, 245, 246;
    cultural appropriation of, 19,
    192–193, 221, 235, 241; defined, 7;
    disease among, 20, 48–49, 52;
    dispersal of, 9, 52, 66, 68, 79, 91,
    128, 143, 144, 161, 170–172, 187,
    217, 230, 232, 236, 240–241;
    education of, 18, 104, 140–142,
    177, 182, 186, 220–221, 224,
    232–234, 236, 243; in fur trade,
    86–87,219; identity of, 9, 21–22,
    24, 52, 55, 59–61, 83, 91, 116, 138,
    142, 145, 146, 149, 151, 160,
    164–165, 180, 190–192, 201, 202,
    204, 222, 224–225, 236, 237; as
    interest groups, 9, 18, 22, 38–39,
    107, 119, 145, 152, 154–156,
    191–192, 196, 202, 224, 231, 244,
    251; labor of, 16–22, 50–51, 67,
    174, 181–187, 214, 219, 230, 232,
    234, 236; land use by, 20, 89–90,
    126, 134, 154–156, 164–165, 167,
    168, 217–218; marginalization of,
    58, 59, 64, 107, 122, 139, 146, 152,
    176, 179, 221–222, 224–225;
    persistence of, 19, 107, 108, 112,
    140, 178, 225, 243; political
    strategies of, 22, 91, 108, 116–123,
    145, 148, 149, 151, 156–160, 190,
    195, 226–227, 234, 243–244;
    reactions to Europeans by, 20,
    85–86, 90–91, 96, 100, 101–102,
    125, 163, 167, 168, 201, 202, 226,
    229–230, 246; relocation of, 9,
    98–99, 106, 121, 146, 154, 167,
    182, 204, 206, 216, 217, 225, 236;
    removal of children of, 232–233;
    resistance among, 16, 19–24,
    53–55, 68, 73, 80–84, 91, 101,
    104–106, 117, 144–160, 165, 166,
    170, 171, 201, 202, 206, 207,
    211–212, 221–222, 225, 226, 243;
    rights supported by United
    Nations, 24; taken to Europe, 29,
    125; as "wards," 144
indirect rule, 113
Indonesia, 203–206, 227, 228, 229,
    231; colonial background, 203;
    in East Timor, 204–205; in Irian
    Jaya, 205–206; population of,
    203; resources in, 204; size of
    territory, 203
Industrial Revolution, 31, 32, 161
Innu, 247

Inquisition, 49
Institutional Revolutionary Party
   (PRI), 77, 78, 83
Instituto Nacional Indigenista, 76
interest groups: defined, 5; in
   Australia, 166, 170, 173, 175–176,
   181, 189, 195–196, 198, 231; in
   Canada, 139–140, 143, 146, 150,
   160, 231; competition among, 6, 7,
   17, 38–39, 57, 93, 108, 146, 150,
   166; co-optation of indigenous
   groups by, 18; dependency theory
   applied to, 35; indigenous groups
   as, 9, 18, 22, 38–39, 107, 108, 119,
   145, 152, 154–156, 191–192, 196,
   202, 224, 231, 244, 251; in Mexico,
   14, 52–53, 55–56, 60–61, 63–64, 66,
   68, 73, 83–84, 231, 244, 246, 248;
   shifting parameters of, 40, 248,
   250–252; states' role in balancing,
   7, 39, 108; in the United States, 88,
   91, 94, 108, 111, 112, 122–123;
   varieties among, 6, 7, 14
International Work Group for
   Indigenous Affairs, 212
Inuit, 130, 149, 152, 154, 155, 156,
   159, 160
Inuit Tapirisat, 155, 246
Inupiat, 115
Inuvialut Final Agreement, 160
IRA. *See* Wheeler Howard Bill
Irapuato, 79
Ireland, 91, 161
Irian Jaya, 5, 205–206, 231
Iroquoian speakers, 89–90, 92–94,
   124–126. *See also* Cherokee, Erie,
   Huron, Neutrals, Susquehannock,
   Tionontati
Iroquois, 29, 86, 90, 92–94, 117,
   125–128, 230, 235, 237. *See also*
   Hodenosaunee
Isabella, Queen of Spain, 45
Italian interests, 218
Iturbide, Agustín de, 56–57, 61
Ixtapalapa, 49

Jaba River, 210
Jablow, Joseph, 100
Jackson, Andrew, 98–100

James Bay Project, 154–156, 160. *See
   also* La Grand Complex
James Bay, Quebec, 154–156, 160
Japan and New Guinea Timbers
   (JANT), 208
Java, 202
Javanese, 204
Jay Treaty, 129
Jefferson, Thomas, 94, 96
Jenness, Diamond, 147
Jennings, Francis, 93
Jesuits, 14, 46, 51, 125, 238
jornada del muerto, 101
Josephy, Alvin M., Jr., 85, 118
Juárez, Benito, 64, 65, 69, 240
Ju/'hoansi, 213–217

Kairys, David, 22
Kalahari Desert, 213
Kamba, 217
Kanehsatake, Quebec, 156
Ka'o'olawe, Hawaii, 246–247
Katherine Times, 185
Katz, Friedrich, 47, 80
Kavango, 215
Kawerong River, 210
Keesing, Roger M., 210
Kehoe, Alice B., 29, 60, 85, 106, 111
Kenora, Ontario, 152
Kenya, 217–218, 227
Kenyatta, Jomo, 217
Khanty, 221, 222
Kikuyu, 217
Kimberlys, Australia, 184
King, Peter, 208
King Philip's War, 22
Kingston, Ontario, 129
Kino, Father Eusebio, 51, 54
Kinzua Dam, 119
Kiowa, 98
Kiowa Apache. *See* Naishan Dené
Klamath, 111
Klein, Alan M., 105
Klistinaux. *See* Cree
Koppes, Clayton R., 114
Koriak, 221
Krech, Shepard, III, 87
Kruger, Linda, 116
Kupferer, Harriet Jane, 100

Kwajalein, 247
Kwakwala speakers, 129

labor: as motive for state expansion, 13; boarding schools as producers of, 18, 107, 141; British plantations, 17, 28; convict, 16, 162, 163, 168; in dependency theory, 35; devaluation of, 250–251; in England, 31, 161–162; forms of, 21, 67; reserve indigenous pool of, 18, 20, 60, 67, 107; Spanish appropriation of indigenous labor, 16, 17, 50–51, 53, 55, 60; transnational corporations and, 79–80, 191, 249; underemployment, 17, 20, 67, 107, 122, 249; in world systems theory, 36
Labrador, 124, 130
Laclau, Ernesto, 6
ladinos, 58
La Grand Complex, 154–156. *See also* James Bay Project
Laguna, 70, 74
Lake Erie, 126
Lake Huron, 134
Lake Ontario, 126
Lake Superior, 129, 134
Lake Texcoco, 47
Lakota, 96, 97, 98, 105, 108, 117, 119, 227. *See also* Sioux, Teton Sioux
Lamphere, Louise, 35
Lamu, 217
Land: appropriation of, 15, 51, 60, 64 66, 67, 68, 73, 74, 79, 94, 99, 109–110, 118–119, 128, 139, 142, 144–147, 154–156, 172–173, 176, 181, 182, 183–185, 187, 190, 211, 241; claims cases, 120–121, 151, 154–156, 157, 159, 195, 197–198; considered uninhabited, 15, 166, 176, 179–180, 182, 197–198; indigenous rights to, 11, 15, 91, 92, 137–138, 140, 148, 151, 154–156, 157–158, 164–165, 184, 189, 195, 245; individual allotments of, 109–110, 121, 144, 146, 151, 196; as issue in Mexican independence, 56; as motive for conquest, 28, 88, 161; negotiations for, 16, 134–137,

154–156, 189, 195–198; ownership of, 15, 16, 91, 92, 134–135, 137, 154–156, 164–165, 172, 176, 195, 197; restoration of, 74, 76, 120–121, 151, 159, 160, 197–198, 239, 243; use rights to, 15, 134, 184
Landor, Edward Willson, 234–235
Langton, Marcia, 195
Las Casas, Bartolomeo de, 26–27, 51
law, 22, 39, 42, 57, 95, 99, 100, 114, 120, 137, 138, 139, 142, 155, 157, 158, 160, 171–173, 176, 177, 184, 186, 189, 195, 197, 225, 250
Law of Nations, 15
Lawrence, Peter, 207
Leacock, Eleanor, 154, 155
League of Indians of Canada, 148
League of Nations, 206
Lee, Richard B., 213, 216
Leni Lenape, 93. *See also* Delaware
Leon-Portilla, Miguel, 45
Lerner, David, 33
Leslie, John F., 146, 147
Lethbridge, Kirk, 124
letrados, 63
Levin, M. G., 219
Levy, Daniel, 69
Lewis, I. M., 12
Lewis, Meriwether, 96, 101
Libby, Ronald T., xiii, 42, 189, 196
limpieza de sangre, 49. *See also* racism
Little, J., 173
Little Big Horn River, 105
Littlefield, Alice, 18, 88, 107, 234
Littlefield, Daniel F., 99
Little Pine, 145
Liverpool, 31–32
Locke, John, 15
Lodagri corporation, 218
Loft, Frederick O., 148
Lone Wolf v. Hitchcock, 120, 230–231
Louisiana, 127
Louisiana Purchase, 86, 96
Lowenthal, Richard, 91
Lower Canada, 124–125, 128, 143
luluais, 207
Luxemberg, Rosa, 35
Lytle, Clifford M., 95

Maasai, 217
Maa speakers, 217. *See also* Maasai, Samburu
Mabo Case, 197–198
MacDonald, Sir John, 145
Mackenzie River Delta, 160
Macklem, Patrick, 236
MacLeod, William Christie, 91
Macquarie, Lachlan, 174
Maddock, Kenneth, 195
Madero, Francisco, 69, 70, 71
Madrid, Miguel de la, 79
Maguire, Ron, 146, 147
Maisterra, Manuel de, 54
majimbo, 217
Major Crimes Act, 107
Malaysian Archipelago, 164
Malinche, 52
Malindi, 217
Mandan, 96
Mande, 36
Mandelbaum, David G., 96
Mandok, 225
Mangas Coloradas, 31, 117
Manitoba, 133, 136–138, 143, 151, 158
Manitoba Act, 136
Manitoulin Island, 134
Maori, 31
maquiladoras, 77–78, 107
Marshall, John, 12, 95, 99, 107, 120
Marx, Karl, 31, 35
Mascarene's Treaty, 134
Mau Mau, 217
Maya, 7, 23, 47, 48, 53, 58, 81
Maxmillian, 63, 65
Mazatecan, 48
McCaskill, Don, 152
McClelland, David C., 33
McCormick reaper, 68
McNab, David T., 143
Me, 206
Medicine Creek Lodge Treaty, 105
Meech Lake Accord, 158, 246
Meggitt, M. J., 165
Melanesians, 211
Menomini, 111
merchants; as interest group, 14, 47
Mescalero Apache, 114, 122
mestizaje, 9, 52–53, 59–60

mestizos, 52–53, 58, 60, 69, 73, 82, 83, 88, 101, 138, 180, 237, 239
Metacom, 22
Métis, 23, 132–133, 136–138, 149, 152, 159, 180
México, 47, 48, 58. *See also* Aztec
Mexicali, 74
Mexico, 7, 45–84, 138, 139, 180, 201, 202, 232, 233, 234, 235, 236, 237, 240, 243; church role in, 49, 50, 65, 73, 237; as colony, 10; conservatives in, 58, 60–61, 63–64, 67, 233, 239; Constitution of 1857, 65; Constitution of 1917, 71, 72, 79; disease in conquest of, 48, 49; foreign interference in, 60, 62–63, 65, 69, 70, 73, 75–78; independence of, 55–57, 244; indigenous population of, xv, 48–52, 64, 88, 201–202, 239; indigenous states in, 10, 50; indigenous zones in, 239, 241; interest groups in, 14, 52–53, 55–56, 60–61, 63–64, 66, 68, 73, 83–84, 231, 244, 246, 248; intermarriage in, 27–28, 52–53; labor in, 21, 27, 50–52, 54, 77–78; liberals in, 58, 60–61, 63–65, 67, 69, 75; mining in, 52, 66, 67, 69; Mixtón Wars, 23; the *porfiriato* in, 65–68, 73, 76, 78; privatization in, 78; the *reforma* in, 64–65; relations with the United States, 61, 62, 66, 69, 70, 72, 76–80, 84, 100, 102; revolution in, 68–72; "War on Drugs" in, 78
Meyers, William K., 70
Miantonomo, 91, 117
Michalenko, Gregory, 208
Michels, R., 6
Michoacán, 48
Micmac. *See* Mi'kmaq
Mi'kmaq, 125
Milirrpum v. Nabalco Pty, supra, 195
millenarian movements, 207
Miller, H. V., 185
Miller, J. R., 23, 86, 125, 127, 130, 132, 141, 142, 143, 145, 147, 153, 158
Miller, Jay, 93
Millon, Rene F., 47
Milloy, John S., 142, 144

Mills, C. Wright, 6
Mimbres Apache, 117
mining: in Australia, 23, 181, 184, 189–190, 196; in Bougainville, 210–213; in Papua New Guinea, 208–211
Minneconjou, 105. See also Lakota
Minnesota, 96
missionaries, 22, 51, 54, 125, 133, 140, 141, 167, 180–182, 237, 238, 243
missions, 21; Australian, 23, 180–182, 190, 238, 241; Mexican, 50–51, 54, 101
Mississauga, 129
Mississippi River, 90, 96, 99
Missouri River, 90
Mitterand, Francois, 247
Mixtec, 47, 51, 84
Mixtecan, 48
Mixtón Wars, 23, 246
Moctezuma, 49
modernization: as concept, 33, 73; associated with 19th-century ideas of progress, 34
Mohawk, 93, 94, 122, 125, 129, 156–158
Moi, Daniel Arap, 217
Mombasa, 217
Montagnais, 20
Montaigne, Michel de, 29
Montana, 110
Montreal, 125, 127, 132, 157
Mooney, James, 106
Mooney River, Australia, 171
Moore, John H., 98
Moors, 27, 46, 49, 50, 239
Moran, Albert, 193
Morelos, 70, 71, 81
Morelos, Father José María, 56
moriscos. See Moors
Morisett, Jean, 136
moros de paz, 239
Morris, Barry, 18, 185, 186, 187, 191, 193, 235
Morris, C. Patrick, 121, 243
Morse, Bradford W., xiii, 194, 195
Mosca, Gaetano, 6
Mount Graham telescope
Mount Kare mine, 209
Mulroney, Brian, 152, 158, 191

multinational corporations. See transnational corporations
Mulvaney, D. J., 164
Munn, Nancy, 165
Murray, Charles A., 32
Murtupo, General Ali, 205–206
Mururoa Atoll, 247
Muskogean, 90
Myall Creek massacre, 170–171, 172
Myers, Fred, 165, 192

Nabalco corporation, 195
NAC. See National Aboriginal Conference
NAFTA. See North American Free Trade Agreement
Nahuatl, 48, 81
Naishan Dené, 98
Namibia, 213, 215–216
Napoleon III, 55, 63
Napoleon Bonaparte, 86
Nasioi, 210–211
Naskapi, 20, 160
Nation, The, 251
National Aboriginal Conference (NAC), 195
National Aboriginal Consultation Council, 195
National Action Party, 77
National Congress of American Indians (NCAI), 23, 118
National Democratic Front (FDN), 78
National Front of Indigenous People, 84
National Park Service, 108
National Public Radio, 251
National Indian Brotherhood, 151
nationalist movements, 11
nations, 11–12; differentiated from state, 12
Native Brotherhood of British Columbia, 148
NATO, 27
natural gas, 153, 222
Navajo, 232, 245
NCAI, 23, 118
Neate, Graeme, 195
Nenets, 222
Neolin, 128
Netherlands, 85, 202

neutrals, 126, 129
New England, 22, 89, 91, 126
Newfoundland, 85, 124, 127, 170, 231
New France, 125–126
New Guinea, 164, 205, 207, 248. *See also* Irian Jaya, Papua New Guinea
New Mexico, 101
New Orleans, 86
New South Wales, Australia, 16, 166, 170, 174, 187, 191, 193, 196
New Spain, 11, 14, 47, 97, 237; co-optation of indigenous leadership in, 53; diseases in, 48; indigenous resistance in, 53–55; interest groups in, 47, 52–53, 55–56; population of, 50
New York, 94, 118, 155, 156
New York Times, 32, 206, 248
New Zealand, 23, 247
Niagara Falls, 119
Niagara River, 184
Nielson, Erik, 152, 191
Nietschmann, Bernard, 203, 205, 206
Nigh, Ronald, 81, 82, 83
Nishga case, 158
Nixon, Richard M., 111, 114, 121
noble savage: as concept, 29
Non-Intercourse Acts of 1790, 95
North American Free Trade Agreement (NAFTA), 79, 80, 224, 243
North Atlantic Treaty Organization (NATO), 247
Northern Territory (Australia),161, 169, 179, 184–186, 189, 195
Northern Territory Department of Mines and Native Affairs (Australia), 189
North West Company, 132
Northwest Mounted Police, 136, 145
Northwest Ordinance of 1789, 95
Northwest Territories (Canada), 133, 144, 145, 153, 159
Nor'westers. *See* North West Company
nuclear testing, 190, 247
Nunavut, 159, 160
Nyerere, Julius, 218–219

Oaxaca, 47, 51, 54
obrajes, 67
Obregón, Alvaro, 70–71, 73

Ocozocuautla, 54
Ohio River, 90
Ohio Valley, 246
oil. *See* petroleum
Oil Producing and Exporting Countries, 212
Ojibwa, 96, 129, 134, 135. *See also* Anishinabek, Chippewa
Oka, Quebec, 156–158, 243
Okanagan, 129
Oklahoma, 99, 100
Ok Ma River, 208–209
Ok Tedi Mining, 208–209
Ok Tedi River, 208–209
Oliver, Douglas, 210
Oliver, Symmes C., 98
Oneida, 93, 143
Onondaga, 93
Ontario, 143, 152, 154
O'Odham, 48, 51, 54, 246
Opata, 48
OPEC, 212
Operasi tumpas, 206
Operation Annihilation, 206
Orara River, Australia, 171
Oregon, 111
Orilla, Ontario, 141
Otomanguean, 48
Otomí, 75
Ottawa, 128, 135, 136, 140, 147, 153, 155
Ottawa River, 127
Ovambo, 215, 216

Pacific Coast, 139, 145, 148–149
Pacific Forum, 212
Pacific Islands, 247
Pacific Island Monthly, 209
Paiute, 20
Palmer, Kingsley, 194
PAN, 77
Pangura Mine, 210–211
Papua New Guinea, 33, 206–213, 225, 228, 229, 232; in Bougainville, 210–213; colonial history of, 206; mining in, 208–210; resources in, 208–209
parcialidades, 239
Party of the Mexican Revolution (PRM), 76, 77

Pastry War, the, 62
Peace of Paris, 127, 128
Pembina, 135
peninsulares, 47, 53, 56–57, 59, 63
Penner Committee, 152
Penner, Keith, 152
Pennsylvania, 119, 234
peones acasillados, 67
Pequot, 91
Pequot War, 91
Perdue, Theda, 88, 99
perestroika, 221, 222
Pérez de Ribas, Andres, 55
Perry, Richard J., xiii, 103, 107,
    118, 171
Perth, Australia, 235
Peterson, Nicolas, 195
petroleum, 66, 67, 69, 70, 75–77,
    109, 113, 115, 120, 153, 154, 205,
    212, 222
Philip II of Spain, 50
Philippines, 32
Phillips, George Harwood, 101
Philp, Kenneth R., 114
Phipps, Helen, 66
Piapot, 145
Piegan, 129. *See also* Blackfoot,
    Blood, Siksika
Pigeon Hole, Australia, 183
Pilling, A. R., 164
Pillsbury, 79
Pima. *See* O'Odham
Pine Ridge, 108, 119
Pinjara, Battle of, 170
Pinto, Constancio, 201
Pitjandjatjara, 190
Pitjandjatjara Land Council, 196,
    224, 246
Plains. *See* Great Plains
Plan of Iguala, 57
Plan of San Luis Potosí, 69
plantations, 28
Plateau, 20, 90, 101, 129
Poison Creek, Australia, 183
Pokot, 217, 218
political class, 6
Politt, Katha, 251
Pomponio, Alice, 225
Pontiac, 23, 128, 224, 225
Pontiac's War, 128

Pope, 54
porfiriato, 65–68, 73, 76, 78
Porter, Joseph C., 104
Port Fairy, Australia, 172
*Portland Messenger-Normanby
    Advertiser*, 172
Port Phillip District, Australia, 174
Portuguese, 203, 216
positivists, 12, 63. *See also cientificos*
Potapov, L. P., 219
potlatch, 145
Poulantzas, Nikos, 6
Powell, J. M., 184
power elite, 6
prairies, Canadian, 132–138
presidios, 54. *See also* Tubac,
    Tumacacori
PRI. *See* Institutional Revolutionary
    Party
Price, John, 155
primitive: as concept, 29, 32
Princess Augusta Bay, 210
PRM. *See* Party of the Mexican
    Revolution
progress: as concept, 12, 13, 29–31,
    63, 108, 187, 189; as justification
    for colonialism, 32; implicit in
    dependency models, 38; implicit in
    underdevelopment models, 33
Project 4.1, 247. *See also* nuclear
    testing
Protectors of the Aborigines, 186
Prucha, Paul, 98
psychic unity: as 19th century
    concept, 30
Puebla, 63
Pueblos, 54–55, 101, 113
Puritans, 91, 237

Quakers, 238
Quebec, 143, 150, 154–157, 158,
    243, 246
Quebec City, 125
Queensland, Australia, 174, 185, 197

racism, 17, 28, 31–32, 34, 49, 53, 64,
    84, 98–100, 102–103, 112, 118,
    157, 169, 175, 176, 178–182, 185,
    186, 193, 196, 198, 201, 202, 214,
    232, 240, 248, 251

Rainbow Warrior, 247
Rainbow Warrior II, 247
Rashid, Yanus, 247
rational thought: in Enlightenment, 29; in social Darwinist thought, 30–31
Ray, Arthur J., 87
Reagan, Ronald, 77, 84, 111, 116, 243
Red Cloud, 105
Red River, 134, 135, 136, 137
Red River Resistance, 136
Red Tent program, 220–222
reducción, 16, 50, 100
Reece, R. H. W., 23, 172, 173, 174
Reff, Daniel T., 55
reforma, 64
Regina, Saskatchewan, 136
Remote Area Dwellers Office (Botswana), 216
repartimiento, 21, 54, 55, 73
Republic of Marshall, 247
Republic of South Africa, 213, 214, 216
reservas, 239
reservations, xiii, 103–104, 106–109, 110–112, 116, 120, 121–122, 222, 226, 236, 240, 248
reserves, 18, 138, 140, 144–146, 172–173, 187, 222, 226, 237–240
resources: as variable in conquest, xv, 32; contested, 9, 97, 103, 106, 109, 139, 146, 153, 154, 168, 178, 189, 193, 221–222, 227, 228, 229, 230, 231, 246; in dependency theory, 35; in Mexico, 66, 73; as factor in state development, 5; in United States, 113, 114–116, 119–121
Reynolds Aluminum, 122
Reynolds, Henry, 20, 169, 170
Riding, Alan, 56, 60
Ridington, Robin, 154
Riel, Louis, 136, 150
Río Blanco strike, 67
Rio Grande, 54, 101
Rio Tinto Zinc corporation, 212
Robie, David, 208, 210, 211
Robinson, George Augustus, 170
Robinson Treaties, 134
Rockefeller corporations, 69
Rocky Mountains, 129

Rodney, Walter, 37
Rogers, Edward S., 154
Roosevelt, Franklin Delano, 111, 112
Rose, Deborah Bird, 161, 169, 182, 183, 184, 185, 186, 187–188, 191
Roseau River Reserve, 135
Rousseau, Jean-Jacques, 29
Rowley, C. D., 20, 23, 170, 171, 173, 182, 190
Royal Commission on Aboriginal Peoples (Canada), 124
Royal Dutch Shell, 76
Royal Geographic Society of London, 247–248
Royal Proclamation of 1963, 92, 95, 128, 135, 137, 142–143, 145, 177, 244
Ruiz, Ramon, 46, 50, 53, 58, 63, 64, 67, 74, 75, 77
ruling class, 6
Rumsey, Alan, 165
Rupert's Land, 132, 133, 135, 144
Rus, Jan, 58
Rush-Bagot agreement, 129
Rushforth, Scott, 153
Russia, 219–222
Rustow, Dankwart A., 11
Ryerson, Egerton, 141

Sahtuot'ine, 153. *See also* Athapaskan, Dené
Said, Edward W., 27, 32
Salinas de Gortari, Carlos, 78, 79, 83
Salt Rock Cave, Arizona, 171
Samburu, 217
Samoyedic speakers, 219
San. *See* Ju/'hoansi
San Carlos Apache, xiii, 104, 106, 118, 120
San Carlos Reservation, 104, 106, 118, 120
Sand Creek massacre, 105, 160
Sanderson, Steven, 68
San Jacinto, 62
San Luis Potosí, Plan of, 69
Santa Anna, Antonio López de, 61, 62, 65
Santa Fe Trail, 100
Santee Sioux, 96. *See also* Dakota
San Xavier del Bac, 51

Saskatchewan, 23, 136, 138, 145, 152
Satz, Ronald N., 98
savage: as concept, 29–32, 172
Schreyer, Frans J., 80
Schwartz, E. A., 113, 114
scientific racism, 30, 32, 188
Scotland, 91, 161
Scott, Duncan Campbell, 147–148, 150
Scott, Thomas, 136
Sealaska Corporation, 116
Secoy, Frank R., 97
Select Committee of the Legislative
    Council on the Aborigines, 182
self-determination, 114, 121, 193–195,
    226, 242–243
Selkirk Treaty, 134, 135
Seminole, 98, 99, 113
Seminole Wars, 98, 99
Seneca, 93, 119
Sergeyev, M. A., 220
Service, Elman R., 4
settlers: in Africa, 213, 217; in
    Australia, 166–173, 175, 177,
    178, 179, 181, 184, 193, 235; in
    North America, 88, 91, 94, 95,
    103–104, 115, 125–129, 133,
    135–137, 148, 150; settler societies
    defined, 42, 167
Seven Oaks, Battle of, 133
Sharma, Davendra, 212
sheep stations, 23, 168, 183
Shenon, Philip, 33
Shkilnyk, Anastasia M., 154
Shoshonean, 90
Shuswap, 20, 129
Siberia, 219–222, 228; compared with
    Canada, 219–220
Sierra Madres, 48
Sierra Zapoteca, 52
Sifton, Clifford, 139
Siguenza y Góngora, Carlos de, 64
Siksika, 129. See also Blackfoot,
    Blood, Piegan
silver, 13, 27, 28, 52
Simpson, Eyles, 65
Sims, Beth, 78, 84
Siouan speakers, 96, 129, 132. See
    also Assiniboin, Crow, Dakota,
    Lakota, Santee Sioux, Teton
    Sioux

Sioux, 96. See also Lakota,
    Teton Sioux
sisal, 68
Skalnik, Peter, 4
Skraelings, 85
slavery, 21, 28, 31–32, 36, 51, 61, 62,
    86, 88, 89, 91, 94, 95, 99, 101, 162,
    219, 229
Slezkine, Yuri, 219, 220, 221, 222
Slotkin, Richard, 88
smallpox, 48, 96, 128
Smith, Marvin T., 11
social contract, 11
social Darwinism, 30–32, 34, 73, 139,
    170, 176
social forces, 6
Social Services Act of 1959
    (Australia), 188
Soldier Settlement Board (Canada), 146
Solomon Islands, 210–211. See also
    Bougainville
Sonora, 22, 54, 62, 70, 102, 239
Soto, Hernando de, 20, 85
South Africa, 22, 172
South Australia, 174, 195–196
South Dakota, 108, 119, 160
Southern Africa, 213–217. See also
    Botswana, Namibia, Republic of
    South Africa
South West Africa, 215
South-West Africa People's
    Organization (SWAPO), 215–216
Soviet Union. See Union of Soviet
    Socialist Republics
Spain: appropriation of land and labor,
    16, 101–102; in competition with
    other powers, 85, 98, 99; ideology
    of Conquest, 27; interest groups in,
    14, 45–46; in Mexico, 10, 16, 47;
    power of Crown in, 40, 45; quest
    for precious metals by, 13, 27; use
    of caciques by, 18, 174
Speck, Frank, 154
Spencer, Herbert, 30, 31
Spicer, Edward H., 16, 22, 51, 54
Spry, Irene M., 135
St. Catherine's Milling Case, 137
St. Lawrence River, 20, 86, 89, 93,
    124, 125, 127, 129, 130, 202
St. Lawrence Valley, 10, 126, 229, 238

St. Louis, 96, 100
Standard Oil, 69, 75–76
Stanford, Lois, 80
Stanley, George F. G., 137
Stanner, W. E. H., 165
state, 3–24; autonomy of, 6; characteristics of, 5, 11, 226; compared with
nations, 11–12; as competitive
arena, 8, 38; concreteness of, 7;
consolidation of, 230–231; expansion of, 13–14, 226–229; and food
production, 5; ideology of, 7;
infrastructure of, 7; and interest
groups, 5, 38, 203, 223, 229–230,
244, 246, 248, 250; internal diversity
of, 5; legitimacy of, 7, 18; origins of,
4–5; as pattern of relationships, 7;
population size as factor of, 5;
proliferation of, 4; reification of, 7;
resource regulation by, 5, 11; role of
government in, 11, 223; similarities
among states, 7, 223–244; use of
violence in, 229–230; in world
systems theory, 36
Steele, Chief Justice Donald, 137
Stevens, F. S., 170, 179, 181
Steward, Julian H., 4
Stone Age: as concept, 32, 206
Stubben, Jerry D., 120
sugar, 28, 31, 87
Sulpicians, 156
Sun Dance, 145, 149
Susquehannock, 126
Swahili, 218
Swain, Tony, 164, 165, 182
SWAPO, 215–216
Sydney, Australia, 167, 170
Sydney University Peace and Conflict
Studies Centre, 208
Sygden, R., 40
Szekely, Gabriel, 69

Tacuba, 49
Tahiti, 247
Taimyr Peninsula, 219
Taita, 217
tamemes, 21
Tanganyika, 218
Tannenbaum, Frank, 69
Tanner, Adrian, 154, 155

Tanzania, 218–219
Tarahumara, 48, 75
Tarascan, 48
Tasaday, 32
Tasman, Abel, 162
Tasmania, 166–167, 170, 231. *See also*
Van Diemen's Land
Tasmanians, 31, 166–167
Tecumseh, 117, 129, 225
Tehuantepec, 54
Tenochtitlán, 47, 49
Tenskwatawa, 117, 129
Tepehuane, 48
termination, 110–111, 116, 121,
191, 240
Teton Sioux, 96. *See also* Lakota,
Sioux
Texas, 59, 61, 62, 63, 100
Texcoco, 49
Thayendanagea, 94. *See also*
Brant, Joseph
Third World, 27, 33, 35, 203, 213
Thompson, Liz, 249
Thrapp, Dan, 103
Thunder Bay, Ontario, 152
timber, 21, 111, 115, 116, 204, 208,
209; as motive for state expansion,
13, 15, 28
Timor Gap Treaty, 205
Timorese, 201, 204
Tionontati, 126, 129
Tiwi, 164
Tlaxcalans, 21
Tlingit, 115, 116
tobacco, 28, 32, 87
Tobias, John L., 133, 143, 145, 149
Tobin, P., 177
Todd, Walker F., 84
Todorov, Tzvetan, 27
Tok Pisin, 208
Tonkinson, Myrna, 197, 198
Tonkinson, Robert, xvi, 165, 197,
198, 236
Tooker, Elisabeth, 126
Torres Straits, 197
Totonoc, 47
Trail of Broken Treaties, 119
Trail of Tears, 100
transnational corporations, 39,
121–122, 153, 159, 189, 208–209,

212, 216, 218, 223–224, 227, 242–243, 249, 250; defined, 40; in dependency theory, 36; in Mexico, 66–68, 69, 75–79
Treaty of Córdoba, 57
Treaty of Guadalupe Hidalgo, 100
Treaty of Paris, 128
Treaty of Utrecht, 127
triangular trade, 31
tribal colleges, 121, 243
tribe: as concept, 12, 113; as used in Australia, 13; tribal governments in United States, 18, 113–114, 117, 120, 121, 235, 241
Trigger, Bruce G., 93, 125, 126
Trigger, David S., 174, 182, 185
Trotsky, Leon, 76
Trudeau, Pierre Elliot, 149–151, 191, 231
Trutch, Joseph W., 148, 173
Tsimshian, 129
Tswana, 215
Túbac, 51
Tuck, James A., 126
Tucson, 103
Tultuls, 207
Tumacácori, 51
Tungus, 219
Tupinamba, 29
Turkana, 217, 227
Turkana District, Kenya, 218
Turkwell Dam, 218
Turkwell River, 218
Turnbull, Clive, 167
Turner, D. H., 165
Tuscarora, 118–119
Tuxtla, 54
Tzeltal, 54, 81
Tzotzil, 54, 81

Uganda, 219
ujamaa, 219
Ulura-Kata National Park (Australia), 249
Uncas, 91
underdevelopment models, 33–35
Unger, Roberto Mangabeira, 22, 120
Union of Soviet Socialist Republics, 219, 220–223, 228, 231, 232, 241

United Nations, 23, 24, 204, 205, 206, 212, 216
United Nations Human Rights Committee, 204
United Nations Special Commission on Decolonization, 212
United States, 85–123; boarding schools in, 104, 106–107, 236; Civil War in, 103, 104, 105, 231; colonial era in, 10, 86–89; conservatives in, 110–111, 251; Constitution of, 95; early state societies in, 90; egalitarian indigenous societies in, 89; fur trade in, 87; ideology toward indigenous peoples, 94, 110–111; imposition of tribal governments, 18, 113–114, 117, 120, 121, 235, 241; independence of, 93–94, 128–129; indigenous coalitions in, 22, 23; indigenous labor in, 17, 18, 20, 21, 23; indigenous land rights in, 95; industrial interests in, 103–107; interest groups in, 88, 91, 94, 108, 111, 112, 122–123; land claims cases in, 120–121; policies toward indigenous peoples in, 111; racism in, 94, 99–100, 102–103, 112, 118; railroads in, 104; relations with Indonesia, 205; relations with South Africa, 214, 216; reservations in, 94, 103–104, 106–112, 116, 120, 121–122, 146, 236, 240, 247; social boundaries in, 88; status of indigenous peoples in, 95, 99; treaties in, 94, 118, 120; use of "tribe" in, 12, 113, 117. *See also* Air Force, U.S.; Army Corps of Engineers; Bureau of Indian Affairs; Department of Interior; Federal Bureau of Investigation
United States Department of Interior, 108, 113
United States Public Health Service, 232
Unity Act (Canada), 143
Upper Canada, 128, 129, 139, 143
uranium, 232
Uto-Aztecan, 48

van de Velde, Pieter, 4
Van Diemen's Land, 166, 167. *See also* Tasmania
Van Kirk, Sylvia, 132
Velasco Agreement, 62
Veracruz, 62, 70
Vestey corporation, 184, 186
Victoria, Australia, 170, 174, 196
Victoria River Downs, Australia, 161, 183
Vikings, 85, 124
Villa, Pancho, 69–70, 71
Voltaire, François Marie Arouet, 30
Von Sturmer, J. R., 197

Wagoner, Jay, 103
Wallace, Noel M., 190
Wallerstein, Immanuel, 10, 36, 37, 52, 227–228
Wampanoag, 22, 91
War of 1812, 129
Warren, J. Benedict, 48
Washington, D.C., 119
Washita River, 105
Washo, 20,106
Wasserstrom, Robert, 18, 52, 54
Watt, James, 111
Wave Hill Station, Australia, 184
Weaver, Sally M., 195
Weber, Max, 7
Wells, E. A., 182
Wendat, 90, 125. *See also* Huron
Wesleyans, 235
West Africa, 36
Western Australia, 174, 184, 189, 196
Western Desert, Australia, 170, 190
West Indies, 91
West Pokot District, Kenya, 218
Wet'suwet'en, 158
Wheeler-Howard Bill, 112–113, 235
White, J. Peter, 164
White, Richard, 35
White Guards, 74
White Mountain Apache, 114, 120
Whitlam, Gough, 194, 195
Wilkinson, Charles F., 95
Williams, Eric, 32, 162
Williams, Ian, 212

Williams, Nancy, 11, 13, 15, 176, 177, 195, 235
Williams, Robert A., Jr., 95
Wilmsen, Edwin N., xiii
Wilson, Edmund, 119
Wilson, John, 191
Winnipeg, 135
Wisconsin, 111
Wittaker, Elvi, 249
Wittfogel, Karl A., 5
Wolf, Eric R., xii, 32, 60, 65, 66, 67, 68
Wollaston, Alexander, 247–248
Womack, John, Jr., 70
Wood Buffalo National Park, 146
World Bank, 77, 213, 216
world systems theory, 35, 36, 38
World War I, 110, 146, 147, 148, 167, 210
World War II, 110, 115, 184
Worsley, Peter, 38, 207
Wounded Knee, 105–106, 108, 160
Wrobel, David M., 109

Yamasee, 22
Yaqui, 12, 22, 48, 51, 54, 68, 70, 74, 75, 76, 239
Yellowtail Dam, 118
Yirkalla Case, 195
Yolngu, 195
Young, Linda Wilcox, 80
Yucatán, 21, 53, 54, 58, 59, 67–68, 74
Yugoslavia, 232
Yukon, 153
Yukon First Nations, 160

Zacatecas, 23, 52, 246
Zaldívar, Antonio de, 54
Zanzibar, 218
Zapata, Emiliano, 69–70, 71, 73, 81, 243
Zapatista Army of National Liberation (EZLN), 23, 80–85, 243
Zapotec, 47, 51, 65
Zavala, Lorenzo, 58, 62
Zedillo, Ernesto, 83, 84
zona indigena, 239
Zoque, 54
Zózola, 47

DATE DUE
